A Culture in Conflict is a study of continuity and change in the lives of skilled workers in Hamilton, Ontario, during a period of economic transformation. Bryan D. Palmer shows how the disruptive influence of developing industrial capitalism was counterbalanced by the stabilizing effect of the associational life of the workingman, ranging from the fraternal order and the mechanics' institute to the baseball diamond and the "rough music" of the charivari. On the basis of this social and cultural solidarity, Hamilton's craftsmen fought for and achieved a measure of autonomy on the shop-floor through the practice of workers' control. Working-class thought proved equally adaptable, moving away from the producer ideology and its manufacturer-mechanic alliance toward a recognition of class polarization. Making ample use of contemporary evidence in newspapers, labour journals, and unpublished correspondence, the author discusses such major developments in the class conflict as the nine-hour movement of 1872, the dramatic emergence of the Knights of Labor, and the beginnings of craft unionism after 1890. He finds that the concept of a labour aristocracy has little meaning in Hamilton, where skilled workers were the cutting edge of the working-class movement, involved in issues which directly related to the experience of their less-skilled brethren. More remarkable than the final attainment of capitalist control of the workplace, he concludes, are the long-continued resistance of the Hamilton workers and their success in retaining much of their power in the pre-World War I years.

Bryan D. Palmer has taught at the State University of New York, Binghamton, N.Y., and Queen's University. He has published a number of articles on working-class history and is a member of the editorial board of *Labour/Le Travailleur*.

A CULTURE IN CONFLICT

Skilled Workers and Industrial
Capitalism in Hamilton, Ontario,
1860–1914

Bryan D. Palmer

McGILL–QUEEN'S UNIVERSITY PRESS
MONTREAL

© McGill-Queen's University Press 1979
ISBN 0-7735-0346-3 (cloth)
ISBN 0-7735-0347-1 (paper)
Legal deposit third quarter 1979
Bibliothèque nationale du Québec

Design by Naoto Kondo
Printed in Canada

This book has been published with the help of a grant from
the Social Science Federation of Canada, using funds
provided by the Social Sciences and Humanities Research
Council of Canada

For some friends:
Tom, Russell, Heidi

History has remembered the kings and the
warriors, because they destroyed; Art has remembered
the people, because they created.

William Morris

Contents

Illustrations

Preface

What follows is a study of skilled workingmen in Hamilton, Ontario, in the years 1860-1914. It attempts a three-tiered task. First, to establish the importance of the skilled workingman as an historical presence, and to outline the essential context within which the craftsman assumed this importance, that of industrial-capitalist development. Second, the study seeks to explore the culture of the skilled worker, as manifested in various forms of associational life, traditional forms of enforcing community standards and morality, patterns of shop-floor control, and strains of working-class thought. Third, an attempt is made to chronicle the emerging patterns of class conflict, revealed in the nine-hour struggle of 1872, the upsurge of the Knights of Labor in the 1880s, and the "new unionism" of the pre-World War I year.

While each of these themes is explored in self-contained units, composed of various chapters, it is the relationship among the sections that is perhaps the most important and interesting. Thus the processes of continuity and discontinuity in working-class life are central to the overall discussion. So too is the phenomenon of nineteenth-century workers' control, an important component of shop-floor life in any number of North American communities. Finally, it is the way in which culture is used, adapting to the changed environment of industrial capitalism, that predominates in much of this examination of skilled workers in Hamilton. Indeed, if there is a central concern in this study it is with the way in which working-class culture sustains a persistent protest against industrial-capitalist disciplines and development, enriching the process of class conflict, bringing workers and employers into battle with one another, despite the apparent inevitability of working-class defeat.

Workers, of course, have seldom left articulate statements making these kinds of links, arguing that their culture and their struggles were part of an essential unity. We could hardly expect them to provide future interested parties with such a neatly arranged analytical framework. This makes the historian's task that much more difficult, piecing together fragments of a story posterity has left in a shattered, incomplete form. Nevertheless, the relationship between culture and conflict *is* critically important, if problematic. In this study culture and conflict are regarded as complementary processes or working-class life in an age of industrial capitalism. If much of the argument regarding this relationship rests upon reasonable inference and informed speculation, sceptics should be aware that the price to be paid for eliminating such procedure is, quite simply, the continuation of our refusal to confront these important issues.

This preoccupation with culture and conflict defined the parameters of the study. Skilled workers were chosen as the prism through which to view these processes because they tended, in light of their workplace power and organizational strength, as well as their history of cultural involvement, to serve as the cutting edge of the working-class movement as a whole.[1] I have attempted elsewhere to outline the unique historical presence of the skilled workingman, and his leading role in class conflict, and there is no necessity of dwelling further on the significance of this stratum of the working class.[2] Needless to say, skilled workers, despite their unique place in the world of the working class, cannot be analytically isolated from other segments of the labouring population — women, children, and the unskilled — and attempts have been made to weave the historical experience of these groups into the pages of this study; at the same time, there is no denying the focus on the skilled.

In other ways, too, an interest in culture and conflict dictated certain research paths. Hamilton, as opposed to other Canadian cities, seemed an appropriate target of study because it exemplified the transformation from handicraft production to modern industry, a locale where class polarization and struggle were essential features of the nineteenth-century past. And the apparently cumbersome chronology, 1860-1914, was deemed necessary for it seemed important to witness the craft workers' last stand against skill dilution, managerial innovation, and technological change, forces gathering strength in the first decade of the twentieth century.[3] Against these developments, skilled workers posed the practices and panaceas of the late nineteenth century. The war years, with their more consciously revolutionary activity, and the example of the Bolshevik Revolution of 1917, would cultivate new perceptions, forms of struggle, and political solutions. But in the years 1860-1914 the craft response remained something of a unity, albeit one that reflected, in the later period, distinct changes.

Lastly, the concern with culture and conflict dictated a specific approach to the subject, and the utilization of certain kinds of evidence as opposed to other sources. Hamilton, as many social historians are well aware, has become one of the most intensely studied communities in North America. Michael B. Katz and his ongoing Canadian Social History Project have utilized quantitative data to launch one of the more sophisticated community studies in the history of social scientific inquiry.[4] While Katz's work demands respect, particularly his structural analyses of inequality, transiency, and social mobility, it remains an open question as to how much numerical data can tell us about culture or conflict.[5] It thus seemed fitting to probe traditional sources (newspapers, manuscript and archival holdings, and local records) to see what they could offer. While such material is truly impressionistic, it has yielded an impressive collection of data that tell us much about obscure corners of the nineteenth- and early twentieth-century world.

Beyond the data, however, looms the theoretical framework within which this study evolves. While sections of the book have been somewhat influenced by my wrestling with a kind of structuralist theory — chapter 2 can be read as a discussion of culture as structure — the attachment is to a structuralism rooted in historical analysis, informed but not dominated by the approach of the anthropologist. It is, in short, the structuralism of Lévi-Strauss, rather than the structuralism of Althusser.[6] Where one has, at least, a partial respect for history and empirical findings, the other is unashamedly antihistorical, masking abstraction with the reification of theory.[7]

This study, then, is no marriage of the social sciences and history. If it does not totally accept the judgement of Richard Cobb that it is unlikely that historians will ever get much profit from the company of social scientists,[8] it cannot argue with Elizabeth Fox-Genovese's and Eugene D. Genovese's recent remarks on the dangers inherent in promiscuous "borrowing" from other disciplines.[9] Far too often, the historian's own lack of rigour has moved him toward the sociologist, the psychologist, the economist, or the anthropologist; and the theoretical gains have been minimal. These advocates of the interdisciplinary approach have often succumbed to the worst kind of defeatism, for in looking for answers to history's interpretive problems they have subordinated Clio to the jargonistic antihumanism of the social sciences, replete with their clinical sterility and elaborate control mechanisms. The past, however, was never so tidy.

What really informs this study, therefore, is not social scientific theory as handed down to the historian by the sociologist or economist, but rather a tradition of empirical Marxism. This tradition takes history itself as the basis of an inquiry that seeks to refine and reformulate theory, rather than positing theory as the basis of an abstract and general history. E. P. Thompson, probably the foremost author within this tradition of empirical Marxism, has written briefly on this relationship between history and theory. In an early review of Raymond Williams's *The Long Revolution*, he argued that "to adumbrate a theory of culture it is necessary to proceed from definitions to evidence and back from evidence to definitions once again; if the anthropological and historical evidence is not fully consulted, then we may not know what it is that we must define."[10] Fifteen years later, Thompson seemed confirmed in his earlier judgement. "The *real* history," he maintained, "not only tests theory, it reconstructs theory."[11] Thompson also linked the processes of culture and conflict, themes central to much of the following discussion of Hamilton workers:

Any theory of culture must include the concept of the dialectical interaction between culture and something that is *not* culture. We must suppose the raw-material of life experience to be at one pole, and the infinitely complex human disciplines and systems, articulate and inarticulate, formalized in institutions or dispersed in the least formal ways, which 'handle', transmit, or distort this raw material to be at the other. It is the active *process* — which is at the same time the *process through which men make their history* — that I am insisting upon: I would not dare, in this time of linguistic hypertension, to offer a new definition. What matters, in the end, is that the definition will help us to understand the processes of social change. And if we were to alter one word in Mr. Williams' definition [of culture] from 'way of life' to 'way of growth', we move from a definition whose associations are passive and impersonal to one which raises questions of activity and agency. And if we change the word again, to delete the associations of progress which are implied in 'growth', we might get the 'study of relationships between elements in a whole way of *conflict.*' And a way of conflict is a way of struggle. And we are back with Marx.[12]

And, indeed, virtually all of Thompson's work, from his political polemics, through his celebrated discussion of class formation in the period 1792-1830, to his current concerns with eighteenth-century forms of plebeian protest, revolves around these themes of culture and conflict. It is the most sophisticated statement of a tradition of Marxist inquiry confronting "the collisions of evidence and the awkward confrontations of experience."[13]

Thompson's approach rests on an essential historical sensitivity. Theory is meant to inform historical inquiry and, in turn, to be informed by historical research. This kind of orientation cautions against the adoption of models or immutable laws of historical development.[14] What this approach poses is the differing perspectives of the social historian and the sociological historian. Social history, based upon empirical research, uses the sharp detail of limited chronology or restricted region to illuminate the human dimensions of the past.[15] Sociological history unfolds in a more grandiose fashion, peering down at large segments of the past from the lofty heights of imposing abstraction and generalization.[16] This distinction between social and sociological history is not meant to deny the extent to which the two approaches have drawn dramatically close to one another, nor is it meant to imply that either orientation is the particular territory of any ideological camp.[17] Rather, the distinction is made to highlight the potentialities of each approach, and to place this study within a specific framework.

Sociological history, for instance, seems particularly adept at chronicling transformation and change, in their epochal sense, interpreting the development, over long periods of time, of specific modes of production and systems of economic and social organization.[18] Marx's work, largely structured within the confines of an ongoing debate with the orthodoxies of classical political economy, can be considered within this framework, *Capital* being primarily a discussion of the development of the capitalist mode of production *as a whole*, an overview of the long march toward bourgeois hegemony. Dominated by an understandable concern with the emergence of capitalism as a social system, Marx could hardly have developed a coherent conception of culture and its relationship to class conflict. His view of culture was also necessarily restricted by the limited vision of the period within which he wrote.[19] And this interpretive gap has continued since Marx, Raymond Williams arguing that what is

> evident in some of the best Marxist cultural analysis is that it is very much more at home in what one might call *epochal* questions than in what one has to call historical questions. That is to say, it is usually very much better at distinguishing the large features of different epochs of society, as between feudal and bourgeois, or what might be, than at distinguishing between different phases of bourgeois society, and different moments within the phases: that true historical process which demands a much greater precision and delicacy of analysis than the always striking epochal analysis which is concerned with main lineaments and features.[20]

Sociological history, despite its promise, thus remains inhibited in certain important realms, where only the detailed, empirical approach of the social historian can intervene.

One such realm, where the approach of the social historian bears important fruit, is the study of class. And it is the approach to precisely this question of class that is obviously central in the following discussion of skilled workers, culture, and conflict. There is, of course, a significant and voluminous theoretical literature on class, a literature that, because of its concerns and method, can be described as sociological. Within this tradition, class is often a static structural category or, worse, a mere expression of self-perception. Thus class can be identified as a literal quantitative measurement located beyond empirical findings; a category totally determined by productive relations, expressed as so many wage-earners, white-collar workers, industrial capitalists, and so on. This approach, to be sure, has its validity, and its superiority to the Lloyd Warnerian approach of American sociology, which negates class by constructing status hierarchies resting upon people's proclaimed self-images — where the questionnaire and the survey reign supreme — goes without saying. But regardless of the level of sophistication, the sociological approach to class often cannot avoid entrapment. It is all too easy to believe, while reading much of this literature, that the refinements of theory take precedence over experience. Class becomes little more than an argument among academics. It takes place, not in the arena of the past, but in our own minds, books, articles, and footnotes.

This study seeks to demonstrate an alternative approach to class. Class, in this sense, is inseparable from class struggle. The process of confrontation conditions an understanding of class and of people's place in the larger social order, an understanding mediated by a particular cultural context. Class is thus defined by men and women as they live through the historical experience. It is class struggle and culture, not class itself, as an analytical category, that are the primary concepts upon which classes themselves arise and assume importance. One task of social history, and certainly one purpose of this book, is to address the class experience in such a way as to force consideration of the central place of conflict and culture in any historical and/or theoretical discussion of class.[21]

Social history, drawing upon the delicacy and precision of local research, grounded in a thorough understanding of the developments of a limited chronological period, and attentive to the importance of culture and conflict, can thus enrich Marxist theory, offering the potential of new, essentially *historical* insight.[22] Moreover, unlike sociological history, which grapples with social change writ large, social history raises the possibility of a different kind of understanding, a "feel" for the human context of historical development: "The analogy of certain other sciences makes it natural that some of those engaged in history should be preoccupied, at times to excess, with questions of change, development, and causation. That approach has its uses, but to view either an individual or a society as a problem is to make certain of misconceiving them. Sympathy is a form of knowledge."[23] It is this sympathy that enables the social historian to grasp the importance of cultural continuities in the midst of economic transformation, to glimpse the tenacity of common people struggling against increasingly harsh realities. It is this sympathy that moves the historian to understand the resistance that has characterized the plebeian response to the last three centuries of developments in the industrial-capitalist world. Finally, it is this sympathy that pushes the social historian toward the link between culture and conflict, the recognition that continuity and change are but halves of a dialectical unity.[24] And it is this kind of sympathy, and these kinds of concerns, that underlie this study of class, culture, and conflict in Hamilton, Ontario.

This study owes much to other people. I would like to thank James Rinehart, John Herrick, and Elizabeth Anne Macdonald for their early encouragement. While a graduate student at SUNY at Binghamton, working on an earlier version of this study, I was sustained by many friends and teachers: Peter Friedlander, Philip McMichael, Philip Kraft, Sarah Elbert, Charles Freedeman, and Mary P. Ryan.

As I pursued my research I incurred the customary debts to librarians and archivists. The staffs of the Public Archives of Canada, the Public Archives of Ontario, the McMaster University Special Collections, the Tamiment Institute, the Trent University Archives, and the Wayne State Archives of Labor History and Urban Affairs were cordial and helpful. Brian Henley of the Hamilton Public Library deserves a special note of thanks.

Michael B. Katz, Robert Storey, Wayne Roberts, John Weaver, and Craig Heron graciously provided me with access to materials I would otherwise have had difficulty locating. Numerous individuals read drafts of various chapters, contributing critical assessments that forced me to rework portions of my argument. Among them I would like to thank Craig Heron, Douglas P. McCalla, David Levine, Heidi Solz, David Montgomery, Edward Shorter, Leon Fink, Gus Richardson, Wayne Roberts, and James Rinehart.

Peter Warrian contributed fundamentally to chapter 4, allowing me to borrow extensively from his unpublished studies of labour's conservative political economy in the late nineteenth century. Craig Heron and I collaborated on an article "Through the Prism of the Strike: Industrial Conflict in Southern Ontario, 1901-1914," *Canadian Historical Review* 58 (December 1977). Appreciation is expressed to the editors of the *Canadian Historical Review* for permission to include sections of that article in chapter 7. Sections of chapter 2 first appeared in "Discordant Music: Charivaris and Whitecapping in Nineteenth-Century North America," *Labour/Le Travailleur* 3 (1978), and I thank the editor for allowing me to use that material here.

My greatest debts are to Gregory S. Kealey and Russell G. Hann. Hann and Kealey read and reread a number of drafts of various chapters, and the prompt and fraternal critical suggestions that they forwarded to me provided the balance between the support someone writing a book desperately needs and the hard-hitting criticism that saves a writer from self-indulgence, lack of clarity, and factual error. Finally, both Hann and Kealey also shared research with me, epitomizing the kind of selfless commitment to scholarship that is all too rare in academic life.

Melvyn Dubofsky read an earlier version of the manuscript, supervising its progress. His demands for improvements in form and content were consistently on the mark. Although my prose remains flawed, it was under Dubofsky's supervision that I first learned to appreciate the art of elegant writing.

While writing and researching a previous version of this book I was supported by the Canada Council, which granted me fellowships in 1975-76 and 1976-77. Only those who have existed upon the largesse of the council can appreciate the material support sustaining so much intellectual activity in Canada. Queen's University provided me with a small grant that offset the costs of typing the final manuscript. My thanks, finally, to George Rawlyk, who urged me to submit the manuscript to McGill-Queen's University Press and offered me wise counsel, and to the Social Science Federation of Canada, which agreed to a subvention to offset publishing costs.

So many errors in spelling, grammar, and punctuation appear in the contemporary sources that I have omitted the conventional [*sic*]. Thus the appearance of such errors in passages of quotation merely reflects an error in the actual source.

This book is dedicated to three people, none of whom typed the manuscript, darned by socks, arranged my notecards, cooked my dinners, did my research, cleaned my house, or bore my children. Despite their lack of intimate proximity, as it is usually defined in ritualized dedications, they were all important to me as I wrote this book. Tom Reid provided the kind of principled commitment to revolutionary politics that will lead to the emergence of socialist alternatives to capitalist decay. His direct involvement will some day bear fruit for those on the fringes of the struggle. Russell Hann's service to Canadian social and working-class history has remained unacknowledged for too long; although a dedication is small thanks to offer for his sacrifices it is appropriate that, for once, he be given some small measure of credit. Heidi Solz, who now has her own row to hoe, made the burdens of my task much lighter. I hope that she realizes why this study is, lastly, dedicated to her.

Part I

CONTEXT

What is true of the constitution of historical facts is no less so of their selection. From this point of view, the historian and the agent of history choose, sever and carve them up, for a truly total history would confront them with chaos. Every corner of space conceals a multitude of individuals each of whom totalizes the trend of history in a manner which cannot be compared to the others; for any one of these individuals, each moment of time is inexhaustibly rich in physical and psychical incidents which all play their part in his totalization Even history which claims to be universal is still only a juxtaposition of a few local histories within which (and between which) very much more is left out than is put in. And it would be vain to hope that by increasing the number of collaborators and making research more intensive one would obtain a better result. In so far as history aspires to meaning, it is doomed to select regions, periods, groups of men and individuals in these groups and to make them stand out, as discontinuous figures, against a continuity barely good enough to be used as a backdrop.

Claude Lévi-Strauss (1966)

1

Disciplines and Development

> ... the historical movement which changes the producers into wage-workers, appears, on the one hand, as their emancipation from serfdom and from the fetters of the guilds, and this side alone exists for our bourgeois historians. But, on the other hand, these new freedmen became sellers of themselves only after they had been robbed of all their own means of production. ... And the history of this, their expropriation, is written in the annals of mankind in letters of blood and fire.
>
> Marx, *Capital*, I

A Hamilton workingman's diary, in the year 1846, would likely have expressed little foresight with regard to the future economic growth of the city. All seemed as it had always been, and few who ventured to look forward would discern patterns of development notably different from those of the past.[1] More than half a century later the city's workers knew well the price to be paid for "progress." A depiction of "Johnny Kanuck," a carriagemaker who had landed in Hamilton at the foot of John Street in 1851, travelling from the eastern districts of the colony to seek his fortune in Western Canada, reveals something of the uneasy transition effected in these years. The sketch portrays an independent artisan, on the tramp, who tarried but a few days in the Ambitious City, as Hamilton was then and later known. Shouldering his handkerchief, containing his extra shirts and socks, he struck out on foot for London, a leisurely three-day trek. For three years he toiled in the carriage factories of that city. In 1854 he returned to Hamilton to work in the Great Western Railway shops, drawn by the promise of $1.50 a day, paid regularly every two weeks. War interrupted his stay, and he joined the 100th Regiment, Hamilton's recruits for the Crimean War. Habits acquired as a soldier stuck with him, and after returning to Canada on completing his stint defending the British flag, he never married. Instead, he wandered from one end of Canada to the other. In 1908 he returned to Hamilton. He found his old home caught in the midst of a recession similar to, but not as severe as, the economic downturn that had gripped the town in the late 1850s. "His old eyes," claimed the account, saw "great changes." Even in the context of an economy slowed by the impact of layoffs, he could discern workers with money for leisure. But for the old carriagemaker himself there was no place, "for nearly everything that [was] used in building a carriage [was] made by machinery." Employers had no use for "older men, no matter how skilful they may have been in their younger days." "Johnny Kanuck," the old craftsman, was one of the many casualties of the coming of industrial capitalism.[2]

As late as the 1840s, however, there were few signs of the radical alteration in social and economic relationships characteristic of industrial-capitalist development. Production, in city, town, and country, evolved around local exchange and barter mechanisms in which used value figured prominently. Craftsmen, either individually or in small groups, wielded the traditional tools of their trades to fashion the goods necessary for everyday use in a society only recently removed from the frontier stage of development. Those characteristic features of industrial-capitalist society, an impersonal labour market and large-scale, mechanized production, were conspicuously absent.[3]

Despite their superficial tranquillity, these were formative years in the evolution of Canadian capitalism. They witnessed, for instance, the initial construction of a basic transportation network. Integrating fragments of a national economy and linking it to the outside markets of the world, the early canal and railway endeavours of the 1840s and 1850s stand as milestones in the launching of the process of capitalist development.[4] Important, too, was the transformation of work necessitated by the building of these arteries. Unruly gangs of Irish navvies, imported to labour on construction sites few British craftsmen would venture near, first raised the spectre of indiscipline before the eyes of men of property and standing. Openly rebellious, viciously exploited by unscrupulous foremen and subcontractors, huddled together in close, unsanitary quarters, and rigidly segregated from any but the most indirect relations with employers, canal and rail navvies early demonstrated the potential of the dangerous classes.[5] In his early study of one violent confrontation precipitated by such men, the Lachine canal strike of 1843, H. C. Pentland concluded that the 1840s were a "decade of transition, marking the rise of wage labour on a large scale, and of a milieu that would forge labour into a self-conscious independent force."[6]

Although the seeds of industrial-capitalist growth had thus been sown in the 1840s, they would germinate slowly. Throughout the 1850s many localities remained divorced from market considerations, and the typical productive concern, even in large cities like Montreal and Toronto, approximated more closely the artisan shop rather than the factory. Diversity characterized the economy, and industrial predominance, as this occupational breakdown reveals, was far from secure:

> In analysing the Professions, Trades, and Occupations it would appear that the adult male population of Canada West pursuing Trade and Professions — are ... 228,567 and 1,116 persons living on private means. Of these there are 86,224 farmers, being only three-eighths of the whole. By this it appears that Canada West is far from what is generally denominated a 'solely agricultural country' ....The trades and occupations occupying the greatest numbers are, Carpenters and Joiners, 8,122, about one-twenty-eighth of the whole; Blacksmiths, 4,235, one-thirty-fourth; tailors, 2,662; merchants, 2,794; clerks, 3,100; coopers, 1,935; millers, 1,083; weavers, 1,738.[7]

Industrial-capitalist development would remain restricted throughout the 1850s, retarded by the severity of the economic downturn of 1857 which left many municipalities debt-ridden and financially crippled, and many early manufacturers wary of further involvement in an economy providing scant protection against ruin and destitution.[8]

With the 1860s came consolidation. Those years, proclaimed *The People's Journal*, "set agoing an industrial revolution."[9] Stimulated by a shift in the terms of trade with its southern neighbour occasioned by the Civil War, and the stabilizing impact of Confederation, industrial capitalism sank deep roots in Canadian soil.[10] The hallmarks of capitalist production, large factories employing workers by the hundreds, dotted the landscape of many early industrial cities.[11] With time the process accelerated. Between 1870 and 1890 establishments capitalized at $50,000 and over increased by about 50 per cent, and machines became increasingly common.[12] By the 1880s a period of concentration had begun, marking the demise of the manufactory and the rise of the corporate concern, centralized, bureaucratized, and linked to its suppliers and distributors through a complex network of horizontal and vertical integration.[13] The process would near completion with the rise of the iron and steel industry, the establishment of cheap hydro-electric power, and the emergence of important new industrial sectors in the prewar years of the twentieth century.[14] Firmly entrenched, industrial capitalism would remain the basic context within which Canada evolved in the twentieth century.

These are the contours of a prolonged development, and it was within their confines that everyday life, both on and off the shop or factory floor, unfolded in Hamilton and other south-central Canadian cities. To fully comprehend this process of growth, however, it is essential to link the specific, historical emergence of capitalism in Canada with a theoretical understanding of capitalist development in general.[15] And, if we are to transcend the limitations of an abstract, sociological history, realizing the potential of a truly human, social history, we must not push the actual people involved in industrial development too far into the background. What follows, therefore, is an outline of a theory of capitalist development particularly suited to the concerns of the historian exploring the social and cultural lives of working people in an age of capitalist transformation. The remainder of this introduction then explores the concrete, historical developments that this theoretical understanding seeks to illuminate: the particular emergence of capitalism in Hamilton, and the essential human consequences of that process, the struggle over the question of work discipline.

The theory of capitalist development upon which we rely is outlined in the works of Karl Marx, most explicitly in *Capital*, but also in the *Grundrisse* and a host of other minor texts. It proves especially attractive to the historian for it is based upon a rigorous historical analysis of the logic of capital over the course of three centuries. As a unique blend of case study and theory construction, it is deserving of close scrutiny by all those professing an interest in capitalist development. Marx's theory is distinguished by an exceptionally acute awareness of the stages of capitalist development: the "so-called primitive accumulation"; the period of manufacture proper; and the culmination of capitalism's protracted development, modern industry.[16]

Few concepts within economic history have been so fundamentally misunderstood and so unjustifiably maligned as Marx's concept of the original, or primitive, accumulation. David Landes, an otherwise astute and sophisticated commentator, once saw fit to caricature Marx's notion of primitive accumulation as nothing more than the channelling of early capital into industrial forms of activity, an obviously insignificant causal factor in the development of the Industrial Revolution.[17] Primitive accumulation, within Marx's analysis, bears little relationship to the actual mechanisms of capital accumulation. Rather, as an historical process it is noteworthy in that it establishes the preconditions necessary for the realization of those mechanisms, thus giving rise to social forms and historical conditions favourable to the *future* accumulation of capital and consequent development along capitalist lines.[18]

Marx argued that primitive accumulation, and its "secret," provided the foundation of capitalist development:

> The capitalist system pre-supposes the complete separation of the labourers from all property in the means by which they can realise their labour. As soon as capitalist production is once on its own legs, it not only maintains this separation, but reproduces it on a continually extending scale. The process, therefore, that clears the way for the capitalist system can be none other than the process which takes

from the labourer the possession of his means of production; a process that transforms on the one hand, the social means of subsistence and of production into capital, on the other, the immediate producers into wage labourers. The so-called primitive accumulation, therefore, is nothing else than the historical process of divorcing the producer from the means of production.[19]

In another context Marx noted the importance, within this process, of the dissolution of a number of concrete historical relationships, among them "relations which presuppose ... ownership of the instrument of labour, and which presuppose labour itself as a craftsmanlike, specific, skill, as property."[20] Focusing upon the British experience, Marx was able to locate much of this process in the expropriation of the peasantry, conveniently attained via the enclosure movement. In Canada, the United States, and Australia, where feudal ties to the land were largely nonexistent, the process would operate under different conditions, but the result — the creation of a propertyless labouring class — would be the same.[21] Marx thus took a vital transformation in social relationships, in which skill dilution figured as a central component, as the starting point in his theoretical discussion of capitalist development. For the social historian of the working class the importance of such a point of departure should be eminently clear.

Primitive accumulation involved much more than the creation of a wage-labour force, however. As Richard Garrett and Philip McMichael, in work currently in progress analysing capitalist development in the American South and Australia, have argued, the process of primitive accumulation encompassed a range of developments within precapitalist economies which, at one and the same time, brought social forms to the brink of capitalist production while erecting barriers to the ultimate development of a mature capitalism.[22] Merchant capital, interest-bearing capital, and concentrated agricultural holdings were three such transitional forms, deeply embedded within the precapitalist world, that fostered the development of productive capital at the same time as they inhibited its full-scale emergence. It was in this context — the emergence of irresolvable and fundamental contradictions within European feudal society — that E. J. Hobsbawm presented his analysis of the "crisis of the seventeenth century," a crisis precipitating England into the vanguard of international capitalist development.[23] Primitive accumulation, then, may be regarded as the nemesis of the precapitalist order.

Out of this crisis of precapitalist society emerged the first real stage in the development of capitalism, the period of manufacture proper. Its defining characteristics were the harnessing of productive power through the cooperative employment of labour, and the emergence of a rudimentary division of labour carrying to an extreme the specialization inherent in most forms of handicraft production. Marx plotted two routes into this period of manufacture:

> On the one hand it arises from the union of various independent
> handicrafts, which become stripped of their independence and spe-
> cialized to such an extent as to be reduced to mere supplementary
> partial processes in the production of one particular commodity. On
> the other hand it arises from the cooperation of artificers of one han-
> dicraft; it splits up that particular handicraft into its various detail
> operations, isolating, and making these operations independent of one
> another up to the point where each becomes the exclusive function of
> a particular labourer. On the one hand, therefore, manufacture either
> introduces the division of labour into a process of production, or fur-
> ther develops that division; on the other hand it unites together han-
> dicrafts that were formerly separate.[24]

Despite the socialization of labour and heightened productivity flowing from this development, capitalist production remained inhibited. Binding the potential of the period of manufacture, "a productive mechanism whose parts are human beings," was the retention of forms of specialized labour linked to precapitalist craft practices. While the transition to manu-facture proper had thus effected a quantitative break with the past by gathering labour into large cooperative units and refining the craft divi-sion of labour, a qualitative transformation had been postponed. "The subjection of labour," Marx explained, "was only a formal result of the fact that the labourer, instead of working for himself, works for and con-sequently under the capitalist."[25] The real subjection of labour to capital, and the qualitative transformation to a period of total capitalist control, awaited another historical epoch.

It was with the second stage in the development of capitalism, a period Marx referred to as Modern Industry, that this transformation was effected and the fetters on production violently removed. The period of manufac-ture itself provided what Marx called "the immediate foundation" of this development. With the division of labour, upon which manufacture rested, arose a refinement of the instruments of labour. This refinement, in turn, transformed the tool into the machine, and with the development of machinery occurred a fundamental change in the historical develop-ment of the productive process: the breakthrough into the Age of Modern Industry.[26] The transition occurred in the following manner:

> Manufacture produced the machinery, by means of which Modern
> Industry abolished the handicraft and manufacturing systems in
> those spheres of production that it first seized upon. The factory sys-
> tem was therefore raised, in the natural course of things, on an inade-

quate foundation. When the system attained to a certain degree of development, it had to root up this ready made foundation, which in the meantime had been elaborated on the old lines, and to build up for itself a basis that should correspond to its methods of production . ... Modern Industry had therefore itself to take in hand the machine, its characteristic instrument of production, and to construct machines by machines. It was not till it did this, that it built up for itself a fitting technical foundation, and stood on its own feet.[27]

Technical change and the pulse of mechanization, according to Marx, precipitated the productive process into the final stages of capitalist development.[28]

Marx's conception of capitalist development proves remarkably applicable to the Canadian case. The years prior to 1853 can be seen as a period in which the process of primitive accumulation ran its course, establishing a propertyless labouring class, consolidating merchant capital, and concentrating land in the hands of a few leading families.[29] Between 1853 and 1870 the rise of the factory and the demise of merchant capital mark the period as one especially suited to the conditions Marx outlined under the stage of manufacture proper.[30] Finally, with the full-blown emergence of large-scale, mechanized production in the early 1870s, we can envision Canada entering the period of Modern Industry.[31] In its groping from "the ambitious little city" of the 1850s to the "Birmingham of Canada" in the 1880s and 1890s, Hamilton reveals the process of this development, perhaps more vividly than any other Canadian city.

As early as 1837 Adam Hope, a prominent Hamilton merchant, chronicled the frenzied activity characteristic of an era of primitive accumulation:

The Great Western Bill has passed the Legislative. Hamilton is to be splendidly illuminated tonight. Processions are to march in less than an hour from the time I write & a large Cannon has been produced for the occasion and everything is in preparation for great demonstrations of joy. Schemers, planners, and jobbers are in ecstasies. Speculation in town lots is rife and some will burn their fingers for all this some day. Flags are flying in all directions. It is the first thing of the kind in this part of the country, if not in the Province.[32]

Hope's phrasing was apt, if guarded: fingers would indeed be singed, but whole bodies would also be charred. The debacle, however, was two long decades away. In the interval land speculation proceeded[33] and, under the cover of the chartered banking system, merchant capital continued in its rise to predominance.[34] These, then, were important years in the consolidation of merchant capital. Illustrative of this was the meteoric rise of the

House of Buchanan throughout the 1840s and 1850s. As Canada West's most distinguished merchant wholesaler, it stood at the centre of Hamilton's credit structure and lent force to the city's growing reputation as a leading wholesale centre.[35]

Then, too, the 1840s saw the establishment of numerous small-scale stove molding concerns which would, in later years, serve as the cornerstone of Hamilton's industrial structure. The most prominent was that of Edward Gurney, the elder of two brothers who came to Hamilton from Steuben, Oneida county, New York, in 1842. A year later the brothers commenced making stoves "in a small way." In later years E. & C. Gurney and Company would operate factories in Montreal, Toronto, and Winnipeg, as well as Hamilton, and Edward Gurney would have interests in insurance, banking, and loan companies, besides controlling the Gurney Manufacturing Company and the Gurney and Ware Scale Works. "Restless, tireless, pushing to the last," Edward Gurney was remembered as an ardent protectionist, an advocate of the National Policy long before it became popular, and a stern Methodist. He began with "his own hands and ended by employing hundreds of others."

We could perhaps dismiss Gurney and his appearance in these early years were it not for the fact that he was only one of many. Preceding him had been John Fisher from Warsaw, New York, a Presbyterian who would occupy the mayor's chair in the 1850s, and Calvin McQueston, another New York Presbyterian quick to establish a local foundry. Soon after the Gurneys' appearance, Dennis Moore, Edward Jackson, and a Mr. Dickerman settled in the city to engage in the molding and tinware trades. In the words of the *Hamilton Spectator*, these were "the men who made Hamilton's stove foundry business. They were all from New York State, became the loyalest of Canadians, were all either Methodists or Presbyterians and always took the greatest interest in their respective churches."[36]

Hamilton's early iron founders serve as examples of what Marx referred to as "the really revolutionising path" to capitalist development, the process of the producer usurping the traditional role of the merchant and becoming a capitalist, offering his products for sale in the market.[37] Thus the real significance of the 1840s and early 1850s, as a period of primitive accumulation, lies in the realization of inherently contradictory developments: on the one hand, the dominance of merchant capital over economic and social life; on the other hand, the emergence of a sector of industrial capitalist production independent of the sway of commercial capital. Commercial supremacy had become linked "with the prevalence to a greater or lesser degree of conditions for a large industry." From there, the path to capitalist development was easily followed, and the late 1850s and 1860s would see "the subordination of merchant's capital to industrial capital."[38]

Only the lack of a propertyless labouring class blocked the passage to capitalist development. But this restraint was also well on the way to being overcome. Indeed, if we can believe one disgruntled "Emigrant," complaining that land in Canada was priced at double the cost of comparable plots in the United States, land speculation in the Hamilton district had produced just the situation E. G. Wakefield's "systematic colonization" desired. Blocking the immigrant's access to the land, it had forced him to engage in wage labour.[39] Our "Emigrant" spoke of a common disappointment: "In the first place, there are vast tracts of land in different parts, held by speculators who leave it, as they term it, 'in pickle' — that is, waiting until the country around is settled — when they hope to get a high price per acre. . . . these poor people [recently arrived immigrants], who have unfortunately spent their all on a location, under the impression that the adjoining land would soon also be located, find out when it is too late, that it is 'pickled land', and that years may elapse before it is fit for the pickler to put it in the market."[40]

Another process swelling the ranks of a propertyless labouring class was the massive tide of Irish pauper immigration, much of which rolled up to Hamilton's shoreline.[41] On 2 September 1852 Fowler and Morrel, Hamilton contractors on the Great Western Railway, advertised for labourers to fill their construction gangs. Just over one month later the city received a contingent of Irish families from Limerick county, their fares paid as far as Hamilton by their old country landlord. Destitute of all means of support, the Irish newcomers were deposited on the wharf where, it seemed, "nought but privation and distress . . . look[ed] them in the face, even worse then they had already gone through." One of their number would drop dead on a city sidewalk a few days later. Straits such as these moved people willingly into the labour market, and Fowler and Morrell undoubtedly obtained their workers.[42]

Finally, the same year witnessed two developments indicating that another stratum of labour was also experiencing an uneasy entrance into the capitalistic labour market. In March 1852 the mechanics of the city launched an attack on the truck system of payment, desiring cash for their work, rather than script redeemable in goods at local stores.[43] Such an action spoke to the acute realization on the part of the mechanics that on the eve of capitalist development the outmoded social relations of an era clearly on its deathbed held little benefit for them. Better, they contended, to move into the impersonalized realm of the cash nexus, with all its pitfalls, than trust merchant and master to look to their interests. Yet the movement toward capitalist social relations was not always initiated by the skilled workingman; more often than not it was imposed from above and resolutely opposed. "With feelings of sorrow and of reprobation," the *Gazette* reported the emergence of one such crushing blow to the status and well-being of the workingman, "the ill omened practice of sweating." This deplorable tactic involved nothing less than the attempt to "procure the utmost of labor from journeymen tailors for the smallest possible remuneration." It was a "most inhuman ... most unChristian iniquity," but one that was apparently there to stay.[44] It was, of course, only a taste of what was to follow.

The apparently widespread practice of "truck payment" and the indignation with which the *Gazette* greeted the introduction of what would become, in later years, a common feature of capital-labour relations, attest to the precapitalist contours of the local economy as late as 1852.[45] At the same time, the mechanics' opposition, and the emergence of sweating as a common practice, indicate that the social order was on the brink of transformation. The mid-to-late 1850s can thus be construed as years of transition in Hamilton, years in which the contradictions bred of many years of primitive accumulaton gave way to the period of manufacture proper. While any date chosen to denote this transition necessarily strains the essential awkwardness of the transformation, 1853 seems an appropriate point initiating a new, introductory stage in capitalist development.

That year, for instance, saw the coming of the Great Western Railway to Hamilton, and its impact in stimulating the rise of large-scale manufactories, employing labour cooperatively, rather than individually, cannot be ignored.[46] One traveller, commenting on the industrial progress of the city, noted: "Among other establishments which show the size and flourishing condition of the city is that of Mr. Lawson, the tailor, who employs 100 workmen and two sewing machines (an American invention I believe). It is the largest in Canada."[47] Three years later Daniel G. Gunn, formerly a freight superintendent at the Great Western rail yards, formed a partnership with two Englishmen and engaged in the production of Canada's first locomotives, the Shem, Ham, Johet, Bacchus, and Achilles.[48] Commenting on the quickened pace of industrial development, the *Hamilton Gazette* praised the city's rapid advancement: "This onward progress is rapidly gaining for Hamilton a higher standing amongst Western cities than more favoured and older communities can boast of."[49]

The emergence of the cooperative employment of labour, however, was not the only factor demarcating the emergence of manufacture, for the post-1853 years saw the relentless erosion of merchant capital. Much of this story has already been told, albeit implicitly, in Michael Katz's discussion of the vagaries of the fortunes of what he rather nebulously referred to as Hamilton's "entrepreneurial class" of the 1850s.[50] What Katz failed to perceive is that many of the business failures of this period were, in reality, the demise of independent commodity producers, often skilled artisans, whose economic security in the marketplace depended upon credit from merchant wholesalers. As long as merchant capital remained secure, so too was the place of the independent producer. But when crisis hit the mercantile community, as it did so forcefully with the economic downturn of 1857, the first to feel the pinch of the tightened belt was the small, independent master craftsman with an overdue account at a large wholesale house. Douglas McCalla, in his analysis of the Buchanan businesses, states succinctly the mercantile challenge on the eve of the 1857 depression:

> the period from 1854 to 1857 was a watershed in this business, and for Canadian business as a whole. The wholesalers' techniques were now to be tested by a commercial crisis, prolonged liquidation in the Upper Canadian economy, and the intensified competition that these events brought. For the Buchanans' business just to survive in these circumstances, it would have to secure funds from its overdue accounts. It would need to reduce its dangerously heavy reliance on borrowed funds and accommodation paper, secure a more secure and satisfactory clientele, develop tighter and more efficient buying practices, and move with the time in marketing its merchandise. ... The business was ultimately unable to adjust to the new circumstances.[51]

And, as McCalla then goes on to detail, the Buchanans and their partners, Hamilton's merchant princes, were never able to respond adequately to this basic challenge. They were to be bankrupted in 1867, and again in 1872. It was to be a common pattern throughout the third quarter of the nineteenth century.[52]

It was in this context that so many of the independent artisan producers on the fringes of Katz's "entrepreneurial class" failed. Katz's major source, the records of R. G. Dun and Company, a New York concern providing international credit ratings, reveal the pattern of chaotic dissolution precipitating so many of Hamilton's master artisans into the ranks of the wage-earning class. A sample of credit evaluations conveys the point:

> R.L.G. (tinware): 1 Jan 51, has a ... store and does a very trifling business, will hardly ask for credit out of Hamilton, if so should not be credited ...; 12 May 1858, Failed last winter.

> George H. B. (Hamilton tinsmith): 11 Aug 57, Does small business, practical tinsmith of good character and habits, very industrious and attentive ... never sued, in good credit and considered quite safe; 25 July 59, Winding up and going to leave (Not as good as formerly).

> Alexander S. (Hamilton cabinetmaker): 31 July 55, ... believe he will do well, believe his standing is good & that he may be trusted, no R.E. Sept 56, Can't compete with the states or with our penitentiary

works, though a good workman; 7 April 56, Has left Hamilton for
London leaving some debts unpaid. . . . 19 Sept 56, Has left town for
London or Toronto, we are not sure which.

John R. (Hamilton gilder/painter): 16 Dec 57, . . . a prudent, hard-
working man; 1 June 58, Good for small amount; 6 Oct 59, Drinks
hard. . . . 25 Nov 62, Very dubious.

James R. (Hamilton cabinetmaker): 24 June 58, Is a man of some
property, is frequently sued, his standing is not very good; 13 June
59, Doing pretty good now, but means not large, and he is sometimes pressed for money; 6 Oct 59, Is honest, hard-working man,
but poor, his ability endorses for him.[53]

Even the manufacturer of Canada's first locomotives was not spared the
agony of financial ruin:

Daniel G. G. (Hamilton Car Factory and Foundry): 14 July 56, Was
formerly in the employment of Great Western Railroad as freight
superintendent. Has lately purchased Williams' car factory and is
establishing a locomotive foundry. Has brought into partnership two
young men (Englishmen) . . . is a very industrious man . . . may be
credited; 31 Aug 57, Is engaged in the manufacture of locomotives . . .. Has a large establishment and is doing a good business. His
credit, we believe, is very good; 8 Feb 58, Is understood to be
embarrased to a considerable extent at present, the expenses of his
business have been large, and the depression in trade and the money
market has affected him. . . . 12 May 58, His work is at a stand-
still . . . 17 March 59, All to pieces.[54]

To the men experiencing such dramatic reversals, it was a question of
much more than downward mobility.

The early 1860s, following closely on the heels of the decline of merchant
capital, the increasingly precarious stature of small-scale craft production,
and the early cooperative employment of labour of the 1850s, represent the
last stand of the period of manufacture proper. William Edwards, editor of
The Journal of the Board of Arts and Manufactures for Upper Canada, commented on the rise of manufacturing in the face of much adversity:

Whatever depressions or discouragements may hitherto have
affected the material interests of Canada, nothing has thus far
retarded the progress of manufactures. They, as a rule, have been
continually advancing, as well in extent and variety as in quality of
articles produced. Considering the limited extent of the Canadian

market, the small amount of capital seeking investment in this direction and, especially, the absence of experienced and skilled labour, we may well regard as remarkable the advance which has been made in Canada in this particular branch of industry during the last five years.[55]

Epitomizing this stage of development in Hamilton were the Great Western Railway (GWR) shops where, in February 1860, the skilled mechanics in the employ of the sprawling concern completed the construction of the workshops' first locomotives.[56]

With a labour force of well over three hundred, and productive relations operating on the basis of a well-defined division of labour, the GWR shops marked the zenith of manufacture as a stage in Hamilton's capitalist development. Yet, despite the complexity and scale of the endeavour, this was not the full realization of capitalist potential. As scattered surviving pay lists from the locomotive department attest, the diversity of craft skills lent the shops the appearance of an artisan manufactory, enlarged to grandiose proportions. Fitters, turners, molders, machinists, smiths, boilermakers, masons, and patternmakers, some on day rates, others paid by the piece, worked sporadically and at highly differentiated scales of remuneration. Under many of these skilled mechanics, and most certainly paid directly out of their pockets, were a mass of assistants, helpers, and "lads."[57] The craft essence of productive relations in this large manufactory emerged clearly in an account of a "Grand Festival" held at the Mechanics' Institute, attended by six hundred mechanics, their wives, and numerous friends. There, after toasts to the Queen, the President of the United States, and the Governor General of Canada, the chairman, an official of the GWR, rose to propose the final salutation, "To Mechanism, its rise and progress."[58]

The later Sixties would be something of an Indian Summer for the craft-based manufactory. As early as 1864, however, a significant industrial-capitalist sector had already emerged in Hamilton. In that year, for instance, 2,300 workers (in a total populaton of 19,000) were employed in 46 factories, 43 per cent of which operated with the aid of steam-powered machines.[59] By 1866 one authority saw south-central Canada on the brink of a new age: "We Canadians are to all appearances about passing into an altered condition of things. A new era will shortly dawn upon us. It will be ours to determine its character, and if we are wise we shall make it the MANUFACTURING ERA OF OUR HISTORY."[60] By the early 1870s, when Hamilton first attained the reputation it would vigorously defend in later years, as "the Birmingham of Canada," the transition to the final stage of capitalist development, what Marx referred to as Modern Industry, was completed.[61]

No concern typified the full-blown realization of capitalist development more than Wanzer's sewing machine factory, whose accomplishments the *Hamilton Spectator* lauded in humble appreciation:

The division of labor is here carried to the last point of perfection; each particular part of the sewing machine is handed over to a series of lathes, drills, punching machines, emory wheels, and no end of similar ingeneous devices for lessening labor and giving accuracy to the work.[62]

Here men sit in front of emory wheels revolving at the rate of 3,000 revolutions per minute, polishing needle bars, the dust from the latter flying off at white heat from the rapidity with which the machine works. ... Next are lathes for woodwork, machines for finishing and polishing screws, machines for milling or slabbing the clothe plates, a very complicated and beautiful piece of machinery for cutting irregular forms, the only one in Canada, and a perfect gem of a planer which is self regulating ... and which works so smoothly and so silently that a penny set on edge is not jarred off. This is also the only machine of this kind in Canada.[63]

Nor was it the only Hamilton concern producing sewing machines on a large scale. Besides Wanzer's, employing 266 hands, the city also boasted of Wilson, Bowman and Company, with 220 hands, and a recent acquisition, Gardner's, destined to become a leading Canadian manufacturer. These three establishments, employing no less than 513 workers, paid out $167,960 in wages a year, producing more than 900 machines weekly.[64]

Between 1864 and 1871 the number of workers in Hamilton's factories increased by 52 per cent, while the number of steam-powered plants jumped by 32 per cent.[65] This process was of crucial significance in the history of skilled workers, as Katz and the Canadian Social History Project have documented. Between 1851 and 1871, for instance, the machinists' trade increased numerically by almost 800 per cent, growing from 53 to 468 members. This group, combined with other workers in the metal trades, stood second in size in 1871 to the 871 building trades' workers, a craft experiencing a 92 per cent increase during the two decades of industrial growth since mid-century. Traditional trades — shoemaking, blacksmithing, butchering, watchmaking, tailoring, marble working, baking, and others — struggled to survive, increasing their numbers from a mere 8 per cent to 55 per cent, despite a general population increase of 47 per cent.[66]

Firms like the Copp Brothers' Foundry, MacPherson's Boot and Shoe Manufactory, the Hamilton Rolling Mills, Beckett's Locomotive Works, the GWR shops, the Gurney works, Sanford, McInnis and Company, and the sewing machine factories illustrated this development. Such firms, employing anywhere from 60 to 984 workers, operating with amounts of fixed capital ranging from $40,000 to £138,726, producing goods valued anywhere from $140,000 to $680,000 and up, and driven by

TABLE 1
Industrial Development, Hamilton, 1871-1911

Year	Capital Invested	Hands Employed	Yearly Wages	Value of Products
1871	$ 1,541,264	4,456	$ 1,329,712	$ 5,471,494
1881	4,825,500	6,493	2,246,127	8,209,486
1891	8,175,551	9,609	3,244,118	14,044,521
1901	13,494,954	10,196	4,054,592	17,122,346
1911	58,013,768	21,149	11,600,898	55,125,946

Source: *Census of Canada, 1871*, III, 448; *1881*, III, 503; *1891*, III, 384; *1901*, III, 328; *1911*, III, 352.

steam-powered machines, went beyond the stage of manufacture and pointed to the emergence of Modern Industry. Interspersed with innumerable smaller concerns, which remained integrated into the local economy, but existed at the margin of the international marketplace where the larger establishments functioned, these capitalist enterprises set the pace for future development. Whereas in 1851 only about 24 per cent of the workforce laboured in firms employing ten or more people, by 1871 the proportion had increased to 83 per cent. Industrial capitalism, by the 1870s, had established itself in Hamilton.[67]

There would, of course, be no turning back. While depression would temporarily stifle development in Hamilton with striking regularity over the course of the next four decades, industrial capitalism was never really threatened to any serious extent. With the stimulus flowing from the National Policy, implemented in 1879, Hamilton saw unprecedented industrial expansion in the early 1880s. Citing the prominence of labour-saving devices and modern machinery, the increasing output of many factories, the expansion of old mills and shops and the establishment of new ones, and the impressive consumption of coal, a key indicator of capitalist development, the *Monetary Times* stressed the pivotal place of the city in the Canadian economy. "In manufactures," it noted in 1887, "Hamilton takes a prominent place." A local source reiterated this theme in 1892, calling attention to the city's 14,000 artisans and 170 factories. "Manufacturing almost every article required for use in the Dominion," it contended, "Hamilton is the great centre for skilled labour."[68]

By the turn of the century the iron and steel industry, enticed by lucrative bonuses and tax exemptions gleefully offered it by the city fathers, had established itself in Hamilton.[69] And by 1914, with the realization of cheap hydro-electric power and the presence of such powerful American-based firms as International Harvester and Westinghouse gracing its industrial landscape, in conjunction with the continued expansion of the steel industry, the city became dissatisfied with earlier comparisons of it to Birmingham. Pittsburgh, it proclaimed, was a more appropriate likeness, and a good choice it was, for Hamilton stood as the undisputed centre of the metal trades in Canada, as well as the focus of the country's heavy industry.[70]

All of this has carried us a long way from our starting point. More to the point, in attempting to delineate the stages of Hamilton's capitalist development, we have been dealing in categories that often convey little more than a sense of impersonalized, ongoing change. Yet we must never forget the impact of such transformation upon the lives of those who lived through it, an impact that often drew blood and left a nasty scar. The process of capitalist development involved much more than gross expansions in the size of workplaces and productive output, far more than the celebrated rise of the machine. If this development has its economic history, its political economy, it also has its social history. If one focuses upon a core of indices and measures, the other has as its central concern "the history of groups, collective destinies, and general trends ... whose subject is man, human beings, and not 'things'."[71] This essentially human context is an all too often forgotten component of the process of capitalist development.

Those experiencing "the great transformation" in Hamilton, however, knew well the loss occasioned by the rise of the factory and mechanized production. A vivid recollection of the passing of "The Old Blacksmith Shop" summarizes much of what we have previously outlined:

It was in full blast some twenty five years ago — that old blacksmith shop at the head of James Street on the mountain brow.... The setting of tyres was a grand carnival at the old blacksmith shop, for the juveniles of the neighbourhood at least. They were then given the envied privilege of making themselves useful by gathering chips for the fire, but though they might gather them, no hand but the blacksmith's own must set them round the tyres, they must be placed at an angle that no eye but his own could detect. When the fires had brought the tyres to the requisite degree of expansion, the blacksmith's hat was thrown aside, the vest followed, the leather suspenders were girded over the top of the leather apron, and amid the uprising steam and smoke he bounded like an antelope, from hammer to tongs, his teeth firmly clenched and the perspiration coursing down the furrows of his cheeks. At such times he became to the youthful imagination a veritable Tubal Cain — a man of might.

The last time we saw the blacksmith he was riding sorrowfully from the funeral of one of his brothers. 'I am the only one left now,' said he, 'of a family of as fine boys as ever left Ireland,' and a manly emotion struggled up from the depths of his heart and overspread a countenance not given to the melting mood. He was not long the last, for he, too, was soon gathered to his fathers. No vestige of the old blacksmith shop is left. It is gone with much that was contemporaneous with it, but as well as things of a more picturesque aspect it serves as a rallying point for old memories, and struggles to the surface 'in the silent resurrection of buried thoughts.'

Work and life had enjoyed a symbiotic relationship in the old blacksmith's shop; with the smith's ultimate fall that unity suffered a harsh defeat.[72]

Many craft workers located the cause of their decline in the growing number of machines displacing their skill, an appropriate conclusion if one accepts Marx's assessment of the forceful impact of technical change on capitalist development. William Collins, a machinist "of the old school," who had learned "the whole art or mystery of mechanics — that is, so far as human skill ... could accomplish it, either wood, iron, brass, blacksmithing, or anything," groped with uncertainty towards an explanation of the degraded status of the skilled worker in the modern era. Retired from the Great Western Railway since 1872, he testified before the Hamilton sessions of the Royal Commission on the Relations of Labor and Capital, articulating the sentiments of many of his peers:

> You see the effect of the introduction of machinery by the manufacturers is to abridge labor and cheapen everything. That must necessarily be against the interests of the man who has his labor to sell, because an unskilled kind of labor can be introduced by the application of mechanism, whereas it is by his skill that the skilled artisan lives. ... In my opinion, the introduction of machinery has been detrimental to the interests of the employe, inasmuch as the introduction of machinery reduced the labor required. ... There is some hocus-pocus about this that I cannot exactly get at the bottom of myself. I feel somehow or other that the employee is run out in this question — he is not considered. He is just a pawn in the game, and there is where the trouble lies, and until the employe awakens he will lie there.[73]

Throughout the course of the nineteenth and early twentieth centuries mechanization would pose a vital threat to many of Hamilton's crafts. While some trades escaped the more destructive consequences of its impact, few failed to recognize the aftertaste it inevitably left: skill dilution; debasement of apprenticeship training and regulation; the flooding of the shops with "green hands"; an accelerating pace of work; and a constricted labour market depressing general wage levels and fostering long hours.[74] Out of the inevitable antagonism following in the wake of such developments, skilled workers often voiced a contempt of the social order bordering on an outright rejection of much that comprised capitalist development.[75] The problem of disciplining such overt dissidents, and others who simply failed to endear themselves to the new rigour of work relationships, would prove the essential human task of the process of capitalist development.[76] It was not to be accomplished easily.

Certain trades, for instance, were notorious for their resistance to their employers' crusade for strict adherence to the tenets of capitalist production. Canada's pioneer iron founder, John Mason of Potter's Creek, early commented on the incorrigible nature of his work force:

> But the greatest difficulty I have to overcome is iron men, as we call them, who are the very worst sort of men to manage, colliers not excepted. Not one of a hundred of them will take every advantage of his master in his power. If I have just the number of hands for the work, every one of them will know that I cannot do without every one of them, therefore every one of them will be my master, anxiety and trouble will be the consequence; and if I keep more hands than are necessary, so as I have it in my power to turn those away who will not do right, this is expensive.[77]

Similarly, a Coburg manufacturer warned an apprentice about the habits of foundry workers: "they are a drinking, carousing set, and their associates are of the same stamp. They seem to have organized the very worst elements of society into a social band for convival and depradatory purposes. If any mischief is done in the town, they are looked to as its perpetrators."[78]

James Rose, an English carpenter, later to achieve prominence in the Toronto labour movement of the 1880s, expressed violent discontent with the rigidity of work relations in his newly adopted country. Three weeks after leaving Liverpool, he obtained his first Canadian job in the Almonte, Ontario, cabinet factory of W. McGuire. He found certain aspects of the work disconcerting:

> I have worked here now 16 days and not received my money I dont feel very comfortable for I cant get my desired answer what I am to have he wont come to any agreement until I have finished my job. I come to the determination to try to have tonight for I found this morning the Shop posted with Rules which are very one-sided and obnoctious in every way and never having worked under any restrictions before dont seem inclined to do so now. It appears by these Rules that Two months money are kept in hand that is on the last Saturday of each month the money due up the the last day of the previous month is paid. If I had of known there was any Rules to this shop I should not have gone for a job.

Rose's capacity apparently won him concessions, for McGuire waived the restrictive rules, allowing the carpenter relative autonomy on the job. "I gave him to understand," Rose related, "I should not agree to stop any particular time as most of his hands were under agreement for twelve months and so on and that I should not think of giving a months notice at leaving that I had always been used to one hours notice and I felt it was quite sufficient now so that any time he was tired of me I was quite agreeable to one hour. He told me that those Rules did not affect me that they were mearly put up to keep the Boys in order that if he did not have something of the sort he would not be able to keep them at work half their time."[79]

Malcolm MacLeod, the "Lancashire Artisan" featured frequently in *Fincher's Trade Review*, the *New York Trades Advocate*, and the *Manchester Examiner and Times*, and prominent in the North American International Union of Machinists and Blacksmiths, the New York Working Men's Union, and the Engineer's Emigration Association, questioned an English artisan recently arrived in Canada. When asked as to the possibility of his returning to the Old Country, the mechanic replied, "Go back, to be snubbed by them petty foremen and masters? Why, sir, a man is a slave in England."[80] Indeed, the English workman was recognized by all employers as a thorn in the side of work discipline. Manager Callaghan, of Hamilton's Canada Works of the Steel Company of Canada, reported in the aftermath of an April 1912 strike: "Owing to the scarcity of labor we are compelled to hire all nationalities. The English workman is the cause of more labour difficulties than any other nationality."[81]

The story is well documented for the 1880s in the testimony before the Royal Commission on the Relations of Labor and Capital. Canadian employers raged against indiscipline and intemperate workers, who often honoured the traditional craftsman's holiday of Saint Monday, a day given over to recovery from or continuation of the weekend's bout of drinking.[82] Hamilton shops and foundries presumably fared no better, for Saint Monday was kept alive by shoemakers and coopers, to name but two crafts, well into the 1880s.[83] Employers found these practices irritating, and by the turn of the century demanded sober workmen. "The time was when the idea prevailed that the bright young men and the most capable mechanics were those who drank freely," noted a Hamilton newspaper in 1908. "That fool notion has long since been exploded, and employers are very particular as to the habits of their workmen." On Hamilton's street railways, for instance, employers' concern went so far as to forbid workers to indulge in a glass of beer even if off duty.[84] "I simply say this," a St. Hyacinthe mill manager bluntly concluded, in words that won approval among Hamilton industrialists, "unless there is a certain amount of discipline in a factory where two hundred hands are employed, you cannot run it."[85]

Employers' efforts to curb lapses in work discipline emerged clearly in the 1880s testimony, especially in terms of their reaction to rebellious children.[86] These youngsters, thrust into the "dark, satanic mills" of early Canadian capitalism, seemed intent, if we can believe their employers, upon carrying out a protracted guerrilla warfare against the rigidity of their work.[87] Children who played in the aisles of factories, talked to one another, tormented foremen, or disobeyed orders bore the brunt of a harsh discipline. At Fortier's Montreal cigar factory, vicious beatings, promiscuous fines, and confinement in a basement "blackhole" were utilized to inculcate submission to authority. A special constable stalked the works, supervising the children and inflicting punishment for poor work, talking on the job, and infractions of countless rules.[88]

Fortier may have exercised excessive and atypical measures against his child workers, but in other realms he was no different than numerous employers. His posted workshop regulations were representative of those hanging in many Canadian establishments:

RULES AND REGULATIONS OF THE FACTORY
10 Hours Constitute a Day's Work

From 1st April to 31st September, all employes working by the week must be to *work* at 7 o'clock A.M. and 1 o'clock P.M. and from 1st October to 31st March 7:30 o'clock A.M. and 12:30 P.M. Doors kept open 15 minutes later for piece work employes.
No one allowed to stop work during working hours.
All employes to be searched before leaving factory.
Loud or profane talking strictly prohibited.
All employes wasting or dropping tobacco on the floor will be fined
    for each offence.
No tobacco to be left on the tables after *work*.
Anyone breaking these rules will be subject to a fine.
No one allowed to comb their hair in the factory.
No one allowed to leave their department.[89]

Such methods may have worked well with children, but even that is doubtful. For the skilled and sensitive men of the crafts they were hardly the right approach. As late as the first decade of the twentieth century, the problem of labour discipline remained acute. One of the most protracted struggles in the molding trade, a 1905 strike at McLary's London foundry, for instance, grew out of the men's defiance of their superintendent's order not to enforce a half-holiday and attend a picnic.[90] A brief glance at the question of labour discipline in Hamilton and its environs in the years 1860-1914 reveals the critical dimensions of the problem, as well as the range and scope of forces marshalled in the interests of work discipline and productivity.[91]

Posing the problem forcefully, once again, were the children. The records of apprenticeship of the Hamilton Orphan Asylum prove invaluable as a source revealing the depth of the disciplinary crisis of the late nineteenth century. Apprenticeship was probably not the appropriate term for many of the relationships entered into by the asylum and regional farmers and townsfolk, for often the children involved were simply adopted, and there are abundant indications of the most admirable of motives, love and genuine compassion being only two of many. Other cases, however, rested more firmly on a well-defined series of labour obligations and compensatory payments, to be deposited with the asylum until the term of indenture expired, when they were to revert to the child. The boys and girls involved in these contractual arrangements, often little more than babies, proved remarkably difficult to control.[92]

George Grove, for instance, was indentured to a Port Burwell farmer 5 July 1878. The ledger told of his future action: "Ran away from Mr. McCollom, his sisters having enticed him, for the sake of living in the city, to leave his good master in the month of February 1883, and by this conduct forfeited his money, which was refused him tho' he tried his utmost to obtain it." A Simcoe woman, Mrs. Vincent, undertook the indenture of Georgina McKay in the autumn of 1879. The relationship was to prove short-lived: "Ran away and came to Mrs. Pratt, Hamilton, in the summer of 1880 and forfeited her money." William Cuthbert, indentured 7 July 1879, ran away 28 March 1882, "being dissatisfied." Beside the name of Jenny McAndrew, indentured 15 December 1879, the asylum books recorded, "found unmanageable."[93] Murray Glover, hired out to James Anderson, a Guelph farmer, left him promptly, apparently without cause. The asylum's matron noted that he had probably been enticed by his brother George. Another inmate indentured to a Guelph farmer, William Rutherford, severed his contract because the farmer's wife was "particular about his being in the house at night." Mary Anne Camden, eight years old, was twice apprenticed in July 1884 and April 1885, and was twice returned. "Unsuitable" was her disgruntled employers' only comment. Other cases abound: an apprenticed brass founder running away from parents who sought his return to "his home & trade"; a sickly girl, once an inmate of a Toronto training school, whose apprenticeship was disrupted by "an inherited terrible temper and an unmanageable will"; a dressmaker whom the Asylum's committee found plagued by a troublesome "self-will."[94]

One of the more detailed, and certainly the most tragic, cases was that of Emily Gertrude Catchpole, a two-and-a-half-year-old infant first "let out" to George Catchpole. Catchpole unfortunately died in 1888, three years after the indenture. His wife not being able to keep the girl, she was returned to the asylum. Sent to Mrs. Agnes Meiklle of Brantford, she soon found her way back to the Hamilton Asylum once again. From then until 1896 she was shunted from one home to another, none of which could keep her. Finally, a few days before Christmas in 1896, she "was taken by Miss Jones to Toronto Industrial School for girls who are hard to control." Sentenced to an indefinite period of detention, her fate was quickly passed over by her former overseers: "we hope she may remain there till her good common sense will dictate a proper course of life; the inmates are most carefully trained for future life."[95]

But the most interesting case was that of Willy Williams. First indentured 4 February 1887 to a farmer, Willy proved to be less than satisfactory: "Willy doing well ... [but] requiring someone to work with him to insure his working well. ... Willie Williams through disobedience to Mr. Anderson was the cause of Wm. Anderson's barn being burned and a heavy loss was the result. Still Mr. Anderson bears patiently with the boy. Willie finally ran away giving Mr. Anderson great trouble." By 4 November 1895, however, Willy seemed to be progressing well. Perhaps his change of masters sat well with him, for he was now learning a skill: "Willie Williams has settled down and is now doing well—living in Rockwood where he is learning the trade of blacksmith. He writes for information regarding his parentage so that he may get life insurance."[96] The young Mr. Williams, it seemed, had imbibed a measure of the work ethic. Yet we should exercise restraint before arriving at such a conclusion. A letter to his former matron at the Hamilton Asylum, written three years after the above entry, conveys the point:

> I am now working in Guelph at J. B. Armstrong's Manufacturing Company manufacturing buggies I am working what they call the rollers making springs I am fireman and getting 13¢ an hour I have been working their for 4 weeks I was coming down on good friday but all of us men at Armstrong's had to work that day when I started to work at J. B. Armstrong's I weight 1.67½ lbs and I only weight 1.52 so you may know how hard it is it is the heat more than the work I dont know whiter to stay at this job or not but if I stay at it for a nother week or so I shall stop then till the harvest is on it is a very hot job hottest Ive ever struck[97]

It was perhaps ironic that Willie's first exposure to labour discipline had resulted in a fire causing his employer much anguish and considerable cost, while his own entrance into industrial work would be as a fireman, where the flames would take their toll in 15½ pounds of his own flesh. For William Williams, a childhood aversion had blossomed into an adult dilemma; attaining a modicum of skill eased the discomfort only a trifle. True, he had turned to industrial labour, but it was a labour of duress not of love. Come the harvest he would be gone.

Behind these case histories of orphans' indenture lie an obscure but important history of resistance to work discipline. Factors contributing to its potency would be complex: kinship; the lure of the city; an under-current of sexual maturation; a knotty individualism manifesting itself as self-will; and, to the nineteenth-century mind, inherited traits reflecting unfortunate parentage. Who, for instance, can fail to sympathize with children like John Brown, aged nine years, who was apprenticed to a farmer, Lachlan Taylor, and proved less than adequate: "Mrs. L. Taylor called today to say she & her husband had tried to do their utmost with the boy, who seemed very slow to learn, very timid, and consequently inclined to tell stories; which is not surprising when one considers that Father and Mother were drunkards." Or John Glenn, "returned to the Orphan Asylum having run away as Mrs. Gorman would not let him go to school."[98] The orphans' resistance to discipline has bequeathed to us a vivid story of human struggle against forces much larger than young children. It is noteworthy in itself, but also because it reflected a wider process.

A Dundas watchmaker, for instance, reiterated Willy Williams's distaste for the routine and rigour of industrial society. His credit rating suffered accordingly: "An idle lazy man just gets subsistence and that with the aid of his gun and rod."[99] Besides the young orphans, other apprentices took to their heels in resisting the incursions of work discipline. They usually ended up in court, the losers for their trouble: "Mr. R.A. Pilgrim summoned Henry Hanson before the Police Magistrate on Saturday, for leaving his service without notice. Hanson pleaded that he was taken ill and was obliged to go home. Mr. Pilgrim said Hanson was ill too often, that it was his old dodge to get rid of work. His Worship inflicted a fine of $10; and Hanson in default of payment was sent to jail."[100] The aftermath of the strikes for the nine-hour day in May 1872 saw similar actions, and similar victories by employers.[101]

Throughout the 1880s the problem of runaway apprentices continued to plague manufacturers,[102] but one of the most notable testimonies of youthful rebellion was a strike at the Wanzer sewing machine factory, which had taken to employing young boys for basket weaving. Working by the piece, often as many as nine hours a day, the twelve-year-olds at Wanzer's averaged $3.82 a week, a sum, they said, hardly sufficient to keep them in food let alone clothing. They boldly marched into the offices of the *Palladium of Labor*, organ of the Hamilton Knights of Labor, figuring that the editor would be interested in their plight and the strike they intended to initiate. There was only one "scab" in the lot.[103]

Wanzer's young basket weavers, of course, emulated those much older and more experienced than themselves. Between 1860 and 1914 Hamilton's skilled workers would utilize the strike consistently to ease the pinch of labour discipline. Their frequent clashes with their employers formed a central component of an ongoing struggle for control of the workplace. If their childhood allegiance to an imposed work ethic had been fragile, their later years would prove only slightly different in this respect. Where in youth they had often engaged in individualistic action, in their more mature years they would cultivate a collective response.

Employers, understandably enough, saw the problem as one of crucial importance. "Workmen who do not keep up their compliment of five hundred a week," read a sign in Wanzer's shop, "are expected to return to work at night."[104] When such blunt demands failed to elicit compliance, manufacturers often resorted to mockery. During the early stages of the agitation for the nine-hour day, in February 1872, 145 Hamilton manufacturers closed ranks, determined to countenance no reduction in the hours of labour. Their resolution betrayed a bitter resentment of their employees' actions:

> Resolved, That the 'workingmen' in our employ be respectfully requested to attend, in future, at our respective establishments at ten o'clock, a.m., and amuse themselves therein, in gentle exercise at the forges, benches, lathes, etc., till noon; that at noon they be humbly solicited to accept of a cold collation of boned turkey, ham, tongue, etc., and thereafter indulge in a 'weed' (real Havana), and champagne, and a 1 o'clock they be again most respectfully requested to continue their amusement at the forges, lathes, benches, etc., aforesaid, till three o'clock, and then to return to their respective homes to improve their morality. The 'consequential damages' to be borne out of our profits and, when these are exhausted, out of funds raised on mortgage of our property.[105]

Men who passed such a resolution took their cues on labour discipline from many sources, but often from strange quarters:

> It is painful to the industrious and moral portion of our people to see so many loungers about the streets and such a multitude whose higher aspirations seem to be to waste their time in idleness, or at base-ball, billiards, etc. . . . While we should by no means unreasonably restrict 'healthy recreation' we should remember that 'time is money', that idleness leads to immoral habits, and that the peace, prosperity and character of a city depend on the intelligence, integrity, industry, and frugality of its inhabitants.[106]

The speaker was none other than P. T. Barnum, digressing on the evils of "Idleness, Base-Ball and Billiards" and the contribution they were making to the Great Depression of 1873-74. The depression would end, but, as is so often the case, the ideas would live to a later age. They remain with us yet. It was significant that the man who popularized the circus, an important element in nineteenth-century working-class leisure activity, also provided industrial capitalism with welcome words on the sanctity of the work ethic.

The range and scope of forces working on the side of employers, and in favour of the inculcation of labour discipline, were subtle and complex. Poverty, for instance, must often have bent the workingman's will in the direction of submission to authority.[107] In Canadian cities like Hamilton, where skilled wage rates remained well below those of the United States, this problem must have been exacerbated.[108] Recurrent depression, and the rise of short time, unemployment, and a labour market flooded by tramping mechanics, often forced Hamilton's skilled workers to swallow indignities they would not have stood for under less adverse circumstances.[109]

Disease, a potent force in the social history of the early Canadian working class, must have rendered many of Hamilton's skilled workers severely incapacitated in their day-to-day resistance to the encroachments of factory discipline. Among most skilled trades death came early, often the result of a sickness bred of the conditions of work in a particular craft. "Stone-cutter's consumption," the consequence of inhaling particles and dust over the course of many years, decimated the craft in Hamilton as early as the 1880s, few members of the trade surviving beyond the age of 40.[110] Molders and glassblowers, prominent among Hamilton's skilled workers, tended towards problems related to their employment in situations necessitating proximity to intense heat and cold draughts.[111] Among printers, and in the "sweated" trades of the garment industry, tuberculosis was a dreaded killer.[112]

Beyond these well-known cases of specific occupational hazard lay an even more generalized pattern of ill-health affecting most of Hamilton's workers, skilled as well as unskilled. Hamilton hospital records for the mid-1890s provide only a glimpse into what was all too often a gruesome chapter of working-class life. Charles Landry, a thirty-year-old blacksmith, was admitted to the hospital 17 September 1894, his past medical history indicating an earlier contact with malaria. "Feeling ill for over two weeks," he suffered from "weakness-depression," as well as fevers and perspiration. He died September 28.[113]

A Scots workingman, Robert McKay, entered the hospital 2 October 1894 only to die on 21 October: "Patient has always enjoyed fair health until about a year ago. He has been employed latterly in a piano factory — in younger days was employed about mills. Has been troubled with cough in fall of years for 4 to 5 years and more or less continuously for past year, during this time patient was unable to secure employment and has not received medical attention — patient contracted syphilis in early life." John McAllister, also a smith, entered into confinement complaining of a spell of giddiness on 7 November 1894. He was discharged 22 November, "feeling a little better," but his symptoms indicated a sealed fate: "40 years ago was laid up in bed with a venereal disease."[114] A weaver by trade, James Cloughly, forced into the foundries as a common labourer since coming to Canada fifteen years earlier, was admitted 11 January 1895 and released 14 February. While much improved, his medical history detailed frequent attacks of the *grippe*, an affliction imposed on many Hamilton residents.[115]

Another blacksmith subject to recurrent colds, a miller troubled with respiratory problems attributed to dust inhaled in his trade, a molder bedridden with severe back pains and a leg infection oozing an offensive pus, an anemic labourer, a carpenter immobilized from a fall he took on the job, a rolling mills worker, a syphilitic merchant tailor, and a series of women plagued with the "female disorders" so characteristic of nineteenth-century medical diagnosis complete the list. If the specific disease did not kill them, the hospital might. Edward Linder died 14 October 1896 after Dr. Baugh prescribed a fatal dose of "morphia." Small wonder that the records detail only the presence of the labouring poor.[116]

These harsh realities of working-class life must be construed as disciplines of a sort, albeit not of the same order as those consciously employed by factory and workshop owners. They supplemented the plethora of "obnoxious" rules, petty fines, child beatings, and rigid supervision characteristic of work discipline; their effect was to move the worker into the labour market and keep him/her there. Patrick Hayes, aged fifty, admitted to the Hamilton hospital 24 September 1894, left abruptly, apparently before cured: "informed me that he would not stay as his wife was kicked out of house for not paying rent. He was well and wanted to go and earn money and pay rent." Yet, despite the forces mounted in its favour, discipline was far from secure. Even the hospital complained of the problems associated with disciplining patients who rejected the restrictions imposed upon them, expressed dissatisfaction with the poor diet, and openly threatened to leave the institution.[117]

Moreover, such harsh realities may well have operated to discipline's disadvantage at certain points. The school, many have contended, was a major vehicle for preparing children to accept the disciplines of the new industrial order. The late nineteenth-century crusade for compulsory attendance, led by zealous reformers, was simply an acknowledgement that too many working-class youngsters were escaping the net of industrial discipline cast by the early institutes of public education. Ian Davey, in a brilliant study of the rise of school reform in Hamilton in the years 1851-91, has documented all this and much more. But his conclusions are startlingly revisionist, for he argues that as a disciplinary agent, in Hamilton at least, the school proved distinctly inept. Despite the strictures enforcing compulsory attendance, the practice was less than satisfactory. Winter months saw school desks vacant as sickness and inclement weather took their toll. Other seasons often saw the children engaged in employment necessary to the family's economic survival. In short, it was difficult for the school to develop submission, deference, and an ethic of work appropriate to industrial-capitalist society if working-class children seldom sat in its halls.[118]

Not all forces tending to breed acceptance of the new conditions of industrial society took their toll in working-class sweat and blood, nor were all rejected by the workingman. Some, to be sure, drew workers into the ambit of capitalist social relations via the carrot rather than the stick. George Tuckett, Hamilton's leading cigar manufacturer, introduced a host of reforms into his factory that gained him a reputation — nationally and internationally — as an eminently fair man. His hands worked nine hours a day, while other firms kept their workers at the benches as many as twelve hours. Christmas-time was brightened by regular bonuses and, of course, the traditional turkey for each household. Upon those cigarmakers remaining in his service for a twenty-one-year stint, Tuckett bestowed deeds to city lots and $225 in cash to enable them to erect a house. In an age of excessive labour turnover, the fact that significant numbers of Tuckett's men received such compensation attested to the cigar manufacturer's foresight. We need not impute any sinister motivation to men like George Tuckett, while realizing that their paternal concern for their employees paid good economic dividends. Tuckett testified before the 1887 Royal Commission on his short-hour system:

> We found that by starting in the summer time at 7 o'clock and working until 6, and giving them a half holiday on Saturday, so that they could get off and enjoy themselves, they worked steadier and with more vigor. In the winter time we start at 7:30 and work until 6 o'clock, allowing them one hour at dinner, and giving them from 4 o'clock. This allows the mothers to do the marketing in the daylight and we find that they can do the same amount of work in the nine hours, and then they appear more healthy and strong than when working the longer hours.[119]

Tuckett, however, was likely exceptional in his success, and in his willingness to innovate. Another Hamilton employer, the stove manufacturer Edward Gurney (son of the earlier iron founder), found his molders less grateful for his efforts to better their conditions, and lost all faith in "such foolishness": "When I built the present foundry I built a room (against the opinion of my father, who had more knowledge of such things than I), so that the men might have a place to wash in. I fitted it up with warm and cold water and everything of that kind. The men would not go there; they washed in the pots in the foundry, as they always had done, and as their fathers did before them. I got well laughed at, and by none more so than the men."[120] Custom, it seems, could prove a rigid barrier to many paternalist innovations.

Pointing to the continuities in the crisis of labour discipline were the immigrant upheavals rocking Hamilton in the years 1895-1914. While the Irish navvies of 1852, drawing the ire of the city's early men of substance,[121] first posed the problem, the "new immigrants" of the later period perpetuated it. Where stood labour discipline amidst scenes like these?

> There was trouble on Section 20 of the T.H. & B. on Saturday afternoon. When the men discovered that they were not to be paid they all quit work and the operations had to be suspended. When the night gang came on the strikers took the tools away from the men and would not let them work. Had the men attempted to work there would have been a riot, as the strikers, being in need of the money coming to them, were desperate. . . . Some of the men had a wild time Saturday night and Sunday. They did nothing but drink beer. Five kegs of beer were sent out this morning.

> A strike occurred on the T.H. & B. today. . . . No damage has been done yet. The trouble arose among the Italian contingent, and they forced every other laborer to quit. They carried a red handkerchief on a pole and marched up the track.[122]

And from a 1910 strike at the Iron and Steel Company of Canada, a conflict involving Sicilians protesting the extortionate demands of sub-foremen for weekly payments to ensure continued jobs, the following note on ethnic solidarity:

> Last night the strikers were holding secret meetings. The minute an English speaking person begins to ask questions they become suspicious and shut up tighter than a clam. Around the district known as 'Little Italy' little groups of foreigners were assembled, apparently discussing the situation, but directly a Britisher hove in sight not a word was heard until he had passed out of hearing distance.[123]

As Herbert Gutman has persuasively argued, and as Donald Avery is currently demonstrating in the case of Canada, the influx of immigrant cultures into a context of industrial capitalism often raised severe problems of labour discipline.[124] Hamilton proved no exception to this general pattern.[125]

Hamilton's skilled workers also continued their resistance to labour discipline into the twentieth century. Craftsmen, as Craig Heron and I have argued elsewhere, continued to struggle for control of the workplace in the years 1901-14 in many southern Ontario communities; at the core of this conflict was the issue of work discipline.[126] Hamilton was to prove a centre of this confrontation, and even at this late date the proponents of discipline would be far from victorious. But the writing was on the wall, and the back of craft resistance was about to be broken. In Hamilton, as in other early twentieth-century industrial cities, a matrix of developments and forces — a fierce employer's offensive, personnel management, welfare capitalism, and detailed rationalization of the work process by efficiency experts — bred skill dilution, vanishing autonomy, and displaced discontent. That the craftsmen hung on through it all, to mount a last offensive during the war and immediate postwar years, was a testimony to their resiliency.[127]

Disciplines and development, then, are the background against which the remainder of this study evolves. They form halves of a complex whole, feeding off one another and buttressing the process of their mutual continuity. As the basic context of the period 1860-1914, they are a large part of the setting in which Hamilton's skilled workingmen built a movement of opposition, a movement we shall chronicle in the rise of the shorter-hours movement, the Knights of Labor, and the aggressive "new unionism" of the early years of the twentieth century. Capitalist development, bred of many years of primitive accumulation, had called into being a wage-earning class, but proved incapable of fashioning it in its own image; it faced a persistent disciplinary crisis. It was this crisis that reflected the human dimension of the process of capitalist development, a process captured in verse by "Janet":

Oh, the Mill of the Gods grinds slow,
When we smart with a sense of wrong;
When justice cometh not with the years,
And the bread of labor is salt with tears,
And the night is dark and long,
But all through the hours of the night and day,
The Mill of the Gods grinds away;
The seasons come and the seasons go,
But the Mill keeps grinding sure and slow.[128]

But the city's skilled workers would not be totally ground down. They were to prove less malleable than the iron forged in its foundries, more resilient than the steel smelted in its mills. They, after all, possessed a culture, and it is to this culture, rich and complex, mediating the impact of capitalist disciplines and development, and generating opposition to them, that we now turn.

Part II

CULTURE

The workingmen once held in dis-esteem — looked upon as unhonored and unhonorable — as a serf, a thrall, fit only for merest drudgery — now comes to be recognized in his true claims. Labor being so fundamental and necessary, all ingenuous, noble minds feel that the workingman is worthy of double respect. He is worthy because he is a man — and because he promotes that which is fundamental to the advancement of society. Nor can anyone doubt the importance of self-culture to that class. It may be that the workingman is undistinguished — obscured by his position and must always remain so. That all men are to be distinguished — and great, no one can reasonably imagine, and yet wherever you find human nature, that which makes a man, you find elements of greatness. The workingman has intellect, judgement, conscience; is capable of affection, sympathy, love, can exercise fancy, imagination, perceive the grand, the beautiful, as well as the statesman, the philosopher or student; what he wants is inward culture — development — and he will be prepared to put forth outward influence of the highest character. ... Men and especially workingmen are so absorbed in small details that they sometimes grow unstable; are like children who turn from one thing to another. What they want is something broad, permanent, something established, fixed, that alone is found only by culture.

The Workingman's Advocate, 2 June 1866

2

In Street and
Field and Hall

Once at a social party, Madame K.
(A foreign actress of especial note
For reading well what other people wrote,
And writing ill what few can truly say
They ever read at all) said, with a sneer,
When C. was called a genteel *artisan*,
'What! a mechanic and a Gentleman!
Pray, tell me sir, are such things common here?'

'Why, no,' replied the wittiest of men —
Looking the while serenely in her face —
'Perhaps 'tis not a very common case,
And yet such things do happen now and then,
Just as in your trade one may chance to be
An *actress* and a LADY — don't you see?'

"The Artisan and the Actress,"
Journal of the Board of Arts and
Manufactures for Upper Canada (1866)

Thomas Briggs, a Grand Trunk rail worker, died in early April 1904. As the funeral procession wound its way through city streets, it reflected social ties that had been of importance during the mechanic's lifetime. Numerous friends and relatives, of course, gathered to pay their last respects, but it was perhaps a closer, final, proximity to Briggs that tells us something of the loyalties dominating his years of residence in Hamilton. Carrying him to his grave were two members of the Ancient Order of Foresters, two members of the Sons of England, and two of his former workmates at the Grand Trunk yards.[1]

The response to the death of Thomas Canary in 1885 also typifies the skilled workers' reaction to the loss of a fellow craftsman. As an active member of Hamilton's Cigar Makers' International Union, a delegate to the 1885 Cincinnati convention, and prominent in the Emerald Beneficial Association, Canary's funeral was attended by scores of the city's workers. Eulogized by his union as an "earnest, intelligent, and foremost worker in our struggles," Canary was the recipient of a solemn tribute: after his burial the Cigar Makers would drape their charter in mourning for a period of thirty days, a mark of respect for a man of substance and worth.[2]

These men were not atypical, and in Hamilton, as well as in other Canadian communities, the funeral procession was one of many persistent continuities in the culture of the skilled workingman.[3] It was a moment of appreciation of the accomplishments of ordinary men, as well as a chance to celebrate the ties that had meant so much over the course of a lifetime. Funerals, in fact, were often regarded as the touchstone of solidarity. "Men who fail to show respect to the dead," argued the *Palladium of Labor* in 1884, "seldom or ever respect anything outside of their own precious selves."[4] Fire companies,[5] baseball teams,[6] fraternal lodges and friendly societies,[7] and reform clubs[8] all mourned the loss of working-class brethren. Among the membership of craft unions or assemblies of the Knights of Labor attendance at a funeral was a matter of principle and pride, a collective as opposed to individual choice; "in a body" was the usual manner in which they paid their last respects.[9] The funeral procession, then, hints at the strength of the associational life of the Victorian workman, a key component of his social and cultural existence. In the sheer size of the mourning procession, or the unanimity of the trade union turn-out, we are reminded of the tenacious bond of solidarity cementing the working-class community.[10]

So prominent, indeed, was working-class attendance at funerals that the event came to occupy a place within the language of the trades. An "Old Timer" reminisced:

> I would tell what I know about team shoe making. The men are a jolly set and have their own little rackets. A team is composed of a laster, healer, burnisher, and finisher. The best thing is to get a steady team, for unless you have that luck you are never sure of a full weeks work. Shoemakers have more 'uncles' and 'aunts' than any other mechanic. If in the summer the day be fine, some one of team gets the 'flem', and the others cannot work without him, so they are obliged to stop, and as a rule, they get the 'hines'. He may turn up next day. Ask him where he was? "To be sure, to a funeral." His 'wife' died. I knew one man to bury a wife every other week. The funniest thing is that all the wives died to order, always Sunday so they can take Monday to attend the funeral. What work the laster gets out for the week the other four will get paid for, and it happens that the other men will get paid for work not finished.

The boys call that 'dead horse', after him the team must pay for it, so it is in their interest to keep him until he finishes the work. The Dutch shoemakers call it 'swine' and it is now left for the French to give it a name. Tell all who desire to become shoemakers to see that the team are steady men; but look out for 'dead horse', 'swine', and 'funerals', and you may succeed.[11]

This "Old Timer's" account of resistance to work discipline in the shoe industry suggests another context in which to view the customary attendance of funerals. Relief from the drudgery of work may well have prompted the exodus from the workplace accompanying the burial of a shopmate. An iron molder, "J. C.," outlined the consequence of this alternative, the deterioration of the long-standing practice of funeral attendance among foundry workers:

In former years it was customary for the shop's crew, and even the entire union to take a day for attendance, not altogether because of their grief or affection for the brother, but because of the custom that had been established in years gone by, and often I regret to say because the members desired to take in a ball game or other athletic event or visit a neighbouring town. It was frequently happened that not one-fourth of the men have attended the funeral services, and one instance came under my notice where, out of 173 molders working in six shops, but eleven were present, the others spending their time in other ways.

In the midst of this kind of inattention to tradition, some craftsmen undoubtedly advocated the abandonment of the obligation of funeral attendance. This was "J.C."'s solution, and he must have had his followers.[12]

Historians with an acute urge to pigeon-hole, and a finely honed sociological bent, will perhaps perceive a modernist-traditionalist divide separating "J. C." and the "Old Timer." It is a neat categorization, and one that will appeal to those who crave order and precision, but working-class culture knew few such tidy distinctions. The old and the new, the residual and the emergent — to use Raymond Williams's terms — were much more likely to exist symbiotically, and in Hamilton, at least, it is the continuities in the cultural lives of nineteenth-century workingmen that are striking.[13] The tradition of funeral attendance, for instance, lived on, albeit in a less rigorous form. When David Ross, a printer once prominent in the Hamilton Trades and Labor Council, died in Toronto in the winter of 1898 his body was returned to Hamilton, members of the city's International Typographical Union attending the funeral in large numbers. Nonresidency had done little to stifle their sense of obligation, and Ross's funeral spoke of the persistence of an established tradition.[14]

More than the funeral, of course, persevered. The culture of the nine-teenth-century skilled workingman embraced a rich associational life, institutionalized in the friendly society, the mechanics' institute, sporting fraternities, fire companies, and workingmen's clubs. Complementing these formal relationships were the less structured but equally tangible ties of neighbourhood, workplace, or kin, manifesting themselves in the intimacy of the shared pail of beer, or the belligerence of the charivari party. Lingering at the edge of this culture, and illuminating its contours, stood events of importance to the community of the skilled: Confedera-tion, marked by celebration and trade procession; self-proclaimed work-ingmen's holidays, later legitimized by government proclamation, and declared Labour Day; or less momentous happenings, such as the coming of a circus, or the visit of a minstrel troupe. By the early twentieth century, it is true, realms of this culture would be emasculated, if not destroyed. The mechanics' institute, poisoned by the condescension and contemptuous patronage of the city's elite, had withered and died, while professionalization siphoned off much of the cultural essence of the base-ball teams and fire companies. Yet the passing of institutions or the sub-limation of once specifically working-class activities hardly signified the obliteration of a culture. Much lived on, transplanted to other formal set-tings, craft unions being particularly fertile ground; other cultural forms and traditions continued to thrive in their own right.

Cultural continuities, then, testify to the basic resiliency of working people in the face of the industrial-capitalist transformation of the nine-teenth century.[15] It was perhaps this fundamental continuity which lent coherence and stability to the working-class community, mediating the disruptive impact of massive population turnover, pervasive upward and downward social mobility, and the chaotic upheavals associated with the transition from handicraft production to modern industry — all prominent in the years 1860–1914. And, finally, this essential cultural continuity may be seen as the background of coherence against which new forms of working-class protest evolved, forms that in Hamilton assumed impor-tance in the struggle for the nine-hour day, the rise of the Knights of Labor, and the emergence of an aggressive craft unionism in the pre-World War I years. For culture is nothing if it is not *used*: a process that constantly brings into relief the specific social relationships of a given society, relationships that often reflect basic antagonisms under industrial capitalism.[16] What is too often seen as trivial and commonplace in the cultural arena may be, as Henri Lefebvre points out, an important source of creativity and inspiration, perhaps even a sustaining force underlying the process of resistance:

As a compendium of seemingly unimportant activities and of pro-ducts and exhibits other than natural, everyday life is more than something that eludes natural, divine and human myths. Could it represent a lower sphere of meaning, a place where creative energy is stored in readiness for new creations? ... It is not a chasm, a barrier or a buffer but a field and a half-way house, a halting place and a spring-board, a moment made on moments (desires, labours, pleasures — products and achievements — passivity and creativity — means and ends, etc.), the dialectical interaction that is the inevitable starting point for the realization of the possible.[17]

It was, perhaps, in just this kind of way that culture operated in past times in Hamilton's community of skilled workers. Despite the irksome fact that working-class involvement in friendly society and fire-engine hall, mechanics' institute and baseball team, is shrouded in obscurity, a ubiquitous anonymity being imposed on historical knowledge by the lack of surviving sources, it is possible, and even probable, that the associational life of skilled workers cultivated a sense of solidarity that strengthened the ability of the skilled to resist the encroachments of industrial-capitalist disciplines and development. And it is undeniable that within a shared cultural context there were age-old customs and traditions — the charivari, to name but one — that could be turned to the purposes of protest. Historians who by-pass this culture, denigrating its importance, miss a complex component of nineteenth- and early twentieth-century life.[18]

Clearly one of the most visible corners of associational life in Hamilton in the years 1860-1914 was the fraternal lodge. Friendly societies attracted the city's residents with striking regularity: Orangemen met to celebrate the Battle of the Boyne, or reminisce over dinner on Guy Fawkes Day; Masons often found themselves attracted to festivals honouring the traditions of their ancient craft; and the Foresters, Emerald Beneficial Association, Sons of England, Workmen, Odd Fellows, St. George's Society, and Knights of Pythias all sank deep roots in Hamilton's soil.

These voluntary associations can be viewed in different ways. Some have suggested that they were primarily bases of community power, led by men of property and standing.[19] Others have looked in another direction, focusing instead on the involvement of many working-class elements.[20] Both perceptions touch on important truths. On the one hand, merchants, professionals, clerks, and propertied men did indeed exert disproportionate amounts of influence in many friendly society circles, although it is important to realize that this hegemony was uneven, varying from society to society as well as within different lodges of the same organization. On the other hand, skilled workingmen certainly, and even some labourers, were common in all of the societies, and in many their role was far from subservient.

There was much to draw the skilled worker into the halls of the fraternal order. We have already noted the important contribution of the friendly societies in time of death. Beyond this the very language of the fraternal order was often borrowed from the crafts, appealing to a sense of dignity and pride of workmanship well understood by the mechanic.[21] For the wandering emigrant, on a "tramp" of unnatural severity, the comforts of shared sympathies and impressions must have drawn many a Scot to the St. Andrew's Society, a number of Englishmen to the St. George's Society, and not a few Irish to the St. Patrick's Society or the Orange Lodge.[22] The elaborate ritual and solemnity of the secret oath undoubtedly cultivated a sense of fraternity cherished by men of the trades and, in the case of an old Crispin or a dedicated Knight of Labor, thoroughly familiar.[23] And, as a means of transcending the tight bounds of economic insecurity, many nineteenth-century workingmen might well have been attracted to the charitable impulse so important in the germination of the voluntary society.[24]

All of this, and more, pushed the skilled worker towards friendly society halls, an environment in which cooperation, fraternity, and equality thrived. The motto of the Ancient Order of United Workmen, for instance, proclaimed their adherence to mutual aid: "The one needs the assistance of the other."[25] Among the Odd Fellows an old axiom—"In union there is strength"—achieved a place of prominence. "A single individual," proclaimed the *Correct Guide in all Matters Relating to Odd-fellowship*, "if he labor with a will, may accomplish much in the field of fraternity, but a host, united in solid phalanx in the service of Benevolence, may revolutionize the world."[26] Class distinctions were to have no place within their order: "we aim to abolish all considerations of wealth or poverty in our fraternity; to make all feel that as Odd Fellows, at least, they are not only brethren, but equals."[27] Small wonder, then, that the Odd Fellows aimed their sights directly at a working-class constituency: "It is probably the most adapted to working men, who from changes in locations of trade, and other causes, are daily becoming more migratory in their habits, and who are also emigrating in great numbers from our shores to our colonies and distant lands."[28] This was an attractive package to the workingman of the Victorian city.

Few indeed were the Hamilton men prominent in trade affairs who had no connection with a fraternal lodge or benevolent association. John Pryke, whom we shall encounter again as president of the Hamilton Nine Hour League, and a staunch Crispin, was an active member of the Orange Lodge.[29] A machinist, William Derby, Grand Master Workman of the Hamilton District Assembly of the Knights of Labor, and an early pillar of the Trades and Labor Council, was a leading official of the Young Men's Protestant Benevolent Association.[30] A leading activist in the organizational drive of the pre-World War I years, Harry Obermeyer, was prominent in a number of societies.[31] Among printers the penchant for involvement seemed particularly acute. Cornelius Donovan, a typographer serving as president of the Hamilton Trades Assembly in 1872, assisted in the founding of the St. Patrick's Society.[32] Two printers — A. T. Freed and David Hastings — stood out as dedicated members of the Acacia Lodge of the Ancient, Free, and Accepted Masons, documenting its early history.[33] Probably the most ardent supporter of the friendly society, however, was William J. Vale. Vale, whose experience in the working-class movement included participation in the Toronto printers' strike of 1872, a term as Grand Master Workman of the Hamilton Knights in 1883, scurrilous indictment as a member of the notorious "Home Club" in 1886, long affiliation with the International Typographical Union No. 129, and leadership of the Trades and Labor Council in the late 1880s and early 1890s, also found time to patronize the Foresters, Odd Fellows, and St. George's Society. He viewed the fraternal order as the practical embodiment of the principles of the cooperative movement; his intimate connection with and understanding of Hamilton societies won him a position as insurance inspector in 1892.[34] Vale's associate in the printers' union, the workingman's alderman William C. McAndrew, was the recipient of a "past preceptor's jewel," an honour attained by few Orangemen.[35] Men like these prompted the working-class press to keep abreast of fraternal society activities, allocating columns to the progress of the secret orders. "A large number of union men are members of the Woodmen of the World," noted the *Industrial Banner* in 1907.[36]

The most convincing evidence of the skilled worker's presence in the friendly society, of course, would be complete membership listings, which could then be used to formulate a conception of the occupational structure of specific lodges.[37] Such data are extremely rare. Only two such compilations exist for Hamilton societies in the years 1860-1914 and these, unfortunately, are from a body — the Ancient, Free, and Accepted Masons — which, along with the St. George's and St. Andrew's Societies, had a particularly weak working-class constituency, one factor, no doubt, contributing to the survival of these lists.[38] Between 1855 and 1905, 709 Hamiltonians joined the Acacia Lodge of the Ancient, Free, and Accepted Masons; of these, the occupations of 489 could be determined.[39] Within this latter group a clear majority, 282, belonged to a social stratum distinctly removed from the world of the skilled workingman, led by merchants (14), manufacturers (5), and proprietors (29), and supported by a vast body of clerks (45), accountants (23), and salesmen-travellers (30), and a retinue of doctors, bartenders, managers, insurance agents, architects, brokers, bank tellers, teachers, and barristers.[40] The skilled worker, however, was not without a voice in Acadia Lodge: approximately 36 per cent of this identified sample, or 176 members, belonged to the skilled trades, among them 21 machinists and 19 carpenters.[41] Rounding out these figures were 31 members from the ranks of the unskilled and service occupations: labourers, mariners, sorters, checkers, watchmen, and teamsters. In the Barton Lodge the story was almost identical. There, of the 159 identified members (269 joined in the years 1845-1911), 36 per cent, again, belonged to the skilled trades.[42]

In the absence of comparable data from other societies, we can only speculate as to the extent of the involvement of the skilled worker. There are, however, indications that many fraternal bodies housed significant numbers of craftsmen and other working-class elements. James Hennigan, president of the Hamilton branch of the Emerald Beneficial Association and an advocate of the cause of the Knights of Labor, wrote to Terence V. Powderly requesting him to speak at a gathering of his association, which apparently contained large numbers of Powderly's followers.[43] When William Vale was asked "What kind of membership constitutes these societies?", he replied bluntly: "Working classes—nine-tenths of them."[44]

Listings of friendly society officials, common in the daily press and in city directories, are also useful as barometers of working-class involvement. A few examples suffice. The Ancient Order of United Workmen, often confused with the Knights of Labor in the parlance of the 1880s, boasted a tinsmith, a conductor, and a printer among its officials in 1881, two brief years after its founding in the city.[45] A glance at the 1901-10 minute book of Lodge No. 49 of the Hamilton Workmen depicts an organization overwhelmingly working class in composition in which picnics, lectures, banquets, and sporting rivalry figured prominently.[46] The hegemony of the skilled manifested itself blatantly in the Commercial Lodge of the International Order of Odd Fellows in 1863. Daniel Black, a saloon-keeper patronized by many early unionists, shared the leadership of the lodge with his brother William, a machinist at the Great Western shops, John Williams, another machinist, and William J. McAllister, a printer.[47] Officers of the Lodge Britannia No. 8 of the Sons of England in 1883, similarly, included two labourers, a printer, painter, fitter, porter, machinist, butcher, and carpenter.[48]

The organization with the most substantial following of skilled workingmen, however, was undoubtedly the Orange Lodge. Between the years 1863 and 1878 the officials of various Orange Lodges included representatives from virtually every Hamilton craft, the machinists being especially visible. And, if there was a threat to the hegemony of the skilled, it was posed from below rather than from above, common labourers being the single most prominent occupational category in positions of responsibility.[49] By 1895 the situation was much the same, the officers of the city's Orange Order including two machinists, two cabinetmakers, and a bricklayer, carpenter, molder, and packer.[50] In 1911 the officials themselves had changed, but the trades persisted; among the officers printers, molders, machinists, iron workers, labourers, and carpenters were to be found.[51]

What are we to make of this presence and involvement? It is a thorny question, and one that defies simplistic answer. Workingmen sought many things in the halls of friendly societies: a measure of security against sickness and death; association with their peers or, perhaps for some, the chance to cultivate ties with their betters; simple recreation away from the confines of family and work, often realized in a game of carpet ball or quoits, or an excursion on the steamboats of Burlington Bay; an affirmation of their status as respectable members of the community, dispensers of charity and good works, and not just, as in occasional times of great need, recipients. The lessons they learned would be equally varied: the benefits and attractions of equality, fraternity, and cooperation, on the one hand, all deeply embedded within the consciousness of the emerging labour movement; or, on the other hand, deference, accommodation, and an exclusionary contempt for those less attuned to the practices of sober thrift and appropriate propriety.[52]

William J. Vale, in a paper delivered before the Hamilton Trades and Labor Council, stressed the positive contribution of the benevolent society in the evolution of working-class consciousness. Such organizations had, he maintained, done much to further the cooperative impulse, providing a mechanism of collective protection for the lower orders. His views were vehemently opposed by John A. Flett, a Hamilton carpenter later to emerge as a central figure in the rise of the American Federation of Labor in Canada. Flett considered these associations "merely poultices on the cancer" of the social system, and concluded that "[if] there were no benevolent societies there would be a revolution among the workingmen of the country. The sooner the country comes down to actual want, as a matter of fact, the sooner we'll have change."[53] Both men caught something of the truth, and if we seek a hard and fast explanation — a sociological model — behind the popularity of the fraternal order in working-class life, we will only stifle the diversity of human motivation and complexity of consequence surrounding the skilled workingman's participation in lodge and chapter.

In one realm of fraternal order activity, however, there was no mistaking the potentiality of divided loyalties that could foster antagonism between two distinct working-class groups. Orange and Green were badges worn by many nineteenth-century workingmen, and if Toronto can be taken as any standard, conflict between Irish Protestants and Irish Catholic workers was common and violent.[54] The Jubilee Riots of 1875, for example, stand as one of the most virulent sectarian clashes in the history of Canada.[55]

Yet, in Hamilton, at least, Orange and Green rarely met in violent confrontation. Scattered references to individualized combat do, of course, exist. George Douglas, a boot and shoe maker, was viciously beaten by his neighbour, John Halloran, who while wielding the iron bar he used so effectively upon his opponent's head, was heard to scream, "I'll take your life! I'll take your life you b----y Protestant!" He did not succeed, but it was not for want of trying.[56] In the fall of 1860 many local Orangemen were outraged when the visit of the Prince of Wales and the Duke of Newcastle was marred by the appearance of "the Romish Bishop, in full canonicals," and the St. Patrick's Society, bearing aloft "*a green flag and green badges*."[57] And the flooding of the city by the Toronto 'Prentice Boys in 1887, celebrating the Relief of Derry, gave rise to a brawl, Hamilton's Green contingent apparently having been not at all pleased with the invasion of their turf.[58]

The only serious affair occurred on the night of 6 August 1878, and it was overblown by the local press. Orange-Green relations in the city were apparently at a low point, for there were rumours circulating that the Emerald Beneficial Association was planning to burn an effigy of King William III in retaliation for some insulting acts perpetrated by the Orange Young Britons. The timing of the outburst was conditioned by a visit of some Toronto friends to the King Street rooms of the Emerald Association. After escorting their confrères to the steamer bound for Toronto the Catholic body returned to their rooms, only to be confronted with a large number of men and young boys. A row appeared imminent, and when the Emerald Association's band dispersed, the True Blue Fife and Drum Band appeared, 300 to 400 bringing up the rear. After a brief flurry of yelling, singing, and marching around the Gore, the procession headed towards James Street, during which time it was interrupted by cries of "Fight! Fight!" Almost immediately two carters, Dan Collins and Tom Brick, found themselves surrounded by a sea of unfriendly Protestant faces. It was not long before Collins and Brick, armed only with their whips, and the stones thrown at them by their adversaries, were engaged in a battle with the crowd. One must give them their due; they fought admirably. Police eventually extricated them from the street war, and they drove off in the direction of Corktown.

The crowd, "yelling and maddened," was not so easily put off, and it headed for Brick's house, which was "reached in a few minutes." Windows were soon being smashed as the crowd stoned the Brick residence, driving Mrs. Brick, an infant clutched to her breast, to shelter in a neighbour's house. Two or three policemen eventually arrived, but even then "it was sometime before quietness could be restored. The whole region was in a ferment, women and children running hither and thither and the mob hooting, yelling, swearing and conducting themselves generally in a most outrageous style." After an abortive attempt to continue the fun at Collins's residence, the crowd finally dispersed, but not before they saw Collins and Brick drive down from the Mountain, denouncing the "Orange body, whom they blamed for all the trouble." Brick had not even been in his house during the melee.[59]

Some of the actors met in court the next day, and the testimony, as in most courtroom theatre, was both revealing and humorous.[60] Dan Collins swore that "there was 600 or 700 there, but I didn't have time to count them; the tune the band played didn't annoy me a bit; you can bet your life I didn't make any remarks, thinking it better to keep my mouth shut." Michael Begley, a GWR policeman charged by Brick and Collins with assault, insisted that Collins called him an "Orange s-- of b----," but denied that he had said that he had "stood enough of the d----d Papist row," and that he "wasn't going to have any Montreal here." Brick seemed undaunted by the whole affair, informing the court that he did not recall "how often I have been before the Police Magistrate for acts of violence; I guess I have been up twenty times." The Irishman then assured those gathered to witness the proceedings that "if there hadn't been 600 or 700 they wouldn't have tackled us."[61] Brick apparently had not learned an elementary lesson in court etiquette, for his belligerence cost him $10 and costs; the other cases were dismissed. Both Collins and Brick, however, would resurface in the 1880s as members of the Knights of Labor, the latter serving as a workingman's alderman for many years.

This, of course, was a major battle, but a war waged against two carters should not be overdrawn. It should be abundantly clear that there may have been something more to this skirmish than Orange-Green antagonism. Many a man must have had a score to settle with men of the bearing of Dan Collins and Tom Brick. Nevertheless, the event stands out as the most prominent case of aggravated sectarian assault in the city in the years 1860-1914.[62] As such, Hamilton's experience pales in comparison with the upheavals common in Toronto, New York, or Belfast. Part of the reason for this lack of conflict was undoubtedly the strength of the Protestant community. Like London, Ontario, Hamilton was most emphatically a Protestant city, and this hegemony may have gone unquestioned.[63] Equally important, however, was the strength of the working-class movement, and the solidarity it conditioned; Hamilton's Orange and Green workers apparently knew how to keep their divided loyalties in perspective, and their allegiance to their class may have mediated many hostilities.

Richard Trevellick said as much in a letter to Terence V. Powderly, comparing the Hamilton Knights of Labor with the Toronto assemblies. In Toronto, Trevellick maintained, the Order was a failure: "The large assembly of shoemakers as a class are Orangemen and Ladies and if they are not Orangemen they are self-conceited flunkeys and not fit for Heaven." Hamilton, however, had many trustworthy workers, and meetings were well attended and properly run: "our house is doing well," Trevellick assured the Grand Master Workman.[64] Workers such as "Unity," "Anti-Bigot," and "Pinkerton" urged upon Hamilton mechanics the politics of class unity, rather than division, and with the realization that Orange-Green antagonism was "the bloody shirt" waved in the face of the working-class movement, the cause of unity won important victories.[65] Sectarian conflict would impinge only peripherally on Hamilton's workingmen in the years 1860-1914, and virtually never after 1887.

Rivalling the friendly society as a centre of the skilled worker's associational life, and less ambiguous both in terms of its class composition and its impact, was the fire company.[66] The history of the Hamilton companies commences in 1833, following a devastating conflagration in 1832. They remained peripheral to community life until the early 1850s when the growing awareness of the importance of manufacturing to the city's welfare prompted an expansion in the number of companies as well as an increase in the number of volunteer firemen. By 1857 the force stood at eight companies, with a combined membership of 518 officers and men. A series of disputes and disbandings weakened the brigade; by 1867 membership had dropped to 220, consisting of a hook and ladder company, one hose company, and three engine companies. By the mid-1860s manufacturers and merchants had reacted to this decline, questioning the competency and efficiency of the volunteer corps, advocating the establishment of a professional fire-fighting force. It only required a major loss to prompt them to action. With the burning of the D. McInnes and Company warehouses on 1 August 1879 they received their stimulus, and a professional, standing fire department was created, supplemented by volunteers.[67]

For over twenty years, however, the fire companies were created, led, and staffed by Hamilton workingmen.

> On the brakes of the old machine
> They worked from day to day,
> Putting out the raging fire,
> Although they got no pay.

A successful craftsman, like the carriagemaker John Amor, who would establish a lucrative agricultural implements works in the city in the 1860s, often played a prominent role, but the majority of firemen were skilled workers of small means.[68] In the Hook and Ladder Company, embracing a membership of thirty, the key officers were M. W. Attwood, a watchmaker, A. Green, a brush manufacturer, P. Colvin, a carter, and H. E. Eliot, a tailor. A salesman, an engineer, a compositor, and a shoemaker served as officials in the forty-member Hose Company, while Rescue Company, with forty-five members, was led by a scalemaker, a machinist, and a brushmaker. John Amor and his brother William, a fruit dealer, seemed to control the No. 1 Company, but even there they were aided by a hatter and a foundry helper.[69] Nothing had changed by

1867.[70] The composition of the Great Western Brigade in 1867 states the case clearly: the hose company was led by a millwright and two labourers; the No. 1 engine company's officers were a painter, a machinist, a boiler-maker, and a fitter; the officials of No. 2 Company included a foreman, an upholsterer, a clerk, a carpenter, and a cabinetmaker; while the steam engine company was presided over by four fitters and a turner.[71] Of the ninety-three fire company officials classified occupationally in the years 1860-1872, fully sixty-five were from the skilled trades, eleven came from unskilled occupations, with the remaining seventeen falling into a category composed of clerks, foremen, manufacturers, contractors, and merchants.[72]

Like the friendly society, the engine house had much to offer. Some were attracted by the opportunity to serve the community in a time of crisis, for the nineteenth century knew few fears worse than that of fire. Others were undoubtedly drawn to the rich texture of engine-house life, accentuated by the oyster suppers and alcoholic refreshment indulged in by many companies, or the festive gatherings marking the end of a suc-cessful year.[73] Fierce rivalries, bred of neighbourhood jealousies and rein-forced by the maintenance of separate companies for each ward, must also have attracted some, for there was no company which did not count as a high accomplishment the honour of arriving first at the scene of a fire. So ingrained was the competitive impulse that firemen sacrificed their wages, dropping their tools at the shout of "Fire!" or the clamour of the bell. In their haste to arrive first on one unfortunate occasion, the Hose Reel Company trampled a young boy underfoot on their dash to a fire.[74] For others the lure of a uniform (consisting of cap and belt, red shirt, light blue coat, and white staff and badge of office), displayed in the handsome torchlit procession of a summer evening, or in the spring parades celebrating the Queen's Birthday, must have been irresistible. Finally, for many the fire company reinforced other realms of associa-tional life, bringing together patrons of similar causes, Orangeism and temperance being only two of the more obvious.[75]

Richard Butler, reminiscing on the "History of Hamilton Fire Depart-ment," recalled many an evening spent in the engine house, polishing the equipment and passing the time with other volunteers. His memoir tells us much about the texture of life in a mid-century fire company. At the time of his service in Cataract Company No. 2, in 1854, he described the brigade as

a department of four engine companies, a hose company and a hook and ladder company, comprising an active membership of about three hundred, mostly all young men who did not own a dollar's worth of property in the city, and gave their services without fee or reward for the benefit of their home town. Day or night, when the fire alarm bell called, the boys answered promptly, leaving their work in daytime, at a loss to themselves, for their employers as a general thing charged up the lost time they were absent from the workshop; and at night they would turn out in a cold winter storm, half dressed, buttoning up their clothes as they raced to the engine house. It was the pride of every fireman to pull on the drag rope, and if possible, get to the fire before the other company and have the first stream on the burning building.

Butler also noted the distinctive social character of each company. "The boys of No. 3," he remembered, "were a convival set, and often indulged in crackers and cheese and beer, especially after a fire." Business meetings were often the scene of hotly contested debates over the beer bill accumulated since the last meeting, a thorn in the side of Charley Smith, captain of No. 3, and a teetotaler who worried "to think his Company had such an appetite for beer." No. 4 Company was composed solely of young Orangemen, "a wild lot of boys" occupying an engine house on James Street North at the Railroad Bridge. Butler's own company, No. 2, had started out as a temperance venture, but found it difficult to adhere to the cause; the heat of the flames cultivated a thirst water could not quench. And apparently No. 2 was sufficiently devoid of competent leadership to give rise to this early indictment:

> It is a reflection upon the character of our town that as miserable a piece of machinery is, called Engine No. 2, no better person can be found to manage it than that buffoon, Bill Morin, who at the late fire appeared as Captain of it in some kind of grotesque coat, said to have been taken from a Yankee deserter, and afterwards trimmed with shilling-a-yard red flannel. When he could amuse himself no longer with throwing water on some burning rubbish, he commenced trying experiments with his double and twisted thousand dollar Jim Burke engine at some persons who were placed on the roof of Sam Kerr's store, to prevent it taking fire. How can it be expected that fire companies can be efficient with such men to conduct them.

The author concluded his harangue with the observation that in many companies "there was not much attention given to fire fighting."[76]

Such disorder was not likely to continue to prevail in the aftermath of the economic expansion of the 1850s and 1860s, nor were employers likely to continue to accept the infringements on labour discipline posed by the volunteer brigades. As employers sought to rationalize and standardize fire-fighting procedures they turned to the panacea of a municipal fire department.[77] Butler remembered the shift in character of the No. 2 Company as businessmen joined its ranks, and men of the type of Bill Morin got the shunt.[78] During the late 1860s clashes between the volunteer companies and the City Council became increasingly common as firefighting methods, inefficiency, and the personnel of the brigade's leadership came under attack. By the early 1870s it was clear that professionalism had won the day, and local officials saw a trained, standing force, paid by the municipality, as the solution to the many problems posed by the workingmen's volunteer companies.[79] It was a process opposed by many a "Hoseman," but it was destined to run its course, and by 1879 the volunteer brigade had been replaced by a permanent, paid force, headed by a professional fire chief.[80]

Even after the demise of the fire companies, however, old ties retained some force. Firemen's celebrations and reunions continued to draw many skilled workingmen well into the 1880s, and as late as 1908 the *Industrial Banner* paid tribute to Larry Clark, a London fire chief who had been a charter member of Hamilton's Federal Labor Union and an ardent unionist.[81] As thinly disguised workingmen's clubs, the fire companies would be replaced by other associations of workingmen throughout the 1870s, 1880s, and 1890s. Discontinuity would be compensated by a fundamental functional continuity.

Closely approximating the experience of the fire companies was the rise and fall of the Hamilton and Gore Mechanics' Institute, founded in 1839 and disbanded 25 April 1882, its library sold in small lots to appease its many creditors. Originally convened in an engine house, the Mechanics' Institute grew in size and importance, its purpose of "diffusing scientific and literary knowledge, by a library of reference and circulation; by the formation of a museum of specimens in zoology, geology, or other subjects of nature, science, or manufactures; by lectures, by philosophical apparatus; by conversations; and by any other method the committee may judge necessary," apparently exercising considerable appeal. By 1852 the institute had erected a building composed of a library, reading room, and public hall. Ranked as one of the foremost associations of its kind in the Dominion, Hamilton's Mechanics' Institute would serve as a centre of community life until its collapse in the early 1880s.[82]

Like many realms of working-class associational life, the mechanics' institute has been the focus of much recent scholarly work. The tendency is to view the institute as a vehicle through which the crusading, rational middle classes successfully controlled both program and clientele, utilizing the halls of the mechanics' institute to inculcate a submissive respect for authority and an appropriate attitude towards work, offering courses and lectures designed to attract clerks and accountants, rather than working men and women. Foster Vernon, in an unpublished study of the development of adult education in Ontario, states the case baldly: "they were essentially a middle class organization run by people with middle class values which they constantly sought to impose on members of the lower class who came to the institutes searching for help with their learning problems."[83]

In fact, however, such a generalization distorts as much as it clarifies. For mechanics' institutes cannot be divorced from their local context, in which the strength of the working-class movement would contribute to the vibrancy of the working-class presence in these early buildings of adult education. Nor must we mistake the hegemony of propertied elements, so common in many institutes, for an acquiescent working-class constituency. Merchants, manuacturers, and clerks could often control local institutes, while workingmen utilized the services and facilities for their own purposes, often expressing distinct dissatisfaction with the policies and practices of the directors. It is necessary to recognize both the dreary demise that so many institutes suffered, stifled by the efforts of men who knew all too well what was best for other men, and the submerged involvement and struggle of workingmen, who learned much in the process.[84]

Hamilton's Mechanics' Institute was directed by men far removed from working-class life. There is no mistaking this basic continuity of control. Prominent in the history of the Hamilton Institute were men like Dr. William Craigie, a wealthy surgeon; Archibald Macallum, a principal active in educational reform; and Thomas McIlwraith and C. W. Meakins, local businessmen and promoters. Sir Allan MacNab, a "pillar of the community" and prominent in early railroad construction and speculation, was the Mechanics' Institute's Honourary Patron. There was little of working-class leadership here, although an aberrant upholsterer or isolated painter often occupied a position of responsibility.[85]

Such blatant control was not without an effect. In 1861, with membership standing at 396, Adam Brown, president of the local institute, and Archibald Macallum concluded their report on the Hamilton and Gore Mechanics' Institute with a sorry refrain: "The profound object ... is the improvement of our artizans and working classes ... but there is reason to fear this design has in many instances been lost sight of ... as other classes of the community other than operatives constitute not infrequently the majority of subscribers and attendants."[86] After 1861 the directors frequently complained of the apathy of their constituents, and the membership declined year after year.[87]

In the absence of membership listings we can only speculate as to the degree of working-class involvement in the Hamilton Institute, or the extent of the mechanics' utilization of the facilities. It must have been significantly greater, however, than working-class activity in the Mutual Improvement Association or the Mercantile Library Association, bodies catering to merchants, manufacturers, and clerks.[88] There are indications that many more mechanics used the facilities of the local hall than actually joined the Mechanics' Institute,[89] and the books prominent in the library must have drawn more than one worker into the reading-room to thumb the well-worn pages of *Les Miserables*, or study the arguments of classical political economy.[90] The Great Western Railway, for instance, subsidized the local hall, on the condition that fifty of its mechanics receive reductions in their membership fees. It withdrew its support in 1866, after its employees built their own reading-room to accommodate their needs.[91] Undoubtedly the most common form of working-class patronization of the Mechanics' Institute, however, was attendance at the many festivals, reunions, readings, lectures, minstrel troupe performances, and evening classes so prominent in the late nineteenth century. As a community centre, Hamilton's Mechanics' Hall knew no rival.[92]

If the extent of working-class participation in the affairs of the institute is veiled in ambiguity, working-class opposition to the directors often seethed below the surface of seemingly tranquil relationships. The *Hamilton Times* hinted at the manipulation of key positions that characterized the election of officials.[93] "A Mechanic" complained of the poor workmanship so common in repairs to the local hall, and implicitly raised the questions of graft and corruption, positing profiteering by the directors on contracts undertaken by the Mechanics' Institute.[94]

Often the critics touched on more substantial issues. A series of letters to the *Hamilton Spectator* in February 1860 complained of the degeneration of the institute, and the deterioration of the library. "W" objected to the board's policy of "objecting to this paper or that periodical because it happens to advocate views or express opinions which do not coincide with their own." A similar theme was reiterated by "an incorporated member," who objected to the Board of Directors because of their prejudices and narrow vision.[95] In the aftermath of the withdrawal of the Great Western Railway's $200 yearly grant, occasioned by the exodus of the GWR mechanics to their own reading room (itself an act of protest), one workingman was scathing in his indictment of the directors, whom he feared would utilize the financial loss to cover their own blunders. "Men of ease, who lack enterprise," he wrote, "should not be permitted thus to sacrifice the best interests of the society; if they have not time and are unwilling to meet manfully the difficulties of their position, let them at least make room for others who both can and will." He also criticized the directors' willingness to sacrifice the library at the first sign of economic stringency, while they took pains to maintain the newsroom, used by mercantile and professional men who were able to spend their time away from their homes. The library, on the other hand, served the interests of more humble men, who borrowed books to read in the privacy of their dwellings, in brief hours of leisure enjoyed after a day's labours.[96] Less than a month later, on the eve of an election of the Board of Directors, "Watchman" argued in like fashion, calling for evening classes and library improvements.[97] But such a mundane purpose gained few adherents among those at the helm, and the institute stumbled along, apparently blind to the needs and desires of common labouring men and women. When it eventually foundered in 1882, the *Spectator* correctly concluded that "the people had lost confidence in the management of the library."[98]

Oddly enough, the working-class response to the fall of the local institution is perhaps the most substantial indication of the importance of the hall in the lives of the city's workingmen. Few causes were more dear to the Victorian workman than that of self-improvement, cultivated in the reading-room, and nourished by the holdings of an accessible library. When the means to this end were threatened, Hamilton's mechanics reacted with vigour. In October 1881 a petition supporting the Mechanics' Institute was signed by 865 persons, a total far in excess of the registered membership.[99] After the institute's collapse, "Humanitas" condemned the city for the lack of a library which it had once possessed "before some of [its] citizens became too wealthy to care for the comforts of their less fortunate brethren."[100]

Throughout the 1880s Hamilton workingmen threw their support behind the free library movement, and it was largely because of their efforts that the cause was won. With the establishment of a Free Library Board in 1889, of which Fred Walters, long-time member of the International Iron Molders' Union No. 26, and a delegate to the Central Labor Union, was a member, Hamilton's workingmen had finally rid themselves of the irritable taste of class distinction and manipulation that the Mechanics' Institute's Board of Directors had left in their mouths for so many years.[101] With that achievement gained, and their library secure, they had won a victory dear to their hearts.

Completing this structured realm of associational life so ardently patronized by Hamilton's skilled workingmen was the baseball club. Baseball remains an unexplored component of the working-class experience. Craft unions were seldom without a team, and across North America weekend and after-work games among printers, cigarmakers, molders, butchers, and other craftsmen attracted workmates, friends, and families to local fields, where the tensions of life dissipated with the excitement of a close match, the clowning of a particular player, or the refreshment of a glass of beer, a keg of which was usually within easy reach.[102] Unlike sports that would find a ready place within university curriculums, and unlike those games attracting clerks and professional men (football, cricket, rowing, for example), baseball was a distinctively working-class activity.[103] The emergence of professional teams in the late 1870s and 1880s would siphon off some of this early enthusiasm, but the adherence of the working-class community to active participation on the fields and diamonds of the city was startlingly resilient. To Hamilton's mechanic ballplayers sport was to be something more than a spectacle.[104]

One early account in the *Hamilton Evening Journal* conveys something of the importance of baseball in the lives of ordinary men: "The east end of the city presents a lively appearance every evening. All the avenues in the vicinity of the commons, as well as the commons themselves, are occupied by baseball clubs. ... There is also a club from the workshop of McPherson & Co., who are well up in the game and no doubt will, ere long, compete favourably with any 'professional' club in the city. ... It is understood that the shoemakers intend playing a match with the Hat-Factory Club in a few weeks, and no doubt it will be well contested."[105] Hamilton's working-class enthusiasts thus played their baseball as members of a club, employees of a specific shop or factory, or practitioners of a particular craft.

The clubs, apparently the most disciplined of the groupings, were prominent in the 1860s and 1870s, although the Young Mechanics Ball Club was active in the early 1880s. They were presided over by a serious group of officials, practised diligently, and bred a strong bond of personal loyalties and friendships, reinforced at annual suppers held in prominent city hotels. Organized by two brothers, William and James Shuttleworth, a clerk and a shoemaker, the Maple Leaf Club dominated the early scene. Those officials and players whose occupations could be determined included five clerks, three shoemakers, two turners and two labourers, and one of each of the following: coach manufacturer, broom manufacturer, saloon-keeper, hatter, painter, hammerman, foreman, butcher, machinist, marblecutter, brakesman, carriagemaker, boilermaker, tinsmith, horse-collar maker, teamster, watchmaker, cigarmaker, cabinetmaker, grocer, bookbinder, plasterer, tobacco worker, carpenter, sailor, and wool sorter.[106] Other clubs — the Star, Independent, Eagle, Mechanics, Rising Union, Ontario, Social, and Dundas Mechanics — were even more firmly in the grip of the skilled worker, as their names often suggested. The 1868 roster of the Star Club, for instance, included three molders, a turner, a tobacco worker, a cigarmaker, a labourer, and two men whose occupations could not be determined. On the Independent's 1867 team were three boot and shoe makers, a molder, a tinsmith, and four others whose occupations could not be ascertained. Among the Young Mechanics of 1881 were a mason, a trunkmaker, and two shoemakers.[107]

Games between various shops and factories complemented the activities of the clubs. Wanzer's, MacPherson's, Copp's foundry, Reid's furniture works, and other local businesses all fielded teams, and judging from the scores of some of the contests — 73-54 and 58-35 — these were raucous affairs, punctuated with much merriment.[108]

But the most persistent participants were craft unionists. The printers exemplify the case. In the fall of 1871 the Hamilton printers initiated an attachment to baseball that would continue for over forty years. "The Great Typographical Base Ball Match" was the billing attracting many to the Maple Leaf grounds to watch the nines of the *Spectator* and the *Times* compete, and Bauer's brewery transported large quantities of ice and beer to the park "to quench the thirst of the large crowd anticipated." After the game the printers retired to a local pub where they enjoyed a hearty meal and abundant refreshment. By 1884 the city's typos had established a baseball club, and games between married men and bachelors, as well as contests involving printers from other towns, were commonplace throughout the 1880s and 1890s. In September 1911, in what may well have been a commemoration of their 1871 match, the local union held a stag picnic, at which the major attraction was a baseball game, interrupted by bouts of drinking. A month later the printers challenged the cigarmakers in the traditional Labour Day ball game.[109]

Small wonder, then, that baseball was Hamilton's "favourite game" and the city known as "the baseball centre" of Canada.[110] Despite disenchantment with the deterioration of old practices, and the growing commercialization of the game,[111] skilled workers owed a strong allegiance to a sport many of them had known intimately in their youth; attendance at strictly amateur games often exceeded 1,000 persons.[112] the Knights of Labor knew the drawing power of a good game and attracted city workingmen to rallies and demonstrations with the promise of a baseball match.[113] Even within the professional teams an awareness of their origins must have stirred, for in December 1884 a Cooperative team was formed; members of the Clippers had grown disgusted with their management's practices and sought just compensation for their labours on the diamond.[114] While "Old Sports Pabulum" could mourn the passing of the "regalia, long ovations, rabid fans, and west end vs. east end rivalry" characteristic of ball games in an earlier period, the sport nevertheless remained embedded within working-class culture.[115] Assuring its continuity was the union picnic, where a baseball game was almost a matter of course. "Picnics as a rule," noted the *Hamilton Spectator*, commenting on a past gathering of the Bricklayers' and Masons' Union, "now have little interest manifested in them unless there is a baseball match."[116] The demise of the mechanics' baseball club, and the transferral of its function to the union picnic, thus leads us out of the structured, institutionalized realm of associational life and into a more eclectic, but equally pervasive, domain.

At the centre of this more diffused culture stood the craft union, its disciplined apparatus organizing events of importance and meaning to its membership. In the late nineteenth and early twentieth centuries spring, summer, and early autumn months were a time of picnics and outings and among certain crafts, such as the printers, these undertakings had a long history.[117] Winter nights were often warmed by festive gatherings of craftsmen, commemorating the founding of their union, paying their respects to a workmate moved out of the shop by promotion or old age, or simply enjoying a hearty meal. Also conspicuous were dances and balls, attended by members of the fraternity and their wives.[118] Parades, in which the workers often appeared in uniform, proudly displaying their wares, and always "in full number," were common occurrences, marking the celebration of a major event or prefacing the sports, speeches, and frolicking of "labour's holiday," later to be officially proclaimed Labour Day.[119] In Hamilton these events constituted an important aspect of the skilled worker's everyday experiences.

Picnics were perhaps the most numerous. After the traditional skirmish in late April and early May over wage increases and job conditions, Hamilton's crafts settled into a summer of labour, pleasantly interrupted by trips to the Oaklands, Dundurn Park, or the Crystal Palace Grounds. A weekend in mid-August 1886, for instance, saw countless small picnics, as well as gatherings of the Bricklayers', Masons', and Labourers' unions, an outing by the employees of D. Moore and Company and the Burns and Robinson manufacturing company, an excursion to Niagara Falls by 700 Grand Trunk workers, and trips and picnics by the workers of the Ontario Cotton Mills and two assemblies of the Knights of Labor.[120] Throughout the years 1860-1914 virtually every Hamilton craft held regular summer picnics and outings. These excursions were complemented by gatherings of workers of specific shops and factories and assemblies of the Knights of Labor. Occasionally the city's skilled mechanics formed committees to organize grand workingmen's picnics encompassing all of the crafts, as well as the unskilled. These were gala events, drawing anywhere from 3,000 to 5,000 people, whose presence was often taken as an indication of the strength of labour's cause.[121]

Like picnics, banquets, dances, balls, and festivals were exceedingly common. A plumbers' gathering in the winter of 1874, a year of severe economic downturn, must have done much to lift the spirits of men exposed to the pinch of hard times.

> Come, all ye mechanics, for no dreadful panics
> Will meet you with grim spectre-faces.

A local newspaper noted "the hilarity manifested by members of the craft," and judged the gathering a success, "tending greatly to promote good feeling and sociability in all branches of the trade."[122] Pride in their work and recognition of their place in the community were also common themes and consequences of these craft gatherings.

> Come, each son of labour, and do us the favor
> Of tasting the good things provided.
> A truce to your moiling! for hard daily toiling
> Gives Rank that must ne'er be derided.

John Hargreaves, foreman of the locomotive works of the Great Western Railway, toasted the mechanic at an 1860 festival: "The mechanic was a progressive being and he would, bye-and-bye, take the lead; he was strong and his object should be to endeavor to elevate himself in the highest scale of mental culture." Another speaker noted the fraternal relations predominating: "Here they behaved themselves like men, and no coldness was visible among them; they all appeared like brothers; and if the aristocracy can have their assemblies, and enjoy themselves, he could not see why the mechanics should not have their reunions also."[123]

Molders, cigarmakers, glassworkers, stove-mounters, brushmakers, printers, carpenters, engineers, masons, and skilled workers associated with various assemblies of the Knights of Labor apparently agreed, for they appeared only too willing to organize a ball or socialize over dinner.[137] Typical of these festive occasions was the celebration of International Typographical Union No. 129, commemorating its sixtieth anniversary with a "Feast of Oratory and Good Eatin" at the Strand Cafe in March 1914. Old hands reminisced about "washing rollers" and "bucking wood," common chores in their early days as apprentices. Extolling "the art preservative of all arts" were two charter members of the Hamilton Typographical Society, A. T. Freed and Reese Evans. Talk eventually turned to an early conflict: "The reminiscence of the first strike in Hamilton told by Mr. Butler was interesting; how there were no railways running between Hamilton and Toronto then; but Mr. Smiley who owned the daily that refused to yield, went to Toronto and brought the 'rats' by boat, only to be captured by the big Tom Cat of the 'Vigilance Committee'. The men won after being out ten days. They asked for a raise from 9 to 10 dollars a week." For the printers, at least, the commemorative supper was one means of preserving a rich heritage.[125]

The most striking assertion of the craft unionist's presence, however, was the trade procession.[126] One of the earliest and certainly one of the most impressive instances of the forceful presence of the Canadian Victorian workman was his avid enthusiasm for the union of the Canadas, and skilled craftsmen presented a united front in Hamilton's Confederation parade. Many skilled mechanics would have marched in the ranks of the Fire Brigade on 25 May 1867, under the banner "Success to Confederation."[127] In late June preparations began in earnest, the Crispins, butchers, and tailors, in concert with the St. George's Society and the Kalithumpian Klan (a motley crew of pranksters that must have included some skilled tradesmen and some young apprentices), pledging their support for the scheduled events of 1 July 1867.[128] On the "Celebration Day" the trades turned out in force, the *Hamilton Spectator* describing the unionists, preceded by the fire companies, splendidly attired in colourful uniforms:

> Then came the butchers who made an excellent show. The ox which had been profusely ornamented with red and blue rosettes and artificial flowers (furnished by Mrs. Ridder), was in a wagon from which he surveyed the admiring spectators with a mild and placid gaze.

Round him clustered the sturdy butchers, all of them well mounted and exceedingly 'old countrified'. . . . The Iron Moulders were not a showy looking, but an exceedingly respectable set of men, and they marched well and preserved good order. The Shoemakers with King Crispin and his champion and sundry other worthies grotesquely habited were a decided attraction. The King was dressed in robes of pink, with a crown of gold upon his head, while the champion looked decidedly like a warrior of olden time. The Bakers, next, made a good display. In fact, they attracted more observation perhaps, than any other body. The process of breadmaking, etc., was carried on during the progress of the procession.

It was a proud moment for Hamilton's workingmen.[129]

The labour parade resurfaced in the 1880s, amidst the general festivities surrounding the celebration of "labour's holiday," the prelude to the officially sanctioned Labour Day of later years. In a procession honouring the birthdate of Uriah Stephens, founder of the Knights of Labor, Hamilton's crafts assumed a place of prominence. At the head of the throng, 2,000 strong, embracing skilled and unskilled, marched "the flag bearers, blending in one breeze the Union Jack, the Stars and Stripes and the flag of our own Dominion, emblematic of the international fraternity of labour." Then marched the Molders, the Carpenters and Joiners, the Shoemakers Assembly of the Knights of Labor, the Art Assembly, composed of Woodworkers, the women of the shoe factories, riding in union hacks, the Telegraphers, currently embroiled in a bitter struggle with their employers, the Tailors Assembly of the Knights of Labor, the Amalgamated Association of Iron and Steel Workers, and the Ontario Rolling Mill men, complete with a decorated wagon. The Bricklayers and Masons came next, "present[ing] a solid front on holiday, as they [did] on every other occasion, the secret of their organized success. They wore the apron, symbolic emblem of their craft." Completing the procession were the Glassworkers, the Hatters, Local Assembly 2225 of mixed callings, largest in the city, Vulcan Assembly, the Brushmakers, the Brickmakers, and the Harnessmakers. The printers were represented by the staff of the *Palladium of Labor*, borne in Dan Collins's wagon, proclaiming "the press as the defense of Labor and the medium of intellectual elevation of the masses," distributing a sheet entitled, "The elevation of Labor is the advancement of the State." It was a stirring spectacle, involving over 3,000 working men and women. "Union is strength," concluded the *Hamilton Spectator*. "This old adage was never more forcibly illustrated in Hamilton than yesterday afternoon, when the monster procession of the city's artisans filed its way through the street. . . . the present occasion will long be recollected, marking as it does a memorable epoch in the history of trades unionism."[130]

Parades celebrating "labour's holiday" and "labour's carnival" continued to draw the city's workingmen in the 1880s and 1890s. With the institutionalization of Labour Day in 1894 their energies were directed to similar ends, and if Hamilton failed to launch a procession in honour of its mechanics, the city's unionists often travelled to neighbouring towns — Buffalo and Brantford to name two — to march with others who shared their sympathies. Festive celebrations, these parades often prefaced a gigantic picnic or a well-attended baseball game.[131] With the early years of the twentieth century, however, Labour Day suffered a serious emasculation, and the older practices often seemed regrettably remote. The tradition lived in the customary baseball game or the union picnic, but the autonomous class activity of a self-proclaimed holiday had been shattered by government proclamation. Many of Hamilton's craft workers mourned the passing of the Labour Day parade, a visible reminder of previous carnivals and festivals.[132]

These were not insignificant or minor events, inconsequential in the grand context of class conflict or the progressive expansion of the labour movement. Baseball games, mechanics' festivals, union balls, commemorative suppers, picnics, and parades formed a vital part of the very stuff of everyday life, important in their own right, and too long ignored by labour historians lusting after the episodic or the explicitly political. They were part of a culture that bred and conditioned solidarity, a prerequisite to any struggle attempting to better the lot of working men and women. Their continuous presence in the years 1860-1914, despite shifts in their locale and importance, lent strength to the working-class community, providing a coherence and stability that had important ramifications in other realms.

Baseball clubs and weekend games, for instance, cultivated fraternal relations that were welcomed by men active in the working-class movement.[133] Moreover, sport could illuminate class inequalities, and generate fierce opposition to the fundamental wrongs of the social order. "Why does the law allow a millionaire to play golf on Sunday," queried the *Industrial Banner*, "and arrest a mechanic for playing baseball?"[134] Games were often a subtle means of popularizing labour's cause, as with the Cigar Makers' Union, utilizing the baseball diamond to advertise the merits of the Blue Label, or to raise money for striking comrades.[135] As in the case of London, Ontario, where iron molders were locked in a protracted conflict with the McClary Stove and Range Works in 1906, baseball leagues, firmly controlled by union men, often stood staunchly behind skilled workers in their battles with employers:

> Last year the McClary base-ball team won the pennant after an exciting contest. The question that now arises, is whether the other clubs, who are largely composed of union men, will feel disposed to play with a club who are largely acting as an advertisement of the McClary firm. Union men throughout the city, while they have no antagonism to the McClary team, say they don't propose to patronize a league that advertises said firm. ... It is a well known fact that

the patronage of the City League comes largely from union men and in the past the iron molders have taken a great interest in the game, in fact take away union support for the league and it would not pay rent for the park.[136]

"Old Sports Pabulum" could even link the cause of the shorter-hours movement to the interests of baseball, predicting greater attendance at games if the eight-hour day was won.[137]

The importance of festivals, dinners, and workingmen's balls should be even more clear. In the formative years of Hamilton's working-class movement, the Iron Molders' Union utilized a ball to attract molders to their ranks, as well as to cultivate ties with other organized crafts.[138] Throughout the 1860s the GWR mechanics periodically met over a glass of beer at Dan Black's Fountain Saloon, which attained a reputation as the favourite haunt of "the Western boys"; in later years Black's Club House would be a focal point in the emergence of the Nine Hour League.[139] Balls and suppers, as well as picnics, were often used by Hamilton crafts to raise funds for other unionists, suffering the anxiety of unemployment or the plight of a prolonged strike.[140] A union ball could be the scene of a stark reminder of class relationships, as in 1883, when the molders offered thanks to their employers for a recent wage reduction with a printed program entitled "To Our Generous Employers."[141] Even a supper presided over by an employer, a situation geared to foster deference, could give rise to dissent. Four hundred Ontario Rolling Mills workers booed and hissed a speech-maker at such a function when he insisted on extolling the achievements of the Tory government.[142] But the most forceful impact of such gatherings was the "cementing together [of] the bonds of unity," a consequence of great importance in future years of arduous struggle.[143]

Picnics, of course, were a major means of attracting workers to craft bodies, or solidifying ranks in times of crisis.[144] The *Palladium of Labor* championed their role, congratulating the carpenters and joiners on a picnic success:

> Such outings do far more good than is generally supposed — they bring together members of a craft and make strangers into fast friends, and any person of common discernment can see the benefit of common mechanics knowing each other. It is of the greatest benefit to them to do so, either in fair weather when clouds are gathering, or when they burst. For that reason we hope that tradesmen will never fail to have their annual outings in the summer season and social gatherings in winter, as it all tends to make them more united and competent to fight the monster (Capital) when occasion requires.[145]

One of the most vehement turn-of-the-century industrial conflicts, the 1905-1906 McClary molders' strike mentioned earlier, was precipitated when men defied their foreman by attending a Saturday afternoon picnic, held under the auspices of their union. The molders were consequently fired, their places taken by nonunionists, and a struggle that was to last well over two years initiated. As late as the summer of 1909 no union men worked in the London shop, and its products were boycotted by Canadian unionists.[146]

Workingmen's parades, aside from their significance as moments of exhilaration and craft pride, also possess an inner history of importance. Two brief months after their participation in the Confederation procession, Hamilton's shoemakers would play an important role in the creation of an Ontario-wide boot and shoemakers organization.[147] And behind the parades and processions celebrating "labour's festivals," in an age when an officially sanctioned Labour Day was scarcely considered a possibility, lay a history of toil and trouble no government proclamation could appease. "That parliament has made Labor Day a national holiday," thundered the Hamilton engineer Edward Williams, "is a tardy recognition of those noble beings who in the past, through vituperation and calumny, suffered persecution for defending the rights and liberties of men, and who claimed that the Trades Union was destined to develop the highest type of manhood in the march of civilization, and as feudalism followed barbarism, so education and enlightenment would tend slowly but successfully to bring about the freedom of thought and action which asserts the equality of rights before the law."[148]

Beyond this context of collectivist culture, institutionalized in mechanics' institute, friendly society, fire company, and baseball club, and buttressed by the social activities of craft unions, stretched an informal network of associations bred of neighbourhood, tavern, and workplace. Enmeshed in an obscurity that inhibits precise analysis, either in terms of its meaning or its class composition, the nuances of this cultural activity suggest that here too the skilled workingman was an important figure. And once again it is the continuities in this realm of associational life, set against a background of economic change and transformation, that are significant.

Artisans and apprentices, for instance, had historically figured prominently in ritualized forms of mock ceremony, aimed at undercutting the solemnity of constituted authority, building an arena of legitimized dissent that struck sharply at the rigid inequality of social relationships.[149] It would have been surprising if some of Hamilton's craftsmen, or their younger apprentices, had not been present at a ribald outing of 1863, described as a strictly private picnic. Members of "the worshipful company of chislers" met at the Railroad wharf and sailed to the beach. After a game of baseball a mock trial was conducted upon constitutional principles, the county attorney, judge, special high sheriff, and police magistrate coming in for particular derision. This was a gathering at which little was sacred, and few prominent local officials escaped its ridicule.[150]

More conspicuous was the Kalithumpian Klan, a New England political variant of the age-old ritual of charivari. The Klan, and its presence in Hamilton, suggests strongly the process of cultural diffusion. It paraded city streets on notable days of celebration, such as the Queen's birthday: "First came the General, bearded like a bard, and equipped in a cocked hat of gigantic dimensions. Then came an individual of 'exceedingly suspicious appearance', and as the Police Report says, looking very much like the pictoral representations we have seen of the Prince of Evil; then came a large crowd of all kinds of grotesque characters ... going through a number of salutory exercises upon a platform, which was placed on wheels for their accommodation."[151] Always led by their Generalissimo, "a ferocious looking military official," their shouts barely audible over the din of a perpetual "discordant music," the Klan marched in a manner that hinted at its class composition. It was not likely to be a meeting ground for men of property and standing.[152]

Both the Company of Young Chislers and the Kalithumpians had lapsed by the mid-1870s; their social and cultural role, however, was perhaps assumed by the rise of the workingmen's clubs. First appearing in the city in the 1870s, the clubs may well have arisen in the context of the decline of the volunteer fire companies, which had served as workingmen's clubs throughout the 1860s. Hamilton's workingmen had praised the British club movement as early as 1864, but little apparently came of this endorsement.[153] The first Hamilton clubs, other than the sporting associations of the 1860s, probably had their roots in the desire for conviviality and good fun. This was most likely the case in the club of "Jims," all over six feet tall, who met regularly in rooms over the Market Square. Each member was known as Jim, with a prefacing sobriquet suggestive of his appearance, character, nationality, or line or work (Pretty Jim, Dumpy Jim, Railroad Jim, Dutch Jim, or Slim Jim). Their rooms had been "neatly fitted up and supplied with books and papers." Only those capable of giving and receiving a good joke were allowed to join.[154] From this innocent beginning the clubs mushroomed.

They were of various persuasions, but in many clubs activities were reputed to centre around drinking, gambling, and the subtle art of seduction, young sewing girls and domestics being particularly attractive prey. All of these acts aroused the ire of both local and working-class newspapers.[155] Other clubs, more respectable in nature, including the Maple Leaf Social Club, a probable outgrowth of the early baseball club, the Workingmen's Club Room, and the Patience Athletic Club, drew their strength from workingmen with a social or sporting bent.[156] Yet even these more acceptable bodies generated opposition. The Patience Athletic Club, whose leaders included a wagonmaker, a shoemaker and a mason, was routed by the police early one Sunday morning, three of its patrons charged with vagrancy. The charge collapsed, however, "as they work[ed] every day and [paid] their way." In its stead, the police substituted charges of keeping a common gaming-house, and the men were eventually convicted. Regarding their arrest as just one more case of police subservience to wealth and position, the *Palladium of Labor* stressed that many of Hamilton's prominent citizens belonged to clubs, including the chief of police, yet these men went unmolested; it was the workingman who was subjected to abuse. Taking a stiff jab at the constables involved in the arrests, the paper concluded: "Ignorant, crawling, syncophants clothed in authority are dangerous animals to run at large. ... It is no wonder that the wealthy tyrannize over those in the (what is called) lower walks of life when such parasites are to be found amongst them."[157]

The police quite possibly did an excellent job in their repressive assault, for there are no indications that the Patience Athletic Club survived into the 1890s. But they may also have been overly zealous in their work, for replacing the numerous small clubs of the 1880s, organized around athletic and social activities, were the turn-of-the-century East and West End Workingmen's Clubs. In their halls workingmen also fraternized, but the activities were more structured, more explicit political in their orientation. It was there, for instance, that Hamilton workingmen debated the questions of overtime work, wages on civic projects, shorter hours, and the effects of offering manufacturers tax exemptions and bonuses to locate in the city. There too they heard papers on socialism and the relations of labour and capital. In 1904, in the midst of a strike at the International Harvester Company, the Workingmen's Club would serve as the headquarters of the embattled machinists.[158] By 1910 the Workingmen's Clubs were no longer in existence; they had been replaced by the May Day Committee and the Marx Club.[159]

The continuities in club life—from the informal Company of Young Chislers of the 1860s to the early twentieth-century Marx Club—thus hint at an important process of adaptation. While the 1860s and early 1870s, when club life centred on the jocular, were years of an emerging working-class movement, the later decades of the nineteenth century saw the development of class polarization and an accelerating pace of industrial conflict. In this context it is quite possible that workingmen once drawn to the company of pranksters transferred their loyalties to informal groups more dedicated to the protection of working-class interests. Their sons were even more likely to do the same. We have already noted one early instance of this, the Typographical Society's "Vigilance Committee," led by Tom Cat, surfacing in an early strike. From the 1880s to the early years of the twentieth-century workingmen's clubs would assume an increasingly political role, opposing certain tenets of the emerging capitalist order. Club life in the years 1860-1914 brings into relief the importance of cultural continuities as a force sustaining working-class protest. A similar process, illustrating the adaptation of traditional cultural mechanisms and activities to explicitly working-class purpose, was also at work in the arena of the enforcement of community morality.

One of the most persistent of cultural traditions was the charivari, a ritualized mechanism of community control with historical roots penetrating back to the medieval epoch. Known throughout the Atlantic world (as skimmertons in eighteenth-century New England; as shivarees in the nineteenth-century American Midwest; as skimmingtons in the English countryside from the late eighteenth century onwards; and as *Haberfeldtreiben, Katzenmeishiken,* or *Schnurren* on the European continent), the charivari was used to expose sexual offenders, cuckolded husbands, wife and husband beaters, unwed mothers, and partners in unnatural marriage, to the collective wrath of the community. Many variants were possible, and the phenomenon had a rural as well as an urban presence, but the essential form was usually cut from the same cloth. The demonstration was most often initiated under cover of darkness, a party gathering at the house of the offender to beat pans and drums, shoot muskets, and blow the proverbial horn, which butchers often rented out for the occasion. Sometimes the guilty party was seized, perhaps to be roughly seated on a donkey, facing backwards, and paraded through the streets, passersby being loudly informed of his or her transgression. Sometimes the charivari party was led by youths, on other occasions by women; in seventeenth-century Lyon and eighteenth-century France we know that journeymen and artisans were particularly active, as were rural tradesmen in eighteenth- and nineteenth-century England. As a constant check on misbehaviour, the charivari served an important purpose in many communities, in many different cultural contexts. Its demise, generally considered to have occurred after 1850 at the latest, has been interpreted as an indicator of the potent rise of the nuclear family, which no longer required the collective surveillance of neighbours and townsfolk to assure its stability and continuity.[160]

In Hamilton, however, where the late nineteenth century certainly saw the consolidation of the nuclear family, the charivari survived, often functioning in its traditional manner, but also turned to new purposes.[161] There is incontestable evidence that in sixteen separate instances, between the years 1865 and 1895, various parts of Hamilton and its environs were noisily awakened by the clamour of rough music. This must be only the tip of an iceberg, long since melted into back woodlots and dark alleys. Many of these occurrences were rural affairs, but King and John streets, to name but two major city thoroughfares, were not spared the hoots and cries, the thumping of tin pans, and the unmistakable bellow of the fishhorn, characteristic traits of the charivari party.[162] Hamilton must have been well acquainted with such acts, for Isaac Buchanan entitled his 1858 election appeal to the city's workingmen, *Hamilton Charivari: An Election Fly Sheet.*[163]

The origins of the charivari in Canada remain obscure, but the ritual was certainly well established in the 1830s. Susanna Moodie, an Englishwoman "roughing it in the Canadian bush" at the time of the 1837-38 rebellion, was informed by a neighbour that the

> charivari is a custom that the Canadians got from the French, in the Lower Province, and a queer custom it is. When an old man marries a young wife, or an old woman a young husband, or two old people, who ought to be thinking of their graves, enter for the second or third time into the holy estate of wedlock, as the priest calls it, all the idle young fellows in the neighbourhood meet together to charivari them. For this purpose they disguise themselves, blackening their faces, putting their clothes on hind part before, and wearing horrible masks, with grotesque caps on their heads, adorned with cock's feathers and bells. They then form a regular body, and proceed to the bridegroom's house, to the sound of tin kettles, horns and drums, cracked fiddles, and all the discordant instruments they can collect together. Thus equipped, they surround the house where the wedding is held, just at the hour when the happy couple are supposed to be about to retire to rest — beating upon the door with clubs and staves, and demanding of the bridegroom admittance to drink the bride's health, or in lieu thereof to receive a certain sum of money to treat the band at the nearest tavern.

The neighbour then told of a rowdy crew that had once extracted thirty dollars from a tight-fisted old shopkeeper, recently married to a handsome young widow. Bargaining was to no avail: "Thirty! Thirty! Thirty! old boy!" roared a hundred voices. "Your wife's worth that. Down with the cash, and we will give you three cheers, and three times three for the bride, and leave you to sleep in peace. If you hang back we will raise such a 'larum about your ears that you shan't know your wife's your own for a month to come." Astounded that such hooligans had won their demand, which they promptly dissipated at a nearby tavern, Mrs. Moodie asked, "And do people allow themselves to be bullied out of their property by such ruffians?" "Ah, my dear!" replied her informant, " 'tis the custom of the country, and 'tis not so easy to put down. But I can tell you that a charivari is not always a joke."[164]

Mrs. Moodie's neighbour may well have simplified the origins of the charivari, for the ritual had English as well as French ancestry, but her assessment was not far off the mark. Hamilton experienced a number of similar cases, the charivari usually being mounted against those managing their households in a manner frowned upon by the community, or against old men who took younger women into their matrimonial bed. A village widow whose "mode of managing her household affairs did not come up to the social standard of moral ethics," a newly married couple that had offended the neighbours' sensibilities, and an old widower who took a woman thirty years his junior as his wife, were typical targets of the charivari party in the Hamilton region.[165]

The Nineties saw the passing of the charivari. In 1890 three hundred young men, boys, and girls, assembled at the corner of Catharine and Hunter streets, charivaried Charles John Williams and his bride, "considerably his junior in years," Miss Elizabeth Reid. Yelling, blowing fish-horns, and singing parodies of "Annie Roonie," the crowd was eventually dispersed by the police, but not before they had physically assaulted the old storekeeper.[166] One of the last charivaris to take place in Hamilton occurred in 1894. "Old Man Christie" had married "pretty Widow Andrews," and attempted to settle in his old home, formerly occupied by himself, his late wife, and his daughter. Leading the charivari party was Christie's daughter, who claimed the house as her own, insisting that it had always been the property of her mother, and that it had been left to her. Devoid of any daughterly sentiment, the woman vowed that if her father ever again attempted to enter her abode, he would exit in a coffin.[167]

Blackened faces, voices obscured by the perpetual din, and shadows illuminated by moonlight do not lend themselves easily to identification, and the threat of legal action, always present in this period, pushes the participants of the charivari further out of view. We would be hard pressed to place Hamilton workingmen at the scene of any of these boisterous gatherings, although what we know of the practitioners of rough music in other settings suggests strongly that apprentices, mechanics, and craftsmen contributed to the proceedings. It would be strange indeed if a crowd of "300 young men, girls, and boys" gathered on Hamilton's street corners on a Sunday afternoon contained no workers. Finally, the harassed victims, generally from the lower orders or petty shopkeepers, suggest that the charivari was utilized by the labouring poor. The rich, after all, were likely to keep their houses in better order, at least visibly, and would at this late date shy away from any form of public exhibition. Fortunately, there is more than a suggestion that the charivari was employed by working men and women.

On 29 April 1890, 150 weavers, threatened with a wage reduction of 25 per cent, struck the Ontario Cotton Mills. Half of the strikers were women, and their earnings were already depressed, the majority making only $1 or $1.25 a day. For over a month the strike continued, the firm obstinate, the weavers determined.[168] Some women, among them a Mrs. Trope, returned to work. The first week of June saw the weavers respond violently to these cases of strike-breaking: among their tactics, the charivari, waged against Mrs. Trope and another woman, Anne Hale, on two separate occasions. Charged with assault and intimidation, "the charivaring weavers" were sent up for trial. Mrs. Trope, suffering from "nervous prostration," charged Elizabeth Wright, Mary H. Kingsley, and William Carlyle with assault and, in another case, had George Maxwell, Robert Irwin, and Carlyle brought before the bench to answer a charge of intimidation. Similarly, Mrs. Hale accused Moses Furlong, Richard Callan, Henry Dean, and Anne Burke of intimidation. Mrs. Trope testified

> that she had worked at the mill for eight years. The mill had been shut down for five weeks because of the weavers strike. She did not attend any meetings of the strikers and at the request of Manager Snow she went to work last Monday. When on her way home that evening she went along Ferrie Street ... followed by a crowd of men and women. The defendants Maxwell and Irwin had fish-horns and were blowing them. She estimated the crowd at a couple of hundred, many of them weavers. Mrs. Trope turned down Catharine Street and was followed by the crowd. She stopped to let the people pass and Mrs. Wright struck her. She tried to strike back and Mr. Carlisle pushed her into the road, and she fell down, injuring her hip. Trope found his wife surrounded by the crowd, and took her home.[169]

With Mrs. Hale's charges it was "the same old case of fish-horn blowing, shouting, and general disturbance," the crowd bearing a likeness to a "procession of Grit schoolboys."[170] The charivari, as Mrs. Moodie's informant rightly concluded, and as Mrs. Trope and the strikers, who drew fines ranging from $2 to $5, well knew, was no joke.

Charivaris, as traditional forms of community control, proved resilient in Hamilton, apparently falling into disuse only with the coming of the twentieth century. Yet even here the process of cultural continuity was evident, for another cultural phenomenon followed quickly on the heels of the charivari's decline. E. P. Thompson has argued that in nineteenth-century England rough music was increasingly used against wife-beaters.[171] North American communities, however, employed another ritualized mechanism of community control to curb wife-beating and other violations of community standards and morality. The White Caps, an organization obviously patterned after the Southern vigilante groups attempting to preserve white hegemony in the aftermath of black emancipation, thrived in numerous American and Canadian communities in the years 1890-1905, fulfilling the traditional function of the charivari.[172]

Whitecapping was probably a fusion of a number of nineteenth-century experiences. It may well have drawn its intense appreciation of moral purity from Ellice Hopkin's White Cross Movement, a religious crusade of the 1880s that raged against prostitution, lewdness, and manifestations of social impurity.[173] It certainly borrowed heavily from the tradition of Southern vigilantism, the white caps and masks of the Ku Klux Klan often being the badge of the White Cap. In the South, at least, racism may also have been a potent force in the history of whitecapping, black share-croppers and contract labourers being prominent targets of abuse.[174] White-cappers may also have drawn upon the rituals, oaths, and secret ceremonies of the friendly societies or Knights of Labor to bind members to the pur-poses and promises of the association.[175] This kind of cultural coalescence bred strong attachments, and the White Caps exercised a significant pre-sence in many North American communities.

Within this presence two features stand out: first, the extent to which whitecapping was an intensely regional or local experience; second, the degree to which the phenomenon could be turned to working-class ends or, less explicitly, the extent to which the movement functioned within the working-class community's conception of social order and acceptability.

The regional or local essence of whitecapping was most pronounced.[176] Nothing indicates that any ties existed among the White Caps of various North American communities, only that informal associations mush-roomed spontaneously in diverse settings, adapting themselves to local situations: Trenton, New Jersey, White Caps directed their attacks against wife-beaters; in Berlin, Ontario, a stepmother accused of ill-treating a stepchild was tarred and feathered; in New Mexico the White Caps fought large cattle ranchers and landowners who fenced the best grazing lands, threatening the existence of small squatters.[177] Whitecapping in Sevier county, Tennessee, was one of the more virulent forms. Originally con-vened to rid the county of adulterous perons who had avoided legal prose-cution, the Sevier county White Caps grew in influence and size until they controlled local juries and politicians, thus assuring themselves immunity from the law. People judged to be leading immoral lives were sent threat-ening letters, signed "White Caps," promising them a "switching" if they did not leave the community. A bundle of hickory switches were often deposited on their doorstep as an additional warning. An opposition group, the Blue Bills, said to be allied with some local prostitutes, battled the White Caps openly for a number of years. From 1892 to 1896, con-tended one commentator, "there prevailed a reign of terror in the county which has long harbored memory known as the White Cap Era."[178]

Beyond this local context, whitecapping appeared to be a plebeian movement, and one that was easily channelled into forms of working-class protest. Mississippi whitecapping, for instance, was a movement of small farmers, initiated in the early years of the depression of the 1890s; although its main targets were black sharecroppers, its real grievances were the credit and landholding practices of the local mercantile elite. Threatened by foreclosed farm mortgages and an influx of Negro contract labour, the small Mississippi dirt farmer attacked a familiar scapegoat.[179] In New Mexico the class nature of the movement was exceptionally ex-plicit. Always an association of small squatters, the Nevada *Gorras Blan-cas* (White Caps) burned the cattlemen's fences and cut their barbed wire, claiming to "protect the lives and property of our people." The organization apparently embraced over 300 members, posing as a bona fide assembly of the Knights of Labor. During the building of the Santa Fé Railroad, the White Caps, incensed by the low wages paid to labourers, burned railroad ties and harassed section foremen. Charlie Siringo, a cowboy Pinkerton detective later to attain notoriety in the Coeur D'Alene strike, infiltrated the New Mexico White Caps in the early 1890s, finding the group a political adjunct of the Populist Party.[180]

Hamilton's White Caps may have had their beginnings in the mid-1880s, with the rise of the White Cross Army, a movement dedicated to the protection of maidenly virtue and wifely chastity. The *Palladium of Labor* saw the preservation of such attributes as important, but cautioned that the real problem was the low wage structure and consequent poverty characteristic of women's work: "If the white cross army would strike at the root of the evil and protect women from wrong and degradation they should seek to secure her industrial position, to abolish the evils of starvation pay and long hours."[181] Throughout the 1890s and early years of the twentieth century, Hamilton's White Caps remained an obscure grouping. Their presence, however, was established by a number of street confrontations and assaults, as "Whitecap gangs" battled local police constables and youths.[182] Robert and George Ollman, two brickmakers, apparently headed the Hamilton White Caps.[183] As in other communities, the city's White Caps were known for their willingness to defy constituted authority and their readiness to by-pass proper channels in the enforcement of popular standards. Forces like these could be harnessed by the working-class movement in times of crisis.

The winter and spring months of 1892 were just such a moment of crisis for Hamilton's iron molders. In a fierce contest precipitated by their employers, the Iron Molders' International Union was being tested in a strike which, if lost, would spell their extermination as an organized craft. The founders, led by the Gurney and Copp brothers, had imported non-unionists to man their foundries, but the molders had resisted, hanging on with grim determination.[184] One nonunionist, William Clendenning, was prosecuted by a local constable for carrying a loaded revolver. He claimed it was a necessary precaution, taken after he noticed that whenever he stepped out of his room he was followed by gangs of unionists. Moreover, along with another strike-breaker, named Fleury, Clendenning had been the recipient of a chilling, threatening letter, written in pencil and headed with a skull-and-cross-bones, a whip, and a club: "Scabs, beware! We have formed an association to go and club the life out of scoundrels if you don't cleare this town before Wednesday night, Ye will a lashing such as white man never got before what you are looking for badly." The note bore a sinister signature, "WHITE CAPS." Given a suspended sentence for his crime, Clendenning was told that it was not necessary for him to carry a revolver, for the nonunion men were afforded every possible protection. Bound over for six months by the court, the "scab" molder expressed his pessimism: "If the union men get their way I won't be here for six months."[185]

Both the charivari and whitecapping thus illustrate a process of cultural continuity and adaptation. Traditional mechanisms of community control had become converted into tools of working-class protest. Other realms of working-class culture also highlight this process of continuity and adaptation. The workingmen's clubs, for instance, in their evolution from the jocular associations of the 1860s and 1870s to the organized forums of radicalism in the 1898-1914 years, exemplify an important trend. Even such superficially mundane activities as baseball games, picnics, and suppers could bring into relief the class interests of Hamilton workingmen. Finally, the institutional sphere of associational life, centred in the friendly society, mechanics' institute, fire company, and craft union, provided a stability and coherence to working-class life that, over time, fostered an important solidarity. It was in this context that events like the nine-hour movement of 1872, the Knights of Labor parades of the 1880s, or the Hamilton street railway strike of 1906 would draw universal support.

This, then, was a rich and vibrant culture; its subtle interconnections speak of an important continuity. Conscious of the transformation of economic life over the course of the nineteenth century, historians have perhaps emphasized change too much, ignoring the cultural continuities in working-class life.[186] And these continuities were not without meaning, for they could soften the blows of industrial-capitalist development, ease the strain of the many disciplines seemingly engulfing the Victorian mechanic. In certain circumstances, too, cultural continuities could be adapted to new purposes, confronting directly the harsh realities of the new order. But even this was not enough. The impingements of capitalist society were often too oppressive, the strains of everyday life too exhausting, the toll, in human terms, too great. It was in this kind of context that "Vincent" could write to the *Labor Union*, an organ of the Hamilton Knights of Labor:

Culture ... is a grand thing for the workingman. ... There is often a vast difference, however, between theory and practice; between the ideal and the real. The ideal workingman never has any stomach or nerves; is never hungry, or tired, or cross, or discontented, and has no more passion nor temper in him than a yellow sunflower in an idiot's buttonhole. His wife is a sort of faded wallflower who never disagrees with him; his boys are goody-goody little cherubs, and the girls, bless their little hearts, they are just like primroses, and they always hold their mouths just so, and they keep their handkerchiefs ready so they can burst into tears when any of the great ladies con-

descend to speak kindly to them or offer them charity. Suffice it to
say that workingmen and such families are phantoms and not realities;
they don't exist in nature, they only exist in the imagination of certain
fine people, such as those who honour the home of poverty occasionally with an official visit in state dress, when they want to collect missionary money for the poor heathen. The real workingman is a different article than this. He is not a phantom, he is a *fact* and I hope some
of those fine people who are making a living out of him now, and
honoring him with a little of it back sometimes by way of charity, will
find him a stubborn fact before they get through with him. His wife too
is a reality, probably has a temper of her own and surely has feelings.
His children are not too well clothed, and have democratic tendencies
which are very hard to control. The real workingman always has a
stomach, which is necessary. After his day's work he is hungry and
tired; sometimes he is discontented, especially Saturday night if he
can't get any money. Sometimes he has nerves, which are not necessary. He has to work ten hours a day; sometimes he walks a mile or
two before and after work, and saws wood when he comes home. In
that case he has not much energy left for culture and education, especially if the children have the whooping cough, and his wife is worn
out working. As far as culture is concerned, mental labor, if severe,
is worse than bodily labor, as it leaves the mind so exhausted as to
be incapable of further effort after the day's work is done. So you
can see in case of severe labor, either bodily or mental for small
wages a man's whole existence is necessarily a sacrifice for the
mean's of sustaining mere animal life. All culture or improvement
of mind is out of the question. Life becomes a barrier, and hopeless
slavery, the only release from which is death and the only result of
which is to prepare a few more lives for a fate possibly similar. The
above picture is not overdrawn, it is true to life. I am a workingman
myself, and I see such cases everyday; I can put my finger on a
dozen of them. The object of a labor union is to remove the cause
and the necessity for such cases, and to make it possible for a man
to live by his labor independently as a man ought to live.

Bitterly resentful, "Vincent" at least had not lost hope, and his solution
to the problems besetting the workingman lay in organization.[187]
    Hamilton's skilled workers lived their culture in street and field and
hall. But as "Vincent" so passionately argued, this was not enough. They
had other realities to contend with, many of them far from pleasant. The
workplace in which they spent so much of their lives was also the arena of
a culture vigorously enforced by Hamilton's craft unions, a culture that
sought to defend and extend the boundaries of workers' control.

chapter

3

The Culture of Control

The mechanic who built all creation,
Who spanned earth and sea with his arch,
Gave the 'plumb-line' and square to
Trades Unions,
And sent progress with them on the march;
It was he made the craftsman a noble
Before even Kingdoms were born;
God gave to Trades Unions his warrant
This globe to enrich and adorn.

Iron Molders' International Journal (September 1884)

The notion of workers' control did not enter the vocabulary of the international working-class movement until the World War I years, a period of escalating syndicalist struggle which saw British shop stewards and Western Canadian miners articulate radical demands for national, democratic, working-class control of basic industries and services. Yet, despite the dating of this phenomenon, workers' control had a long history, constituting a fundamental feature of the shop-floor experience of nineteenth-century skilled craftsmen. A British shop steward hinted at the long-standing existence of certain forms of workers' control when he told Carter Goodrich: "People talk as if the demand for control was something that had to be created among the workers by a slow process, but it's there already!"[1] Even the most cursory glance at nineteenth-century work relationships suggests strongly that both skilled workers and their employers considered control of the shop-floor to be of vital importance. Moreover, while such a glance reveals the drawing of firm battle lines, it *does not* suggest that employers necessarily controlled the workplace.[2]

The *Brockville Daily Times*, commenting on an 1884 strike at the James Smart Manufacturing Company's foundry, asserted: "The question at issue is simply one of 'control'. It is a fact, however humiliating, the acknowledgement that during the past three years of the company's existence, the business has been practically controlled by the Moulder's Union." Robert Gill, manager of the concern, concurred: "If the conditions are such that 'control' cannot be gained by the proprietors, then Brockville will lose the industry which we are trying to carry."[3] A Montreal founder seemed to agree with Gill, discharging all of his molders in 1883 for "dictating to him how he should conduct his establishment."[4] *John Swinton's Paper*, in discussing a prominent trade dispute, called attention to the importance of control and its relation to union strength: "The fact that the manufacturers hope to crush the Troy Union shows that the Union is not as strong and firm as it ought to be. If it were, they would not indulge in their hopes. The employers of Pittsburg entertain no hope of breaking up the Amalgamated Association of Iron and Steel Workers, to which they have just surrendered. It is too strong for them. It controls the trade, as the Window Glass Workers' Association controls that trade." Swinton continued, in a later issue of the paper, to extol the virtues of workers' control: "It was even said of Pittsburg by the old iron masters, that Trades Unions have such a grip upon their industries that they are crippled."[5] Thorold, Ontario stonecutters apparently exercised an equally forceful control, for their contractors reacted with vigour in the depression years of the late 1870s, locking them out of work. "The reason for this," wrote H. J. O'Neil of the union, "was distinctly stated by the contractors to be that they could get the work done in winter time for much less money, and they were not going to be dictated to by any union, that the stonecutters had been bosses long enough, and the contractors were going to try it for a while." After a long and hard battle, in which they were sustained by their International Union, the Thorold cutters returned to work on their own terms.[6] A Toronto boss painter decided against such tactics of resistance, acquiescing in the pernicious control his own men practised:

> Paint pots empty — brushes dry,
> Jobs unfinished — and for why?
> Men dictate — then I kick,
> I'm the cheese — I'm a brick.[7]

Organization, of course, was usually the preliminary stage in the realization of this limited form of workers' control. "The first step for wage-earners," wrote "Imogene" in Hamilton's *Palladium of Labor*, "is to organize every industry, and thus obtain control of their wages."[8] Workplace confrontations, arising out of this struggle over organization, fed directly into labour's political consciousness by bringing the issue of control to the forefront. Potters in East Liverpool, Ohio, for instance, clashed with their employers over their affiliation with the Knights of Labor. "We desire to be clearly understood by all citizens of the United States that this is not a strike or lock-out on account of any dispute about wages," they noted. "It is a stand taken by us in support of the principle of liberty, that was achieved by our fathers in the Revolution and by ourselves in the Rebellion. We are not slaves, to be prohibited by our employers from joining any organization we see fit to become members of, whether religious, political, or for mutual protection. Grant our employers the right to dictate to us in this point," the potters concluded, "and they can with equal justice dictate to us how we should vote, or worship God."[9] From this kind of perspective it was but a short step to a more explicit argument.

Speaking for most trade unions, the Cigar Makers' International posed the question, "Have the Unions A Right to Control The Shops?," answering it with an emphatic yes:

> Every time a union is formed the employers say it is an attempt on the part of the workingmen to control the shops. ... They believe in hiring whom they please; they believe in private contracts and will suffer no dictation from the union. ... Dictatorship must exist either in the employer or the man, and the organization of the men is only an attempt to restrict the absolute dictatorship of the boss. He has not the right to do as he pleases in his shop or business affairs, for every act he does has an influence on his fellow men, and if his self-interest is not foiled by the counter self-interest of the men, he would soon have them in a condition where human beings would be lower than beasts.

"Human rights," concluded the *Official Journal*, "are more sacred than the rights conferred on dead matter, on property. Therefore men organized in unions have a right to control the shops and interfere in business affairs, ... the right to a voice in ... management."[10]

Hamilton cigarmakers found these words particularly attractive, and among the city's other tradesmen — molders, glassblowers, tailors, machinists, building trades' workers, engineers, blacksmiths, iron and steel workers, and shoeworkers — the argument was no less appealing. The *Hamilton Spectator* saw the essential feature of work relationships as a conflict between capital and labour, each camp struggling for control: "This is the war between capital and labor: Capital continually withdrawing itself from healthful work because it is afraid of losing its price, continually at difference with its one friend, without whom it must perish; Labor striking, demanding shorter time, more wages, dictating imperious rules about piece-work and apprentices, quarreling with its one friend, without whom it must die or seek the poor house. To adjust these difficulties is the problem of the day."[11] For the skilled worker the "problem" was easily overcome, Hamilton's *Palladium of Labor* proposing a blunt solution:

> Monopoly must not control,
> The Labor Market heart and soul.[12]

The *Palladium of Labor's* predecessor, the *Labor Union*, also saw the issue of control as an important aspect of the solution of the "problem of the day." It noted that a "revolutionary agitation" had been initiated, and that everywhere "the claims of labor to control production are being debated by knots of workmen."[13]

The *Labor Union* had correctly identified workers' control as a central concern of masses of skilled workers, but it had erred in suggesting that their attachment to control was revolutionary. Rather, in its nineteenth-century variants, workers' control meant adherence to commonplace practices and workplace customs. Thus, in the summer of 1883 a fireman on the *Southern Belle*, James Foren, was brought before the police court on a charge of mutiny. Foren had been ordered to "trim coal" at another man's boiler and had agreed to do so provided he was to have the customary fee of fifty cents extra, a long-standing practice on the ship. The *Southern Belle*'s owners, however, had chosen this moment to break the tradition of extra payment, and ordered Foren to proceed without compensation. He staunchly refused, and for his resistance received a sentence of three weeks in the common jail and a fine of one dollar. "Custom doth breed a habit in a man," concluded the *Palladium of Labor*.[14]

Other workers, however, succeeded in preserving their customary workplace rights. In such trades as nailmaking, glassblowing, and molding, for instance, no employer could exercise dictatorial power over skilled hands whose craft knowledge was the only assurance of an acceptable product. Technology itself had made few inroads on these crafts prior to 1890 and employers often had to settle for workmen whose desultory work habits they deplored, but whose skills they needed. Coremakers who added molasses to sand in the creation of molds judged their recipe according to "taste"; glass bottle blowers relied on their "sure touch" to turn "the smouldering brew of glass and soda" recently extracted from the "glory hole" into a container. Craftsmen like these could not be driven to produce, and their skill, a recognized and valued commodity, assured them of a measure of control over their work.[15] In this sense, workers' control was nothing more than the functional autonomy of the skilled worker, a workplace practice flowing out of the craft worker's knowledge of the production process.[16]

Workers' control, however, was much more than a mere technological phenomenon, for in trades where mechanization did make inroads, craft unions often proved capable of "controlling" the machine, successfully demanding that only union labour be allowed to operate the new "labour-saving" devices. Printers perhaps best exemplify the case, although glass bottle blowers after 1896 (when the blowing machines were introduced into the trade) were also reasonably successful.[17] "Labor must control the tools," declared Toronto's *Labor Advocate* in 1890, endorsing the International Typographical Union's policy of manning all typesetting machines with union printers. Other crafts would follow suit.[18]

The essence of nineteenth-century workers' control lay in the restrictive powers exercised by the trade union over the employer. Carter Goodrich long ago recognized three types of workers' control: restrictive control, shop control, and control of an entire industry. The last-named came to prominence only with the emergence of ostensibly revolutionary movements, such as the British shop stewards or the One Big Union of the Canadian West. Restrictive and shop control, however, thrived in the late nineteenth century in the rules and regulations of the trades.[19] Limitations on the number of apprentices per shop and institutionalized restriction of output were important features of workplace life in both Canada and the United States; they formed the key components of restrictive control.[20] Shop control was a more complex practice, involving the use of union foremen in some trades and shop committees in others; both mechanisms controlled hiring and firing, secured adherence to trade regulations, parcelled out work to members of the craft, and set prices and negotiated agreements with employers.[21] While both restrictive and shop control would and could be practised by workers outside the pale of trade unionism, skilled as well as unskilled,[22] the real bastion of workers' control was the craft union. Indeed, among Hamilton's craft unionists, workers' control thrived as something of a culture of the shop-floor.

As a culture of the shop-floor, control was bred within the context of industrial-capitalist development. Unlike the continuous culture of the community, which exhibited the persistence of many cultural forms and traditions with roots in precapitalist times, control was an essentially new phenomenon. It manifested itself most blatantly in moments of conflict, when the workingman's conception of control clashed sharply with his employer's views of work relations. Control was, essentially, the skilled workers' response to the realities of workplace organization within a society transformed by industrial capitalism. Against industrial-capitalist work discipline, the skilled worker posed the rules and regulations of his trade.

Glass workers, for instance, exemplified the case of nineteenth-century workers' control. Virtually every international craft union praised their record of achievement. John Swinton's laudatory appraisal of the glassblowers of Pittsburgh knew no bounds. His enthusiasm for their restriction of output (each man's weekly labour was limited to forty-eight boxes of glass), their adherence to limited hours of labour, and their summer stop rule, by which the union dictated that from 1 July to 1 September each year the fires in North American glass works be extinguished to give the men a well-deserved rest, was striking. "Control is a bitter word to the manufacturer," concluded Swinton.[23] In Hamilton, where glass workers were associated with the Amalgamated Flint Glass Blowers' Union No. 13 and Branch No. 45 of the United Green Glass Workers' Association, the

summer stop rule and institutionalized restriction of output were honoured practices in the trade.[24] As day workers, few Hamilton glass men
laboured more than seven or eight hours a day during a six-day week.[25] So
complete was their control of the trade that Hamilton glass workers were
rarely challenged by their employers, and virtually never found themselves involved in strikes or lockouts. To the *Palladium of Labor* this was a
record of achievement worthy of emulation. "What is possible in one
trade," it noted, "is presumably so in another."[26]

Few trades would develop the art of control to the level attained by
the glass workers, but all crafts exercised some form of restrictive or
shop control. M. A. Pigott, a Hamilton contractor, wrote to the city's
member of Parliament, Adam Brown, prior to the release of the 1887
Royal Commission on the Relations of Labor and Capital findings. The
contractor's theme was the negative impact of the restrictive practices of
Hamilton's skilled workers. He first attacked the system of apprenticeship regulation:

> The apprentice restrictions *practically prohibits* boys from learning
> trades, for instance I may have 25 or 30 masons & bricklayers, the
> union will only allow *one apprentice in three years* to each employer
> regardless of the number of men he employs. *Moulders* one appren-
> tice to every 8 men in four years. *Stonecutters* same as masons. The
> object is, since they cannot boom the demand, they can by the
> above restrictions reduce the supply.

Then, to conclude, he railed against restriction of output:

> Another matter regulated by the unions that must soon become in-
> jurious to trade is the reducing of the standard quantity of work per
> day in the matter of daily paid employees for instance, you may have
> a number of workmen engaged on a similar class or kind of work,
> among the gang be one or two slow coaches, it then becomes the
> duty of the faster men to adapt themselves to the slower motion of
> their slow companions, to save them from reprimand and possible
> discharge & also to provide against a scarcity of work by not pushing
> on, it helps to keep good the supply of work, which assists them in
> obtaining their increased demands.

Pigott's own stonecutters, in fact, had blocked work on the city's Custom
House in late 1883 over the enforcement of their union rule limiting the
daily output of trade members. While the *Hamilton Times* found the situation deplorable, the *Palladium of Labor* again came to the men's defence.[27]

Judging by the disdain with which Hamilton's skilled workers regarded
workingmen who "rushed," "hogged," or "speeded up," Pigott's charges
were rooted in the real practices of craft unionists.[28] Indeed, contempt for

the "hog" who ignored collective control of daily output was, as David Montgomery has suggested, one badge of the craftsman's "manliness," a concept that connoted independence, respectability, and a cultivated sense of self-worth. "A hog union man," wrote the editor of the *Industrial Banner*, "is a thing that takes union wages and spits tobacco juice over a scab pair of shoes, and a scab suit of clothes."[29] "Junius Junior" wrote of three workers in a Hamilton factory, caught in the midst of a rush order from their foreman:

> They worked like demons once the rush started; came back nights, and piled up a wages bill that fairly made their eyes bulge out when they got the money. In their haste to push along the good thing, they shortened the noon meal hour to fifteen minutes, and 'beat the clock' at the starting hour in the morning. By dint of these efforts they managed to nearly double their output. That was all right, while the rush lasted. After it was over they were rewarded by a 50 per cent cut in the price. They protested and the cut was reduced to 40 per cent.

"And they blamed the boss," noted "Junius Junior." "I don't," he countered.[30] The *Palladium of Labor* voiced a similar sentiment: "It is to the fact of the existence of hoggish workmen more than any other cause that nearly all wage differences are brought about, and trouble between employee and employer occasioned. On men guilty of such actions a heavy fine should be imposed by each union for every offence; two or three doses of which would probably bring most of them to their senses. If this failed to convince them they should be fired out of the union altogether."[31]

But the real conflict over the question of control was not the craft workers' disapproval of the "hog," for the aberrant "rusher" was merely the exception proving the rule of craft solidarity. Conflict over control, in its restrictive and shop realms, was almost exclusively a clash involving craft workers and their employers. Molders, building trades' workers, and cigarmakers, for instance, were often drawn into struggles turning on the question of apprentice regulations. On rare occasions mechanization would pose a threat to skilled craftsmen, and in an attempt to preserve their control mechanisms workers would strike rather than succumb to the machine. More common were control struggles waged against the dismissal of union foremen or workmen, or the hiring of workers who had defied union authority, either by acting as strikebreakers or by failing to fulfil their craft obligations. Finally, in many union shops, where control was related to the "standard rate," and its enforcement by shop committees, employers' attempts to stifle union power by wage reductions led to violent strikes and lockouts that went well beyond the limited question of wages.[32] It was within these broad parameters that Hamilton's skilled workingmen and their employers became locked into a struggle for control.

One of the first recorded instances of a control struggle occurred in 1856, when the mechanics of the Great Western Railway yards struck work in protest over the dismissal of a shop mate. While the company claimed the man "had been drunk while on duty," the workers contended that "a capable workman had been abruptly dismissed to make a job for a friend" of one of the superintendents. Over 500 workers turned out, demanding the reinstatement of the worker, and the discharge of the supervisor. "A valued principle had been violated," they claimed. At a time when strikes were a relatively new, and exceptional phenomenon, the men's action spoke of a deeply entrenched solidarity. In the face of potential legal prosecution for violation of the conspiracy laws, the mechanics instituted negotiations with their employer. A few days later the dispute was settled, and the discharged man was back at his place in the company's yards. Although the strikers did not secure the superintendent's dismissal, an early victory had been won.[33]

By 1864 a number of craft unions had surfaced in the city, and, led by the Iron Molders' International Union No. 26, they banded together to form a Trades Assembly, the first of its kind in Canada.[34] This body apparently had wide-ranging local powers. When the city's carpenters and joiners struck work in the late spring of 1864, they first sought the approval of the Trades Assembly, receiving the assurance of a "rate ... to provide for the maintenance of those who may be compelled to remain on strike."[35] At this early date craft workers had institutionalized mechanisms to support their control struggles, mechanisms which crossed craft lines, binding one trade to the cause of another.

These were also years which saw the beginnings of conflict between the founders and the molders. As early as 15 December 1864, Copp's foundry was the scene of a confrontation over the apprentice question.[36] By February 1866 the rift had widened, developing into an escalating struggle between the employers and the union. The founders' tactic, as one molder recounted, was to break the union and secure, once and for all, control of the shops:

> Most of the foundry-men of Hamilton, as well as of other places in Canada, sometime since formed themselves into a union for mutual protection against the encroachments of labour, and in the plentitute of their power, they enacted a law to be enforced by penalty, that no member was to hire a moulder who had of his own accord left the employment of another member, no matter what the cause of his leaving or under what conditions. To leave voluntarily was to make himself within the jurisdiction of the boss' union a proscribed man, thus depriving the working man of that personal liberty which is the necessary consequence of living in this free country; and Mr. Editor, that law has been enforced in Hamilton at least three different times

during the present winter. Sir, would you believe it possible for a committee of three gentlemen to drive gaily down in a sleigh to hound a poor man from his employment.

Faced with this kind of opposition, the molders struck work, only to see the founders flood the community with "men from the United States." For the molders it was a battle against "slave law."[37]

Less than a month later, Hamilton's founders had made common cause with their American counterparts. Many Canadian foundrymen, undoubtedly more than a few from Hamilton, helped to draft the preamble of the *Proceedings of the National Convention of Iron Founders*, a statement which left no doubts as to the founders' views on workers' control:

Whereas the Iron Moulders in different sections of the country are seeking, by concert of action and union amongst themselves, to change the relations which exist naturally between employer and employee, assuming arbitrarily to dictate the prices which shall be paid by the employer, and to direct the government of the workshop and the management of the business of their employers ... [we resolve] to proceed to introduce into our shops all the apprentices or helpers we deem advisable, and that we will not allow any Union committees in our shops, and that we will, in every possible way, free our shops from all dictation or interference on the part of our employees.

Among the iron molders' most offensive rules and practices, the founders listed: (1) the apprentice restriction of one apprentice to every ten molders; (2) the closed shop, allowing no nonunionists to work in the foundries; (3) the presence of shop committees at each foundry to set prices on work and enforce the rules and regulations of the trade; (4) the molders' "control" of the labour market, the shop committees "giving all necessary information to applicants for work, and whether their services are required, and if so, whether it be proper for such applicant to apply either to the employer or his foreman for employment"; (5) the prevalence of strikes resulting from the founders' inability to live with such restrictions.[38] Troy became the centre of the founders' offensive, but the unionists there stood firm, registering impressive victories over their employers.[39]

In Hamilton the molders won no such victory in 1866, their fight carrying on into the autumn months. Well after the May settlement in Troy, Hamilton molders continued to face the resistance of their employers, who demanded the right to introduce as many apprentices as they thought appropriate. While the "obnoxious" rules of the founders were eventually withdrawn from many iron works, and the apprentice ratios of the union reestablished, the pages of the *Iron Molders' International Journal* indicated that the price for these concessions had been high. "Scabs" abounded in two city shops, and reports from the Hamilton local to the international union indicated that the closed shop had been dealt a strong blow. Not until January 1867 was the dispute in Hamilton settled, and then only with the intervention of William Sylvis, president of the International Union.[40] Many Hamilton molders had grown dissatisfied with their shop committee, and sometime after the settlement of the protracted contest of 1866 Hamilton's Molders' Union retreated into obscurity, contenting itself with activities such as balls and picnics, apparently lacking the confidence to test its employers again.[41]

By the winter and spring months of 1872 the Molders' Union had revitalized itself, playing an important role in the strike wave aimed at securing the nine-hour day.[42] The union had begun to rid the shops of the many nonunionists who had originally flooded the city in the late 1860s.[43] Then, too, the organized molders reestablished their control over the labour market, all travelling molders being instructed to apply for work at the Clyde Hotel, whose proprietor John Miller was an honorary member of the union.[44] Recovery, however, was far from complete; moreover, it was to be stifled by the economic downturn of 1873-74 and by the flooding of the Hamilton shops with unemployed molders from the United States. "There are too many molders here at present," wailed Fred Walters, and the pages of the *International Journal* bristled with an exchange of letters debating the "Invasion of Canada."[45] With the labour market glutted, and the economy moving toward recession, the founders imposed a 10 per cent wage reduction in December 1873.[46] By March 1874 Hamilton's union was informing molders from many North American cities to stay away from the foundries "as we expect trouble."[47]

Even the molders' limited attempts to secure a measure of control over their work spurred the foundrymen to action. When the union asked for a resumption of their former wages — the abandonment of the 1873 reduction — in the summer of 1874, the employers reacted forcefully. At the Burrow, Stewart and Milne foundry the molders received a terse reply: "While regretting any serious consequences such as a strike, from our refusal, we can only say if such is resorted to in either of the two shops you have made the demand from, or any other, there is not an iron foundry in Hamilton that will not be instantly closed thereafter." To add force to this pledge, the Hamilton founders issued a complimentary communication, signed by D. Moore and Company, Burrow, Stewart and Milne, A. Laidlaw and Company, Copp Brothers, James Stewart and Company, E. & C. Gurney, and L. D. Sawyer and Company.[48]

With the battle lines drawn, the conflict commenced. After two brief strikes, the employers turned to a general lockout. Led by the Gurney brothers, whose shop employed only nonunionists, and backed by the Canadian Founders' Association, presided over by the Hamilton founder James Stewart, the foundrymen presented a formidable front. But the union also stood firm. "The fight is forced on us. Let us meet it like men," declared the *International Journal*. From late August 1874 through the early winter months of 1875 the struggle raged. For both the employers and the unionists the conflict turned on the open shop.[49]

Edward and Charles Gurney posed the issue clearly, demanding that all employees sign an "Iron clad" contract:

I, the said _____, in consideration of the said Messrs. E. and C. Gurney hiring and employing me, as they hereby do, upon the terms hereinafter mentioned, convenant and agree to serve the said Messrs. E. & C. Gurney, as a molder, at such work, and in such manner, as they, or their foremen for the time being, shall assign or direct me, for the period of one year from this date, at the current rate of wages, for such work, payable from week to week during such year, and faithfully and diligently, to the best of my ability, and without interruption, other than by sickness, bodily injury, or such like accident; and that during said year I will wholly abstain from being a member of, and being in any way connected with, and from any manner, or to any extent, contributing to or toward the funds of, or any object of, or any connection with any Molders' Union, or any such like combination or association of persons; and in any case of any breach or breaches by me of this agreement, or for any other cause as to them may seem just, said Messrs. E. & C. Gurney and their foremen, for the time being, and any of them, are hereby empowered to discharge me immediately, or whenever they see fit, and also after discharging me, or without so discharging, to take such proceedings against me under this agreement, as to them may be advised.

J. Campbell, president of the Hamilton Iron Molders' Union, commented on the Gurney agreement: "The agreement is worthy of the veriest tyrant, and the men who would sign it would degrade themselves below the standing of a Chinese coolie or African slave." The *International Journal* concluded that "wages are not the only thing a man looks to or for in a foundry; but the poor cowardly things that sign such an agreement put themselves at the mercy of an employer's idea of justice, and we hope they may get it."[50]

The outcome of the 1874-75 lockout was ambiguous, but it seemed that once again some of the shops remained under union control, while others were run with nonunion labour. Victory rested securely with neither employers nor union. With the onslaught of depression, however, the employers were given the upper hand and, for the molders at least, the struggle for control would be submerged. Tailors also engaged in a brief skirmish with their employers over the trade's bill of prices, but they likewise foundered in the context of economic downturn.[51] The struggle for control was temporarily halted, as craft unions faced the disruptive impact of depression. The economic recovery of the early 1880s, however, was around the corner, and with it came an impressive assertion of the craftsman's penchant for control.

Leading the craft workers back into the struggle for control were the "bottomers" of the MacPherson and Company's shoe works, who struck work in the fall of 1879, protesting against the employment of a painter who had never "served his full time at the boot and shoe trade."[52] By the summer of 1881 Hamilton craftsmen had used the relative prosperity of the early 1880s to reestablish positions of strength. Bricklayers extended a fine net of control over their trade, refusing to work for contractors who remained unfair to union workers.[53] Hamilton tailors secured a new and more favourable price list, averting a strike.[54] Shoemakers managed to gain a 15 per cent wage increase.[55] Iron molders, who had been granted an advance of 10 per cent in 1879, struck for a further 10 per cent in April 1881, all the shops eventually giving in to the men's demands.[56] Three months later the Molders' Union felt sufficiently strong to strike the Stewart foundry, demanding the removal of two nonunion men.[57] Similarly, in July 1881 bricklayers and masons struck work against the contractor D. & C. Cripps, protesting the contractors' employment of their brother, an incompetent nonunionist.[58] The upheaval drew even the unskilled into battle with their employers: coal heavers struck work for higher wages and, when police arrived to protect a new force of men, routed the constables as well as the strikebreakers;[59] municipal labourers employed on the water mains left work, demanding $1.50 a day;[60] teamsters on the Grant Western Railway took job actions to secure a raise of $2 a month.[61] "The effect of the labour movement is already making itself felt in a general rise in everything," concluded the *Hamilton Spectator*.[62]

Relations between skilled workingmen and their employers were perhaps exemplified in the cigarmaking trade. Hamilton's Cigar Makers' International Union No. 55 determined to demand an advance of $1 per thousand cigars, on hand work, with a proportionate increase on "fancy brands." On 28 May 1881 the union issued a communication to the manufacturers:

> Gentlemen: In view of the present advance in the cost of living and rents, we conclude it is but justice to ourselves and families to present to you a bill of prices, which has a tendency to equalize cigarmakers' wages with mechanics and other artists of the Dominion of Canada and the United States. We most respectfully hope you will give the subject your most careful consideration. All we ask is compensation for our labour. Please do us the kindness to inform the shop committee man of your conclusion.

The manufacturers replied in kind: "We beg to acknowledge receipt of your favor of May 28, accompanied by the list of prices adopted by your board. In reply we are willing to meet your views; provided it is to be provincial and strictly carried out in every shop in the city." In times of economic recovery employers were evidently prepared to acquiesce in shop control of the union, and the strike wave of 1881 attested to the craft workers' quickness in judging a moment ripe for the reintroduction of control mechanisms, securing the union shop and the standard rate.[63]

March of 1882 saw the continuation of the 1881 spring offensive. The molders once again secured a 10 per cent wage increase, their third such hike in three years. Their employers, however, were beginning to balk. Burrow, Stewart and Milne acceded to the 10 per cent, "but no more." Laidlaw, Bowes, and Company made it clear that this was the last increase they would tolerate. "We want to get a little of the profits," said the company spokesman. And at E. & C. Gurney's foundry the manager granted the 10 per cent advance, "but no more, no matter what the consequence would be." When some employers refused the increase, the molders simply sought work elsewhere and, in order to keep men in the shops, the Hamilton employers eventually gave in. It had been a significant show of strength on the part of the International Union.[64]

Tailors and nailers, following in the wake of the molders, instituted similar demands.[65] The custom shoemakers' shop committee presented their employers with a new price list, which was quickly accepted.[66] The early spring of 1882 also saw conflicts involving lathers, painters, bakers, and carpenters.[67] At the Ontario Rolling Mills 150 men sent a note to their foremen stating that they were walking off the job. They demanded the reinstatement of a discharged employee, and won their request four days later.[68]

Two brief months after this first settlement at the Ontario Rolling Mills, members of the Amalgamated Iron and Steel Workers' Association again struck work. The union's major grievance was the superintendent, a Mr. Whitehead, whom they claimed was dedicated to "overthrow[ing] the union." Among Whitehead's transgressions had been the firing of union workmen, the hiring of nonunionists, and the assignment of union men as helpers to nonunion labour. All of these acts violated the "rules of the organization." Words ensued between Whitehead and Lloyd, the chairman of the mills committee, and the workers' representative was discharged for verbally abusing the overseer. A strike resulted. Whitehead then terminated the employment of the president of the Workers' Association. Eventually the dispute was settled, Lloyd securing work elsewhere and agreeing not to press the matter. All of the other unionists returned to their places.[69]

Amidst this kind of strike activity, both workers and employers sought institutionalized means of protection. The Trades Assembly, active in the mid-1860s and in the 1872 upheaval, was reborn in late March 1882 when delegates from various unions and labour organizations met to form "a trades and labor assembly, whereby all branches of labor could act unitedly on all questions which affected any one branch of labor in this or any other locality." Hamilton's workingmen were thus building bridges linking them to other centres of working-class agitation; moreover, the interests of skilled and unskilled had been united in one organization.[70] Employers too were on the move. When the builders and contractors met to form "a union both offensive and defensive," they turned aside a resolution urging that they not "combine against the workmen." Their associations, it seemed, were also born with the aim of control in mind.[71]

With the emergence of the Knights of Labor in Hamilton in 1882 much of the story of workers' control is transferred to the context of the Order's development.[72] But skilled workers continued to resist the encroachments on their shop-floor power, struggling to retain control mechanisms. In April 1883 members of the Hat Finishers' Union and the Dominion Hat Factory became embroiled in a controversy involving apprentice ratios in the shop.[73] The following month the bricklayers and the Master Builders' Association were at odds, the bricklayers demanding $3 a day and the contractors complaining of the union's arbitrary rules. Most offensive to the building contractors were the union's refusals to allow injured men to work at reduced rates, the union's practice of allowing bricklayers to take independent contracts up to $100, and the craft's apprenticeship regulations, which restricted the master to one apprentice, regardless of the number of journeymen employed. By the end of May, after considerable negotiation, the bricklayers emerged victorious, their rules intact and the $3 a day standard rate secured.[74]

By the closing months of 1883 the economic boom of the early 1880s was clearly waning. In December the molders were forced to accept a 20 per cent reduction.[75] The Ontario Rolling Mills became the site of a hotly contested control struggle in January 1885, one that would see the destruction of the Amalgamated Iron and Steel Workers' Association. Iron workers objected to changes in the method of work, changes which reduced earnings severely and forced men to work with poor quality scrap iron. A shop committee approached the company's manager, but when no satisfaction could be gained the men struck work. With rolling mills across North America idle, and workers in the trade desperate for employment, the company easily won the day, and filled the strikers' places immediately. Craft control in the Ontario Rolling Mills had succumbed to managerial authority.[76]

Seth J. Whitehead, manager of the rolling mills, saw the strike of 1885 as the consequence of his offensive strategy:

Q. Do you have any trouble with strikes?
A. No.
Q. None?

A. We had in the Ontario Rolling Mill. We had a union in connection with the Amalgamated Association in the United States, but it became necessary to upset it. The management bore it as long as they could, but the men acted very foolishly; we thought they began to dominate, and the gentlemen who run the place con-cluded that they would be better off without it, and they just sat upon it and squelched it out.

The employer's aggressive retaliation, however, was not directed against the union's wage policy, but against customary workplace practices, against the irksome presence of routine aspects of workers' control:

Q. Was the difficulty for an increase of wages or shortening of hours?
A. No; it was not. It was for matters that didn't amount to anything. In fact, a great part of the trouble was that they would get drunk and try to run things their own way, and shut us down and go on just as it suited them.

But even in the aftermath of the employer's victory, Whitehead recog-nized that the penchant for control died hard:

Q. Did any of the men object to the association being wiped out?
A. Well, they did and they didn't. There is a sort of terrorism in con-nection with that thing that a man does not dare to speak.[77]

Nor were the ironworkers the only "defeated" craft still harbouring memories of their lost control and the "manly" stand accompanying it. Coopers at the Ontario Nail Works, a craft displaced by mechanization and devoid of organization, refused a 12 per cent reduction and bluntly told their employer they would not countenance the year-long contracts con-temptuously forced upon them.[78] Shoemakers, who had faced the disrup-tive impact of technological innovation throughout the 1860s and 1870s,[79] could still mount offensives in the 1880s, securing significant control over workplace settings. At the Hamilton factory of MacPherson and Company, shoe workers affiliated with the Knights of Labor launched "a determined stand" against an imported nonunionist and apprentice. Although their employer agreed to pay the two recent arrivals the regular scale of prices, "the shop committee called a meeting of workmen on Monday evening, at which they took these facts into consideration, and refused to go to work with them." The shoemakers apparently exercised considerable power, for they received a polite reply from their employer the next day: "Gentlemen: Having no other course to pursue, we are obliged to accept your terms, as our samples must not be delayed." A shoemaker's lament of the depres-sion-ridden years of the mid-1870s,

> Whats our trade a coming to
> for I am used up how are you
> I hav little work and Less money
> to live on that is very funny,
> for shoes are cheaper than the leather
> and it still remains a query weather
> they'ell be any alteration
> in this our stagnate Nation,

had been replaced by a more positive refrain.[80]

Organized craft workers affiliated with international unions, however, continued to lead the way. A strike wave in March 1888, involving the building trades, indicated just how securely many trades retained their control mechanisms, and how staunchly they would defend them from attack. Carpenters initiated the upheaval, demanding that their employers hire only union men and that all foremen be affiliated with one of the two carpenters' unions in the city.[81] On 9 March 1888 a conflict developed at Hancock's stone quarry, where the Bricklayers' and Masons' Union objected to the use of nonunion labourers, the long hours imposed on the men, and the practice of importing stonecutters to work the stone to be used in the construction of the new city hall on Ontario Street.[82] Ten days later union labourers at the construction site of the city hall quit work, declaring that they would not work with stone drawn from a quarry employing nonunionists; masons on the same job followed suit. The contractors, members of the Builders' Exchange, attributed the trouble to agitators, particularly condemning the unions' policy of controlling foremen on all jobs, and expressing irritation at the restrictions imposed on all contractors by trade regulations. "Many of these restrictions are so arbitrary," claimed the *Hamilton Spectator*, "that the bosses find themselves completely in the hands of the men, and they decidedly object to the men running their business."[83]

On 28 March 1888 the contractors, led by the quarryman Hancock, took the offensive, informing the building trades' unions:

> Whereas, certain labour organizations or unions in connection with the building trades have in the past and are now using the power they have acquired by combining together for unjust and arbitrary purpose, having no reference whatever to wages; and, whereas, serious loss must result to the employer and the building trade generally by the abuse of power ... the Builders' Contractors, and Dealers' Exchange ... resolve that on and after March 28, all known union men of every branch in the employ of members of the Exchange shall be and remain suspended from work until the satisfactory removal of the difficulty between the Laborers' and Bricklayers' Unions and the Master Builders' Association, when work will be resumed.

Replying to the Builders' Exchange, the Amalgamated Association of Carpenters and Joiners condemned the notice as, "one of the most unjust and arbitrary actions ever perpetrated in the city of Hamilton, in that without any warning previous to Tuesday they discharged their old and faithful hands for the crime of belonging to a society banded together for mutual improvement and beneficial purposes. It is well known to us that they have combined for the purpose of crushing all the trade societies of this city if they can."[84] By the end of March 1888 over 700 men were locked out of work, and a Council of Building Trades — composed of delegates from two carpenters' unions, a plasterers' union, a stonecutters' union, a teamsters' union, and a building labourers' union — had convened and censured the Builders' Exchange.[85]

Dragging on well into April 1888, the stalemate revolved around union restrictions and the crafts' support for one another. Hancock, president of the Builders' Exchange, explained that all trades had been locked out because of their shared demand that union foremen be hired. Moreover, he added, the Exchange resented the conspiratorial thrust of the unanimous trade union support for the Bricklayers' and Masons' Union. Finally, he stressed the cumbersome rules of each craft, restrictions which had even been adopted by the unskilled members of the Builders' Laborers' Union. In that category of work, for instance, a man was not to carry more than fourteen bricks in a hod; a man carrying bricks was not to carry mortar; a man carrying mortar was not to carry bricks; and none were to carry sills, planks, or anything other than what they were particularly engaged in handling.[86]

By early May 1888 some trades had settled with their employers, but other crafts remained out. M. A. Pigott, a contractor whom we have seen to be a rabid opponent of craft restrictions, became involved in a conflict with the Stonecutters' Union on 25 April 1888. Pigott claimed that he had "a decided objection to have the union run his work and propose[d] to show them that he [could] be independent."[87] The struggle took a turn in another direction shortly after the stonecutters' run-in with Pigott. As contractors filled job sites with nonunion men antagonism built between the organized and unorganized workers. To protect their interests, the nonunionists formed an Independent Workingmen's Association, open to all nonunion building trades workers. Its first meeting was physically disrupted by craft workers affiliated with the union, although the strikebreakers promised to continue their "organizational" efforts.[88] Three members of the Bricklayers' and Masons' Union — William Mitchell, William Littlejohns, and David Gibson — were charged with conspiracy in the context of their union's efforts to boycott a job site where a nonunionist was employed. On 21 June 1888 they were convicted. Even in the midst of these setbacks, however, the building tradesmen stood firm, gaining their point in many cases.[89] By mid-August the conflict continued to excite the passions of union men, but only M. A. Pigott's city hall construction site still employed nonunion labour.[90]

Outside of the building trades, the late 1880s and early 1890s saw similar struggles. Nailmakers struck work 5 July 1888, objecting to a change in the work process.[91] In the spring of 1891 brickmakers fought a losing battle against the mechanization of their trade.[92] And in 1892 and 1895 Hamilton's cigarmakers opposed their employers over the union price list and the apprentice ratios in a major city cigar manufactory.[93] But once again the struggle for control was sharpest in the city's foundries.

Hamilton molders had utilized the relative prosperity of the late 1880s to reestablish their prominence in the city's foundries. Engaging in almost ritualized yearly confrontations with their employers, the molders had won wage advances in 1887 and 1888. By the spring of 1888 the union's shop committee controlled the labour market, and all applicants for work reported directly to it.[94] Things remained relatively peaceful until 1892, when the employers struck back with a vengeance.[95]

In early January 1892 the Molders' Union was notified that the founders intended to reduce wages 10 per cent on all piece and day work. Complaining that they could not compete with the open shops of London, Brantford, and Toronto (where Hamilton's Charles Gurney owned and operated a foundry on nonunion principles), the employers contended that "Hamilton [was] the only place governed by the union." Over 350 union men were thus faced with lay-offs following the traditional Christmas break, for the foundrymen claimed that they would run their shops with nonunion men if the molders resisted the reduction. By the end of January the clash appeared inevitable. Union molders resolved to oppose the reductions, preserving their commitment to the union shop as their *only* protection. The founders dedicated themselves to the realization of the open shop and further wage cuts.[96]

A local founder saw the cause of the dispute as the union's policy of "dictat[ing] terms to the Hamilton manufacturers"; he outlined the new manner in which the shops would be run:

> What the stove firms intend to do is run their shops on new principles. Instead of paying wages according to a fixed scale, we will pay each workman according to his work. the good workman and the poor workman will not be paid alike, as in the case under union principles, but good workmen will be paid more than the poor workman. ... Another change will be that we will be able to distribute work in such a manner as to secure better results, to give fine jobs to good workmen, and coarse jobs to those who are unskilled. Heretofore we have not been allowed to distribute the various pieces of work: that is done by the men themselves and the results are often unsatisfactory. Another change will be in the direction of specializing

the work — that is, keeping certain men at certain pieces and nothing else, thus ensuing a greater average skill and rapidity of workmanship in the total results. I anticipate a long struggle, and a bitter one. But the foundrymen realize the gravity of the issue involved in it, and they will not yield any longer to the dictation of the union.[97]

The founder's statement left no doubt that the conflict hinged on the restrictive powers of the craft unionists.[98]

By mid-February 1892 the struggle was well under way. Many Hamilton molders left the city, securing employment in Detroit and London shops. Others stayed behind to "welcome" the influx of "scab" workmen from Salem, Ohio, and Toronto, and to deride the efforts of incompetent apprentices and "botch" workers who manned the foundries. While the founders refused to pay union men more than $2 a day, they contracted with nonunionists, promising them $2.50-$3.00 for the duration of the year. Despite these lucrative terms, the union was often able to induce the nonunionists to leave town, and the city's foundries appeared to be stifled by the conflict.[99]

The union continued to persuade molders to leave the city, coaxing them with cash (as much as $30-$50 a strikebreaker), whiskey, threatening letters, and, in more than one case, physical violence. To replenish their diminishing stock of nonunionists, the foundrymen secured the services of Joseph Payette, a Gurney molder who acted as the founders' agent in Montreal, delivering French-Canadian molders to the Hamilton shops. Ironclad agreements, driven from the molding trade in the 1880s, reappeared. Crowds of workingmen, numbering over 500, gathered each evening outside D. Moore and Company's foundry and followed the nonunion workmen to their boardinghouses, hooting, jeering, and yelling all the while. Burrow, Stewart and Milne rented a frame house next to their shop to house their labourers, fearing that it "won't be long before there will be mobs around our foundry as there have been at Moore's." Arsonists succeeded in igniting a small fire at the Moore foundry. Assault cases involving nonunionists and craft workers — molders as well as other skilled workers — were frequently tried in the city courts. Boardinghouse owners often refused to rent accommodation to strikebreakers. Street fights became an everyday happening. By early May 1892 the community stood polarized, but neither union nor employer had given way.[100]

For the unionists, indeed, the struggle for control had been transformed into a struggle for existence. John Jennings, secretary of the Molders' strike committee, wrote to the Peterborough Molders' Union, explaining the desperate situation No. 26 found itself in:

In answer to how we are geting along I might say there are four shop runing with scab labor & Boys Gurney shop as about forty boys and twenty five scabs Burrows eleven french canadians and Boys Copps 8 men and boys Moore shop 4 french men and boys and the other as not started as yet — we have sent away about 46 scabs since we began and still they come they are a hard class to deal with they tell you straight they are going to stay here and them that wants to go we cannot touch them for they want the earth the main thing is to keep our employers Just were they are but it takes money to do it we have to get it somewhere or we are going to loose which means crushing the Banner Union of this Dominion of ours or otherwise Unionism in Canada Trusting you will still continue to help us for its money against money[101]

Jennings's argument was restated in a North American circular, "Labor Against Capital," issued by the Hamilton Union:

This trouble of ours has been gradually coming on for the last four or five years. The Manufacturers' Combine have closed down, on an average, from twelve to fourteen weeks each winter, and have been doing their best to limit the production and starve us into submission. ... We are the BANNER UNION of Canada, and second to none in America as competent workmen. ... They are determined, as we said before, to wipe us out of existence. In order to fight them successfully, *we must have money*, we therefore appeal to every union molder throughout the length and breadth of the land, to give us a helping hand, and to do it *as soon as possible*. No time should be lost, as our very existence is involved in this issue.[102]

In August 1892 the two parties remained locked in a stalemate. James A. Laidlaw, owner of a local foundry, consented to hire union molders, but only if they abandoned the restrictions of their organization. "We have made an agreement with our foreman, Hugh Sweeney," said Laidlaw, "by which he is to employ the molders and get so much a ton. If he fulfills his agreement the men can't be union men. We have no objection to the union men, but we want to control our shop." Three days later the union molders walked out of Laidlaw's foundry, refusing to work with nonunionists.[103] But a week later union men were in control, the closed shop apparently in effect.[104]

The crack in the wall of employer resistance exhibited at Laidlaw's did not widen, however, and the struggle between the foundrymen and the molders dragged on into 1893. By mid-February, with only twenty-eight union molders employed in the locked-out shops, the unionists had been out for over one year, and the International had expended $30,000 in their cause. Time proved to be on the founders' side. The 1892-93 conflict would be something less than a victory for IMIU No. 26, and the drift into economic recession would ensure that union control of Hamilton's stove foundries would not be established in the immediate future. But neither had the union given in, and its quest to reestablish control would surface again.[105]

Control, then, formed an essential component of nineteenth-century work relationships. Its importance was revealed most dramatically in conflict situations, when employer and craftsman confronted one another over the question of workplace hegemony. That many of these conflicts revolved around seemingly "economistic" issues—the standard rate, price lists, and wage reductions or increases—should not obscure the essential context in which struggle evolved. Opposition to reductions, demands for wage increases, and the enforcement of union price lists all tested the strength of the craft union and its shop committee. To be defeated by an employer on such bread-and-butter issues spelled the demise of craft control just as surely as a contractor's circumvention of apprenticeship regulations or a founder's attack on restriction of output. Restrictive and shop control thus knew few boundaries, forming the essential context of shop-floor life in nineteenth-century Hamilton. Workingmen struggled to preserve these forms of control, and strikes therefore serve as the prism through which the historian can best observe the process. At the same time, it must be stressed that as a culture of the shop-floor, control thrived on a daily basis, in the routine and mundane practices of the working day. Control, won in the context of class conflict, extended well beyond the episodic.

When Hamilton mechanics read labour and reform newspapers aloud to one another at the workplace, exchanging issues among themselves, for instance, they exhibited a degree of autonomy from their employers.[106] Iron rollers and heaters regularly punctuated their day's work with a smoke and a glass of beer, having twenty minutes between heats "to go where they have a mind." At Hamilton's Duncan Lithographing Company, Robert T. Armstrong recalled the boisterous atmosphere of the turn-of-the-century workplace, where supervision seemed non-existent:

All Bronze work was done by hand also dusting. Many a fight was started by the men and boys by firing bronze at each other. . . . What times we did have. Remember a fight between George Webb and Jim Gray and everybody stopped work to see it to a finish. And again a fight between the fireman and Joe Best. Of course, in those days Jack McCarthy had to be in on every fight. And the booze question!! What a time. There were three hotels on one alley and two on the other, and then we saw the result of drink. It was a common thing on Monday to be short of help. It is to smile when I think of going out the back door, and buying fresh doughnuts for 5¢ a dozen.

Another printer, "Red Ink," recalled the camaraderie of the shop, where young workers constantly aided their older workmates, and "sojering" was the norm.[107]

As men who often hired their own helpers, Great Western Railway boilermakers, glassblowers at the Burlington Glass Works, nailers at the Ontario Rolling Mills, and cigarmakers at Tuckett's factory exercised direct control over much of the work process.[108] Other crafts, like the iron molders, asserted their power against employer demands that unionists work with helpers, contemptuously referred to as "bucks" or "berkshires."[109] Thus in 1892 the Hamilton molders refused any compromise involving "the system of 'brick-shares'."[110] The point is that craft unionists could exercise their workplace discretion in many directions, controlling their helpers by hiring them themselves, or refusing to work with helpers altogether.[111]

Control was also intimately related to pride in craftsmanship, an aspect of working life that thrived in times of peace as well as in times of trouble. Restriction of output often involved much more than simple job security. Against the accelerating pace of work the true craftsmen posed the issue of a quality product, always contingent upon the skilled workers' autonomy:

> The 'hurrah' and 'rush' of American practice in the workshop or on American buildings, is surely destroying skillful workmanship. To do good work requires time, and no man can make a good honest piece of work with the lash of the foreman pressing him on to 'hurry up', 'hurry up.' The writer of this has known of more than one case where first class workmen have been elbowed out of existence by men who did not know half as much, but who have the fatal knack of always appearing to be in a hurry. In these days — in the building trades at all events — there seems to be in most instances no incentive to become a good workman. It is not the quality but the quantity of work a man can do that gives him value in the eyes of his employer. All this has a tendency to make indifferent workmen and to fill up the ranks of the building trades with half-trained men, botches and pretenders.

"It is hurried workmanship which overtasks the strength of the workman," argued the *Palladium of Labor*. The Hamilton labour paper then defended restricting output, claiming that a union rule against, "undue haste [was] directly favourable to improvement in the quality of work."[112] Indeed, each trade had its derogatory term for incompetent workmen: telegraphers dubbed poor operatives "pegs" after the metal implements dividing the switches on the keyboard; printers and jewellers referred to clumsy craftsmen as "blacksmiths'; and tailors labelled incompetent workers "shoemakers," indicative of their inability to work with cloth. Likewise each trade had a specific epithet for the strikebreaker.[113]

The basis of quality work lay in the craftsman's early years of apprenticeship training. Apprentice regulations were far more than a restrictive mechanism aimed at preserving job security. Ratios were also intimately connected with the craft's realization that for skill to be properly cultivated an appropriate balance of journeymen to apprentices needed to be maintained. It was in this context that many Hamilton trades preserved their apprenticeship conditions during the late nineteenth century, despite persistent employer opposition.[114] Then, too, apprenticeship was an intense cultural experience, and one that conditioned solidarity as well as workmanship:

> We knew he had overcome difficulties, often had he been disheartened and dismayed, often he had heard the mocking jest or coarse laugh of his companions, at his imperfect workmanship, often heard the angry words over goods or tools spoiled through his ignorance or carelessnes. He had risen on dark mornings when his neighbours, lads his own age were snugly sleeping; he had toiled on glorious summer days when his indolent companions were resting under green trees, or plunging into the cool waters; he had done the rough work because he was 'the boy'. Yes, but there is another side to the picture. With courage renewed, with eyes and fingers becoming more and more accustomed to the handicrafts of the trade, every month found him progressing, till tonight, as the still bell tells us, he has overcome. His companions gather round him with boisterous mirth, and the 'older hands' feel a certain pride in him, as wringing his hand they know he ranks among themselves, the means of an honest living at his disposal, one of God's great army of working men.[115]

Youths reared in this context often found it easier to oppose their masters than their future shopmates when conflict situations arose.[116]

As a final indication of the craft worker's attachment to control, and all that it symbolized, one need only consider the question of cooperation.[117] Cooperation was first seriously embraced by local craftsmen in the fall of 1862, when the Molders' Unions of Canada West met in the city to discuss the prospects of establishing cooperative ventures on the model of the Rochdale Equitable Pioneers Society. A union molder wrote to *Fincher's Trade Review*, outlining the stimulus behind the cooperative movement: "Our present organization does not accomplish what we want. That is to take us from under the hand of our employers and place us on equal footing."[118]

By November 1864 the Hamilton Trades Assembly was holding meetings of the "friends of co-operation among the workingmen of Hamilton."[119] A month later Hamilton's Co-operative Association was formed, sustained by 160 subscribers, pledging $5 each towards the establishment of a cooperative grocery store. "The objects of this association," declared the constitution, "are to carry out the principles of co-operation between seller and purchaser in the buying and selling of food, clothing, and other necessities, with the view of ameliorating the condition of the working classes, and, in furtherance thereof, to begin with the establishment of a co-operative grocery store."[120] Throughout the 1860s the association prospered, growing to 300 members by 1867. But financial stability did not assure social success, and the founders of the association were disappointed in the response of the working-class community. Led by the proprietor stratum of the "producing classes," this early cooperative venture attracted few actual workingmen, and by the early 1870s had foundered.[121]

Despite this failure, the working-class community persistently raised the spectre of a more militant cooperation before the eyes of its employers, often in times of conflict. A cooperative bakery, for instance, was often seen to be the solution to the exorbitant prices charged by the master bakers.[122] Hamilton molders sought to intimidate the founders in the midst of the 1872 nine-hour lockouts by starting a cooperative molding shop.[123] In the opening months of the 1892 conflict in the stove shops, four union molders — W. J. Kerr and his son W. H. Kerr, George Coombs, and William Coombs — began their own business, running the shop on union principles.[124] The Hamilton Painters' Union established cooperative businesses in 1882, as did cigarmakers embroiled in apprenticeship struggles with their employers in 1883 and 1885.[125] Their craft assaulted by non-union labour throughout the 1880s, the United Hatters of North America founded the Eureka Hat Works in Hamilton in 1889, informing the Trades and Labor Council: "Our capital is very limited and unless the labor organizations of the city make a more decided stand for union made goods, the Hat Industry will be completely dead in about another year and we will have had to succumb long before that."[126] Bricklayers regularly turned to cooperation, employing the tactic in the middle of the 1883 and 1888 spring strike waves.[127] For the city's Knights of Labor cooperation was a widely touted panacea for the evils of monopoly and corporate greed.[128] It was not the success or failure of these efforts that deserves commentary, for none lasted beyond the moment of crisis. What is important is the deeply embedded commitment to workers' autonomy that active involvement in cooperative ventures articulated.

By the end of the nineteenth century the skilled workingman and the employer had repeatedly tested one another. The question of control had loomed large. In the words of the Royal Commission on the Relations of Labor and Capital, trade unions had done much "in promoting a spirit of self-control." With their development had grown "a spirit of independence and self-reliance." Rather than look to government legislation, the unions preferred "to better their condition by united action."[129] Frederick Winslow Taylor's close associate, Henry Gantt, saw a similar process at work, noting that, "There is in every workroom a fashion, a habit of work, and the new worker follows that, for it isn't respectable not to."[130] The mechanical superintendent of the Ontario Rolling Mills chose harsher terms to describe the phenomenon. "There is a sort of terrorism in connection with that thing," he said, "that a man does not dare to speak." All of these authorities had come to know the culture of control intimately.

1 The Industrial City 1871

2 Great Western Railway Engine No. 8 ("Dakin") and workers

3   Wanzer's Sewing Machine Factory 1871

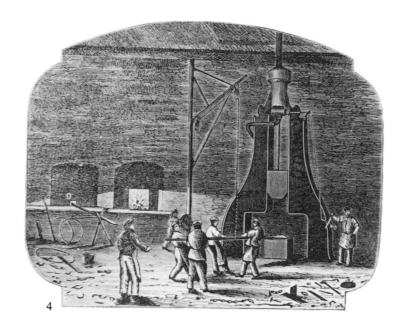

4 Steam Forging Hammer, Great Western Railway Shops 1863
5 L. & P. Sawyer Agricultural Implements Works 1863

6

7

6   The Grand Firemen's Gathering 1874
7   Hose Company No. 2 Pumper, Fire Brigade

8   Great Western Railway Employees' Picnic 1863

chapter

4

Reform Thought and the Producer Ideology

Not by cannon nor by saber,
Not by flags unfurled,
Shall we win the rights of labor,
Shall we free the world.
Thought is stronger far than weapons,
Who shall stay its course?
It spreads in onward-circling waves
And ever gathers force.

Phillips Thompson, "The Power of Thought," in
Marcus Graham, ed., *An Anthology of Revolutionary Poetry*

In a once well-known poem by the Canadian labour reformer Phillips Thompson, a man of letters and a ragged tramp cross paths on an isolated roadway. To the beggar's plaintive cry, "I must have food," the haughty gentleman replies:

'Tis contrary to every rule
That I my fellows should assist;
I'm of the scientific school,
Political economist.

In the end, however, the tramp learned his lessons all too well, succumbing to the political economist's maxim that "The weakest must go to the wall":

The weak must die, the strong survive—
Let's see who'll prove the harder hittist,

This chapter draws extensively upon two unpublished papers by Peter Warrian and represents a cooperative venture by Mr. Warrian and myself.

So, if you wish to keep alive,
Prepare to prove yourself the fittest.

As the poem closes, the scientist is left, penniless, to ponder his fate:

What could I do but yield the point,
Though conscious of no logic blunder?
And as I quaked in every joint,
The tramp departed with his plunder.[1]

Thompson's allegorical treatment of the chance meeting between the economist and the tramp captured the importance of a struggle in the realm of ideas. Workingmen, throughout the late nineteenth century, consistently opposed the tenets of classical political economy.[2] "Let us then hear no more about this vile and vulgar Malthusian doctrine," thundered a pamphleteer in 1880. A mechanic, writing to the *Hamilton Spectator*, denounced the "science of political economy" as "a fraud, a delusion and a snare." The working-class perception of the workings of the "laws" of political economy was discussed by one of labour's poets:

Hurrah for the law of Supply and Demand,
That regulates everything in the land,
The rate of wages, the price of stocks,
And the size of the Vanderbilt pile of "rocks."

It keeps in subjection the dull Labor hordes,
It fills up the chests of our great money lords,
And when for just reasons they're brought to a stand,
They've only to answer, "Supply and Demand."[3]

Indeed, in south-central Canada, workers' opposition to classical political economy burned with particular intensity. By the 1880s, when such potent issues as the development of a Canadian home market and the nature of the people's employment remained to be settled, the foundations of a national producer ideology were laid.[4] From these beginnings, early Canadian working-class thought stressed the mutuality of interests binding manufacturer and mechanic. A loose alliance between the two groups was informally constituted, with a language of social class counterposing the "industrial classes" to the "non-producing drones."[5] Protectionism emerged as the rallying point of "a national industrial class," a conception that obscured the hegemony of nonworking-class elements. As an embryonic form, the working class of the 1860s was not yet capable of articulating its own distinct class interests. It would follow other social groupings, fuelling the fires of the antecedents of the 1879 National Policy.[6]

Breaking down this early harmony of interests was the process of capitalist development itself. The growth of an urban manufacturing population, the rise of large-scale factories, and the increasing use of steam-powered machinery, as we have seen, transformed Canadian social relationships in the 1870s and 1880s. For many, economic development proved to be something less than a blessing, and the increasing polarization of the social order, visible in the growing number of strikes and lockouts, accentuated the collapse of the organic society of producers.[7]

Events in 1872 would clarify the enormity of the transformation and focus the working-class response. Labour organizations, overwhelmingly composed of adult, male, skilled workers emerged as a mass movement in the campaign for the nine-hour day and thereafter became a major political concern.[8] Much of their strength would be sapped by the depression of the 1870s, but the movement would reassert itself in the 1880s, as the Knights of Labor revitalized organizations of the skilled, drawing women workers and the unskilled into the ranks of the working-class movement.[9]

Arising out of this developing working-class movement was a group of self-proclaimed labour reformers in central Canada: the itinerant journalist, Phillips Thompson; the Toronto printers, J. S. Williams and John Armstrong; a cooper, John Hewitt, prominent in the Toronto Trades Assembly; a Grand Trunk machinist-engineer, Hamilton's James Ryan; a London tinsmith, Joseph Marks; and the newspaper editor, A. W. Wright. These men, and others like them, embraced an amalgam of causes and panaceas as eclectic as their social backgrounds, becoming the public advocates of the working-class. Within the context of a growing labour-capital conflict, first in the early 1870s and then in the 1880s, they articulated the strains within, and eventual departures from, the producer ideology of the 1860s and its brittle manufacturer-mechanic alliance. Industrialists, too, distressed by the increasingly autonomous stance of the workingman, gravitated towards their own class interests. Class conflict, we shall see, would prove an acid test that the producer ideology's manufacturer-mechanic alliance simply could not pass and, abandoned by its social betters, the working class would take the first agonizing steps towards defining its own solutions to the problems posed by industrial capitalism.[10]

But the break with the past would be far from complete. Though circumstances of social and economic development forced the working class and its spokesmen away from the conception of the mutuality of interests of all producers, the legacy of the 1860s mediated against any Marxist notion of the essential antagonism of the interests of the emerging working class and the ascendant industrial-capitalist class. Throughout the late nineteenth century the concept of a national economy, grounded upon a critique of classical political economy, remained fundamental to working-class thought. The result was neither economic liberalism nor Marxian socialism, but a populist critique of the new industrial order based on a labour theory of wealth.[11] In a typical attack on the monopolists of the age, "the aristocracy of democracy," the *Hamilton Herald* captured much of this antagonism to the new industrial order:

> they are founding an aristocracy in this democratic country pretty much the same as the good old barons of old, only it is an aristocracy of financial not physical strength. ... Let the observant man of years cast his memory back half a century and think of the gulf that lies between what was and what is. Then let him span the future and he cannot fail to see how surely we are growing away from the simple democratic ideals that are supposed to prevail here.

"Its pretty much the same story the world over," continued the paper. "The locality changes, but the human drama ... is ever the same."[12] Hamilton serves as a useful prism, illuminating the contours of this human drama, and how it played itself out in the realm of working-class thought.

Popularizing the producer ideology throughout the 1850s and 1860s was Isaac Buchanan, a wealthy Hamilton merchant and staunch advocate of protection.[13] A prolific writer and compulsive politician, Buchanan was to suffer bankruptcy in the aftermath of the depression of the 1850s, failing in 1867 and again in 1872.[14] His singular contribution to political economic developments in the 1860s and 1870s has only recently begun to be recognized, an instance of neglect indicative of the important realms of Canadian social and intellectual history that remain to be explored.[15]

Buchanan was intimately connected with the railway boom of the 1850s and the Galt-Cayley tariff changes of 1858-59, milestones in the creation of a Canadian home market, and thus important events in the process of capitalist development. With the opening of the eastern section of the Great Western Railroad, 1 November 1853, Thomas McQueen penned the poem, "The Iron and the Fire," dedicating it to Buchanan. The last stanza sounded the promise of industrialization that many would seek to realize during the next thirty years:

> Hail, Canada! Thy fame in part,
> Is shadowed here today,
> When sounds the steam car's whistle loud
> Round our commercial Bay.
> And hark the whistle sounds again;
> Crowds press, with keen desire,
> To witness Mind's stupendous power
> In iron and in fire.[16]

As early as 1860 Buchanan was championing the cause of railways in no uncertain terms: "If there was any doubt as to these railways being essential to Hamilton being a great mart of commerce—there might be the usual arguments in such cases of a *bad investment*, ... but when the loss is not only money, but existence, the argument seems to me a preposterous one."[17] Mercantile endorsement of rail construction was hardly novel, of course, but his depreciation of mere money hinted at Buchanan's ability to transcend the narrow perspectives of his own business concerns. This penchant to go well beyond the boundaries of personal interest hardened in 1858 with Buchanan's role in the general Hamilton-Toronto agitation to revise tariff schedules.

The Galt-Cayley tariff revisions of 1858-59 apparently coincided with the demands of the Hamilton-Toronto manufacturers and, according to D. F. Barnett, offered sufficient protection to Canadian industry "to set the stage for the development of a broadly based industrial structure in the Province of Canada." Tom Naylor is thus probably mistaken in regarding the tariff revision as a piecemeal reform. Nevertheless, perhaps because of mercantile opposition to the tariff revisions, Galt stressed the revenue-raising purpose of the new schedules, adding that any protection afforded native industry was purely secondary. In the parlance of the times Galt's tariff was known as "incidental protection."[18] This downplaying of industrial protection, coupled with the continuing crisis of the 1850s, must have blinded many manufacturers and mechanics to the positive effects of the tariff revisions. Buchanan himself later referred to the "fair play tariff of 1858," arguing that those who had endorsed it deserved the "support of the workingmen."[19] But in 1859, with the Canadian economy wracked by two years of severe depression, discontent was widespread, and the perceived deficiencies of the tariff must have loomed large.

Across south-central Canada the mechanic-manufacturer alliance of the producer ideology was erected. A group signing themselves "Manufacturers and Mechanics" informed the *Hamilton Times* of their dissatisfaction with the Galt tariff, and pleaded for effective protection: "every workshop ... must at once feel the heavy blow struck at their future prospects, and an uncertainty about entering into any contract for work."[20] Leading this "New Opposition" was Isaac Buchanan, the central figure in the formation of the Association for the Promotion of Canadian Industry (APCI). Until Confederation, and well after, he would be recognized as "*the leader* of the protective movement."[21] Buchanan, who may not have known his economics, knew his politics well, capitalizing on discontent, voicing the policies of industrial development that endeared him to manufacturers and mechanics.

In the free trade community of early Canadian mercantilism, protection was an odd hat for Hamilton's leading merchant to be wearing. Odd, too, was his role as spokesman for a coalition of mechanics and manufacturers. But where Buchanan broke most emphatically with the orthodoxies of his social station and times was in his unqualified support for the workingman, and his ability to integrate the needs of working people with an emerging sense of Canadian nationhood. He consciously directed his appeals for reform to the patriotic workman who had a real stake in the development of a protected Canadian market.[22] While Buchanan was not immune to the practices of the times — he would often court working-class votes with sycophancy, drink, and coin of the realm[23] — he was honestly concerned for people he saw led into threatening prospects by the revolutionary developments of modern industry and the dangerous portent of internationalism.[24] Much of his concern was undoubtedly stimulated by a desire to siphon off the discontent capable of mounting a revolutionary working-class upheaval, but he would never lose sight of the essential integrity of the working people.

> Who dares scorn the swarthy forehead, who dares taunt the horny
>   hand;
> They, have ever been the glory; strength and sinew of the land,
> While in honesty of purpose, nobly daring to be free
> With our strong right arm we win us — the best gifts of Liberty,
> Liberty of thought and action, Liberty of heart and brain.
> These once yielded, tell me Brother, what is worthy to retain.
> Lost to manhood, lost to freedom, croaching hounds and whining
>   slaves,
> Better that our names should perish, better far, be in our graves.[25]

The workingmen had difficulty faulting such a man, a man who had supported the shorter-hours movement in England, defended the striking Grand Trunk trainmen in 1877, and stood behind the election in 1872 of Hamilton's Henry Witton, the first bona fide workingman elected to the House of Commons.[26] "A Free Mechanic" spoke for many of his class in 1867 when he noted the attachment of the Hamilton mechanics to the dissident merchant: "No man has been so open, so sedulous and consistent a supporter of the cause of the working man than has Mr. Buchanan for more than a quarter of a century."[27]

Buchanan's writings were repetitive and ponderous, and flawed by logical inconsistencies, but their central theme — the relationship between monetary reform and tariff protection for native industrial development — appealed to all producers. Stressing "*devotion to the well being of the masses of our country as the first object of our politics*," Buchanan outlined, somewhat immodestly, his contribution to Canadian political economic thought: "I was the first to shew that the question of labor and the question of money are in reality but one question — the solution of the one being the solution of the other — and that the use of Tariffs is to protect the country's currency, while the use of Monetary Reform is simply to secure Fair Play to our Agriculturalists and Artizans."[28] He diagnosed the roots of the economic downturn of the late 1850s in the confluence of those policies against which he had directed his attack—"Free Trade" and "Hard Money"—urging the necessity of establishing diversified manufactures in Canada.[29] If the Empire was to be preserved, he argued, Britain must "yield the selfish principle of *centralizing* which has ruined Ireland and India, so far as such countries could be ruined, and cost us the old American colonies."[30]

His motivation was thus profoundly conservative: to implement measures that would preserve the British connection in a time of economic and political crisis, staving off the incipient rebellion he felt uncomfortably near.[31] Unless the mother country moved immediately against the policies of the political economists, he feared the question, "Can the British Monarchy be Preserved?," would be answered in the negative: "No, emphatically, No, unless the upper classes permit the immediate adoption of measures which their personal interests will, I fear, make them denounce as revolutionary, just as the slave breeding lord of Republican America prefers risking the integrity of the Republic rather than want [the end of] the wretched institution of slavery."[32] By 1865 Buchanan's fears had grown to encompass the proposed annexation with the United States. But his commitment to protection had also widened, placing him in the forefront of the forces advocating confederation of the British North American provinces. What was needed, maintained Buchanan, was "an intimate and indissoluble union of all the provinces comprising British North America," where markets for industry and outlets for trade would ease disloyalty and discontent: "What has true Conservative statesmanship got to offer the work men who are willing to work? One thing ... which is worth ten times all the nostrums that Radicalism ever has offered or can offer, were they all realized and made the law of the land—viz., the opening of the British colonies as fields of all kinds of honest industry. And that is the sole policy by which the workmen, agricultural and manufacturing, can be peacably elevated from their notoriously downtrodden state."[33] In his efforts to secure the preservation of the status quo, Buchanan had thus opened something of a Pandora's box. His conservative critique of orthodox political economy had become startlingly radical in its implications, placing the needs and aspirations of working people squarely on the political agenda of the day.

Early in his writings, for instance, Buchanan couched protection in terms of the social and economic requirements of the labouring poor: "Now as the protective policy is calculated to revive business, and give the labourer the due reward of his toil, we regard it as the poor man's system—as his rightful inheritance."[34] From this statement it was but a short step to the realization that "the question of the employment of a people is THE

GREAT CONSTITUTIONAL QUESTION IN EVERY COUNTRY and one in importance far before all other questions, even those of forms of Government."[35] The vital object of all politics, then, was the "People's Question": "The Employment of Our Working Classes."[36]

Buchanan contrasted his efforts and perspectives with those of "Hard Money" men of the Cobden-Bright variety. While he sought the twin objectives of good government and equal justice for rich and poor alike, they cared less for the labouring poor of Canada or England than the planter of the South cared for his slave. Their error lay in their regard for the people only as *consumers* and their attempt to convince the people that their whole interest lay in *cheapness*. To Buchanan it seemed self-evident that the distinctive characteristic of the people was that they laboured: cheap commodities were only the sorry corollary of cheap wages and dear money. When a man's production did not exceed his consumption there would be no return for his labour and his employment would consequently cease, with drastic implications for the nation as well as the individual. The labourer's production being therefore the larger quantity, Buchanan maintained that workingmen were more interested in the price of it than in the price of the smaller quantity, consumption.[37]

It was this disregard for the essential unity of the labour and money questions that had precipitated England to the brink of Communism. Like a sinking man grasping at straws, the workingman had been forced, by the economies of "Hard Money" and "Free Trade," to look to "Organizations of Labour, Communisms, and Associationisms." Fortunately, Buchanan argued, another possibility existed: "The Working Men now see that *the only possible cause of increased wages, is increased employment*, which can only arise from improving the condition of THE EMPLOYERS OF LABOUR, AS CONTRADISTINGUISHED FROM THE EMPLOYERS OF MONEY ... they see that to increase the number of bidders for their labour, (*the only means of raising their wages permanently*), such an alteration of our Money Laws must be made as will permanently REDUCE THE EXCHANGEABLE VALUE OF MONEY."[38] Posing a political polarization — "The Money Power Versus the Labour Power" — Buchanan attacked the gold standard, the foundation of the monetary system: "our error lies in this, that the circulation is based upon and in proportion to Gold, the rich man's property, instead of upon Labour the poor man's property — that this basis is therefore a thing that cannot be sent out of the country; instead, in a word, of money being the mere handmaid of native industry."[39]

The solution to the political questions of the day thus lay in a dual reform. Recognizing labour as the poor man's property, what was needed was an "Emblematic Money," a paper currency secured by government issue and backing, which would break the monopoly of the rich man's property, gold. This national currency would be the servant of a developing Canadian industry that was, in turn, to be fostered by a protective tariff. A reformed monetary system and a patriotic tariff thus went hand-in-hand, fostering Canadian industrial development and eliminating financial famine.[40]

The institutional mechanism for these reforms was to be an American Zollverein, not unlike that which existed among the German states. Its basis was to be free trade in manufactured goods with the United States and "PROTECTION AGAINST THE DEGRADED LABOUR OF EUROPE."[41] This seemed a rather curious policy for an ardent protectionist to be advocating but, as Tom Naylor has recently suggested, it contained a profound logic. Indeed, economic self-defence demanded that Canada secure free trade for its mechanics and farmers with the United States, a country which would never trade directly with England, but which thrived on Canada's very doorstep. The stimulus to a home market provided by free trade with the United States would lead to the enlargement of cities and the growth of towns, gradually giving rise to an independence from the markets of the southern neighbour. Moreover, only free trade with the United States would ease the rising tide of skilled labour emigrating to the Republic, where higher wages and more secure employment prevailed.[42] At the same time, British capital and labour, eager to share the unique Canadian advantage of proximity to the United States, would be welcomed migrants to the Dominion. "Why should England be jealous or oppose this?" asked Buchanan. "Is not Canada just England in America?"[43]

Buchanan's concern with protection for Canadian industry, and his role as popularizer of the national producer ideology forced him to confront the consequences of continued adherence to the "patriotic maxims called British principles," upheld by free traders like Peel and Gladstone. The Canadian people had suffered much at the hands of such men and Buchanan warned that, like the American colonists before them, Canadian producers would rise in concert: "Am I asked why these people arose in such concert? Because they were people in human shape; because patience under the detested tyranny of man is rebellion to the sovereignty of God; because allegiance to that power that gives us the *forms* of men commands to maintain the *rights* of men."[44] "When bad men conspire," he often declared, paraphrasing Burke's aphorism, "good men must combine."[45]

Buchanan's advice was not wasted on the workingmen, who expressed an early impatience with the inactivity of men of substance:

We have been anxiously waiting for some one to respond to your call, that is: Who will be the first to suggest the means whereby manufacturing will become one of the institutions of Hamilton. We expected that the men who hold real estate would have made a move ere this, but as they have not done so, we hope that asking

you to place our views before the public will not be considered an
act of presumption. In the first place, we propose to establish an
Association, to be named the Hamilton Co-Operative Manufacturing
Company.... Why, we ask, should not this city of the lake become a
hive of industry.[46]

By 1864, the eve of an important election year, the mechanics' discontent
had heightened to a new sense of urgency:

when we see class arranged against class, their interests apparently
dissimilar and their class divided and subdivided by intersectional
rule so that branches of industry become opposed to each other, and
the links that ought to bind us become a matter of dispute, rather
than what is of far more vital importance, viz., our own social development and individual happiness, it is time we straightened our
bended backs and look about us to see what is going on. It is time
our voice was raised to be heard.[47]

It was in this context that *The Workingman's Journal*, the first Canadian
newspaper explicitly devoted to "the Interests of the Producing Classes,"
was established in Hamilton in the spring of 1864.[48] Though short-lived,
the *Journal* proclaimed itself part of a movement of vast social interest
and importance:

Everywhere the industrial classes are organizing societies for the
protection of their interests, and the improvement of their social
condition. In the belief that this movement, if carried out on just
principles, will do an incalculable amount of good, the columns of
the 'Workingman's Journal' will be devoted to its advocacy. The
'Journal' will preach no blind, unreasoning Crusade against the interests of Capital, but will affirm with all the power of reasoning at its
command, the right of the producer to an equitable share of that
which he produces.[49]

Not class conflict, but the promise of the producers' cooperative commonwealth, dominated the pages of this early workingman's journal.

It was an understandable perspective, reinforced in fiction and fact. The
paper opened with a brief novella chronicling the life of Benjamin Brown,
a man who rose in the social hierarchy through hard work, thrift, and the
intelligent and sober application of practical genius. His fall, occasioned by
speculation, frivolity, and reckless abandon — the classical vices of para-
sitical nonproducers — was a reminder to all that success was no excuse for
the abandonment of virtue. On the *Journal's* closing page was a "Trade
Directory" for printers, collarmakers, carpenters, cabinetmakers, cigarmakers, shipwrights, ironworkers, boilermakers, molders, tailors, coop-

ers, stonecutters, painters, plasterers, tinsmiths, bricklayers, machinists, and blacksmiths. The image of the workingman was clearly one of the free labourer capable of engaging or disengaging in employment of his own free will. The ideal and the real seemed to match; the paper listed addresses of skilled workers' organizations in Hamilton, London, Brantford, and Toronto, as well as the locations of 119 trade societies and assemblies in the United States.[50]

To Isaac Buchanan the *Journal* offered a solemn tribute. Reviewing H. J. Morgan's edited collection, *Buchanan on Industrial Politics of America*,[51] the paper praised the singular features of the new book. "One thing cannot fail to secure a place for this work in every Canadian library," concluded the review, "and that is its Canadian spirit, and yet the spirit is not a selfish one."[52]

This early labour publication thus reiterated the themes of national economy and manufacturer-mechanic alliance that had permeated Buchanan's writings, providing the foundation of the producer ideology. These themes surfaced again in *The People's Journal*, founded in Hamilton in 1869, and later relocated in Toronto. Published by John McLean, associate of Isaac Buchanan and an active member in the APCI, it would engage in a consistent critique of free trade, claiming to speak for the manufacturers of the Dominion, irrespective of locality.[53] The *Prospectus* of the new journal, maintaining that "the promotion of home manufactures, and of a self-sustaining industrial policy, being intimately connected with the great question of employment for its people" were subjects of vast importance, focused on issues well known to those familiar with Buchanan's pen.[54] But there was a difference. The industrial development of the 1860s, the American retraction of reciprocity in 1866, and the rising national consciousness bred of Confederation all seemed to render Buchanan's earlier conception of an American Zollverein obsolete. Since "public opinion over the way will not tolerate Reciprocity with Canada," McLean argued, "we had better cease standing like beggars at Jonathan's door ... [and] adopt a policy to suit our own interests, and not those of foreigners, and make the best of the advantages with which Providence had endowed us."[55]

Free trade, *The People's Journal* maintained, was a dismal failure whenever "highly civilized nations on both sides of the trade" were involved. True, between a highly advanced nation and a backward or barbarous one, it sometimes worked quite well. But in order for this to continue one of the parties "*must continue* in this backward or barbarous state." The logic was inescapable: Canada, for long the backward partner in its trade relations with Britain and the United States, must effect an immediate break with past policies if it hoped to sever the chains of subserviency. As a separate community, a distinct nation striving for advancement, it must awaken to a "true perception of its own interests as a *Commonwealth*, to a

practical application of the broad general truth that 'business is war'."[56]
With this realization the producer ideology assumed a new vitality, as
manufacturers, workers, and farmers became participants in the unfold-
ing of a Canadian industrial manifest destiny.

It was the civilizing impact of this industrial progress of nations that so
captivated and inspired *The People's Journal*: modern developments
seemed to point to an inevitable substitution of popular systems of government for the despotic rule of individuals, families, or classes. Such progress was necessarily subversive of free trade doctrines, argued McLean,
for each national commonwealth would strive for self-protection: "The
increasing share of *The People* in government and the increasing pressure of
commercial competition in modern times; — these are the potent and irresistible forces acting against the one-sided arrangement of 'free trade'."[57] In
Canada, however, the path of this evolution was blocked by "the great
representative men of our country." These defenders of Free Trade sought
an easy road to fame, not the best interests of the people. They adopted the
fashionable positions found in their gentlemen's magazines and sought
facile association with prominent statesmen and theorists, whose ideas they
never tired of expounding upon. Yet they never troubled themselves to
give due consideration, in their tiresome homilies, to the relative positions
of "old England" and "young Canada," and it was the producers of the
latter who bore the brunt of often repeated economic crises.[58]

A letter to the editor drew a graphic picture of the "industrial interests"
of Canada — manufacturers, workmen, and farmers — "struggling into
existence" under the most unfavourable of circumstances.[59] Their downtrodden existence was a consequence of the despicable role of the
"drones" of society: the commission merchants, the transporters, and
the insurers. For the producers and consumers, isolation from one
another produced a never-ending inflation of their cost of living, and an
increasing loss of the products of their labour. The middlemen were the
gainers.[60] But the people were far from passive, only requiring education
to become, in the words of one writer, "a lever that never yet failed to
move governments and to influence even Kings."[61]

The People's Journal regarded it as a great step forward, marking the
opening of a "new era" in Canadian social and political thought, when the
House of Commons began a major debate on the question of the tariff in
the spring of 1870. It stated prophetically: "to the politicians who think
that they rule the country and to the literary men who fancy they give
expression to its opinion — this debate gives a rude awakening on their
part to things hitherto undreamed of in their philosophy. ... The debate,
we hesitate not to say, has settled this much — that the question of a
'national policy' for Canada is to be during some years to come the foremost and greatest question before the country."[62] The producer ideology
was thus unmistakably linked to the developing Canadian nation state and

its strategic policies of industrial development. While the workingman had been a willing and acquiescent partner in the evolution of this confluence of ideology and development in the 1860s, he would soon have cause to articulate some fundamental disagreements.

The foremost question in the minds of Hamilton workingmen in the spring of 1870 was not the tariff issue. What captured their attention was the ominous spectacle of Chinese workers being transported across the United States by train to labour in the shoe factories of New England. Rapid and dramatic was the mechanics' response: they would not suffer themselves to be "*worked down*" to the level of the Chinese. *The People's Journal*, ever the champion of the producers' cause, took up their complaint, and in its usual condemnation of the practitioners of the "dismal science" asserted: "It is more important to create a people with the wants and wishes, the capabilities and aspirations of civilized Christian freemen, than that shoes be twenty-five cents a pair cheaper." "*Salus populi suprema lex*": the good of the people was the supreme law of the land, and "cheap goods" were little consolation to a country whose people had no employment and no means to consume.[63]

The threat to Canadian skilled labour, however, was posed in a more direct manner, within the country's borders as well as outside them. Workmen were beginning to realize that the free labour of the economic marketplace was coming to mean freedom *from* their skills, former economic security, and social status. It was, in short, an exceedingly pyrrhic freedom, in which the capitalist had increasingly gained the upper hand. Conflicts between skilled workers and their employers in the late 1860s attested to this fundamental tension, and were illustrative of the initial stirrings of the Canadian working-class movement. Molders, bakers, carpenters, and cigarmakers had played key roles in these early conflicts, Hamilton being an important battleground, but it was relations in the shoe industry that would forcefully depict the rupture of the mechanic-manufacturer alliance.[64]

By 1870 boots and shoes manufacture had become the largest and most mechanized industry in Toronto; in Hamilton the shoe factories trailed only the foundries in terms of industrial importance. Revolutionized by the introduction and refinement of the McKay sewing machine, the shoe industry was led into a concerted assault on the control mechanisms of the autonomous workmen employed in its factories. The workers' response was characteristic: in late 1867, after their participation in the celebrations surrounding Confederation, shoemakers from across the province met in Toronto to form the Boot and Shoemakers Union of Ontario. Two years later they merged with the Knights of St. Crispin, becoming part of the general North American movement.[65]

The Crispins embraced a language of social class that broke fiercely with the conciliatory tone of the producer ideology: "Labor is the interest underlying every other interest, and therefore is entitled to and should receive from society and government protection and encouragement. Recognizing the right of the manufacturer or capitalist to control his capital, we also claim and shall exercise the right to control our labor and to be consulted in determining the price to be paid for it — a right hitherto denied us."[66] Questioning some of the basic premises of an earlier decade, workingmen were shifting their perspective from one of support for protection of the national commonweal to one recognizing the need for protection of labour's rights in the marketplace.

Given this shift in working-class thought, *The People's Journal* left no doubts as to where its sympathies lay: "Trade unions, among skilled labourers, during the past few years, have had a disorganizing effect upon the general prosperity on both sides of the Atlantic."[67] The first stirrings of labour organization had precipitated something of a panic among the upper echelons of the producers' alliance. "If light does not soon break forth," wrote R. M. Wilmot to Isaac Buchanan in the summer of 1870, "I look forward to a frightful social revolution. It is unreasonable to suppose that ... human beings will submit to be starved in the midst of abundance. With the great labour combinations that now exist, we may see an uprising that will astonish the world." Buchanan wrote to President Grant in November 1870, prefacing his remarks on currency reform with a fearful note on "the threatening prospect" among the working classes of Europe and North America.[68]

By 1871 the manufacturers' break with the labour interests would be complete. In that year the Toronto Crispins moved to exclude unskilled apprentices from the shops and control entry to their trade. This attempt at self-protection drew the merciless fire of *The People's Journal*. An outraged McLean attacked the Toronto action as "a piece of monopoly and oppression not to be borne in a free country," finding the "rules of the Society, limiting the number of apprentices, and practically *closing the trade*" particularly obnoxious.[69] This brief moment of class conflict in the shoe industry revealed the brittle substance of the producer alliance. Under attack from above and below, it appeared to rest on a precarious base in 1871. The year 1872 would see it topple.

That year witnessed the inauguration of the nine-hour movement and the birth of the Canadian Labour Protective Association, developments that served to emphasize the emergence of the workingman's distinct perception of class interests.[70] The *Ontario Workman*, organ of the shorter-hours movement, reflected this heightened consciousness when it established itself in Toronto in 1872, advocating the intellectual and physical betterment of the working classes.[71]

J. S. Williams, editor of the *Workman*, stressed the transformation of workers' consciousness attendant upon the rise of the struggle for the shorter work day. "The artizan has assumed the right and privilege of self-assertion," noted Williams. "He takes a far higher place than was his want in the social scale, and as he advances in intelligence, and exercises his political powers properly — which constitutes the source of his strength — he will take a still higher place."[72] Another commentator chose a similar theme when he stressed that "They had no aristocracy here, but the aristocracy of labour, and the man who by the sweat of his brow made himself a position, stood the equal of any man in this country."[73] A "Woodworker" from Toronto, however, surpassed all others in the vehemence with which he broke with the producer alliance in his attack on some Toronto manufacturers publicly opposing the workingmen's purpose: "In looking over the names in the Manifesto that emanated from that Great Mogul the *Globe*, I was highly amused to see among them the names of men that called themselves Master Carriagemakers. What a dignified title. Men that could not make a wheelbarrow. Carriage makers, forsooth! Wood butchers would be a more appropriate term — for butchers I know them to be. Men that a year or two ago could not hold a job in any carriage factory in the city, except to work on repairing, or grease and dust carriages."[74] This, surely, was a statement allowing of no misinterpretation. The mechanic-manufacturer alliance was foundering on the agitation surrounding the struggle for the shorter working day.

Statements such as these articulated a specific sense of the worth and dignity of the workingman, and at their core resided a labour theory of wealth: "The wealth of this country had been increased by the energy, the perseverance, the united toil of the workingmen of this country."[75] There was nothing strikingly innovative in such a formulation. Isaac Buchanan, after all, had rooted much of his earlier writings in just such a conception: "We discern ... that little advancement could have been made in the necessary, useful, or ornamental appropriation of the crude materials of nature, if the efforts of labour had not been made in separate departments of industry, or, as it is called by writers on political economy, the division and sub-division of labour."[76] But the labour spokesmen gave this maxim a new twist. In countering the threat of many manufacturers to withdraw their capital from business and employ it instead in the more predictable trade in money or usury, the labour reformers asserted that it was necessary to touch the nonproductive commodity known as capital with productive labour in order to make it accumulative. And here they introduced the vital connection between class interests and the hours of labour: "The workman has to produce the intrinsic value that money is but the mere representative of, and whether that is done at eight or ten hours there is but one way of doing it, namely, by the productive energies of man."[77] The question of the hours of labour had become entwined with the question of class.[78]

As if to underscore this essential point the *Ontario Workman* reprinted a short excerpt from Marx's *Capital*, the section dealing with "the limits

of the working day." It contains Marx's central contention that labour was
the source of all value and that extraction of surplus value from the
worker was the source of capitalist profit.[79] The ideas of Ira Steward,
leader of the Machinists' and Blacksmiths' International Union, and
prominent in labour-reform circles in the United States, also found
circulation.[80] Steward's argument paralleled that of Marx: "Probably the
working classes are not paid for more than seven hours' labor a day; and
what remains is called profits upon labor, which go into the hands of a
few, who thus become wealthy."[81] Both Marx and Steward broke firmly
with the wages fund theory of capital, the contention that wages were
created out of invested capital, a portion of the gross product which the
entrepreneur, abstaining from personal consumption, reinvested in the
employment of labour. In such a situation the worker was given his job
out of the funds of the employer and should be appropriately grateful.
This, in the eyes of Marx and Steward, was utter nonsense. To them,
wages and the hours of labour were simply what labour could effectively
demand, "the result of a struggle, a struggle between collective capital,
i.e., the class of capitalists, and collective labour, i.e., the working
class."[82]

Neither the ideas of Steward nor those of Marx, however, gained
widespread support among Ontario workers. Against the Marxist notion
of the inevitable class conflict associated with the length of the working
day, the *Workman* urged that moderation in the hours of work would
benefit both master and man through improvements in the latter's productive potential.[83] These early labour reformers failed to rid themselves of
the legacy of the producer ideology. Though the manufacturer-mechanic
alliance disintegrated with the first signs of class polarization, the notion of
the labour theory of wealth proved impervious to decay, an attractive link to
the workingman's past status and world-view. Deeply committed to its
logic, the reformers maintained a naïve faith in the willingness of the
political structure to incorporate their demands. To them, their positions
were only those of eminently reasonable men, and they saw no reason why
the minimal concessions they considered sufficient to improve their lot
would not be granted in the near future. B. Mercer, of the Hamilton
Trades Assembly, put their plea cogently when he suggested that the
workingman refrain from militant job actions, and instead petition the
"Legislature to pass a Law to give to workingmen an equitable division in
the profits of his own productions ... extinguish[ing] for ever the odious
word master."[84] Backing away from the class struggles they had seen en-
acted throughout south-central Canada in the spring of 1872, the labour
reformers drew close to an illusive legislative panacea. They still sought
the cooperative commonwealth, and their quest for it would die hard in
the years to come.

The abandonment of class struggle had developed in the aftermath of the events of 15 May 1872, a virtual general strike on the part of the Hamilton workingmen for the nine-hour day. Craft organizations of skilled workers received an unprecedented stimulus, and workers' bitterness boiled to fever pitch, but the objective of the shorter workday was violently opposed by employers and working-class victories were few indeed.[85] With the economic downturn of 1873-74, even the limited gains of Hamilton's nine-hour pioneers were obliterated.[86] Retreating in haste, the early labour reformers softened their assault on the producer alliance and non-working-class elements once again initiated a clamour in the interests of the producers.

Leading this revival was, once again, Isaac Buchanan. But his appeal had waned significantly; class interests now stood counterposed and among industrial capitalists, at least, there was little support for his appeals. In 1878 he wrote to W. H. Howland, president of the Ontario Manufacturers' Association, urging that group to disband their "class organization of *manufacturers*," and appealing to Howland to support the Dominion League, a revival of the APCI.[87] This new venture, despite its active lobbying role in support of the Tories and the National Policy in the 1878 election, was to have little lasting impact. It drew few workers to its ranks and its ultimate collapse indicated a distinct lack of enthusiasm among manufacturers for a rebirth of the producer alliance.[88]

Portions of the producer ideology retained significant force within reform circles. Particularly potent, in a period of economic depression, were Buchanan's views on monetary reform. Amidst rising unemployment, short time, widespread destitution, and the overrunning of the country by a swarm of tramps, labour reformers found his analysis of the crisis appealing:[89]

> The United States are the only industrial precedent and example Canada has; and we see that their only disadvantage industrially is that they have only carried through *half* the Reform required for the circumstances of a new country, and continue to render Confidence impossible among them (as it is among us in Canada) by ignorantly clinging to that most inveterate and cruel wrong on her people of the Mother Country, in restricting, for the benefit of the *few* whose capital is money, the circulation of *MONEY* among the *many*, whose capital is labor, not seeing that they might as well restrict or diminish the circulation of the blood in the people's veins, and still expect them to be in Health or in Confidence of their own strength.[90]

A. W. Wright, prominent reformer/publisher, for one, found Buchanan's views on the question of currency exemplary,[91] and many prominent Greenbackers in the United States viewed him as an authority of considerable stature.[92] Buchanan's influence, apparently, had not yet run its course.[93]

The pages of *The National*, for instance, established in Toronto in 1874 by Phillips Thompson and H. E. Smallpiece, and later taken over by A. W. Wright, linked the developing "Canada First" sentiment with the causes of currency reform and protection for Canadian industry, measures Buchanan had championed for twenty years.[94] But unlike the exclusive "Canada First Club," which met in aristocratic halls, isolated from the people, *The National* championed a broad range of plebeian causes, taking pains to court the favour of "all the men of the best standing in their respective trades."[95] As an important link between the 1870s and the 1880s, *The National* occupied a unique place in the evolution of Canadian labour-reform thought. Bringing together Phillips Thompson and A. W. Wright, men destined to play central roles in the Knights of Labor upsurge of the 1880s, the paper exemplified the tenuous hold the producer ideology exercised in reform circles of the 1870s. The "new nationalism," of which it was but one expression, owed much to the strains of thought first popularized in the 1860s. And the debt was not forgotten. No contributor appeared as frequently as Isaac Buchanan, championed consistently as the "father of Canadian protection."[96]

Buchanan's influence was perhaps also felt in *The National's* conservative approach to labour conflict. Like *The People's Journal*, its intellectual ancestor, it too would reject working-class attempts to secure control of the labour market, opposing the labour-reform conception of the primacy of labour in all productive relations. "Communism, socialism, and other isms are the outgrowths of this line of argument," editorialized Wright in the midst of an 1878 cigarmakers' strike. "It has led to strikes, lock-outs, rattening, poverty, starvation, bloodshed and murder and yet the real fact of the matter is, that while capital does a great deal for labor, labor in itself does very little for capital."[97] The advocates of the producer ideology, threatened by class conflict, continued to demand labour's acquiescence.

By the early 1880s *The National* had expired. With the publication of *The Commonwealth* in Toronto in 1880, however, Wright continued his efforts to rekindle the dying embers of the producer ideology. Voicing his indignation at the economic hardships of the period, Wright spoke of the need to "Put the Saddle on the Right Horse," and opened with the question, "What Is Communism?": "Communism merely aims at the abolition of the present system which enables a class of idlers and non-producers to filch from industry the fruits of its labors." This, however, was no clarion call for class war. Rather, Wright emphasized, workingmen must never forget that employers of labour are benefactors of their kind, members of the great producing class. The real enemies of all workers, he claimed, were the "usurers" and "money theives" associated with banks and loan societies. At their feet Wright laid responsibility for the currency contraction that was widely regarded as the prime cause of the late depression. It was an argument Isaac Buchanan would have understood well.[98]

The cure for Canada's economic ills lay in a three-point program, the "Beaverback" cause: (1) protection for native industry; (2) resumption by the government of the right, which had unwisely been given over to banking institutions, to issue notes passable as money; and (3) adoption of a system of absolute paper money, based solely on the credit of the Dominion, which would serve as legal tender for all debts, public and private. Additional planks, excluding Chinese immigrants and favouring temperance, were appended to woo the labour and moral reform interests.[99]

George ("Great Beat") Brooks, an itinerant journalist reputed to have been fired from the *Toronto Telegram* by John Ross Robertson in the early 1880s for attempting to organize the news staff into a union,[100] expounded on the meaning of the "Beaverback" — dubbed the "Rag Baby" by its detractors — and focused on the theme "Usury Is Theft."[101] Money, he explained, was but the expression of value, not value itself. As legal tender for debt and a medium of exchange, Brooks contended that money was essentially crystallized labour. But instead of representing the value of all labour (and property, which was only an expression of past labour) money had, by an absurd legal fallacy, been made to represent only the value of gold. Instead of being redeemable or exchangeable in the whole property or labour of the community, money was redeemable only in gold. The many were thus made the slaves of the few; contraction had been rendered inevitable, and the result was misery and want. The "Beaverback," by increasing the supply of currency, served vital needs: "What we want in this country is a money of the people, by the people, for the people, not money of the people, by the people, for the bankers."[102] Buchanan had put the dictum more picturesquely in 1875 when he had stated that "Money is like manure, it's only valuable when it's spread around."[103]

The producer ideology stumbled into the 1880s on the coattails of economic distress and the panacea of monetary reform. Buchanan put it well, when he expounded on the early appeal of the National Policy:

> The proposed National Policy, or in other words the prosperity of our producers in Canada, is the very first and absolutely necessary condition connected with the possibility of Canada building her Pacific Railway by means of paper money, the only way it can ever be done without making Canadians 'hewers of wood and drawers of water' for ever to foreign capitalists who would be her creditors. And such a policy has now happily become possible from the distress and depression of the country having, in a voice, at the late elections, of popular thunder ordered off... the old self-seeking parties with all their dead issues and demanded a National Policy to remove all obstructions out of the way of the producers of Canada. This in fact

has now become the whole essential politics of Canada, as it ought
to be in every country. It is the only cure for the distress and consequent discontent and eventual socialism which is the alarming feature
of the present day ... the people insist that means be taken of securing
justice to the Canadian producer.[104]

It was, however, an ideology embraced by a dwindling number of reformers. Manufacturers and industrial capitalists, alienated by the conflicts of the early 1870s, and enjoying the freedoms of a glutted labour
market, saw nothing promising in a coalition with a group they had come
to regard as part of the "dangerous classes." Sufficiently protected by the
National Policy tariff of 1879, they sat back contentedly to partake of "the
Great Barbecue."[105] The mechanics were restless adherents at best. They
would find the producer ideology, and the National Policy it had pushed
into prominence, less of an inspiration under the recessions of the 1880s
and the depression of the 1890s, when new demands and aspirations
would be posed and felt.

In October 1883 Hamilton mourned the death of Isaac Buchanan, "a man
of great and generous impulses, of superior intellect and irreproachable
character ... who did so much to build up this country, and bring it to the
proud position it now holds among the nations."[106] His passing evoked
little concern among the respectable mechanics with whom he had made
common cause in the 1860s. Their eyes, it seemed, were turned towards
the operators' strike of the Brotherhood of Telegraphers and the phe-
nomenal growth of the Knights of Labor.[107] The closing decades of the
nineteenth century, marred by an unexpected intensity of labour-capital
conflict, would prove decisive in the evolution of Canadian working-class
thought. In the place of the twin panaceas—a protective tariff and the
people's money—characteristic of an earlier producer ideology, the 1880s
and 1890s saw the rise of innumerable proposed solutions to the people's
problems. Indeed, the essential feature of popular political economy
would come to be its fragmentation.

Just how eclectic working-class thought would become was revealed in
the writings and perspectives of Phillips Thompson, probably the most
important labour-reform journalist in late nineteenth-century Canada,
and a familiar figure in Hamilton throughout the 1880s.[108] In the early
1860s, while working for the *St. Catharines Post*, Thompson had penned
an attack on those denigrating the mechanic and the farmer, "the bone and
sinew of the country." Rejecting Buchanan's political conservatism, but
not his imaginative discussion of social economy, Thompson advocated
union of the Canadian provinces along republican lines, "a United British
American Independent Republic."[109] He would later—first in jest, and then
in all seriousness—reassert radicalized variants of the producer ideology in
digressions aimed at popularizing the notion of political reform.[110]

By the mid-1880s, after stints on various reform newspapers, including *The National* and *The Commonwealth*, Thompson had emerged as a major spokesman for the Knights of Labor. In the pages of the Hamilton-based *Palladium of Labor*, under the pseudonym "Enjolras," he discussed a plethora of social issues: Irish home rule; temperance; brainworkers and the Knights of Labor; internationalism; class struggle in the Pennsylvania coal mines; monopoly and its evils; land reform; anarchism; and Canadian culture and national identity. Virtually any subject worthy of consideration, and a good many that were not, were scrutinized by this engaging mind.[111]

These articles would form the substance of Thompson's major work, *The Politics of Labor*.[112] In it he noted the breakdown of the mutuality of class interests of an earlier epoch, and the transformation of the independent self-owning producer into a wage labourer, whose stake in the community and allegiance to national development was mediated by his needs as a toiler. In this context Thompson argued for a revision of the tenets of political economy. For too long, he maintained, it had only concerned itself with the production of wealth and the promotion of the material interests of the nation as a whole. National prosperity had been reckoned only in terms of aggregate production and accumulation, increasing exports and imports, and rising volumes of invested capital. Under these conditions, "Labour [was] just as much interested in the maintenance of capitalism, that is to say, the supremacy of capital, as the slave was in the perpetuation of the slave power." In failing to focus upon the equity of distribution, political economy had neglected the comfort and independence of the masses.[113]

To alleviate this shortcoming, Thompson insisted on the positive contribution of government action, in opposition to orthodox notions of *laissez-faire*:

> The maxim that 'the best government is that which governs least' was excellent when population was sparse and scattered, when land was to be had for the asking, and when men's wants were simple and for the most part supplied by themselves or their immediate neighbours. It is a misleading anachronism in these days of steam and electricity, of complicated and clashing interests, of vast wealth and abject poverty, of giant corporations and swollen city populations, dependent for their very existence on the working of the social mechanism of exchange and transport.

Like the labour reformers in the aftermath of the 1872 strikes for the nine-hour day, Thompson thought legislation could ease the people's burden.[114]

Having established the need for state intervention, Thompson turned to the ultimate causes of the subjection of the workingmen: rent, usury, and profit. Through these devices land, money, and labour had been transformed into commodities, bartered to pay tribute to idlers and schemers:

Land ought not to be a commodity, because like air and water it is
necessary to human existence; and all men have by birthright equal
rights to its use. Money ought not to be a commodity, because it is
used for the exchange of other commodities, and when it is made an
article of trade, the laborer is taxed to pay the dealer in money a
profit under the name of interest for which he receives no value.
Labor should not be a commodity, because it is human life. The difference between the slaveholder, who robs the slave of his whole
time, and the capitalist, who robs the wage serf of a portion of his
time, during which he works for his employer's profit is obviously
one only of degree.

The commodity theory of land, money, and labour therefore stood diamet-
rically opposed to basic planks of the producer ideology, most emphatically
the belief in labour as the foundation of all wealth. By converting the natural
resources of the soil and the mechanism adopted to facilitate exchange into
means of extorting a continually increasing proportion of its product from
labour, the commodity theory stood condemned by all true labour and
social reformers.[115]

Such a perspective naturally drew Thompson to Henry George and his
proposals for a Single Tax on land values. Unearned income from ground
rent was, after all, a concrete example of "capitalist" exploitation. In
cities like Hamilton, where social inequalities seemed particularly acute,
the inability of the workman to acquire his own home stood as a striking
testimony to his debased status, and George's ideas became increasingly
popular. The Single Tax was at once a way to ameliorate social inequalities, eliminate the parasitic recipients of unearned income, and provide a
financial base for the organization of a commonwealth of diversified economic producers.[116] It was a reform measure particularly suited to the
tenets of the producer ideology, and one that Thompson enthusiastically
embraced in the mid-1880s.[117]

Before the Commission on the Relations of Labor and Capital, Thompson testified on spiralling rents in Ontario's major cities, and the impact
on all producers:

Whatever advances may be made in the way of increases of wages
by combinations or strikes, these are offset and more than offset by
the constant tendency to increased value for the land and consequent advances of rent. ... The population has increased, but with
increased population comes increased competition in the different
classes, not only among the laboring class proper, but among tradesmen in a small way and even in a large way. The only real gainers by
the increase of the size of the city are the men who hold land for
speculation or for rental.[118]

Rent as the embodiment of unearned income, represented an "exploitative aristocracy of money." Usurers and speculators abounded, and their monopoly on the land had cost the people dearly. Nationalization of the land seemed to promise alleviation of the problems posed in the 1880s: the government, as the expression of the community, should own the land, or at least secure the right of appropriating its yearly value. In shifting the burden of taxation from the producers to the speculators, a large fund could be obtained for ameliorative reform. This, to Thompson, was "especially a working class measure."[119]

In the mid-to-late 1880s, then, the producer ideology retained significant force. But it had become the ideological orientation of labour reformers only and as such was infused with an explicitly working-class purpose. As Hamilton and many other central Canadian cities became important centres in the North American rise of the Knights of Labor, the reform camp was pushed into the role of spokesman for the developing working-class movement.[120] A. W. Wright, while still a strong advocate of "Buchanan's Baby," currency reform,[121] was no longer publishing *The National* or The Commonwealth, but the *Canadian Labor Reformer*, which functioned as the official organ of Hamilton's District Assembly 61 of the Knights of Labor after the demise of the *Palladium of Labor*.[122] Even the names of the new journals of working-class thought captured something of the transformation of the 1880s.[123] Out of the eclectic reform orientation of the 1880s, articulated most forcefully by the Knights of Labor,[124] labour reformers would turn to a more specific defence of working-class interests.

With the collapse of the Knights of Labor and the persistence of social inequality, exploitation, and oppression into the 1890s, Thompson broke with the panacea of George's Single Tax. "The Single Tax movement is the Unitarianism of political economy," wrote Thompson in 1891, "a brief half-way house where the investigator may rest for a breathing spell but not a permanent abode."[125] Questioning the piecemeal panaceas of men like George, he now looked to a more comprehensive and systematic analysis of the inequalities of the social order. In socialism, with its contention that the real goal was the destruction of the competitive system, the abolition of private ownership of the means of production, and the organization of the industrial commonwealth, Thompson found a program for active involvement.[126] By 1899 his allegiance was unmistakable:

Those who are merely 'social reformers' without a thorough grasp of the principles of Socialism, are always liable to be diverted by side issues and political expedients that promise temporary relief, but do not tend in the direction of Socialism. ... Then again, the 'social reformer' also has an eye only to the immediately practicable, and no adequate idea of the extent of organic change necessary to be effected to insure prosperity on a permanent basis, is liable to be led away by the clap-trap of politicians and to take stock in protection or free trade as the case may be. His social reform is merely an incidental matter while he regards these political delusions as of main importance. The Socialist knows that no prosperity for the masses of the people is possible under any tariff or readjustment of taxation so long as the competitive system exists and he knows, too, that the immediate and practicable reforms which he in common with many others advocates will of themselves do but little in this direction, and that their main utility is not so much in what they will actually accomplish by themselves, but in the direction and momentum they will give to the progressive movement.[127]

By the turn of the century Thompson had abandoned the eclectic orientation of "social reform," leaving behind much of the ambiguity of the producer ideology. From that point on he would embrace one cause only, that of socialism.[128]

Not all labour reformers, to be sure, and certainly not many workers, followed Thompson into the socialist camp. Thompson's rejection of the Single Tax, for instance, elicited a mixed reaction, expressive of the diversity of working-class thought. One reformer, while in agreement with Thompson's views on the limitations of Georgism, turned to Bellamyite nationalism. "By doing away with private property," countered "Belle Amie," nationalism "sweeps out of existence the greed for personal gain, and I consider that the greatest obstacle in the path of some reformers."[129] "The Beaverback party or National Currency Advocates," insisted "Currency Reform," "embraced all the socialists ask for": "Those who control the money control the world. ... With a National Currency taxation of any nature would be wiped out, labor would be sought for, not as now, the laborer seeking money, the wild lands preserved for the cultivator or occupier, plutocracy banished, the credit system no longer harvesting the harvestmen, and rents, profits, and interest would vanish into thin air."[130] For many, land reform remained the essential cause, and despite all the talk about socialism, the Single Tax continued to be a popular panacea in labour reform circles.[131] Others, like A. W. Wright, would need no alternative to Thompson's socialism to justify charging him with dogmatism and sectarianism.[132] Joseph Marks, a London tinsmith in the Grand Trunk shops, would attempt the resurrection of the true principles of the Knights of Labor — reform and organization of the working class — in the formation of the Industrial Brotherhood, which he championed in Woodstock, Hamilton, and London.[133] Many would regard cooperation among workers, largely on a handicraft basis, as the ultimate remedy to the shortcomings of modern industrial society.[134] Even Thompson, before his full-scale involvement in the Socialist League, flirted briefly with a worker-farmer alliance in the mid-1890s, energetically pursuing reform in the name of the producers under the tutelage of the Patrons of Industry.[135] The range and scope of working-class thought was truly impressive, although the degree of fragmentation severely limited its utility.

If the espousal of socialist politics was not overwhelming, neither was it insignificant. *Citizen and Country*, a Toronto reform journal, epitomized a transformation affecting many labour reformers and trade unionists. In the brief period from 1899 to 1901, the journal's masthead, reflecting its editorial opinion, changed from "A Journal of Moral, Social and Economic Reform" to "A Journal of Social and Economic Reform," and finally to "The Leading Exponent of Socialism and Trades Unionism in Canada."[136] Even the church, as Henry B. Ashplant of London's Socialist Labor Party attested, contributed spokesmen to the socialist cause.[137]

In Hamilton, the emergence of socialist politics was unmistakable, capturing the East and West End Workingmen's Clubs, disrupting the Co-operative Commonwealth, and influencing temperance and labour circles.[138] Socialist meetings in the city drew crowds of 1,500, although police intervention and legal prosecutions were apparently commonplace.[139] H. P. Bonny, active in Hamilton's Trades and Labor Council, and a prominent speaker at meetings of the Workingmen's Clubs, was regarded as the most knowledgeable Canadian authority on the classic works of Marx, Engels, and Bebel.[140] Hamilton's Marx Club, located on James Street North across the street from the City Hall, popularized the "Red" cause with picnics at Oakland's Park and sales of the socialist organ, *Cotton's Weekly*; Hamilton residents provided 235 subscriptions to the journal which claimed to "Fight The Battle Of The Plain People."[141] When the Hamilton Trades and Labor Council finally established day work on all municipal projects, overturning the contract system, one local employer could not refrain from an attack on larger subversive activities. "There is," he wailed, "entirely too much socialism in Hamilton."[142]

But it was perhaps "a good liberal" who best evaluated the political situation in Hamilton. Writing to Sir Wilfrid Laurier, this closet Grit urged the Liberal leader to make speeches stressing his concern with the question of industrial development, "the patriotic policy of the government":

> this question is one that will have a great effect upon the voters of Hamilton, which city is considered by many people to be, on account of being largely an industrial and manufacturing city, what one might designate as numbering within her population a large number of 'socialists', who are really, in a large proportion, just plain good hard working men who have not been blessed with a very large degree of education, but are capable of understanding a big question when it is properly and fully presented to them.[143]

What is of prime importance in the evolution of Canadian working-class thought are the processes of continuity and discontinuity. Working-class attitudes towards protection for native industry, a vital issue in the emergence and popularization of the producer ideology, illuminate these processes. Virtually unopposed throughout the 1860s, protection first came under attack with the nine-hour strikes of 1872. In rejecting the *Hamilton Spectator* as the organ of the workingmen, James Ryan attacked "the protective spirit and conservative proclivities" of the paper. "It was felt that there would be a species of incongruity," he said, "in asking an organ of protection as an advocate of the rights of the workingman."[144] As class conflict ebbed in the context of the economic downturn of the mid-1870s, however, protection received a noticeable stimulus within working-class circles, rising in favour as the National Policy gained widespread support.[145] Throughout the 1880s protection retained much favour, but the seeds of opposition were clearly visible, a consequence of the accelerating pace of class conflict and an emerging consciousness of the distinct interests of the working class.[146] By the turn of the century, in the context of an emerging socialist movement, protection would be denounced by most labour and reform journals.[147] "Look at the question how we will," commented *The Observer*, "protection means unhealthy profits for the manufacturers for which the workingmen eventually pay through decreased purchasing power of their wages."[148] As a major plank in the producer ideology, protection had had a long and important history of acceptance within the working-class community. Only with the repeated assault of class conflict, first in the 1870s and then in the 1880s, had it been abandoned in favour of class interests.

The producer ideology, erected on the basis of an early manufacturer-mechanic alliance, thus proved amazingly resistant to corrosion. While the foundation of that ideology, the producer alliance, withered under the strains of early class conflict, the ideology itself retained a persistent place in working-class thought. Not until the 1890s, after three decades of capitalist development, was a real break with the past effected. Even then many, if not most, labour reformers refused to mount the rostrum to champion the cause of the Socialist League or the Socialist Labor Party. Instead, working-class thought often retained its allegiance to causes as varied as monetary reform or the Single Tax.[149] Rooted in time-honoured conceptions of labour's contribution to the wealth of nations, and the dignity of productive work, many labour reformers and spokesmen remained convinced that the evils arising out of capitalist development could be legislated out of existence. Their faith — one that would have made Isaac Buchanan proud — would only be shaken by the sustained wave of class conflict that convulsed Hamilton society in the years 1860-1914.

Part III

CONFLICT

When the capitalist, the merchant, and the manufacturer assume to themselves the unconditional and absolute right of stipulating the prices of labor, and making such deductions from the bills of their workmen, as may suit their own interest, when they assume to themselves the right to extend the hours of labor at pleasure, and compel their workmen to submit to these regulations, it does appear to us the result is certain and inevitable. From such a system, if persisted in and permitted, we can anticipate nothing short of a complete subjection of the working classes to a state of servile dependence on their employers, for a bare and scanty subsistence; and a deprivation of the means of education of their children. It is with regret we witness the rapid prevalence of such an order of things, and we feel fully assured that without some speedy and efficient check, the poor must eventually become the slaves of the rich.

With these impressions, and confident of their correctness, we deem it a duty we owe to ourselves, to our country, and to posterity, to take a firm, manly and decided stand in favor of our rights—to claim the privileges of freemen, and not to have our services demanded by others on their own conditions, and our time disposed of at their pleasure, without consulting our interest or happiness, and without regard to our rightful claims.

Official Handbook of the Rhode Island
District Assembly 99, Knights of Labor and
Protective Association (1894)

chapter

5

Merchants of Their Time

... it is not surprising that man seeks to economize time, and that the most active peoples of our day have taken as their motto, Time is money.

Charles Gidé, *Principles of Political Economy* (1896)

In the early years of craft organization few trades exercised any restraints against the hours of labour, the working day generally being proscribed only in out-of-door callings, where the severity of the season or the period of daylight served as the taskmaster. At the same time, daily work-time was intersected by bouts of leisure and rest, and holidays, festivals, and recurrent days of customary idleness, such as Saint Monday, broke the routinized long hours of the work-place.[1] In 1826, for instance, American carpenters "went to work at six a.m., at eight went to breakfast; at nine to work; to twelve dinner til two; then work to six." Ship riggers worked by the day, with hours flexible, the only established rule being that they receive "grog at 11 and 4 o'clock," or an allowance to compensate for this apparent necessity.[2] Frank Thistlethwaite chronicled the reproduction of work habits in the pottery industry, transferred from the Five Towns of Staffordshire, England, to East Liverpool, Ohio, and Trenton, New Jersey, by migrant potters: "They worked, as they had always worked, in bursts of great activity, spending long hours in the pottery, eating and even sleeping there, and then laying off for several days at a time from sheer exhaustion. They brought their English habits of eating snacks, with 'lunch' in mid-morning and mid-afternoon as well as at regular meal times."[3] Coopers, with their well-known penchant for the "goose egg," a half-keg of beer downed on Saturday pay-days at the shop, and often followed by Sunday and Monday refills, exemplify the nineteenth-century artisan's cavalier attitude towards work-time. "Can't do much today, but I'll give her hell tomorrow," seemed to be the Monday slogan in the trade; the rest of the week saw the coopers banging away with great fervour, until Saturday's "goose egg" slackened their pace.[4] Joseph Barford, prominent in the early struggles of the Iron Molders' International Union, reminisced on the stove plate molding trade, in which the workingmen alternated shifts, casting whenever the furnace was full, day or night, including Sundays, often sleeping in the furnace room at night: "We went to work about 4 o'clock in the morning, but some were there much earlier. We did not get paid in full every week. We had a book account and drew part of our earnings every Saturday and left the rest stand until Christmas time, when a settlement was made and we were paid in full. As we generally had a shut down of seven or eight weeks every winter, this money came in handy."[5]

Such labour practices speak strongly of early craft refusals to internalize an appropriate attitude towards time, articulated, at its vulgar best, by Franklin's maxim, "Time is money," a central component of an emerging bourgeois ethic. Yet this refusal would crumble as the nineteenth century wore on; by mid-to-late century, workingmen's indifference to the question of time would be replaced by an awareness of its importance to the working-class movement. Indeed, as E. P. Thompson and E. J. Hobsbawm have stressed, the cultivation of a protective sense of one's time was an essential component of the working-class acceptance of "the rules of the game" of mature capitalist society. George McNeill, a major figure in the upsurge of the Knights of Labor in the 1880s, expressed the new conception well: "Men who are compelled to sell their labor, very naturally desire to sell the smallest portion of their time for the largest possible price. They are merchants of their time. It is their only available capital."[6]

Conditioning this new sense of time was the onslaught of capitalist development, demanding rigour, punctuality, and disciplined production.

There's a murmur in the air,
A noise in every street—
The murmur of many tongues
The noise of numerous feet—
While round the workhouse door
The laboring classes flock,
For why?—the overseer of the poor
Is setting the workhouse clock.[7]

Pushed to the wall by employers who knew well the value of an hour, nineteenth-century craftsmen embraced their antagonists' view of time, and fought back on the same terms.

Shorter hours were seen as the safeguard of the workingman's cultural existence, a necessity if his life was to go beyond that of a mere animal existence: "The short-hour movement does not, as many people seem to think, mean a restriction on individual liberty. It means that men and women shall not be compelled to give all their energy and time to mechanical drudgery which brings them but a bare living."[8] Hamilton's

Palladium of Labor declared that shorter hours "give opportunities for study, reflection, and mental improvement. They elevate the social and intellectual standing of the laborer. They prevent his being so enervated and depressed by ceaseless toil that all the spirit and manhood is worked out of him and he is ready to submit to anything."[9] James Redpath, writing to the *Journal of United Labor*, put the case bluntly: "The most important products of a republic are not its manufactures, but its citizens. Long hours make shoddy Americans."[10] Mechanization, too, came under attack, the only remedy being a shorter working day: "The continual drive and hurry—the monotonous routine incessant application to tasks which frequently do not of themselves stimulate the faculties or sharpen the intellect if too long continued tends to reduce the modern laborer to the level of the machines among which he works."[11]

The reduction of the hours of labour came to be a primary concern of all those groping for a solution to the "labour problem." Phillips Thompson, under the pseudonym "Enjolras," saw the eight-hour day as a blow against capital's mainstay, the reserve army of labour:

> Let eight hours be the watchword. Eight hours work instead of ten or any longer period, and no overtime labor—not even for double pay for the extra work of today means enforced idleness tomorrow. Eight hours for every man and woman now employed would bring work and wages to the hundreds of thousands out of employment. It would annihilate at one blow the gaunt, ragged, hungry, horde of unemployed ready to work for anything they can get, whose idleness is the result of the overwork of their more fortunate fellows—the 'reserve' force which capital aways has at its command in the event of a strike or a lockout.[12]

Another labour advocate linked the struggle for shorter hours to the fight against the extraction of surplus value, and pictured long hours as a cause of the crisis of overproduction:

> In my opinion as a worker, the reduction of the working day is by far the most important thing, being the key to the whole economic position, since it is by the overwork of the producers that the surplus value is created upon which the idlers live, and as long as two or three million workers are content to produce sufficient wealth to support thirty or forty millions of people, so long must there be idlers, whether these same idlers live in workhouses, hovels, or palaces. ... No time could be more favourable than the present for agitating for a seven or eight hours bill. Everywhere the markets are glutted in consequence of overproduction, everywhere men are being discharged from their employment, or having their wages

reduced, what more just and fair, then, than to demand a reduction of the working day.[13]

An iron molder, less sophisticated in his argument, nevertheless drew similar conclusions, and obviously saw the eight-hour day in the same light: "So let us organize, concentrate — our forces, irrespective of trade or profession, and demand eight hours per day, so that we can put destitute thousands in the way of making a home and a living; and I am confident that once we establish an eight hour system, the great cry of 'a fair day's pay for a fair day's work' will be but a secondary matter — that is, as far as obtaining it is concerned. Let the crying capitalist call us communists or what they will, I would rather be called a communist and have my right, then be called a 'scab' and have no rights at all."[14]

In this context, shorter hours came to be regarded as a central component of the matrix of control mechanisms that we have seen to be of vital importance in the shop and factory life of North American workingmen during the late nineteenth and early twentieth centuries.[15] In the tragic aftermath of the 1886 struggle for the eight-hour day, however, workers learned of the bitter resistance of their employers. The illusion that organization could win workers the shorter day without opposition was forcefully shattered.[16] To be sure, many working-class militants had long known the folly of this misconception, realizing that even a legislative bill was no guarantee that employer subterfuges would not circumvent the law. The only guarantee of shorter hours, as many well knew, was control of the work-place, centralized in trade union regulations, and coordinated throughout the country. No May Day proclamation could win a reduction of the hours of labour from employers fiercely determined to resist such encroachments upon their managerial prerogatives. Almost a decade before the Federation of Organized Trades and Labor Unions adopted a resolution establishing 1 May 1886 as the date upon which eight hours would constitute a legal day's work,[17] a Cleveland iron molder had commented: "The working people should be made to know that a *mere* legislative enactment will not be sufficient to establish an eight-hour work-day. To accomplish this the Trade Unions must centralize their power and work harmoniously all over the country. The labour unions of America must enforce an eight hour law of their own in the mill, mine, and workshop; they must stand constant sentry over that law. .... From one end of the land to the other let our rallying cry be *Eight Hours*."[18] For Toronto's *Labor Advocate*, the relationship of shorter hours to the issue of control was crystal clear: "He who is master of his time is master of himself. When the masses are wise enough to control their time, they will control the world."[19]

Small wonder, then, that the cause of shorter hours, and, particularly in the 1880s, that of the eight-hour day, attracted such universal support. Labour's poets tell the story well:

Wake! sons of toil;
Up! Power-crushed daughter;
Your own are all the hours.
Rescue from Mammon's cruel slaughter
Heav'ns gift of gifts, — arouse to action!
Be Truth your sword, not murd'rous faction.
Onward in column! mass your powers!
For justice, and EIGHT HOURS![20]

Few, indeed, were the labour verses that did not ring with the familiar refrain, "Eight hours for work, eight hours for rest, eight hours for what we will."[21] In Hamilton, the history of the shorter-hours movement provides an insightful commentary on the early years of working-class militancy.

Launching the first attack on the evils of long hours was a Hamilton craft that seldom ventured into the arena of class conflict. On 28 June 1862 the journeymen bakers, "a toiling, hard-used class of operatives," met to discuss "means by which the slavish hours of labour to which they are subjected above every other denomination of workmen, may be shortened to a reasonable time." The bakers wished "their hours of labour to be restricted to within an ample but a limited daily period, namely, from 4 o'clock in the morning till 4 o'clock in the afternoon." They also demanded payment in money, as opposed to the usual practice of their wages being partly paid in board. All of this seemed eminently reasonable, and the *Hamilton Times* had no doubts "that master and man will arrange the matter in question amicably, and to their mutual satisfaction."[22] Its optimism was misplaced.

On 23 July 1862 the journeymen met in the Rob Roy Hotel, where they continued their earlier debate on the merits of day work, and the oppressions of night labour. Although many city bakeries had abolished night work, instituting a 4 a.m. to 4 p.m. working day, some employers must have balked for the operatives, considering unanimity of action essential to their cause, "resolved that, for their common interests and benefit, they unite as a body, in the form of a society, to be called the Hamilton Journeymen Bakers' Association."[23] By mid-August, "perversity, bad and unwilling arrangements, and other causes on the part of some of the masters" had set the cause of the operative bakers back, "the oppressive, unjust, and absurd old night system" being reintroduced, the journeymen working shifts often in excess of sixteen hours.[24]

Isaac Chilman, a well-known Hamilton confectioner, exemplified the resolute stand of the masters. Dismissing his workers, who would not submit "to work any number of hours he chose out of the twenty-four which make the day," Chilman hired Germans in their stead, requiring them to labour sixteen to twenty hours a day.[25] He objected vehemently to the journeymen's independent stand, taking particular exception to their "not asking the masters whether they would agree to their views or not, but took it as a matter of course that they were to continue their employment and do as they pleased." Chilman sneered at the bakers, dubbing them "white slaves." His indiscretions backfired, however, and he earned the scorn of many local interests.[26]

Throughout the city, support for the operatives spread. Many citizens boycotted those bakeries where the night system prevailed.[27] Hamilton's leading craft body, the Iron Molders' International Union No. 26, expressed solidarity with the bakers, passing a resolution that "no moulder should buy the bread of such masters [those still using the night system], and that they should exercise their best endeavours to induce others to follow their example."[28] Other unions followed the molders' example, and the bakers' struggle moved into a larger context, a general meeting of the craft being called, to convene in Toronto to discuss the question of long hours in the trade.[29] Ultimately, however, the employers' concerted power won the day as the masters formed an association to stifle the bakers' rebellion. The journeymen's struggle faded, and long hours continued to plague the trade.[30]

In the spring of 1869 the journeymen bakers again struck work for shorter hours. Once more their main complaint was the pernicious night system; they were "united to a man," preferring "to break stones on the roadside, than work during the summer, sixteen hours per diem, in manufacturing the 'Staff of Life'."[31] The contours of the conflict were much the same as in the earlier clash, the "Bakers' Union" lining up against an employers' offensive led, predictably, by Isaac Chilman. Bakers were imported from Toronto and Guelph to break the strike, and some local journeymen and apprentices were induced to remain at work. The journeymen attempted to drive the emigrant workers off with promises to "pay current wages not to go to work." When this offer was refused, they resorted to anonymous, threatening letters, promising the strikebreakers physical harm if they continued on the job. One Hamilton baker, William McGibbons, was so terrified by such threats that he left his employer, Chilman, to whom he was apprenticed for one year. The master baker wasted no time in summoning the young apprentice before the police magistrate, Mr. Cahill, who inflicted a fine of $15, and "severely censured the action of intimidation particulary, and Trades' Unions in general." Their spirits bolstered by this victory, the employers implemented proceedings indicting "a number of journeymen bakers ... for conspiracy to prevent new bakers supplying their places with their old masters and for threats of intimidation."[32] The bakers returned to work on their masters' terms, their resistance broken by the influx of bakers from other cities, and their cause undercut by the employers' recourse to legal sanction. Not until 1886, when they would comprise the Phoenix Assembly of District 61, Knights of Labor, would Hamilton's bakers win the elusive ten-hour day, and even then many journeymen were bitter in their denunciation of the conditions of their trade.[33]

The bakers' early fight for the shorter working day was not an inconsequential struggle; we have seen that it gave rise to considerable community and craft support and pushed Hamilton workingmen into an organizational effort that transcended their own city's boundaries. It quickly became linked to the cause of Sabbatarianism, which workingmen came to regard as an essential defence in the protection of their time.[34] Moreover, it integrated Hamilton craftsmen into a struggle of North American proportions, the reduction of the working day being a major plank in an emerging continental labour movement.[35] Finally, in the midst of these struggles, we glimpse a major transformation in social relationships, the breakdown of harmonious master-man ties and the emergence of class polarization: "The employee has the idea that the sole object of the employer is to grind him down, to get all the work out of him possible, and for the very smallest compensation, while the employer regards the employee as a mere tool or machine made to labour for his special benefit."[36] The clashes of the 1860s thus serve as a prelude to the more momentous struggle of 1872, when Hamilton's crafts took up the cause of the nine-hour day with unprecedented determination.

Treatment of the Canadian nine-hour movement has generally focused on the struggle of the Toronto printers, an episodic clash involving mass mobilization of working-class elements, fierce employer resistance, led by George Brown of the *Globe*, and the arrest of the Typographical Union's Vigilance Committee, a group of twenty-four printers which included John Armstrong, later international president of the union, J. S. Williams, Toronto Trades' Assembly secretary, Edward F. Clarke, a future mayor of Toronto and MP for York West, and a score of other union members. An examination of the movement in Hamilton in the winter and spring months of 1872 suggests strongly that the city's skilled workingmen played a central role in what Steven Langdon and Frank Watt have referred to as the initial stirrings of Canadian working-class consciousness.[37]

The movement commenced 17 January 1872: "The machinists and blacksmiths of this city held a meeting at Dan Black's Club House on Wednesday evening and adjourned to meet again on Tuesday next, for the purpose, we are informed, of demanding the nine hours labour system. A meeting is also called by placards of the carpenters and joiners of the city to take place at the same house and we learn for the same purpose."[38] This coincides almost exactly with the Toronto Trades' Assembly's resolution of 19 January 1872 that "55 hours be a legal week's work," indicative of the early ties linking unionists of different cities and trades.[39] The question of the nine-hour day was certainly a topic of discussion at the Molders' Union Annual Ball, 20 January 1872, where the city's craftsmen gathered, over 400 strong, to toast "Divided We Fall," "United We Stand," "Unity is Strength," and "Labor is Wealth." President Saffin, of the International Iron Molders' Union of North

America, undoubtedly brought news of the progress of the shorter-hours movement in the United States, and the local heads of Hamilton's Amalgamated Society of Engineers, Cigar Makers' Union, Coopers' Union, Typographical Union, and Hatters' Union likely endorsed the cause. John Dance and William Gibson, representatives of the molders' local No. 28 in Toronto, probably reported on the state of agitation in that city.[40]

The next week saw the continuation of this early organizational drive, the carpenters and joiners meeting at Dan Black's Club Room on Wednesday evening, 24 January 1872. A mixed body of molders, machinists, and blacksmiths met at the same place on the following night.[41] "The agitators of the nine hour movement," apparently also convened, once more at Dan Black's, and made hasty plans for a mass meeting, to be held at the Mechanics' Institute on Saturday evening, 27 January 1872.[42]

The manner in which the city's workingmen flocked to the Mechanics' Hall, on extremely short notice, indicates the extent to which the nine-hour movement, even at this early date, had become a popular cause. By eight o'clock the hall, from which all seats had been removed, was crowded to capacity. On the platform were seated some of Hamilton's major social and political figures, a sign of the esteem in which the workingmen were held. The press, too, was well represented. Hamilton's papers — *The Times*, *Spectator*, and *Standard* — each had delegates on the platform, as did Toronto's *Globe*. Chairing the meeting were the men who would lead the struggle in the ensuing months: C. F. Cole, a Hamilton carpenter; Robert Parker, a Great Western boilermaker; Thomas Scarth, also of the Great Western yards, a machinist; another Great Western machinist-engineer, later to be employed on the Grand Trunk, and described in later years as "the leader in the nine hour movement from the old country," James Ryan; and John Pryke, a cobbler, whose apprenticeship as a working-class leader included early involvement in Hamilton's Sons of St. Crispin, prominence in the formation of the Ontario-wide Boot and Shoe Makers' Union of the late 1860s, active participation in the Hamilton Lodge of the Knights of St. Crispin in the early 1870s, and a place of importance in the city's Orange Lodge and Oak Leaf Baseball Club, bodies patronized by many craftsmen and labourers.[43]

T. C. Watkins, a merchant looked upon as "the workingman's friend" and later a candidate for alderman "on the nine hour ticket," gave the keynote address:

> The main points which it is desirable to study are the reduction of the hours of labor from ten to nine, and the paying of workmen on Friday evening instead of Saturday. The first change will be most directly beneficial to mechanics and artisans; the second is designed to relieve overworked merchants and clerks. If there were a branch

of the Humane Society in the city, it would be proper for its officers
to prosecute the employers of the city *for cruelty to animals* (oh!) in
forcing their men to work ten hours a day and paying them on Saturday
nights, and thus preventing them from doing their shopping until that
time, thereby keeping merchants and their clerks in the shop until unreasonable hours, and unfitting them for attending to their religious
duties on the Sabbath.[44]

It was left to James Ryan to articulate the sentiments of the men:

Our country, though young, is destined to be great and glorious.
Working men want their share in this glory, and seek it in reduction
of labor, not in increase of pay. We want to better our physical con-
stitutions, and increase our mental power, so that if we cannot equal
our Yankee neighbors in the variety of our undertaking, we can at
least compete with them in the artistic finish of our productions....
We want not more *money*, but more *brains*; not richer *serfs*, but
better *men*.... Unremitting and honest efforts for the next three
months will establish the nine hours system of labor, not only in
Hamilton but throughout the Dominion.

Ryan closed with a resolution claiming that the nine-hour day was "a
matter of urgent social necessity."[45]

The movement came under immediate attack. Employers were quick
to deride it, pointing an accusatory finger at the leader James Ryan.

Its sire was a Communist missionar - ee,
An immigrant, late from the Old Count - eree,
Sent out by the great International band
To enlighten the darkness of this savage land.[46]

C. F. Cole wrote to the *Hamilton Spectator* in defence of the movement
and its supporters:

Although a young colony we have had so much introduced by railways and improved machinery that we excell many others who are
our seniors in years. Now, sir, in whom has the progress of this
country rested, and on whom will it depend in regard to her future
wealth and glory? The mechanics are the palace builders of the
world; not a stick is hewn, not a stone is shaped in all the great
dwellings of our rich and princely merchants that does not owe its
fitness and beauty to the skilled hand of the sturdy mechanic. The
towering spheres that raise their giddy heads among the clouds depend upon the mechanic's art for their strength and symmetry. Not

an edifice for devotion, or business, or comfort, that does not bear
the impress of their hands. How exalted is this vocation, how sub-
lime is their calling, and how stupendous the barrier that shuts them
out from the circle of society that it is their right as intellectual and
scientific men to move in, and how hard it is for them to place their
families in a position with regard to education and training equal to
that of the man who holds a place among mankind as a wealthy nonproductive, who spends his money merely to gratify his appetite and
nurse his overbearing pride, and as far as real wealth is concerned, is
of no benefit to mankind in particular nor himself in general.[47]

Under the influence of men like Cole and Ryan, the movement for the
nine-hour day surged forward, the press becoming a battleground for
those with conflicting views on the subject, and Dan Black's and the
Tecumseh House witnessing nightly gatherings of craftsmen and clerks.[48]

Fifty or sixty delegates from various bodies of workingmen assembled
at the Shakespeare Hotel 31 January 1872, for the purpose of forming a
permanent organization, the Nine Hours League. Officers elected included John Pryke, president, James Ryan, secretary, J. McGregor,
financial secretary, and William Walton, an engine-driver, treasurer.
After adopting rules and regulations to govern their organization, the
members of Hamilton's Nine Hours League resolved that "the banding
together of the workingmen of Canada in Trades Leagues is an indispens-
able prerequisite to the success of the nine hours movement." From this
point on the Hamilton League, with James Ryan as its driving force,
would serve as the pacemaker in a central Canadian struggle for the
reduction of the hours of labour.

On 11 February 1872 Ryan issued the first call for an Ontario-wide
movement for the nine-hour day. In "To the Workingmen of Ontario,"
he urged Canadian mechanics to follow their international class brethren,
whose struggles in England and America had elevated the cause of the
skilled workingmen. Exhorting his fellow craftsmen to wage a concerted
fight for the shorter work day, Ryan promised them that their sacrifices in
the ensuing struggle would not be without reward: "You will have
effected a social revolution of great moment, quietly, peaceably, and in
order, have given legislator's another proof of the workingman's capacity
for self-government, have brought employers and workmen socially upon
a more equal footing, have gained additional time for mental culture,
social pleasures and homely joys." Toronto workers responded swiftly to
this call for action, assembling 15 February 1872 to discuss the question
of the nine-hour day. Ryan's efforts were paying dividends.

Talk of "social revolution of great moment," and obvious manifestations of labour solidarity, angered Canadian employers. We have already
noted the Hamilton manufacturers' mock resolution, condemning the

nine-hour men, in our earlier discussion of capitalist disciplines and development. After continued meetings of Hamilton carpenters and joiners, a meeting of the Central Committee of the Nine Hours League gathered at the Molders' Hall to discuss a petition to the employers. But on 19 February 1872 the city manufacturers, builders, and master trades-men circulated a lengthy resolution — signed by 145 of their number — expressing their determination to countenance *no* reduction in the hours of labour.

With the lines of battle firmly drawn, the next day witnessed "the first overt act in the nine hour movement," a strike of 130 machinists at the Wilson, Bowman and Company sewing machine works. An employee named Bland had waited upon the firm on behalf of the mechanics, demanding the concession of the nine-hour day. As Bland had been a delegate to the league and "had made himself very conspicuous in the manufactory as an advocate of the scheme," his employers discharged him. At that point an announcement was made throughout the factory, and the skilled workers walked out in protest. One writer condemned "the blind impetuosity of a *class* the best paid in the universe, but the most dissatisfied."

Even the company's three foremen — George Webster, Andrew Con-nors, and Adam Connell — joined the ranks of the strikers, defending the machinists' abilities as workmen, deploring the employers' efforts to co-erce the men and stifle free discussion. While the foremen recognized Wilson's and Bowman's right to prohibit discussion of the nine-hour question on working time, they took exception to efforts to quash the issue entirely, and found the dismissal of Bland, solely for his role as an agitator, repugnant. "We have to regret," concluded the foremen, "that our late employers should have seen fit to throw the blame for this 'lock-out' off their shoulders, and in a futile attempt at vindication, so far forget their honor as to sacrifice truth and veracity on the alter of a purse-proud position, attained in great measure through, and by the united energies of such mechanics as ourselves."[49]

The strike dragged on for a week, Wilson, Bowman and Company replacing the machinists with imported workmen. These mechanics appa-rently proved far from satisfactory for the strike was settled 27 February 1872, after a series of communications between a "Committee of Work-men" and the company. George Brown termed the settlement a victory for the employers, but the actual negotiated conditions appear less one-sided. Bland was reinstated, and the men were to return to work immedi-ately. Although the sewing machine company refused to dismiss workers who had successfully filled places during the strike, their number must have been small, for most of the strikers were to resume their old jobs. While the nine-hour day was not won, the men themselves were to deter-mine which workers would return to the available jobs, and their employers assured them that reprisals would not be taken against any of the men prominent in the strike. The latter promise, however, rang hollow, as the foreman George Webster and forty others remained unemployed.[50]

Meanwhile, outside of the context of the strike, the movement continued to gather momentum. On 22 February 1872 the Central Committee of the Nine Hours League issued a proclamation, "To All It May Concern," giving notice that "on and after the 15th of May, 1872, 54 hours *shall* constitute a weeks work of six days." "Who is this 'Central Committee'?" raged the *Hamilton Spectator*. "What is this 'Nine Hours League' — that arrogates to itself the authority of determining the times and seasons, of disturbing the foundations upon which society stands, of revolutionizing the entire country, and of curtailing the civil liberties of the people? Whence does it derive its right to command, and its power to enforce obedience to these commands?" James Ryan, his tongue undoubtedly well in cheek, suggested that the paper consult its associate editor on such matters, for he was a member of the league.[51]

William McGiverin, a local politician who had supported the nine-hour movement in its early stages, suddenly took up the reins of opposition. "I am utterly opposed to secret organizations of whatever kind," he proclaimed, "which are calculated to disturb that perfect harmony and those cordial relations which should always exist between employers and employees." When requested to preside at a meeting at the Drill Shed of the Great Western Railway yards, he declined, for he could not approve "the subsequent proceedings of the leaders of the nine hours movement, that is, of the formation of secret leagues, and the expression of a determination to force their employers to comply with the terms demanded."[52] "Occulus" found the sentiments of the nine-hour leaders distasteful: "They smacked too much of the principles of the French communists, . . . of the levelling spirit of Prudhon and the revolutionary action of Gustave Flourens." When an emigrant of a few months' residence in Canada soapboxed in Market Square on the history of Chartism, he was recklessly heckled by the area's farmers. "The Ryan-Cole-Pryke missionary made no converts among the farmers," concluded the *Hamilton Spectator*. "They are made of much sterner stuff than the revolutionist demagogues imagine them to be, and after a longer residence in Canada they will find that out."[53]

Workingmen, however, continued to support the movement. At Dan Black's Club House the city's journeymen tinners organized a union, reading "the preamble of the constitution and by-laws of an organization which had existed in the city years ago but was now defunct." The same tavern was the site of a meeting of the Amalgamated Society of Carpenters and Joiners, chaired by C. F. Cole, anxious for the arrival of their charter from the old country. Walter Greenhill, William Perrin, Benjamin Blair, and James Dodson led the journeymen saddle, trunk, harness, and collarmakers, as they discussed the possibility of organizing a union. At Schuck's Saloon the Tailor's Protective Society met to establish a new bill of prices and review the question of shorter hours, while the Boilermakers gathered at Dan Black's to form a benevolent society. On 29 February 1872 nearby Dundas experienced "the luxury of a nine hour meeting."[54]

Indeed, by this early date Hamilton's Nine Hours League, and its secretary, James Ryan, had become the vanguard of a central-Canadian labour upsurge, with support radiating out from Hamilton as far west as Sarnia, and as far to the east as Montreal.[55] At a mass meeting of Hamilton workingmen, held at the Mechanics' Hall 25 February 1872, Ryan spoke of the spread of the movement, and told of his contacts with workers united in leagues, societies, and unions in a dozen Canadian cities. Andrew Scott, of Toronto's Amalgamated Society of Engineers, addressed the same gathering, outlining the stimulus given to Toronto's working-class movement by the Hamilton example.[56]

On 1 March 1872 the Toronto Trades' Assembly received the first of a series of communications from Ryan, asking for the cooperation of the Toronto workingmen and aid in the struggle for reform. Ryan also travelled to St. Catharines and Montreal, where he spoke on the question of the reduction of the hours of labour, contributing materially to the formation of Nine Hours Leagues in the two cities. At a meeting on 19 April 1872 the Toronto Assembly discussed a memorial to the workingmen of Great Britain, written by Ryan, chronicling the struggle of the Canadian mechanics for the nine-hour day.[57]

The significance of the widening contours of the struggle was not lost on the employers. "A Word of Warning," penned by "Prudence," conveys the point:

Employers of the whole Dominion of Canada pay attention. A vile conspiracy exists at present among a small portion of the working-men in this city of Hamilton to usurp the right you ought to have to manage your own affairs, and to say what rules you will have in your several establishments. What fruits this bare-faced tyranny will bear I know not, but I can assure you if you leave yourselves unprepared till the 15th of May you will be bigger fools than I take you to be. What is sauce for the goose is sauce for the gander and if the working men can form unions, what is to hinder all employers to form unions also, and on the 15th of May shut every shop.... the sooner you show these agitators and demagogues a bold front the better for the country.[58]

With the Toronto printers' upheaval of 25 March 1872, the locus of the nine-hour movement shifted briefly to the nearby metropolis. There is no need to chronicle the massive demonstrations of early April 1872, organized by the Toronto Trades' Assembly, for this important chapter in Canadian working-class history has already received copious comment.[59] What perhaps has not been generally recognized, however, is the degree to which the nine-hour day became the major issue in a series of labour-capital conflicts across the Dominion. In Perth the Journeymen Shoemakers Union led the fight; in Oshawa the molders of the Joseph Howe Works stopped work for the nine-hour day; and in Montreal, where the league would hang on bitterly into the summer months, the brass workers of the Robert Mitchell Company were in the forefront.[60] In Guelph and St. Catharines the month of May saw large demonstrations in support of the nine-hour day, and the Toronto Trades' Assembly discussed the possibility of a general strike. Employers precipitated the conflict in Galt, where skilled workingmen made no organized demands. Molders balked at their masters' attempts to secure signed pledges from the men, declarations that they would desist from any future agitation for a reduction of the hours of labour. By late May the disgruntled workers were attempting to raise enough capital to purchase the Galt Foundry and Agricultural Works, hoping to run it on cooperative principles.[61] At G. Waterous and Company, Brantford, the firm offered the men the option of working five and three-quarters or six days of the week, at no change in hourly pay, and with no reduction in the length of the working day. They further demanded pledges, signed by the workmen, promising that no further agitations would disrupt social relations in their factory. Eighty-nine of their employees promptly left work.[62] In London the struggle took a political turn, as B. Bryan, editor of the *Western Workman*, P. B. Flanagan, a tanner, William Wood, a cooper, and John Skerritt, a shoemaker, played leading roles in the formation of the Workingmen's Progressive Political Party. On 1 June 1872 the city's carpenters and joiners stopped work for the nine-hour day.[63] Striking lumbermen in Aurora, out for the nine-hour day, resisted arrest with crowbars and axes, but eventually succumbed to constables' guns. At Sarnia workingmen gathered above Ebenezer Poole Watson's store to agitate for the nine-hour day. After establishing a committee, the Sarnia mechanics met at the Town Hall, where they heard Colin Cameron denounce "the tyranny of masters in exacting ten hours labor from their *slaves*, winding up with the resolve of the *slaves* that they would be *slaves* no longer."[64]

Across the province employers railed against foreign agitators. British Chartists or unionists and American radicals like Richard Trevellick, prominent in the struggle for the shorter working day in both the United States and Canada, drew their particular ire. One hostile commentator, writing in the *Woodstock Review*, placed these struggles in the context of the more general confrontation over control:

For some time the insidious workings of a few demagogues among the workingmen of Ontario have been apparent. With unions and societies for each branch of industry, they have in large measure controlled the employers and dictated their own terms with regard to the rates they should receive for their labor. Not satisfied with this, a few restless spirits, too lazy to work, have employed themselves at the expense of the industrious workmen — by whom they are kept, in obedience to the rules of the Union — in fomenting a nine-hour movement.

"Justice" took a different approach in a letter to Montreal's *Evening Star*, extending the boundaries of the struggle internationally, noting that "the world is teeming with accounts of the strikes among artizans, workmen and labourers . . . for a diminuition of the hours of toil, and an increase of wages. The justice of these demands is so far admitted that concessions and compromises are being made, generally in favor of the claimants." Where one condemned, another could applaud.[65]

In Hamilton, where the months of March and April 1872 seemed relatively placid after the frenzied activities of late January and February, concessions were the order of the day. The Great Western Railway granted its employees the nine-hour day, as did Wilson, Lockman and Company, a sewing machine manufactory. The *Standard* reported that "all the machine shops of any size or importance in the city, excepting one, have consented to adopt the nine hour system and all the sewing machine firms, excepting one, have also consented." Employer resistance, firm a matter of weeks before, was apparently withering in the face of a persistent workingmen's movement.[66]

The nine-hour men did not let these minor victories go to their heads. Aware of the need for constant vigilance, and desirous of extending the scope of their movement beyond the finite cause of the nine-hour day, "Humanitas" wrote to the *Ontario Workman* of the organizational work proceeding in Hamilton. "In a few weeks," he concluded, "Hamilton will stand foremost among the cities of Canada, both for the number of their Trade Organizations, and the intelligence and earnestness its members possess."[67] By early May James Ryan indicated that preparations were well under way for a mammoth demonstration, scheduled for 15 May 1872, a celebration of the triumph of the Nine Hours League.[68]

To solidify these gains, and to preserve the inter-city solidarity cultivated during the struggle, the Hamilton League convened a "Labour Convention" in the city's Temperance Hall. On 3 May 1872 delegates from five cities and towns met to discuss elevating "the present position of the working class." From the Toronto Trades Assembly came the cooper, John Hewitt, a staunch advocate of the nine-hour day and former associate of William J. Jessup, member of the New York-based Inter-national Workingmen's Association; J. S. Williams, secretary of the Toronto Assembly, and recently prominent in the printers' battle with George Brown; and a third workingman, named Doughtie [Doughty]. Brantford sent D. Buchanan, and William Moore came from Montreal. The Hamilton delegation included Messrs. Pryke, Ryan, Parker, Hedley, Hurley, Ingledew, Conklin, Presnell, Bland, Chambers, Spencer, and Omand. Completing the assembly was John Ballantyne, secretary of the recently formed Dundas League. Letters of endorsement came from Sar-nia, London, Oshawa, Guelph, St. Catharines, and Ingersoll. The body intended to establish Nine Hour Leagues in all the cities and towns of the Dominion, with meeting places to contain "a library and reading room, and having all the requirements suitable for the social and intellectual improvement of the working classes after their hours of labour." Adopt-ing the name of the Canadian Labor Protective and Mutual Improvement Association, the gathering elected John Pryke president, and James Ryan recording secretary. They decided to meet again in early 1873, in Toronto, to impress upon others the strength of labour's newly established organi-zations.[69]

In the aftermath of the birth of the association, Hamilton employers emerged from their brief period of acquiescence to mount a final offen-sive. Manager Tarbox, of Wanzer's sewing machine company, responded to his employees' demands for a nine-hour day by locking them out, post-ing a notice that no further work was available.[70] Finishers at L. D. Sawyer and Company struck work on 10 May 1872, the firm standing pat on its refusal to implement shorter working hours.[71] By 11 May 1872 the city's employers, led by the founders (Gurney's, Copp's, Gurney and Ware, D. Moore, Stewart and Company, Turnbull and Company, and Burrow, Stew-art and Company), had locked out over 1,100 men. Many more were to be cast into the streets in the days to follow, victims of a renewed resistance to the nine-hour movement. "The combination of the employers is as widely extended as that of the men," noted the *Hamilton Spectator*, "and their determination is as great." For the city's molders, most of whom already worked an 8½-hour day, it was a bitter and ironic conflict, precipitated when their request for a 15 per cent advance was denied, the employers counter-ing with a demand that they sign documents pledging themselves to desist from further agitation for shorter hours.[72] "Strikes and their consequences are the only topics of conversation in the city," recorded Toronto's *Mail*. Carpenters, stone masons, bricklayers, painters, saddlers, and marble cut-ters followed the molders into the streets, either striking for shorter hours or locked out by recalcitrant employers.[73]

At Kraft's saddlery the first crack in the solid front demanding the nine-hour day appeared, sixteen harness makers leaving work, not for shorter hours, which they willingly relinquished, but because of their employer's refusal to grant a wage increase. Their petition read: "We, the undersigned, in behalf of the strike of all the trades of this city for the nine hour movement, have come to the conclusion to *take* a raise of 20 per cent on our wages, and work 10 hours per day, Saturday excepted, when we will quit work at 5 P.M., to come into operation on the 19th *inst*."[74] The stage was thus set for the demonstration of 15 May 1872. An event that had been billed as a victory parade would proceed as a virtual general strike for the nine-hour day.

The early morning hours of 15 May (Wednesday) saw Hamilton's streets crowded with workingmen, wearing badges, hastily preparing banners, and urging onlookers to join their ranks. A "marching fever" quickly spread throughout the factories and shops of the city, until by ten o'clock virtually "every workman in the city" had left his work to join the parade, "some with aprons, some with overalls, many with tools." Even those shops where the nine-hour day prevailed turned out, expressing their solidarity with those still in the midst of the fight. "No one worked, everyone marched," remembered Sam Landers. Although the organizers had held nightly meetings in Egener's Hotel to publicize the event, even they were pleasantly surprised by the turnout.[75]

At 10:20 a.m. the procession wound its way out of the Crystal Palace Grounds, over 1,500 men marching four abreast. Leading them was James Steedman, the Grand Marshal, on an impressive steed. Then came the pioneers of the movement, outfitted in black pants and white shirts, proudly bearing a blue ribbon pinned to their chest with a figure nine. Carrying axes, picks, and shovels, symbolic of their hard labours in the building of the shorter hours movement, their numbers most likely included James Ryan, Robert Parker, Thomas Scarth, William Walton, and possibly James Pryke or C. F. Cole. Perhaps the most impressive grouping was the contingent from the Great Western Railway, composed of engineers, molders, boilermakers, carpenters, painters, blacksmiths, and apprentices. Each department displayed the products of their handicraft skill: a highly finished model of a locomotive under a glass case and a stationary engine, both built by Charles Milne, an engine-driver; W. Montgomery's creation, a working model of a traversing engine; two horizontal engines by Silas Wheeler; and a group of engines constructed by Joseph Neville, William Killind, and Isaac Hodgins. All of these minute replications were mounted on a wagon drawn by two horses, and surmounted by an immense crown. Their banners articulated their purpose: "On Time"; "Nine Hours"; "Nec Timere, Nec Timore"; "Wisdom is Better than Wealth"; "United we Stand, Divided we Fall"; and, from the blacksmiths, "We strike the iron while its hot." Marching under a clock indicating the hour nine, the painters proclaimed, "Art is long, life is short." Following the GWR men were the molders, the Dundas League and John Ballantyne, and bands from the Toronto Young Irishmen and

Hamilton's St. Patrick's Society. Wilson's and Lockman's employees
came next, wearing rosettes and ribbons, introducing an "elegantly decorated van, containing six young ladies representing the Provinces of
Ontario, Quebec, Nova Scotia, New Brunswick, British Columbia, and
Manitoba—all running sewing machines." The boys of the establishment
marched under the banner, "By industry, energy and perseverance we
succeed in national enterprise." St. Crispin, "dressed in a pink cloak, with
a crown upon his head," preceded the shoemakers. The Marble Cutters'
Association eulogized the passing of an old acquaintance: a monument,
drawn on a wagon, bore the inscription, "Died 15th of May, 1872, the ten
hour system." Beckett's machinists, an Orange band, and unions of boilermakers, bricklayers, tinsmiths, cabinetmakers, typographers, brushmakers, and tailors followed. Wanzer's workers, appropriately proclaiming,
"Nine hours and no surrender," brought up the rear of the procession.
Even the *Globe*, bitter enemy of the nine-hour movement, labelled it an
impressive event, praising the men's conduct as well as their diligent
application of skill. Cheered on by more than 3,000 onlookers, the
mechanics circled the city, a march of five miles, and returned to the
Palace Grounds.[76]

There the throng was addressed by many speakers, outlining the history of the shorter-hours movement, the relative positions of capital and
labour in the social order, and the employers' opposition which had
forced them into the streets. James Ryan stressed the importance of the
event, noting that the eyes of all the Dominion were now upon them as
pioneers of a new movement for intellectual and social betterment. "Nine
hours was enough for the workingmen of Canada," he thundered, con-
cluding that "it was beyond the power of any capitalist to put the movement
down." J. S. Williams, John Hewitt, T. C. Watkins, and F. T. Roy, a Hamilton molder, concluded the speech-making, and the nine-hour men joined
their friends and families for a celebration dance in the Crystal Palace.[77]

It had been a formidable display, and one that earned the Hamilton
mechanics widespread acclaim.

> Honor the men of Hamilton,
> The Nine Hour Pioneers —
> Their memory will be kept green
> Throughout the coming years,
> And every honest son of toil
> That lives in freedom's light,
> Shall bless the glorious day in May,
> When Might gave way to right.
>
> Your cause was just, your motives pure,
> Again and yet again,

You strove to smooth the path of toil
And help your fellow men;
And Canada will bless your name
Through all the coming years,
And place upon the scroll of fame,
The Nine Hour Pioneers.[78]

The admiration of their peers and the spontaneous exuberance of the moment, however, were not enough to win the workingmen the reduction of the hours of labour they so ardently sought. James Ryan's confident assessment of the inevitability of victory gave way to impassioned pleas to 'hold on, all depends on Hamilton.'[79] What went up with a bang on 15 May 1872 came down with a whimper in the following days of agonizing defeat.

As early as 16 May one authority reported that, "Contrary to expectations, the excitement over the nine hour league demonstration yesterday has entirely subsided, and everything in this city has donned its wonted appearance, with the exception of a certain number of workshops where the men were on strike, and locked out Saturday. The city throughout is extremely quiet, and a number of bricklayers, carpenters, and labourers are at work." L. D. Sawyer and Company continued its lock-out, and Hugh Hennessy, a proprietor machinist, shut his men out after they petitioned him for the nine-hour day.[80] On 20 May the city papers reported that the vast majority of employers were resisting the implementation of the nine-hour day, only nine firms conceding the reduction. Moreover, the spirit of the workingmen appeared to be broken, a number of hands having "returned to some of the shops upon the old terms."[81] In the next two weeks the trend was all too clear, shops reopening, employers suing striking workmen for leaving service, and the nine-hour day being revoked in some establishments.[82] Joseph Hopkins, prominent in the league, and an employee of Wilson, Lockman and Company, was arrested at a scuffle in front of Wanzer's, charged with berating a returning striker with obscene language. Hopkins' "unimpeachable character" won him an acquittal, but it was clear that the court wanted no repetitions of such attacks.[83]

The workingmen made their last stand on a Saturday afternoon, 8 June 1872, when a desperate attempt was made to intimidate one of the key firms opposing their cause. At about five o'clock 200 to 300 men gathered in front of the Wanzer works, yelling, hooting, and groaning, acting in "a manner calculated to incite a breach of the peace and the shedding of blood." Police were called in and one of the more violent demonstrators was arrested. A general cry of "Rescue him" was sounded, but the constables succeeded in placing the man in the cells of the station house on King William Street. Their task was not accomplished, however, until they had subdued another workingman, whose efforts had apparently been turned towards the liberation of his friend. With this second arrest, the crowd "threatened to break into the cells and release their comrades," but the police, armed and ready, defended themselves and dispersed the gathering. On Monday morning John Houghton and Alfred Gladwin appeared before the magistrate to be fined $1 and $2 for their part in the ruckus.[84] The following week saw Wanzer's running full-scale, the building trades booming, workmen apparently anxious to secure jobs, and the Hill and Company Furniture Manufactory abandoning the nine-hour day. Defeat was written on every wall.[85]

To be sure, the movement did not collapse immediately. At a mass meeting in early June, Watkins and Ryan still stood firm, but they were addressing a mere 300 sympathizers, a gross shrinkage in their audience. Ryan continued to stress the importance of skilled labour in the rise of personal fortunes and the advancement of the country: "What is the reason of our large manufacturers realizing immense fortunes in a few years as they do? Is it any personal gift of theirs, by their superior skill, education, energy or attainment of theirs? Certainly not, it is by your labour and perseverance; by your skill and energy; by you workingmen of Canada; by the skill of the men employed in the various departments of handicraft, which a skilled workman alone can accomplish."[86] This, however, would be Ryan's last known public statement. He would play no role in the formation of the Canadian Labor Union in April 1873, the outgrowth of the Canadian Labor Protective and Mutual Improvement Association which Ryan, almost single-handedly, had brought into existence.[87] Perhaps cynicism had begun to take over, for during the working-class community's avid political involvement in the post-May months of 1872 and in 1873, James Ryan was to be conspicuously absent. At a mass meeting of Hamilton mechanics in the spring of 1873, where the leading representatives included members of virtually every Hamilton craft active in the strikes of 1872, Ryan took no part in the discussion of convict labour and its evils.[88] Although he was apparently still living in Hamilton in the 1880s, there is no indication that Ryan played any role in the organizational drive associated with the Knights of Labor.

Ryan's absence in these political struggles is symbolic of a basic transformation. He had stood as the representative of militant job action, and independent working-class agitation, speaking of the Nine Hour League as illustrative of the working classes' capacity for "self-government." His departure marked the demise of that orientation. Hamilton's increasingly political working-class movement seemed to have little sympathy with the tactics of February and May 1872. B. Mercer, of the Hamilton Trades' Assembly, expressed the new view:

> Strikes are contagious and they never stop until they have gone the rounds of all the trades and although a raise may have been con-

ceded in every instance, capitalists are not disposed to abate their profits one jot, and the increase in the cost of production has to come out of the strikers pockets indirectly. Wages are only nominally higher, and strikes leave us where we were before. What is the remedy for this state of things? There is only one, and that is for the Legislature to pass a law to give to workingmen an equitable division in the profits of his own productions. ... It would do away with strikes for ever, as the workman's labor would be his capital invested in the concern, and instead of being an employee, he would be a partner. It would extinguish forever the odious word master.[89]

This new political thrust could, of course, embody independent working-class activity, as well as autonomous class aspirations.[90] The problem was that it was also easily manipulated. Henry Buckingham Witton, and his brief political career, illuminate the point.

Immediately following the Toronto events of April 1872 John A. Macdonald and the Conservative party astutely turned the workingmen's disgust at George Brown's strikebreaking tactics to valuable political purpose, the passage of the Trades Union Bill assuring the Tories of mass working-class support.[91] Hamilton and Toronto were perhaps the central links in the chain of a process that spread across the country.[92] After the failure of the nine-hour movement to secure working-class victories in May 1872, Hamilton workingmen sought political solutions to their problems. Because of a redistribution of constituencies Hamilton had been granted another seat in the federal parliament, and an election was called for August 1872. Seizing the opportune moment, Sir John A. Macdonald paid a visit to the city. The president of the Trades Assembly, Cornelius Donovan, met the Tory leader in his hotel, presenting him with an address from the Hamilton workingmen. The resolution thanked Macdonald profusely for removing all prohibitions against lawfully combining "to maintain our trade privileges and rights of labor," and closed with a polite plea: "while depreciating class legislation as a rule we hope you will continue as promptly as heretofore to remove any special grievances under which the working classes may be forced to labor." The next day, 1,500 people gathered to hear Macdonald speak. When asked what he thought of the nine-hour movement the deft politician ducked the question, stating that, "He did not know what to say ... [but] he worked more than nine hours himself, and he hoped that someday they would petition Parliament to raise his wages." The reply drew cheers and laughter. The Tories had for the moment become the workingman's party.[93]

But just what strategy to pursue in the course of the coming election remained problematic. The man behind the scenes, directing events, was to be none other than Isaac Buchanan. In late June 1872 Macdonald had written to Buchanan: "I have been expecting to hear from you for some

time about election matters, but as the mountain will not come to Mohomet; Mohomet must do the locomotive part of the business. Who are you
going to bring out for Hamilton? I am told that Chisholm & McInnis want
to be the men; or Chisholm and Turner if McInnis will not run. It seems
known that these would make a strong ticket and be sure to win." Macdonald closed with the obvious gibe that "the bullying manner in which
Brown attempted to crush the nine hour movement when it affected his
own establishment and interests should alienate the affections of the
operatives from him and his party."[94]

Buchanan's answer to Macdonald, acknowledging the key place of
workingmen in the politics of the summer of 1872, was given in mid-July.
Opposing the Grit candidates, Charles Magill and Emilius Irving, were
the Conservatives D. B. Chisholm and H. B. Witton. Chisholm, a prosperous lawyer serving a successful term as mayor, was an obvious candidate. Witton, however, seemed slightly out of place as a prospective
member of Parliament. Born in South Lopham, Norfolk, in 1831, he had
emigrated to the United States in 1853, and settled in Hamilton the following year. A self-educated journeyman, keenly interested in the classics
and natural sciences, he earned his living as a carriagemaker, a trade
learned with the Lancashire and Yorkshire Railway Company. In Hamilton he worked for nearly twenty years in the paint shops of the Great
Western Railway, where he was eventually elevated to the status of foreman. He lacked any previous experience in politics—federal, provincial,
or municipal—but was decribed by the *Hamilton Spectator* as "eminently
fit" and in "the fullest sense of the term a workingman." This latter
attribute was to be his ticket to success.[95]

For many, however, Witton and Chisholm as running mates made a
strange political duo.

> Nor could Hamilton Tories a queerer team hit on
> Than that odd combination of Chisholm and Witton.[96]

But Buchanan was capable of using Witton's apparent disadvantages to
good political purpose. While the *Hamilton Times*, a supporter of the Liberals and George Brown, attacked Witton for his affected language and
grammatical slips, Buchanan praised the "better sort of working classes,
more intelligent, and better informed on questions which affected their
conditions than the so-called middle classes." At a meeting of over 1,000
Hamilton citizens, Buchanan pointed to Witton and praised the government's actions in securing justice for all, "not excluding the working
classes." Witton then came to the podium "amid a perfect hurricane of
cheers." His speech could have been written by Buchanan himself. Two
things, declared Witton, were essential to the prosperity of Canada: "a
liberal commercial policy and a safe national industrial policy." This was

the essence of politics and, if elected, Witton promised, he would do all he could to promote harmony between the industrial classes and the employers of labour: "The interests of the two were identical; and he would promise never to use tongue or pen to set master against men, or vice-versa, but should strive to bring them together." Buchanan must have smiled as he heard his producer ideology and the manufacturer-mechanic alliance so ably defended, drawing the support of workers who had a few months before led the assault upon Hamilton's employers.[97] He smugly wrote Macdonald: "Things look very well here for the Mayor and Witton who will I feel satisfied get ¾ths of the working men including those at the Great Western. We did a bold thing of having a mass meeting [illegible] men + supporters on Saty night when the Mechanics' Hall was ¾ths filled. The meeting," Buchanan concluded, "was a great success."[98]

For three weeks the city was caught up in an intense political turmoil. On the official nomination day Buchanan presented Witton as the first "bona fide" workingman ever to contest a seat in the Dominion Parliament. A mass meeting of workingmen followed, addressed by John Hewitt of Toronto and a Mr. Buchanan of Brantford, both formerly key figures in the struggle for the nine-hour day. A motion put forward by Alderman Hurley, a long-standing advocate of the workingman, condemned George Brown and the *Globe*, and praised Sir John A. Macdonald, closing with a declaration "to use all lawful means to secure the election of Messrs. Chisholm and Witton as representatives of the city of Hamilton; these gentlemen having promised to support the present Administration."[99] In the second week of August, on election eve, Macdonald again visited the city. He was the honoured recipient of a torchlight procession. Thousands of workers turned out to march under banners proclaiming "Chisholm and Witton, the Workingman's Candidates," "Equal Rights to All," and "Union and Progress." The thunderous applause that followed Witton's address to the crowd was an indicator that the Tories had not been mistaken in nominating a workingman.[100]

The next day confirmed the sagacity of the Tory strategy: Chisholm and Witton defeated Magill and Irving by a total of 291 votes, amassing a combined vote of 2,870. Macdonald wrote to Buchanan in September, commenting on "the brilliant victory that you gained at the polls." The following days saw the usual charges of bribery and corruption, common since the early 1860s when the *Hamilton Times* had asked of Buchanan, "Will He Buy Us With His Purse?" But the *Hamilton Spectator* closed the debate early, replying that it was "well known that Messrs. Witton and Chisholm owed their allegiance to a large accession of the employees of the Great Western; and the working men of the city." Challenging the *Times*, the Tory paper asked if the Liberal organ would "openly, instead of insinuatingly, say that these men were bribed."[101]

Witton was the first workingman to be sent to the Federal Parliament, and his support had come from the working-class community itself. It seemed to be a great victory, an impressive instance of massive working-class upsurge forcing concessions from the established political structure. But, in fact, it proved to be little more than a veiled defeat. Tory hegemony, not working-class interests and purpose, had emerged the winner. Witton, it seems, assumed an early stance of forceful independence, refusing to jump when the party whip cracked over his head.[102] But it was to be a short-lived autonomy; in a few brief months the carriagemaker turned Tory politician was neatly tucked in Macdonald's pocket.[103] His record in the House in 1873 tells the story well: in April he introduced a bill to incorporate the Dominion Fire and Inland Marine Insurance Company; in May he tabled a petition from the Quebec Typographical Union; and he moved the acceptance of the speech from the throne on 27 October. Lady Dufferin, writing in her journal 29 April 1873, noted the transformation in Witton's appearance, a change that may well have been reflected in other realms of his life: "In the evening we had a large parliamentary dinner. One of my near neighbours was very interesting. He is a 'working man' member; we had met him soon after his election, when he dined in a rough coat, but now he wears evening clothes."[104] Leaving the country in 1873 to travel to the Manufacturers' Exhibition in Vienna, Witton must have seemed to have left behind the class that had nurtured him for years and that had elected him in 1872. His companion on the trip, the "millionaire" Hamilton founder Edward Gurney, well known to city workers as a militant anti-unionist, did little to dispel this belief. Years later, in 1886, the event was remembered with contempt by W. H. Bews, a former editor of the *Palladium of Labor*: "They had a man in Hamilton who was sent to Parliament. What did he do? The first situation that was offered him he took, and went to Vienna on some government exhibition business."[105]

With this kind of record Witton had difficulty securing re-election as a workingman's candidate. Moreover, in 1874 any Tory politician had to contend with the thorny issue of the Pacific Scandal and the obviously approaching problem of hard times. Then, too, the spectre of Chinese "coolies" labouring on the railways threatened many Hamilton workingmen, and hardly endeared Sir John A. Macdonald and his party to them. Working-class support for the Tories was wearing thin indeed. D. B. Chisholm read the writing on the wall and retired from the Hamilton constituency, contesting Halton instead, where he defeated a Liberal candidate only to have the results voided; in an ensuing by-election he was defeated. But Witton pressed on, defending himself against charges that he "put on airs, [wore] ... fine clothes, and refuse[d] to associate with ... old companions since [his] elevation to parliament." D. J. O'Donoghue, Ottawa's workingman representative in the Ontario legislature, travelled to Hamilton to endorse Witton. While he managed to organize one successful meeting, his first effort was broken up by a "riot of knives, bludgeons, stones, and eggs."

The climate of 1874 was thus distinctly different from that of 1872. A Tory, workingman or not, had little chance of success in Hamilton. Witton was decisively defeated, one of his victorious Liberal opponents having been nominated by Fred Walters, a molder active in the nine-hour struggle of 1872, a man who had almost certainly backed Witton in the previous election. After his defeat Witton retired from active politics and from the working class. He secured a position as inspector of canals for Canada, a post he held until he settled into a placid old age, "a dreamy scholar who now spends his leisure hours in the library, one of the best private collections in Ontario." Three sons—one the president of the Tuckett Tobacco Company, another an architect, and a third an instructor at the Hamilton Technical School—survived Witton (who died in 1921), their status indicative of the upward mobility of the man who had ridden the nine-hour movement to political, social, and financial success.[106]

The assessment of Witton's place in the history of Hamilton's working class is best left to a contemporary, "a mechanic".

The workingman who gets a lift
Above his fellows head,
Too often proves no more a friend
To those who toil for bread.

The independence labour won
Is quickly flung away—
His 'fellow workingmen' forgot
Till next election day.

By fulsome flattery allured,
Or hired by Commission—
To praise the Chief with hands *unclean*
He deems his only mission.

When workingmen were vexed by laws
For their oppression meant,
Did Witton lend his aid to those
He claimed to represent?

His sympathies with titles run—
A toady now as then—
His clap-trap is by far 'too thin'
To gull the workingman.[107]

But these words were penned in 1875. The damage had been done in 1872. For as John Pryke, president of the Hamilton Nine Hours League, petitioned "The Working Classes of Ontario" to engage in widespread political action in the summer of 1872, the city's nine-hour movement gasped hard, and the cause of the shorter work-day sank in the stormy seas of political agitation.[108] James Ryan, once labour's militant spokesman, was no longer vocal. Instead, more cautious men came to the fore. In October 1873 D. Craig of Hamilton's Amalgamated Society of Engineers spoke for the Canadian Labor Union on the question of the shorter work day. He endorsed the nine-hour day, but urged restraint when the possibility of securing eight hours as the standard was raised: "If they set out for eight hours they would have the capital of the country arrayed against them."[109] It was not men of Craig's stamp, nor was it statements of this nature, that had sustained the movement in 1872. By accepting the employers' conditions of late May 1872, and by placing their faith in legislation rather than militancy, the workingmen diverted attention away from the workplace and into a political arena long dominated by Tory paternalists. This shift in focus was partly responsible for the ultimate lack of success of the nine-hour men.

It would be wrong, of course, to imply that political involvement itself was at the root of the failure of the nine-hour movement. Rather, it was the immaturity of their political, or class, consciousness that thwarted the workingmen's cause, easing the manipulation of the movement into Tory hands. Nowhere was this more apparent than at Wanzer's, the scene of many an early battle in the uprisings of February, May, and June 1872. J. N. Tarbox, manager of the concern, had played a vital role in defeating the nine-hour rebellion. Yet in a presentation to Tarbox on his retirement in September 1872, the workingmen paid him tribute, depreciating their own earlier struggle: "We also regret that near the close of your stewardship there should have anything happened to mar the good feeling always existing between master and man. That little incident is now passed, and we desire to remember your former kindness and the gentlemanly manner in which you have invariably treated your men."[110] It was a gracious act, and one must acknowledge the mechanics' lack of malice, but their goodwill was not to be repaid in kind. Less than four months later, "Workman" outlined the progress of events in the sewing machine factory: "Man's inhumanity to man has produced a new price list for the piece-workers in the Wanzer Sewing Machine Factory, the immediate effect of which list is to reduce the price from thirty-five to fifty percent. This was very like a new years gift for those men who in the largeness of their hearts went back upon the short time movement and accepted the gilded bait held out to them last summer. These men have found to their sorrow that the way of the transgressor is large."[111]

At the core of the failure of Hamilton's Nine Hours League was the lack of solidarity first articulated by the Kraft saddlers, in attempting to use the nine-hour movement as a wedge to elicit wage gains and accepting the ten-hour day which their brethren struggled so hard to abolish. Sam Landers, reminiscing on the strikes of 1872 forty-two years later, saw the willingness of some to accept high wages in lieu of the shorter day as the tragic source of failure.[112] For James Ryan the problem was central: "The men wish to work nine hours and the engine driver fourteen; but what is the use of the engine driver to work that time if the other men leave or *vice versa*. You must work in union."[113] This lack of solidarity bred, not of exclusionary craft pride, of which there was very little indication, but of an immature class consciousness, conditioned by the early period of capitalist development in which it emerged, opened the doors to defeat. With the strength of the employers' opposition, and the subtle diffusion of militancy occasioned by the drift to Tory political solutions to labour's problems, the outcome was a certainty.

Brantford's "Vera Pro Gratis" chronicled the demise of the movement in his city, where members of workingmen's delegation signed pledges for the Waterous and Wilkes Company, "selling their birthright for a mess of pottage."[114] A Hamilton worker chastised the Wanzer employees for their refusal to stand by a victimized leader, forced to flee the city of his birth to take up a trade in the United States. They paid a high price for their cowardly act, however, for the company soon realized the logic of their victory: "These men who sold their manhood were no longer looked upon as men. They had become the tools in the hands of the masters of retarding for a time the progress of labor reform, and they now find themselves treated as all worn-out tools, namely, cast aside."[115] Such setbacks did not deter some of labour's more staunch reformers, however, and one league member promised future action: "Employers will hear from us soon." But his threat was stifled by the severity of the depression already imminent in 1872. Workingmen were driven to accept work under any conditions, so scarce was employment, and talk of shorter hours disappeared.[116]

With the economic upturn of the early 1880s, Hamilton workingmen once again took up the cause of the reduction of the working day. Carpenters, prompted by the lectures of P. J. McGuire urging them on to the eight-hour day, led the way.[117] Hamilton's District Assembly No. 61 of the Knights of Labor continued to struggle for shorter hours, bricklayers, carpenters, barbers, tailors, and bakers being drawn into the movement.[118] And with the emergence of Hamilton's Trades and Labor Council in the 1880s, many of its members having served time in the strikes of 1872, the cause of the reduction of the working day received further stimulation, riding the crest of a forceful "new unionism" into the twentieth century.[119]

Hamilton's workingmen had thus earned a well-deserved reputation as merchants of their time. Indicative of the trend was the popularity of

"Gibson's Common Sense Time Book," adopted by many labouring men in the 1880s.[120] Their inability to secure the nine-hour day in 1872, however, weighed heavily on the course of their future activities, and had some tragic consequences. The *Palladium of Labor* chronicled the case of "An Awful Death":

> The accident to the young man Charles Kirkwood, who was so suddenly killed in the rolling mills last Tuesday morning, is good evidence that the hours men are required to work, especially in such places as rolling mills, are entirely too many. No person witnessed the accident, but from the position he was last seen in alive, and that in which his body was afterwards found, it is supposed that when the whistle blew for the men to go to work, he got up from a bench on which he was asleep, and being in a dazed and almost unconscious state, fell into the ponderous fly wheel, where his head was torn from his body and instantly ground into atoms. Why is it necessary that men should be compelled to sleep around in such institutions, and work fourteen or sixteen hours out of the twenty-four? Such a system is not only unnecessary but heartless, cruel and wicked; and the sooner it is changed the better. Six hours a day is long enough for any man at such hot and laborious work, as he is called upon to perform in a rolling mill.

Charles Kirkwood's workmates staged a one-day walk-out, protesting his unnecessary death, but the basic problem of long working hours remained.[121]

The magnitude of the 1872 failure can only be appreciated when one realizes that forty-four years later, in the midst of World War 1, Hamilton's munitions industry was rocked by a machinists' and toolmakers' strike for the nine-hour day.[122] Between 1,500 and 2,000 skilled craftsmen, affiliated with the International Association of Machinists and the Amalgamated Society of Engineers, met staunch employer resistance, slurs on their manhood and patriotism, and the cover of a national press censorship, with a general strike for the reduction of the hours of labour. After raging for almost a year-and-a-half, the strike eventually secured half of the men involved the nine-hour day. That such a fight had to be waged, for a demand initially raised in the third quarter of the nineteenth century, spoke of the persistence of workingmen's efforts to secure reductions in the hours of labour, an effort that led out of the uprising of 1872 into the more sustained and broadly-based organizational drives of the 1880s and pre-World War 1 years.

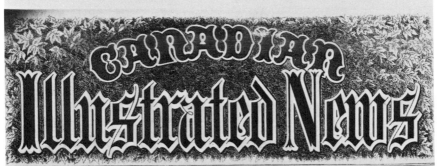

Vol. V.—No. 23.   MONTREAL, SATURDAY, JUNE 8, 1872.   { SINGLE COPIES, TEN CENTS.
{ $4 PER YEAR IN ADVANCE.

9 The Nine-Hour Men 1872

10 Election Procession 1874

11   Knights of Labor Procession 1885

12 The Street Railway Strike 1906: Soldiers charge the crowd
13 The Street Railway Strike 1906: The crowd attacks

14   Dominion Foundries and Steel Castings 1914

15 Isaac Buchanan

16 H. B. Witton

17 Allan Studholme

6

Labour's Lordly Chivalry

Work, brothers mine! Work heart and brain,
We'll win the golden age again!
And love's millenial worlds shall rise
In happy hearts and blessed eyes!
Hurrah! Hurrah! true knights are we,
In labor's lordly chivalry.

Palladium of Labor, 3 November 1883

"I became a member of the Knights of Labor about 60 years ago," recalled John Peebles in 1946, "when I was quite a young chap. I thought its programme would revolutionize the world, not only because of its programme which included Co-operation and State ownership of all public utilities ... and the purification of Politics and of all law and State Administration which also included the full belief in the honesty and sincerity of all members of the order. In short it was a crusade for purity in life generally."[1] John Peebles, a jeweller-watchmaker in the 1880s, was no ordinary member of the Noble and Holy Order of the Knights of Labor. He would play an important role in the Central Labor Union (CLU), representative body of Hamilton's organized working-class movement, where he served as a delegate from his local assembly, filling the position of secretary of the CLU. In the midst of the Home Club affair of 1886, when Hamilton Knights argued over the chartering of the Progressive Cigarmakers — bitter antagonists of the Cigar Makers' International Union No. 55 — as Knights of Labor Local Assembly 7955, Peebles would resign from the CLU, prompted by his fellow Knights' opposition to the CLU's staunch endorsement of the International Union. On 23 May 1887 the Order would appoint Peebles the official organizer for Hamilton's District Assembly 61. Before the Royal Commission on the Relations of Labor and Capital in Canada, Peebles would speak on behalf of the Hamilton Land Tax Club, espousing the doctrines of Henry George.[2] He would later become the city's mayor in the early depression years 1930-33. Yet, despite the uncommon prominence of John Peebles, he embodied much of the common appeal of the Knights of Labor, an appeal manifested in the growth of the Order.

Hamilton early became a centre of Knights of Labor activity, serving as the focal point of the expansion of the Order in Canada. As early as 1875 the Knights of Labor had secured a foothold in the city, establishing Local Assembly 119 on a secret basis. While this early clandestine body had lapsed by 1880, secret organization undoubtedly continued. The first openly active Canadian local assembly apparently had its beginnings in the city in an unfinished basement of the Canadian Life Assurance Building in the fall of 1881, although the actual chartering of the pioneer assembly did not occur until 14 March 1882, when approximately forty painters and gilders, most likely employees of the Grand Trunk shops, banded together in Alliance Assembly 1852.[3] From that point on the Order expanded rapidly. Hamilton became the centre of Canada's first District Assembly, No. 61, which by 1 July 1883 comprised six local assemblies with a combined membership of 880.[4] A year later DA 61 included twelve LA's, embracing 1,054 members.[5] The depression of the mid-1880s, coupled with the emergence of factional strife, checked this expansion briefly,[6] and at the 1885 convention of the General Assembly, held in Hamilton in the autumn of 1885, DA 61 reported only 362 members in eight LA's.[7] With North American labour's upsurge of 1886, prompted by economic recovery, a significant victory of the Order over Jay Gould in the American southwest, and the agitational spurt arising out of the general struggle for the eight-hour day, the Hamilton DA re-experienced a period of intense growth. At the 1887 General Assembly, Hamilton reported a membership of 2,202, organized in no less than thirty-one local assemblies.[8] These gains would prove transitory, however, and the Hamilton Order was soon in a state of precipitous decline. The report to the 1888 General Assembly outlined the contours of a mass exodus of the Hamilton membership: 1 July 1887 (2,070); 1 October 1887 (1,648); 1 January 1888 (1,288); 1 April 1888 (532); 10 August 1888 (386).[9] Although some of the city's Knights of Labor local assemblies would survive into the 1890s, and at least one local assembly would be chartered as late as 1901,[10] the Order's post-1888 presence bore little relationship to its earlier prominence and strength. The essential history of the Hamilton Knights of Labor is thus concentrated in the brief but important period from 1882 to 1887.

At the foundation of the Order's meteoric rise lay the eclectic appeal of the Knights, the promise which had drawn John Peebles to its cause. Incorporating aspects of trade unionism, tenets of political reform movements, the forms, ritual, and associational strength of the friendly society, and the evangelical zeal of a religion of brotherhood and social justice, the Knights of Labor produced a synthesis that transcended the fragments constituting the whole, exercising a powerful attraction that drew many nineteenth-century wage-earners to its ranks.[11]

TABLE 2

Local Assemblies of District Assembly 61, Knights of Labor, Hamilton, 1875-1901

LA	Name of assembly	Membership at peak period	Date established and/or flourished	Source
119	—	—	1875-1880	Garlock and Builder, *Knights of Labor Data Bank* (1973).
1852	Painters/ Alliance	150 painters/ gilders	14 Mar. 1882; lapsed 10 June 1885; reorganized January 1886	F. A. Fenton to T. V. Powderly, Powderly Papers, Catholic University; *Journal of United Labor*, May 1882, 10 June 1885, 10 Jan. 1886; *Canadian Labor Reformer*, 11 Sept. 1886; *Palladium of Labor*, 11 Aug. 1883, 9 Aug. 1884; *Record of the Proceedings of the General Assembly of the Knights of Labor, 1883*, p. 545.
1864	Library/ Literary/ Moulders	150 mixed	9 Apr. 1882; 1882-1887	Fenton to Powderly, Powderly Papers; *Journal of United Labor*, May 1882; *Palladium of Labor*, 23 May 1886; *Canadian Labor Reformer*, 11 Sept. 1886; *Proceedings, GA, 1884*, p. 815; *Proceedings, GA, 1885*, p. 192.
2132	Shoemakers	250 boot and shoe makers	11 Aug. 1882; 1882-1888	Fenton to Powderly, Powderly Papers; *Palladium of Labor*, 11 Aug. 1883, 9 Aug. 1884; *Canadian Labor Reformer*, 11 Sept. 1886; *Proceedings, GA, 1884*, p. 815.

TABLE 2 continued

Local Assemblies of District Assembly 61, Knights of Labor, Hamilton, 1875-1901

LA	Name of assembly	Membership at peak period	Date established and/or flourished	Source
2156	Phoenix	40 bakers	1882-1883, 1886	*Hamilton Spectator*, 19 Apr. 1886; *Journal of United Labor*, 10 Feb. 1886; *Canadian Labor Reformer*, 11 Sept. 1886.
2218	—	telegraphers	1882-1884	George N. Havens to T. V. Powderly, 30 Jan. 1883, Powderly Papers; Garlock and Builder, *Knights of Labor Data Bank*; Eugene Forsey, unpublished data on Canadian Knights of Labor.
2225	Hamilton/Local	580 iron and steel workers	7 Sept. 1882; 1882-1887	Fenton to Powderly, Powderly Papers; *Palladium of Labor*, 11 Aug. 1883, 9 Aug. 1884; *Canadian Labor Reformer*, 11 Sept. 1886; *Journal of United Labor*, October 1882; *Proceedings, GA, 1883*, p. 545; *Proceedings, GA, 1885*, p. 192.
2307	Eureka	100 tailors	18 Oct. 1882; 1882-1889	*Journal of United Labor*, November 1882; Fenton to Powderly, Powderly Papers; *Palladium of Labor*, 11 Aug. 1883, 9 Aug. 1884; *Proceedings, GA, 1884*, p. 815; *Proceedings, GA, 1885*, p. 192.

2450	Cigarmakers	60 cigarmakers affiliated with CMIU No. 55	1883-1886	*Journal of United Labor*, December 1883; *Palladium of Labor*, 12 Apr. 1884; *Proceedings, GA, 1884*, p. 815.
2455	—	letter carriers	4 May 1901	*Labor Gazette* II (1901-1902): 560-61.
2479	—	hatters	1883	*Proceedings, GA, 1883*, p. 545.
2481	Blacksmiths and Machinists	200 blacksmiths/ machinists	1883-1887	*Proceedings, GA, 1883*, p. 545. *Proceedings, GA, 1884*, p. 815. *Proceedings, GA, 1885*, p. 192. *Palladium of Labor*, 11 Aug. 1883, 9 Aug. 1884.
2494 (Burlington)	—	25	1884	*Proceedings, GA, 1884*, p. 815.
2569	Art	80 woodworkers	1882-1884	*Journal of United Labor*, April 1884; *Proceedings, GA, 1883*, p. 545; *Palladium of Labor*, 11 Aug. 1883, 9 Aug. 1884; *Proceedings, GA, 1884*, p. 815; *Journal of United Labor*, 10 Dec. 1884.
2586	Vulcan	134 Grand Trunk Railway machinists and blacksmiths	1883-1887	*Journal of United Labor*, 10 Jan. 1885; *Canadian Labor Reformer*, 4 Sept. 1886; *Palladium of Labor*, 12 Apr., 9 Aug. 1884; *Proceedings, GA, 1884*, p. 815; *Proceedings, GA, 1885*, p. 192.

TABLE 2 continued

Local Assemblies of District Assembly 61, Knights of Labor, Hamilton, 1875-1901

LA	Name of assembly	Membership at peak period	Date established and/or flourished	Source
2741	—	—	1883	Forsey data.
2807	—	—	1887	Forsey data; Garlock and Builder, *Knights of Labor Data Bank.*
3040	Ontario	145 cotton and shoe operatives; men and women	1884-1886	*Journal of United Labor*, 25 Mar. 1886; *Palladium of Labor*, 12 Apr., 9 Aug. 1886; *Proceedings, GA, 1884,* p. 815; *Proceedings, GA, 1885,* p. 192.
3179	Excelsior	75 women cotton and shoe workers	1885	*Palladium of Labor*, 25 May 1885; *Canadian Labor Reformer*, 26 June 1886; *Proceedings, GA, 1885,* p. 192.
4814	Musicians	musicians	1886-1887	*Journal of United Labor*, 10 Jan. 1886, 3 Dec. 1887; *Hamilton Spectator*, 20 Nov. 1886.
5329 (Dundas)	—	mixed	1886-1887	*Journal of United Labor*, 10 Mar. 1886, 4 June 1887.

Number	Name	Trade	Years	Sources
6798 (Thorold)	Mountain	stonecutters	1886-1888	Forsey data; Garlock and Builder, *Knights of Labor Data Bank*.
6931	—	glassblowers	1886-1887	*Journal of United Labor*, 10 June 1886.
6951	—	—	1889	Garlock and Builder, *Knights of Labor Data Bank*.
7522	—	mixed	1886	*Journal of United Labor*, 10 June 1886.
7624	—	hatters	1886	*Journal of United Labor*, 10 June 1886.
7822	Long shoremans	long shoremen/ carters/teamsters	1886-1887	*Journal of United Labor*, 10 July 1886; *Canadian Labor Reformer*, 31 July, 21 Aug. 1886; *Palladium of Labor*, 14 Aug. 1886.
7487	Barbers	barbers	1886-1887	*Journal of United Labor*, 10 July 1886; *Canadian Labor Reformer*, 16 Oct. 1886.
7908 (Thorold)	Stonecutters	stonecutters	1886-1887	*Journal of United Labor*, 10 July 1886.
7955 (also listed as 7956 and 7966)	—	cigarmakers/ packers affiliated with Progressive CMU No. 34	1886-1889	*Journal of United Labor*, 10 July 1886; *Proceedings, GA, 1889*, p. 16.

TABLE 2 concluded

Local Assemblies of District Assembly 61, Knights of Labor, Hamilton, 1875-1901

LA	Name of assembly	Membership at peak period	Date established and/or flourished	Source
7993	—	mixed	1886-1887	*Journal of United Labor*, 10 July 1886; *Hamilton Spectator*, 20 Nov. 1886.
8121	—	salesmen/clerks	1886-1887	*Journal of United Labor*, 10 July 1886; *Hamilton Spectator*, 20 Nov. 1886.
8412	—	—	1886-1888	Forsey data; Garlock and Builder, *Knights of Labor Data Bank*.
8625 (Thorold)	—	women	1886	Garlock and Builder, *Knights of Labor Data Bank*; Forsey data.
8915	—	tailors	1886-1888	*Hamilton Spectator*, 4 Dec. 1888; Forsey data.

This compilation compares favourably with Hamilton and district data in Garlock and Builder, *Knights of Labor Data Bank*, consulted 9 June 1978. The most significant difference is in membership estimates, where the Garlock and Builder data, no doubt resting on official figures computed on the basis of members with paid-up dues, understates the size of various LAs. Relying upon impression-istic estimates of membership, the above table may reflect actual, rather than official, size of the city's assemblies. For precise data on yearly membership, date of establishment, and date of termination of specific assemblies consult Garlock and Builder, *Knights of Labor Data Bank*.

Much of this appeal, especially as it related to the practice of craft unionists, has been touched on briefly in earlier chapters. Molders, glass-blowers, cigarmakers, and machinists, for instance, were all well-versed in the culture of control that thrived in many Hamilton workshops, and which remained embedded in the trade union rules and regulations of the nineteenth-century "autonomous workman."[12] All of these skilled trades were prominent in Hamilton assemblies; their loyalties to various forms of workers' control likely formed an integral part of their enthusiastic participation in the Knights of Labor.[13] Indeed, it is impossible to consider the Knights of Labor in Hamilton outside the general context of the up-surge of North American skilled labour throughout the 1880s. A quick glance at the trades represented in Hamilton's local assemblies, detailed in Table 2, will tell us this much.

This upsurge, as employers realized, was intimately connected with the issue of control. In the midst of the telegraphers' 1883 battle with Jay Gould's North American railroads,[14] a Pittsburgh daily noted that the

Telegraphic Brotherhood is a branch of the Knights of Labor Society; bound by the same oaths and grips and passwords as the rest of that widespread organization. It is essentially a stock company, in which each member holds an equal share and pays the regular stock assess-ment to aid the object of the organization. This object is a strictly business one, viz: to control the labor market of the United States. From this point of view it is as nearly a 'monopoly' in the strict sense of the word as it is possible to conceive of in a free country. Its rules, looking to the restriction of the hours of labor, the limita-tion of apprentices, the embarrassment of all employers who engage outside labor, etc.—are simply the rules of a monopoly which aims to monopolize all the skilled labor of the land, and sell it out at higher prices than would otherwise prevail.[15]

The Knights of Labor would figure prominently in many other conten-tious battles that turned on the issue of control: opposition to employers' attempts to undermine the vestiges of craft control that thrived on the shop-floor; rejection of the often-posted "obnoxious rules" that precipi-tated so many Victorian labour conflicts; and a determined stand in sup-port of unions such as the Iron Molders in their struggle against the intro-duction of bucks and the downgrading of shop and price committees.[16] And in their passionate espousal of cooperative principles, were not the Knights turning to a mechanism well known to many craftsmen strug-gling to realize the full potential of workers' control?[17]

John Sadler, recording secretary of Local Assembly 3305, London, Ontario, wrote to the *Journal of United Labor* enthusiastically endorsing the Order's cooperative coal mine as a means of attaining working-class

self-sufficiency, breaking down the power of the coal rings. He urged all
LAs to contribute their assessment to the mine, as No. 3305 had willingly
done.[18] In Toronto, at the Heintzman and Company's piano manufactory,
seventy-five Knights struck in defence of four discharged workmates,
leaders of the Local Assembly. Responding to the firm's promise to "*fire
all the kickers out of the factory*," the Order launched a struggle to resist
the victimization of its members, a tactic rooted firmly in the tradition of
control struggles.[19] Terence V. Powderly's 1887 "Official Circular No.
17," addressed "To the Order Throughout the Dominion of Canada,"
advised members to "Examine carefully and cautiously into the management of inmates of workshops, mills and factories, and speak out against
such things as are wrong."[20]

In Hamilton the issue of control was obviously central to the experience of the Order. Upon the formation of a Longshoreman's Assembly in
1886, also embracing carters and teamsters, the *Canadian Labor Reformer*
reported that LA 7822 "controls the trade."[21] Phoenix Assembly, composed of bakers, negotiated with their employers in the spring of 1886 on
terms that spoke strongly of their adherence to the basic tenets of workers' autonomy. Their demands included strict limitation of the number of
apprentices, a set ratio of apprentices to the number of journeymen employed, limitation of the hours of labour, an end to night work, standardized wage rates, weekly wage payment, and the regulation of the peddler's
previously chaotic work routines.[22] When the masters resisted these encroachments upon their terrain, a "true K. of L." posed the ultimate
threat: "Now, if the boss bakers of this city think they have full power to
work and pay their men as they deem fit they will find that the journeymen have 8,000 Knights at their back and it would be very easy to raise
$4,000 or enough to start a large co-operative bakery. And if once
started — which I hope it will — the masters may as well sell their wagons
to the peddlars, rent their ovens to the bakers, and get out of business as
fast as they know how, because we will boycott them until they cannot sell
a loaf." It was a powerful inducement, and the master bakers eventually
agreed reluctantly to a compromise.[23]

Closely linked to the issue of control, as we have seen, was the struggle
for the reduction of the working day. Here too craft unionists could feel at
ease in the Knights of Labor, for local assemblies pursued this goal with
staunch determination. Men active in the Nine Hours League of 1872
must have figured prominently in many local assemblies. John Bland,
whom we have met before as the activist at Wilson, Bowman and Company's sewing machine works, whose dismissal precipitated the first strike
in the Canadian nine-hour movement, represented LA 1852 at the third
session of the Canadian Trades and Labor Congress, convened in Hamilton in 1887.[24] Another nine-hour man, William Omand, present at the 4
May 1872 founding of the Canadian Labor Protective and Mutual

Improvement Association, was active in LA 2225 in 1884, when he led a strike at the Gardner Sewing Machine Company.[25] And William J. Vale, one of the most active Canadian workers in the cause of the Knights of Labor, was a Hamilton printer who had served time in the 1872 Toronto strike and conspiracy trials.[26]

Beyond this continuity in the personalities dedicated to the reduction of the hours of labour stretched the Order's organizational role in the 1886 struggle for the eight-hour day. Hamilton's *Palladium of Labor* was the recipient of the 1885 circular urging every "local trade and labor union or Assembly of the Knights of Labor" to establish "the eight hour law passed by your representatives . . . [as] a fixed rule of action from May 1, 1886."[27] The city's Knights of Labor willingly embraced this call to action, and the cry of "Eight Hours" rang out in many local assemblies.[28] One cynic, pointing to the failure of 1872, urged restraint, but was howled down by less conservative forces: "There was the case some years ago when the nine hour movement was agitated in Hamilton. The time was not ripe for the innovation then, and the cause of labor received a set back from the failure of that agitation. My principle is, be pretty sure you will succeed in pushing a matter of this kind, and then work for all you are worth. I raised my voice in the Central Labor Union against the eight hour movement, but I was in a hopeless minority."[29] Michael Conway, CLU delegate from the Flint Glass Workers Union No. 13, probably affiliated with the glassblowers' Assembly 6931, was more representative. "Many of us mechanics," said Conway, "don't work eight hours a day now. I don't work more than seven hours a day myself. When the mechanic's want their hours of labor shortened they are men enough to strike for it."[30] But the eight-hour day was not to be won in 1886, and three years later the Knights of Labor were still agitating for the reduction of the hours of labour, establishing "Time Leagues" in many Canadian cities.[31]

As an avowed supporter of the struggle for control and the eight-hour day, then, Hamilton's Order drew many craftsmen to its ranks. For the skilled workingman, the Knights thus served as a further support for the ongoing pursuit of traditional goals. Beyond this, the Order's chief significance lay in its role in bridging the gap between skilled and unskilled, drawing together disparate strata of the working class into a common body, fighting for common ends. The pragmatic structure of craft organization had inevitably insulated the skilled mechanic from other working-class elements and, aside from any consciously exclusionary ideology, effectively divided the working-class movement. The Knights of Labor did much to overcome this basic problem of labour unity.[32]

Terence V. Powderly, who came to scorn the exclusionary practices of his own organization, the Machinists' and Blacksmiths' Union, saw the Knights of Labor as a potential liberator of the divisiveness bred of separate craft structures.

Aristocrats of labor, we
Are up on airs and graces,
We wear clean collars, cuffs and shirts,
Likewise we wash our faces.

There's no one quite so good as we
In all the ranks of labor,
The boilermaker we despise
Although he is our neighbor.

The carpenter and molder too,
The mason and the miner,
Must stand aside as we pass by,
Than we there's nothing finer.

But some day, some how, things will change,
Throughout this glorious nation,
And men of toil will surely meet,
In one great combination.[33]

Powderly may well have exaggerated the exclusionary practices of the crafts, but there is no denying the importance of the Knights of Labor in uniting skilled and unskilled. Friedrich Engels put the case well in the preface to his 1887 edition of the *Condition of the English Working Class in 1844*:

The Knights of Labor are the first National organization created by the American working class as a whole; whatever be their origin and history, whatever their platform and their constitution, here they are, the work of practically the whole class of American wage-earners, the only national bond that holds them together, that makes their strength felt to themselves and not to their enemies, and that fills them with the proud hope of future victories ... to an outsider it appears evident that here is the raw material out of which the future of the American working class movement, and along with it, the future of American society at large, has to be shaped.[34]

It was a basic premise of the Knights of Labor that "The war between capital and labor won't come on till laborers quit fighting among themselves," and one of the Order's most tangible contributions to the history of North American workers was its role in consolidating labour's ranks.[35]

Phillips Thompson, writing under the pen-name "Enjolras," argued that in an age of mechanization and skill dilution the isolation of craft unionists was both archaic and dangerous:

But if a policy of trade isolation were the rule — each trade looking out for itself only, and the unskilled and half-skilled being left at the mercy of competition, the skilled mechanics would very soon find out that their power to sustain themselves was greatly weakened. Leave the man with a smattering acquaintance with carpentry or printing or black-smithing, the jack of all trades, with a natural bent to turning his hand to anything and making himself generally useful, free to compete with the skilled artisan and free to take his place in the case of labor troubles, as he would be if the spirit of exclusiveness prevailed, and the skilled laborer refused to make common cause with the unskilled, and the isolated union of any particular kind would soon find out class selfishness as mistaken a policy as personal selfishness. In protecting the unskilled in their rights as street car employees, teamsters, rail-road laborers, and similar avocations, the mechanic and artisan are protecting themselves from the competition of many of them who could for a time at least do their work.

"All labor has a common interest," concluded Thompson, "and no arbitrary line between 'skilled' and 'unskilled' should keep apart those who united are all powerful, but divided can easily be crushed by monopoly and capitalism."[36]

It was not a great step to extend this conception of the imperatives of labour unity to other realms of organizational work. "Enjolras" could easily transfer his discussion to the arena of international working-class solidarity and, judging from Thomas Towers's remarks on the subject before the Royal Commission on the Relations of Labor and Capital, internationalism had a strong appeal in Hamilton.[37] The *Canadian Labor Reformer* felt that the Knights were in the vanguard of a movement aimed at purging the divisive element of racial antagonism among wage-earners.[38] Although the Order's position on the exclusion of the Chinese violated this stand, and the existence of "Jim Crow" local assemblies hinted at a continuing degree of racial separation, there is no question that the Knights' attitudes towards the barriers of race and ethnicity were well ahead of their time.[39] Hamilton was almost certainly the site of Canada's first "coloured" assembly, and for the city's black mechanics their affiliation with the order must have been a momentous occasion.[40] Little is known of this black assembly. Whites may soon have joined its ranks, or the LA could easily have lapsed in the mid-1880s, but blacks continued to exist on the fringes of the Order, albeit in the rather stereotyped role of entertainers.[41]

Henry George, addressing a contingent of Hamilton Knights at the Crystal Palace in the aftermath of the Order's 1884 annual demonstration, applauded the organization's efforts, commenting, "This organization has not merely given you power, in association, but in the extirpation

of prejudices. So long as Ten Penny Jack looks down upon Nine Penny
Jim, so long will labor organizations lack power to cope with the opposition they are certain to meet in battling for popular rights. The Knights of
Labor goes beyond the merely local combination. It is an organization that
looks beyond the bounds of nations." By countering the exclusionary
thrust of the crafts, undermining entrenched prejudices, and combating
chauvinism, the Knights' activism pleased Henry George. But the most
striking feature of the day's procession, and one that fitted well into this
context of overcoming inherited barriers to working-class solidarity, was
"the ladies." "The women have a right to come into your organizations,"
argued George. "Why should they not, when they have so much at
stake?" he queried. And, George was pleased to announce, their contribution could be great. One of the Hamilton Knights had told him that
"The women are the best men we have!"[42]

George had touched on an important point, for in their refusal to abandon women workers, many of whom were assuming the places of craftsmen displaced by mechanization, the Knights of Labor did much to
heighten working-class consciousness and thwart the particular oppression of sex. It was the Knights of Labor, for instance, who consistently
supported basic tenets of women's rights throughout the 1880s, advocating universal suffrage, recognizing the important contribution of domestic labour, and condemning the male chauvinism which denied women a
place in the struggles of organized labour.[43] Once again it was "Enjolras"
who succinctly stated the Order's position:

> The idea of the husband's proprietory right to the wife still survives
> in law, and to a certain extent in the public sentiment. It is the basis
> of opposition to woman's suffrage and to the movement for woman's
> suffrage and to the movement for women's enfranchisement gener-
> ally. It reappears in such platitudes as 'woman's sphere is in the
> home' — 'women have no business in politics' — and the like, which
> we hear uttered with an air of superior wisdom as though they were
> original truths promulgated for the first time instead of being worn-
> out and hackneyed falsities.[44]

To overcome these deeply embedded prejudices, the Knights of Labor
enrolled women in many Canadian local assemblies and, where sufficient
numbers of women existed, chartered autonomous women's LAs.[45]

Hamilton was a centre of this drive to organize women workers, the
city being the site of the first women's assembly in Canada, Excelsior
Assembly 3179, composed of operatives in the cotton and shoe factories.
Behind the successful organization of LA 3179 stood Miss Katie McVicar,
a shoe worker.[46] McVicar, daughter of a poor Scots tinsmith and his
English-born wife, joined two older sisters in the Hamilton labour force in

the early 1870s. She began working, like most female factory operatives, while living at home with her parents. Unlike most women workers, however, she never married, and continued working until her early death at the age of thirty, in 1886. Her comparative longevity as a worker helps to explain her prominent place in the history of women's organization. In 1883, writing under the pseudonym "Canadian girl," McVicar corresponded with the *Palladium of Labor*, outlining the need to organize women in factories and domestic service, chronicling the difficulties involved in such thankless labour. She argued that the techniques used in organizing men — holding mass meetings, mounting platforms, and making speeches — would never work for women. Instead she appealed for a few courageous women to come forward, meet with their fellow Knights, and secure aid.[47] Her public appeal was answered by "A Knight of Labor." He suggested that careful, secret discussion among female shopmates be undertaken. When ten women favoured forming a local assembly, he suggested, they should contact him through the pages of the *Palladium of Labor*. A formal organization of a local assembly could then take place. The Order's secret nature rendered it a particularly valuable vehicle for women, he contended, for it allowed them to avoid public notoriety, protecting their modesty. "On behalf of every lover of justice and friend of Labor," this male Knight wished the women "God speed in their noble endeavors."[48] Not long after this exchange of letters, Hamilton's female textile workers and shoe operatives joined with their male counterparts to form LA 3040, organizing the assembly in January 1884. In April of the same year the women shoe workers formed their own Excelsior Assembly, No. 3179. McVicar was long remembered as a key figure in this organizational breakthrough, "the first directress of the first organized Assembly of Women of the K. of L. in Canada."

Hamilton's women workers were not destined to expand upon the base McVicar had done so much to create. Between 1884 and 1885, female membership in LAs 3040 and 3179 declined from 221 to 67. In 1886 Miss McVicar's untimely death dealt women's organization a further blow. Shoemaker's Assembly 2132 sent elaborate floral offerings to her funeral, a mark of respect for one of the few effective Canadian woman organizers capable of playing a public role. Following her death LA 3179, obviously highly dependent upon Katie McVicar, petitioned T. V. Powderly to appoint male Knights from other assemblies to preside over the women of Excelsior Assembly.[49] McVicar's presence would be sorely missed.[50]

In addition to drawing previously excluded sectors of the labouring population — unskilled, blacks, and women — into the working-class movement, the Knights cultivated support by their espousal of political action. Indeed, one authority has seen the reformist thrust of the Knights as a major causal factor in their decline.[51] Aside from the admittedly problematic aspects posed by the Knights' political involvement, tangible and impressive gains were made in many localities.[52] In Toronto, where a long history of labour involvement in both Tory and Grit parties prevailed, the Knights, led by such partisan activists as A. W. Wright and D. J. O'Donoghue, exemplified the potency of the working-class community's political clout. The very existence of the 1887 Royal Commission inquiries into the relations of labour and capital in Canada can perhaps be attributed to the forceful political presence of the Canadian order, whose members played an important role on the commission and figured prominently in many local testimonies.[53]

In Hamilton the Knights of Labor contributed to the establishment of a tradition of independent political action that had its roots in James Ryan's 1872 creation of the Canadian Labor Protective and Mutual Improvement Association, and culminated in Allan Studholme's election to the Ontario Legislative Assembly, under the auspices of the Independent Labor Party, in 1906, 1908, 1911, and 1914.[54] Studholme, a prominent member of LA 2225 in the years 1882-86, first tasted political activity in the early 1880s, as a member of Hamilton's Labor Political Association, a Knights of Labor body headed by the coppersmith, George Collis, of Vulcan Assembly 2586.[55] While discord often divided the Order in some cities where Knights ran for political office on Grit or Tory tickets, Hamilton remained a stronghold of independent, autonomous working-class political action.[56] Edward Williams, a locomotive engineer, Fred Walters, a molder, and Hamilton Racey, a stove-mounter, all represented the Order as workingmen's candidates in various provincial and federal electoral contests.[57] While their victories were few, their success in the municipal field was more pronounced. Thomas Brick, a member of LA 1864, and the Catholic carter we have encountered previously in the 1878 Orange-Green melee, had apparently settled down considerably by the mid-1880s, for he had become a popular alderman, championing the Knights' causes in city council.[58]

Political struggles would later pose problems of a divisive nature within Hamilton's Order, but there is little to indicate that the city's Knights of Labor ever seriously deviated from the principles of independent action. In the midst of one battle, "a Knight of the brush" from St. Thomas defended Hamilton's record: "No matter how many rotten branches fall off, the Order will bear good fruit. Let the wage workers of Hamilton stand by the K. of L. and show these would be Union 'busters' that the ballot will be their dynamite, and that when it explodes, it will blow neither Grit or Tory to the head of the polls, but a wage worker who will take some interest in the welfare of his class."[59]

Hamilton's Labor Political Association epitomized the new mood of political independence. Meeting weekly in the workingmen's club rooms at King and Catharine Streets, it cultivated a collectivist response to the political questions of the day, "apart altogether from partyism." Discussing its positive contribution, the *Palladium of Labor* queried: "Where is the advantage to the laboring class of electing a workingman on a Tory or Grit platform? ... It would accomplish no good to elect a workingman pledged to a servile acceptance of the policy of the party leaders." Editorializing on the Hamilton movement, the *Toronto News* praised labour's orientation: "The headway made by this movement is a good sign. It shows that the people are beginning to realize the evils and abuses of our system, and are dissatisfied with the mismanagement and corruption of both parties. The Hamilton workingmen see that they have been deceived, and their interests systematically neglected by Grits and Tories alike."[60]

The February 1883 campaign of Edward Williams revealed how firmly committed Hamilton's workers were to independent political activity. Conservative politicians sought to entice Williams into their fold, but he refused to be compromised: "if nominated," Williams replied, "it must be as a labor candidate, clear of either political party." Thomas Brick, previously a "good, sound conservative," came forward to endorse Williams. His short speech testified to the distance he had travelled since the late 1870s: "He said that men of all classes, creeds and religions — Catholic and Orangeman — were united in this labor movement, and steadily and surely pulling together to accomplish their object, and they would do it." The engineer's campaign was but one indication that many Hamilton workers had rejected "The two thoroughly rotten, corrupt and ring ridden parties calling themselves respectively 'Conservative' and 'Reform'." Fred Walters, the molder who had likely backed H. B. Witton in 1872, and had switched in disgust to the Grit candidate in 1874, pointed towards the political consciousness gradually taking hold among the city's working class. Casting his lot with Edward Williams, he made some confessions. After fourteen years' residence, he said, "he had, like many others, taken a great deal of taffy from the politicians of Hamilton." But it was "high time a change was made." Let the workers send a representative to Toronto, he urged, "who would more thoroughly adhere to the wants of the people."[61] Walters, disappointed in the 1883 defeat of Williams, would throw his own hat into the political ring three years later, standing as an independent labour candidate. The day was clearly past when a mechanic like Henry B. Witton could be elected as the workingman's representative, while embracing the Tory or Grit banner.[62]

Beyond these conventional attractions for the trade unionist or the political reformer, the Knights extended their appeal, creating an organization that drew on the wage worker's attraction to the associational life of the nineteenth-century friendly society. Men prominent in the early years of the American Order — the founder, Uriah Stephens, or the Crispin, Charles Litchman, for instance — had a long history of participation in numerous fraternal orders.[63] They had seen the powerful ties cultivated by ritual, and cemented by solemn oaths, elaborate grips, passwords known only to the initiated, and the promise of secrecy.[64] George E. McNeill noted the context in which the Knights of Labor came to prominence: "Secret associations, with signs and passwords, were established, the largest point of numbers being the Supreme Mechanical Order of the Sun, an organization with an extensive ritual, having numerous degrees. The Grand Eight Hour League, and other associations whose names were never given to the public, were organized."[65]

Although the Order's growth is generally dated from the abandonment of secrecy in 1881, these aspects of the intimate history of the Knights of Labor remained important.[66] Local assemblies, for instance, continued to receive their charters on a conditional basis:

> And by virtue of this Warrant and Charter the Said Assembly is empowered to do and perform such acts and enjoy such privileges as are prescribed in the Adelphon Kruptos and in the Laws and Usages of the Order of K. of L., and the members thereof are strictly enjoined to bear constantly in mind and always practice the cardinal principles of the Order,
> Secrecy, Obedience, and Mutual Assistance.
> The General Assembly reserves the right to suspend or reclaim the warrant and Charter, and to annul the rights and privileges herein conferred for any neglect or refusal to perform the duties required by the Adelphon Kruptos or by the Laws and Usages of the Order, as adopted and promulgated by the General Assembly, or by any of its officers acting under legally invested authority.[67]

Members of the Order also had to be aware of the geometrical symbolism used to announce the meeting of their local assembly, often a triangle — denoting the three "cardinal principles of the Order" — which enclosed the LA's number and the data and time of the forthcoming gathering.[68] Secrecy had obviously not diminished when, in 1883, Powderly informed Hamilton's John G. Gibson, recording secretary of LA 2307, that the assembly's charter was to be kept hidden from the general membership, in a place known only to the Master Workman.[69] Nor had the ritualistic admission procedure been loosened in Hamilton assemblies; when four blackballs were cast against any candidate his fate was sealed, it being incumbent upon the Master Workman to close the meeting with a formal statement on the rejection of the applicant.[70]

The serious regard in which Knights held the inner workings of their Order is revealed in a letter to William H. Rowe, the Hamilton editor of the *Palladium of Labor*. Investigating the past activities of a member of the Hamilton Knights, E. P. Morgan, Rowe corresponded with J. M.

Brady, Master Workman of DA 47 in Cleveland, Ohio. Brady informed Rowe that Morgan had been a Master Workman of LA 450, the oldest assembly in the city, and that his years of membership had been soiled with "the blackest kind of crookedness." Morgan's crime, which would earn him expulsion from the Knights, had been to publish in the daily press "the aims and objects and secret work of our order." When asked to surrender the secret work to the assembly, he could produce nothing but the tattered covers of the *A. K.* Through his efforts, Brady contended, "the Assembly was nearly disorganized," and much bitterness still prevailed in Cleveland's Order because of his wrong doings.[71] As the object of such loyalties and attachments, the *Adelphon Kruptos* is deserving of a closer look.

At its core lay "the secret work," a collection of signs, passwords, grips, and challenges which outlined the procedures of initiation into the Order, and established means by which members could, in strange company, "ascertain if there [were] Knights present." Both the signs and the language of communication were rooted in a conception of the basic dignity of all labour, and the essential role of work, as a vital human activity, in all social relationships. When admitted to an assembly, the Knight first made the sign of obliteration, a complex act involving the palms, the central feature being the motion of wiping the left hand with the right. The language of the sign — "to erase, obliterate, wipe out" — was related to the process of purging unnecessary thoughts, "as the draughtsman erases useless lines." The same procedure was undertaken upon leaving an assembly, signifying once again obliteration, this time symbolic of the pledge "to keep profoundly secret everything seen, heard, said or done by yourself or others." The sign of obliteration was answered by the sign of decoration, offered by the Venerable Sage, who reminded all that "Labor is noble and holy." Cementing the unity of the signs of obliteration and decoration was the grip, characterized by the locking of thumbs, the thumb distinguishing "man from all other orders of creation, and by it alone man is able to achieve wonders of art and perform labor." Outside the assembly the Knight could determine the presence of other Knights by declaring "I am a worker." A fellow Knight would reply, "I too earn my bread by the sweat of my brow," drawing his right hand across the forehead from left to right, with the back of the hand to the front. In situations of distress a Knight could utter, "I am a *stranger.*" If he heard the response, "a stranger should be assisted," he knew he was among friends. Upon seeing any Knight cheated or imposed upon, or upon hearing a member of the Order thoughtlessly divulge something of a secret nature, a member would form the sign of caution, a movement of certain fingers across portions of the face. To the twentieth-century mind, this kind of ritualistic behaviour appears immediately suspect. Yet in an era of relentless employer hostility these kinds of secret communication clearly had their place. And the isolation and privatization of contemporary life scarcely justify the depreciation of the social ties these customs must have strengthened.[72]

Complementing the ritualistic appeal of the Knights was their profuse use of religious imagery, attracting many North American workingmen whose world view hinged on a conception of social justice, strengthened by an intense pietism.[73] H. A. Coffeen, writing to the *Journal of United Labor*, effectively combined the purpose and symbolism of the Order with fundamental religious principles: "The present civilization has swung through the arc to the utmost limits of competitive business; now let us help start it towards co-operative production and equitable exchange, and surely the experiences of the last few centuries, with the facilities for gathering and distributing information, ought to enable the philosophers of this age, if any exist, to formulate a model government with *equity* and *fraternity* as the two points of the triangle that touch the earth, and as religion recognizing the fatherhood of Deity; as the apex that touches the heavens."[74] For George McNeill, Christ's teachings were still tending to counteract the influences of Mammon, and he had hopes that the movement of labourers towards equality would produce "a new revelation of the old Gospel."[75] A major nineteenth-century labour tract saw true religion as the workingman's emancipation, claiming that "The religion of Christ came out to rectify all the wrongs of the world, and it will yet settle this question between capital and labor."[76] So strong was this religious enthusiasm that many Knights came to regard the labour movement as "a religious movement."[77]

In Hamilton this sense of religion's place in the minds of workingmen affiliated with the Knights of Labor must have been strong. Hamilton Racey, a stove-mounter active for the Knights in the political field in 1886, left Canada to become a missionary in China in 1888.[78] Another political activist, Edward Williams, assured Hamilton's ministry that the workers' disillusionment with the church implied no abandonment of essential religious beliefs: "Labor's faith is strong in the ultimate success of the glorious principles preached by the lowly carpenter and knights of labor who suffered in Labor's cause over 1800 years ago, and Labor's hope will not be in vain."[79] Thomas Towers, a carpenter prominent in the affairs of DA 61, saw labour's duty posed in religious terms.

Brethren, when we fulfil
The Masters just demands;
When we leave unto our children
With pure hearts and clean hands,
The duties he assigned to us
To raise degraded labor;
Be humble as a little child,
Praise God and love our neighbor.

Then will the clouds of blackness
From us fore'er roll,
The knell of crime and poverty
At last begin to toll.
The ploughshare then will turn the sod,
And sheathed will be the sabre,
God's blessing from kind nature's heart
Will bless the Knights of Labor.[80]

"We must depend upon ourselves," Towers later argued, "not as individuals, but as organized labor, inspired by a sympathy born of the natural religion of the soul, the love of humanity which will strengthen our faith in one another, that we can keep our principles ever before us and act up to them without fear of consequence or hope of reward."[81] Towers was perhaps more vocal than many of his fellow Knights, but he undoubtedly captured much of the general sentiment; religious motivation clearly served as a vital plank in the appeal of the Hamilton Knights.[82]

We have wandered a considerable distance from John Peebles' introductory statement, but not without purpose. The eclecticism of the Knights of Labor, their appeal to craftsmen and the unskilled, women and blacks, their political involvement, and their attraction to the religiously or ritualistically inclined, should be apparent, and it was this kind of blending of purpose and passion that marked the Knights for success, however brief. These were the components of a "crusade for purity in life," a cause with few boundaries, and one which therefore gained widespread popular endorsement. For many Hamilton workingmen the Order would represent exactly what they wanted it to, at least for a few exhilarating years.

As crusaders for justice and true religion, as the guardians of the social rights of the oppressed and the downtrodden, the Knights of Labor likened their movement's character to the mythical attributes of a previous age: "A noticeable feature of the strike in which the female boot and shoe operatives are engaged is the ready assistance that has been extended them by other Trade Unions. The age of chivalry has certainly not passed, when we find that men at work at other trades are voluntarily assisting, with money that they can ill spare, the girls that are strong to redress what they consider a grievance."[83] Commenting on the growth of the Order in the fall of 1885, a correspondent in the *Palladium of Labor* placed expansion within a purposeful framework: "I see from the *Journal* that last month saw in the neighbourhood of 190 Locals founded. ... What does it mean? It means this much, at the low average of 20 per local, thirty-eight hundred men and women pledge in honor to each other, and to the cause of social progress toward that goal, on which is inscribed, 'Peace on earth and goodwill toward men', when that is won, then and not until then will the 'modern chivalry' cease from the work to which they have been called by man's inhumanity to man.''[84]

The cause of modern chivalry was given further stimulation by the increasingly impersonalized foundations of an age of rapid capitalist expansion, a process drawing the ire of all true Knights.

> Oh give us one spark of chivalry,
> To illuminate this sordid land,
> Where grubbers save money and preach out,
> The law of supply and demand.[85]

Frank Foster, well known to Knights across North America, drew a vivid picture of the Order's self-conception in a lecture before the Hamilton assemblies at the Opera House in the autumn of 1885:

> The declaration of independence claimed for mankind the right to life, liberty and the pursuit of happiness. But what is life, the dull routine of Labor within the four walls of a factory or the dark corners of a mine as a horizon? No, life should be a great drama, opened up before us by the power of science, art, and education; and in order to enjoy life we must have leisure; and in order to have leisure we must have shorter hours of labor. There is in the heart of every man and woman admiration for the chivalrous, and every true heart who is acquainted with the objects and methods of the Knights of Labor must beat in sympathy for the great ends we have in view. We are now standing where the waves part. ... It is the work of modern chivalry in the persons of the Knights of Labor to save the nations from the fate which threatens it, a fate which, if it comes to pass, will be brought about by the war of irreconcilable elements in society. It is the duty of modern chivalry to champion the oppressed, to wage war against tyranny, and to elevate the type of manhood. It is a nobler chivalry than that of the Knights-errant of old for it knows no race, no color, no creed, and it labors for the cause of humanity everywhere.[86]

In examining the workings of this modern chivalry in Hamilton we will learn much about its successes and failures.

As in many other Canadian communities, Hamilton's Knights of Labor first caught the public eye during the telegraphers' strike of 1883.[87] Organized into a local assembly of the National Trade District No. 45, in October 1882, Hamilton's telegraphers struck work in mid-July 1883, becoming part of a "gigantic movement, the most unanimous ever attempted in this country by any trade organization.''[88] Demanding the total abolition of Sunday work, the implementation of the eight-hour day and the seven-hour night, equal pay for both sexes, and a universal increase of 15 per cent on all salaries, the telegraphers' conflict utilized tenets of "modern chivalry" to wage a struggle against the "tyranny and unjust treatment" of a "soulless corporation."[89] It was to be a hard-fought battle, and with the adoption of sabotage, the cutting of wires, and the harassment of working operatives, it served as an introduction to the similar tactics soon to be employed during many North American street railway strikes.[90] Most important, however, was the bond of strength cultivated by men and women aware of their part in a movement of international importance. Hamilton telegraphers received communications from many American cities, often depreciating the efforts of botch workmen, the "cog-hog" gang, and urging all to remain firm in their stand.

> We're bound to fight,
> Our cause is right,
> Monopoly is sore.
> We have left our keys
> To take our ease,
> Let Jay Gould walk the floor.[91]

Large labour demonstrations in Toronto and Oshawa, to which the Hamilton Knights sent delegations, reinforced the strikers' determination to resist their employers.[92] From London, Ontario, came a word from the Master Workman: "Had a rousing meeting last night and initiated six candidates. We have a committee at every train and are heading off all the 'hams', initiating and sending them back. We number fifteen men, all of whom are in great spirits and show no signs of weakening. We intend to remain out until we go back to the office victorious. Hold the fort boys."[93]

It was not amidst cheers of victory, however, that Hamilton's telegraphers resumed their places at the keys, but in the throes of defeat. By mid-August 1883 the signs of a lost battle were clear, accentuated by the Order's inability to unite the railway and commercial telegraphers. The latter, almost to a man, were affiliated with the Knights of Labor, and bore the brunt of the strike. The railway telegraphers, poorly organized, apparently stayed on the job, hoping that a victory would allow them easy access to the Order. This kind of division, which allowed messages across the wires, undoubtedly undermined the effectiveness of the strike.[94] Coupled with the powerful resistance of an international trust, this basic cleavage spelled defeat. By 15 August 1883 the telegraphers' solidarity of mid-July was beginning to give way to an impatience with the Order. Although many Hamilton Knights refused to acknowledge defeat, insisting that they would continue the strike until directed otherwise by Grand

Master Workman Campbell of the United States, others drifted back to work.[95] At the 1883 General Assembly of the Knights of Labor, the telegraphers expressed a bitter resentment at what they perceived as the Knights' lack of assistance during the strike. By October 1883 National Trade District No. 45, Brotherhood of Telegraphers of the United States and Canada, had withdrawn from the Knights of Labor; with this departure, most of the Canadian telegraphers' assemblies disappeared.[96]

This first international conflict would set the stage for the Order's future inability to protect the basic workplace interests of its members, an inability conditioned by the hostility of employers, the eclectic ties of the membership's affiliation, and, in the eyes of some historians, the Knights' fundamentally ambivalent attitude towards strikes.[97] But in these early days of the organization's growth, other aspects of the strike seemed worthy of recognition:

> Disastrous as the strike has been to a large class of workers whose resources have been exhausted in the unequal fight, we are persuaded that, so far as the cause of labor generally is concerned it is worth all and more than all it has cost. It has given the public at large such a realizing sense of the tyrannous and oppressive nature of the telegraph monopoly, as nothing else would have conveyed. It has done more to hasten the downfall of the system than ten years of agitation could have accomplished. The attitude and conduct of the Brotherhood from first to last has been deserving of the highest praise. The steady adherance of the great majority of operators to their cause in the face of discouragements and difficulties which might well have caused them to swerve, is a bright example to other classes of workingmen and women.[98]

Defeated and blacklisted, the telegraphers found little solace in these words, but in terms of the larger working-class movement, the *Palladium of Labor* had grasped much of the importance of this early conflict.[99]

More successful than the telegraphers' strike, and indicative of the extent to which an appetite for control, usually the prerogative of the skilled, could be demonstrated by other segments of the work force, was an 1884 strike involving women operatives at the John MacPherson boot and shoe factory. The strike was initiated 14 February 1884, fifty-five female operatives expressing disagreement over "a new system of paying wages."[100] At the root of the difficulty was an attempt by the forewoman, Miss Ellicott, to tamper with a long-established scale of prices. The early years of the decade had seen a rapid rise in the cost of living, coupled with increasing profits and rising output at the MacPherson factory. In consequence of these developments, the firm apparently implemented a 10 per cent increase for all hands, and bonuses of from $15 to $60 for all foremen and forewomen. The bonus, however, did not fall equally to all of the women, for mechanized improvements in some departments had enabled some women to increase their output drastically, thus producing large wage differentials, payment being essentially by the piece. This created some discontent, and the firm's response was to attempt to equalize wages by rearranging "the bill in such a manner as to take from those who earn a little and give to them who earn less." Whatever the actual mechanism of wage adjustment, and it appears to have been more complex than the women perceived, the shoe operatives saw the matter in terms of a blunt reduction of 10 per cent: "We did not like this method and consequently refused to submit to the reduction, and we do not believe there is any class of workers in this city that would not have done the same."[101]

It was the women's view of the conflict that is central, along with the widening parameters of the dispute. It was seen, essentially, as a struggle against the "under bosses," who had implemented the reduction, it was felt, to curry favour with the employers, thus assuring themselves of large bonuses in the future. Control was regarded as an important feature of the dispute. Three women workers explained that "the forewoman has said that we run the bindery to suit ourselves, and as she has lost confidence in us is going to run it according to her ideas. With regard to the above, the case is the other way about. We have lost confidence, and believe that if another party had the management all parties interested would be better served."[102] MacPherson and Company, however, soon came to the support of their supervisory staff, stating that the foremen and forewomen were acting on their orders when they implemented the reduction. As from sixty to sixty-five male operatives were thrown out of work, and as other shoe factories, threatening combination, raised the question of a general reduction of 10 per cent imposed on all boot and shoe workers in the city, the strike came to involve more than the women of the MacPherson concern.[103]

Modern chivalry, indeed, had been present at the outset: "They have received promises of financial assistance from the Knights of Labor, although their union is not affiliated with that organization."[104] On 20 February 1884 the shoemakers of the city, members of LA 2132, issued the following declaration: "We, the shoemakers of this city, having examined into the grievances of the female operatives, find that they are justified in resisting a reduction of wages, and pledge ourselves to render all the aid financially and otherwise in our power in assisting them to gain their object."[105] By the first week in March "what seemed at first to be merely a trifling dispute over wages, [had] widened into a serious breach and become a real difficulty." When 125 of the male workers stood by their resolution, refusing to work until the dispute was settled, the firm discharged them, stating that "they were going to get non-union men."[106]

Solidarity eventually won some concessions, a Knights of Labor deputation effecting a reconciliation between the strikers and the firm. Strike-

breakers were given their notice and the old hands — male and female
— rehired. The women, although unable to secure the reinstatement of the
old scale, did reach a satisfactory agreement on new prices which reduced
the severity of the reduction.[107] It had been a victory for modern chivalry,
and undoubtedly contributed significantly to the emergence of Katie
McVicar's Excelsior Assembly of Hamilton women operatives.

Struggles like these, of course, drew the support of many organized
crafts. Indeed, they had followed closely upon the already-mentioned
strike wave of 1882-83, led by molders, cigarmakers, bricklayers, painters, carpenters and joiners, and tailors.[108] The telegraphers' and women
shoe workers' battles thus impressed upon the skilled workingman the
existence of a mutual discontent. More than the Knights' involvement in
strikes, however, cemented this unity.

Equally effective, as a factor tending to unite skilled and unskilled was
the agitation surrounding the exclusion of the Chinese, a cause embraced
by North American Knights with ardent enthusiasm.[109] "Ah Sin," a
pseudonym reflecting the writer's orientation, utilized Hamilton's labour
press to chronicle the degradation all classes of Canadian labour would
experience if Chinese labour were established in the Dominion. It was an
argument filtered through a not-so-subtle lens of racism, but it was also
undeniably true; given the historical experience of the introduction of
Chinese workers, marked by their employers' brutal utilization of their
raw muscle and sheer numbers on railway gangs and dangerous mine
work, Canadian labour not surprisingly saw little to applaud in the coming
of oriental labour.[110] "Who of our community do they benefit?" asked
"Ah Sin" rhetorically. "Why, the capitalist, speculator and manufacturer; none other — they are the great factor in the making of rich men
richer and poor men poorer, marble palaces and dingy poor houses, Great
Britain and Ireland over again, luxurious, licentious, riot and tyranny on
the one hand and penury, degradation, starvation, and death on the
other."[111] While the *Palladium of Labor*, reiterating an argument made in
The National a decade before, could urge that the Chinese be treated as
people, and that the blame for their exploitation be placed squarely on the
shoulders of the capitalist, pragmatists like "Ah Sin," who had spent
fourteen years of his life in "daily contact" and "continual competition
with Chinese coolies," saw the question in less abstract terms: exclusion
of an inferior race was the most expeditious solution.[112]

Widespread opposition to the Chinese culminated in a 1 October 1884
demonstration patronized by "ten assemblies of the Knights of Labor,
the brotherhood of carpenters and joiners, boilermakers union, cigarmakers union, stone cutters union, iron molders union, amalgamated
engineers, glass blowers union, bricklayers and masons union, ... and unorganized and other workingmen." Estimates of the size of the demonstration ranged from 1,500 to 5,000, the latter almost surely an exaggera-

tion. There was, however, no mistaking the purpose of the gathering or the importance of the event. Marching under banners proclaiming "Free Labor — No Slaves," "The Chinese Must Go," and "Never Fulfill a Tyrant's Will, Nor Willingly Live A Slave," the workingmen pelted mud at Chinese laundries on their route, and gathered to hear speeches condemning the government's use of Chinese labour on the construction of the Canadian Pacific Railway. David Gibson and George Collis, leading Hamilton Knights, introduced the key speakers. E. E. Sheppard, popular editor of the *Toronto News*, applauded the Order's stand: "The Knights of Labor have the noblest cause in the land, and the dignity and ability didn't come from the 'Knights', but from the 'labor', and unless the government helped them to uphold their dignity and keep their self-respect that government is certainly criminally to blame, and it was to blame as long as it imported pauper immigrants and Chinese labor." Fred Walters, of Hamilton's Molders' Union, spoke of the honour of being part of such a large demonstration, indicative of the sympathy all workingmen and women had for their brethren on the Pacific coast. "An injury to one is the appeal to all" was a noble rallying cry, and he was proud of Hamilton's working class for its endorsement of the principle. John Brown, of London's Knights of Labor, brought the support of that city's workingmen, and Phillips Thompson, impressed by the turnout, dubbed Hamilton "the Banner Labor City of Canada, whose example was eagerly looked to all over the country." A resolution to curb pauper and Chinese immigration, heartily endorsed by all present, ended the talks. Introducing this resolution was E. P. Morgan. We have met him before, and we shall encounter him again.[113]

The *Hamilton Spectator* was quick to condemn the anti-Chinese cause, claiming that Chinese labour posed no threat to the city's mechanics.[114] This critique, true on its own level, ignored the bonds of solidarity being created among the different strata of Hamilton's working class, and failed to realize the significance of thirty-two labour organizations uniting on a common front. Then, too, the wider implications of Hamilton's support for North American labour escaped the *Spectator's* critical eye. The anti-Chinese agitation, for instance, furthered the cause of independent working-class political action, the Tories' refusal to prohibit the use of "coolie" labour in the construction of the CPR driving one more wedge between Sir John A. Macdonald and the workingman. The Hamilton correspondent of the *Craftsman* condemned the recommendations of the Dominion Chinese Commission, which urged no restrictions on "coolie" immigration until the completion of the CPR: "Of course they listened only to capitalists, whose wine cellars they sampled to their hearts content and stomach's consternation, and Sir John Macdonald told them what kind of report they must present, before they started on their tour of investigation."[115] While the virulent racism feeding on this anti-Chinese sentiment would later pose serious problems for labour unity, the immediate effects of the movement for Chinese exclusion generally contributed towards working-class solidarity and autonomy.[116]

As in the case of the anti-Chinese agitation, the Knights' support for the temperance movement won the admiration of both skilled and unskilled.[117] Temperance had always exercised some attraction for the craftsman, and in the 1860s and 1870s the skilled workers who had stood behind the creation of the *Workingman's Journal* and the Hamilton Co-operative Association were undoubtedly temperance advocates.[118] The officers of early temperance organizations, such as the St. Patrick's Young Men's Temperance Society or the Hamilton Temples of the International Order of Good Templars, were often men prominent in organized crafts, such as Cornelius Donovan, the printer who presided over the Trades Assembly in 1872, while many of the women of the movement were daughters or wives of skilled workingmen.[119] Nevertheless, despite this appearance of working-class support, the organized temperance cause is best viewed as intricately related to the complex of disciplines we have seen to be so essential to capitalist development.[120]

The fury with which Canadian employers raged against drink before the Royal Commission of 1887, as we have seen, suggests strongly that temperance was a key plank in the platform of industrial discipline.[121] A New Brunswick paper stated the case succinctly: "If the workingmen of this country want to see an unparalleled era of prosperity, all they have to do is elect men to office who will enforce prohibitionary laws. Factories will spring up like flowers in Springtime."[122] In the absence of such legislation, however, a major Hamilton concern took matters into its own hands: "Notification has been given to the employees of the Grand Trunk Railway Company that any of them who are seen going into or coming out of a saloon, either when on or off duty, will be discharged."[123] J. W. Bengough, a prominent Canadian social reformer, saw prohibition of intoxicating liquors as a primary lesson for the working classes and advocated the legal suppression of the barroom: "What I mean by the Mask of the Gin Mill is the light and warmth of the Bar Room and its air of joy. This fools vast Crowds and they go in to the trap. They say the Gin Mill is the 'Poor Man's Club'. Yes, it is a Club that beats out his Brains."[124] A Hamilton meeting called to endorse anti-liquor legislation (the Scott Act) in the spring of 1881 drew many mechanics as well as their employers, and the thrust of the prohibitionist supporters was articulated by an employing blacksmith: "The liquor must be crowded out of existence for men were trusted with steam engines and boilers, and the lives of all in factories and other places where machinery was used were in their hands."[125] Such views characterized the temperance and prohibition movements throughout the years 1860-1914; despite efforts to attract workingmen, the leaders of the movements, as well as the purposes of their crusade, were often removed from the context of working-class life.[126]

Extremism of this sort rankled in men whose world view has been summed up by one historian as "nothing on compulsion."[127] Edward H. Hancock, a Hamilton carpenter, spoke strongly against such arbitrary measures, testifying to the distaste Knights felt for this kind of rigidity:

> Q. I am asking you if you consider the law of prohibition that would benefit all classes?
>
> A. I have nothing to do with prohibition. I do not believe in tying a man for nothing.[128]

The *Canadian Labor Reformer* noted the contradictions in the practices of the temperance people: "Our temperance friends are full of touching sympathy for the workingman. They dearly love them, and warmly wish them success in their efforts to better their condition. They also invariably get their printing done at rat offices. A drop or two of practice mixed with their ocean of theory and sentiment would improve the mixture."[129] Joseph Marks, a London tinsmith, and former Master Workman and recording secretary of LA 7110, chronicled the breakdown of London's alliance of organized labour and temperance workers: "The workingmen of London are fully competent to look after their own interests, and wish to point out that in their fight for the eight hour day, the abolition of child labor, and the protection of the working girls, some of their bitterest opponents are ardent prohibition workers."[130] It was in this context that Hamilton's Knights of Labor embraced, as a basic tenet of modern chivalry and their quest for "purity in life," the cause of temperance, while generally remaining aloof from the leadership and organizational bodies of the movement.[131]

Carrying the temperance message into Hamilton were men of prominence in the hierarchy of the Knights of Labor.[132] Terence V. Powderly, for instance, was one of the nineteenth-century's most ardent temperance advocates. Before a gathering at Lynn, Massachusetts, he declaimed: "Had I 10,000,000 tongues and a throat for each tongue, I would say to every man, woman and child here tonight: Throw strong drink aside as you would an ounce of liquid hell."[133] Powderly spoke with similar conviction before Hamilton's Knights of Labor on a number of occasions, arguing at the 1885 General Assembly that "No great reform can be brought about by drunkards, and even when the use of liquor is not carried to excess it generally occasions an expenditure of means and a loss of time, which severely tax the resources of those who could use both to better advantage."[134] Another temperance advocate, Richard R. Trevellick, harped on the same theme, seldom missing an opportunity, when speaking in Hamilton, to depreciate drink and warn of its consequences.[135]

Views like these, reinforced by their reiteration by major Canadian labour spokesmen, gained widespread acceptance.[136] A Hamilton "laborer" condemned intemperance as the gravest danger facing workingmen, a product of "the universal thirst for gain."[137] The *Palladium of Labor* argued that "the working classes do not probably drink more than others, but they experience its effects more." Intemperance undermined "independence and self-control," leaving the workingman "at the mercy of his employer" who, "knowing that he has no savings to go back upon, often takes advantage of his necessities and compels him to accept low wages." As "the cause of the ignominious failure of many a movement on the part of workingmen which otherwise had fair prospects of success," strong drink stood condemned by all true labour reformers.[138] "The man who is not man enough to keep from getting drunk," scolded the *Canadian Labor Reformer*, "has not got manhood enough about him to make a good Knight of Labor."[139]

This kind of opposition to intemperance led to a brief flurry of labour and temperance unity, Powderly himself being invited to speak before the Hamilton gathering of the Royal Templars in the summer of 1886.[140] A leading temperance advocate suggested that "the majority of Union workmen looked strongly upon the Temperance Reform Movement," and urged unity on the political front to secure their common goals.[141] "Tuscarora" acknowledged that "the sturdiest workers in the cause of temperance to be found in Canada" lived in Hamilton, and he phrased his plea for unity in a unique blend of religious imagery and labour-reform rhetoric: "The Temperance Party and Organized Labor should be a unity, and when their leaders call on the enemy to surrender, the walls of Gherico will come thundering down never to be rebuilt. If there was a new prophet come to earth again he would cry from the house-tops, 'Unite and Organize, oh my people!' and the Jesebel of Rome would thirst for his blood. Unite and Organize, oh my people."[142] With the 1886 campaign of the stove-mounter, Hamilton Racey, the labour-temperance alliance experienced a few weeks of common struggle.[143] With his defeat, however, the united front dissolved, to be briefly reconstituted only during Allan Studholme's twentieth-century campaigns. Hamilton's workingmen continued to adhere to many basic temperance principles.[144]

Both the temperance and the anti-Chinese movements, as well as the strikes of telegraphers and boot and shoe workers, fit neatly into the Knights' conception of modern chivalry. As manly stands for the Order's conception of moral purity, often directly related to the defence of others' just demands or essential rights as workingmen and women, they drew the endorsement of many of Hamilton's working people. Moreover, as movements and struggles embraced by the political reformer and the trade unionist, applauded by unskilled and skilled, they helped to cultivate unity in the face of diverse experience. The divisions between

Knights and craft unionists, which have preoccupied so much of the discussion of the Order's history were simply nowhere to be seen on the surface of the history of Hamilton's Knights of Labor, at least prior to 1886. Coexistence was more than a peaceful compromise. It was the essential feature of working-class activity in the city. Responding to a merchant's efforts to depreciate the Order's strength, the *Palladium of Labor* exclaimed in May 1885: "The Knights of Labor in Hamilton have nine Assemblies, one of them has a membership of over 600, and the others will average at least 200 members each. This gives a total membership of 2,200, but there are more. Hamilton has at least TWO THOUSAND FIVE HUNDRED tried and true members in that organization, who work in unison with all the trade unions in the city, and the *Palladium* has the honor of being recognized as their official organ."[145]

With the formation of the Central Labor Union in 1884, this unity was given an institutional expression, delegates from various Knights' assemblies meeting with representatives from the city's craft unions to discuss labour's common problems and priorities. In the midst of the manufacturers' threats to destroy the Cigar Makers' Union, the *Palladium of Labor* could declare: "The Cigarmakers' Union or any other trade union in this city — and there is about thirty of them — do not stand alone. They are linked together in one unbroken chain, and 'an injury to one is the concern of all'. The Organized Labor of Hamilton represent a total membership of over 3,000 men and women.... As a result of the recent formation of the Central Labor Union, all our Labor Organizations are combined more solid than ever before."[146]

Relations between Knights and trade unionists were so close that the official organ of DA 61, the *Palladium of Labor*, was often kept financially afloat by contributions from Hamilton's Iron Molders' International Union No. 26.[147] We have already noted, in our discussion of working-class parades, the trade unionist support for the Knights of Labor celebration of Uriah Stephens's birthdate on 4 August 1883. In the following year, in what was coming to be billed as labour's annual holiday, craft unionists and Knights again marched side by side as Hamilton Local Assemblies 1852, 2132, 2225, 2307, 2481, 2569, and 3040 were joined by Iron Molders' International Union No. 26, Cigar Makers' International Union No. 55, Bricklayers' and Masons' Union of Ontario No. 2, Amalgamated Flint Glass Blowers Union No. 13, International Typographical Union No. 129, Amalgamated Association of Carpenters and Joiners No. 750, Brotherhood of Carpenters and Joiners of America No. 18, International Brotherhood of Boilermakers and Iron and Ship Builders, Branch No. 21, Brotherhood of Locomotive Engineers, Railway Locomotive Firemen, Order of Railroad Conductors, Railroad Brakesmen Union, Hat Finishers, Tobacco Rollers, Stone Cutters' Union, Female Boot and Shoe Operatives, Hat Makers' Union, Custom Shoemakers' Union, Tailors'

Protective Union, Lathers' Union, and the Amalgamated Association of Iron and Steel Workers.[148] On the basis of this kind of unity, the *Hamilton Spectator* predicted a bright future for the Order: "The organization known as the Knights of Labor is comparatively young, but its childhood is mighty; and if in this case it proves true that 'childhood shows the man as morning shows the day', the manhood of the organization promises to be in its profound and far reaching power greater than that of any association that has yet existed for the amelioration and advancement of the working classes."[149]

The Hamilton paper's assessment of the future prospects of the Order would prove unduly optimistic. Within three brief years Hamilton's Knights would be in the throes of decline, its assemblies irreconcilably factionalized, its leadership vilified by the rank-and-file, and the trade unionists of the various assemblies of skilled crafts united in opposition to a clique they would slanderously label the Home Club. By 1888 these developments had taken their obvious toll, and from this time the Knights of Labor in Hamilton exerted virtually no influence in the city's working-class movement. The surface unity of the years 1882-84 gave way to a crisis of disunity in 1886-87. This history of dissension and deterioration tarnished the impressive record of achievement attained by the Order under the guise of modern chivalry.

Despite the solid front presented by Hamilton's Knights of Labor and craft unionists in the early years of organizational growth, the inner history of the Order reveals strains and tensions that would lead to fissures in later years. As early as 6 January 1883, for instance, R. McDougall, recording secretary of Shoemakers' LA 2132, reported to Powderly:

A dispute has arisen in our Assembly, as to the power of the Assembly, levying a tax on its members, and then forcing the same to be paid. The difficulty arose on the strike of Shoemakers in Montreal. Though not belonging to our Order, yet, we believe that a cut in their wages is the first step towards a reduction in ours, as the competition is so keen in our business between Montreal, and Toronto, and Hamilton. We therefore in our own personal interests (as the majority expressed it) called a special meeting for the purpose of considering the question. At that special red letter meeting it was Resolved, That we levy a tax of fifty cents per week on each member, to aid the Montreal strike. The resolution was passed with but one dissenting vote, in a meeting of near eighty members. The levy was collected from all, with the exception of four members. And now the legality of the levy is questioned. The Assembly wishes to know if they can have power to levy for such purpose on its own members and if so can we force the same to be paid.[150]

Powderly, as he often did, waffled, declining to make a ruling. He let McDougall know that the assembly should have made their assessment an appeal, in order not to bind individual members to a contribution to the Montreal strikers.[151] While this was sound advice, offered from the easy chair of distance and hindsight, it did little to heal the rifts in the Shoe-makers' Assembly. The principle of solidarity, even at this early date, was being tested in the halls of one of Hamilton's major local assemblies.

From another quarter came a plea for the defence of trade union princi-ples. Charles Smith, recording secretary of LA 2450, composed of cigar-makers affiliated with the International Union's local branch, No. 55, complained to Powderly about the LaFayette, Indiana, cigar manufacturer August Klingeman, who utilized the Knights of Labor white label to mask his unfair labour practices. Employing "broken down women and incom-petent hands," he ridiculed Cigar Makers' Union No. 158, which had originally lent him $50 to start his business. Smith, enclosing a clipping from the *Cigar Makers' Official Journal*, suggested that Powderly take im-mediate steps to discipline Klingeman, if he was indeed a member of the Order. Otherwise, noted the Hamilton cigarmaker, this case would severely harm efforts to organize cigarmakers not enrolled in local assemblies, and would demoralize those members of the trade who were Knights of Labor.[152] A similar problem preoccupied Eureka Assembly 2307, where Hamilton's tailors discussed the use of the Knights of Labor label in south-central Ontario's hat trade. In Hamilton, where the two hat factories were union shops, the issue posed no immediate problem, but in Toronto the "factories [were] foul and only hire[d] boys." Fred Jones, recording secre-tary, raised this question with Powderly, wanting to know if unfair manu-facturers could be granted the Knights' label; he received no reply.[153]

Another contentious realm was touched upon by E. S. Gilbert, record-ing secretary of DA 61, who wrote to Powderly concerning the possibility of a dispute between Knights of Labor printers and the International Typographical Union: "In London members of the Typographical Union who are also Knights of Labor are working in a union shop when other men belonging to the same Local Assembly of the Knights as the first but not to the Typographical Union apply for and obtain employment in the shop. Would the first mentioned brothers be justified in quitting work in accordance with their union rules and if so what becomes of their pledge of honor as Knights?"[154] Powderly, once again, gave no opinion. He did, however, urge that if the Typographical Union rules regrettably stipulated that its members quit work upon the hiring of non-union men, the Knights of Labor be dealt with leniently. He suggested that the Typo-graphical Union recognize the Knights' role in eliminating the small-town or country printer who had often taken the place of striking union typo-graphers; the Knights' printers, he reminded the unionists, crossed no picket lines and boycotted struck papers. His solution hinged on joint action. Local assemblies and the International Union should work together to thwart capitalist attempts to divide the working class. Let the Typographical Union give Knights of Labor printers a reasonable time to connect themselves with the union, and harmony of action would prevail, assured Powderly.[155] It was a reasonable suggestion, but for the Typographical Union it perhaps posed more problems than it solved.

These issues wuld return to haunt Hamilton's Knights of Labor at a later date. In the meantime, however, the dissension introduced into many local assemblies in 1883-84 would be momentarily sidetracked by the appearance of a man we have previously encountered, E. P. Morgan. Given the nature of the Knights of Labor, and its eclectic appeal, it is not surprising that the organization attracted individuals drawn from a wide spectrum of personality types, men and women whose reasons for affiliation were as varied as the occupations which they pursued in town and country. One of these personality types, however, the opportunistic adventurer utilizing labour's cause for personal gain, found his opening, not in factory or shop, but in the Order itself. The movement's inability to compensate organizers adequately, and the impossibility of maintaining a competent and dedicated staff, contributed to the prominence of such parasitic elements. There is copious evidence, for instance, that A. W. Wright, prominent Canadian member of the General Executive Board of the Knights of Labor, and close affiliate of Terence V. Powderly, often used his position to fill his own pocket. His various schemes for personal enrichment included an insurance plan which Wright contended would be a "great financial success," but which collapsed when prominent Knights and Eugene V. Debs refused to dirty their hands with an endorsement, and the publication of a *Labor Annual*, which brought Wright and Powderly "about $1000.00 to divide up," money secured from prominent reformers and politicians who "bought" favourable accounts of their careers in the *Annual's* pages.[156] Wright, however, was an extremely complex personality, and much of his sordid dealings occurred after the Order had reached a stage of serious decline; in the 1880s he had often been a diligent worker in labour's cause, contributing on a fundamental level to the expansion of the Order in Canada. E. P. Morgan and his partner in crime, F. L. Harvey, made no such contribution. Their role in Hamilton, and apparently in other North American cities, would only be destructive.

Morgan's movements in the years 1877-85 reveal a dimension of the process of mobility seldom chronicled in current treatments of the subject: the bogus "reformer's" perpetual quest for gain. After his Cleveland sojourn, where his involvement in labour-reform circles commenced in 1877 with the railway strikes, and ended with his betrayal of the Knights of Labor's secret work, Morgan travelled to Camden, New Jersey. There, in league with Falconer L. Harvey, he initiated the ploy he would use consistently in later years: the establishment of a newspaper aimed at securing the ready cash of advertisers and subscribers. With this tidy profit in hand, Morgan and Harvey quietly "departed for parts *unknown*."

The pair arrived in Hamilton in the spring of 1884. For the next year they wrought havoc in the Hamilton Order, gathering around them a core of unsuspecting supporters, cultivating dissension in obscure corners of local assemblies. Between April 1884 and August 1885 the two men quarrelled bitterly with W. L. Rowe, editor of the *Palladium of Labor*, were detected by a Hamilton Knight who had been swindled by them in Camden, stood trial in the court of District Assembly 61, suffered expulsion, established a labour-reform newspaper, attempted a bold coup against District Assembly 61's cooperative store resulting in a civil court case, and created an organization to oppose the Hamilton Order, the United Brotherhood of United Labor. It was a record of achievement, albeit of a negative sort, that few men could equal.[157]

Normally an affair of this nature would provide only a footnote to the history of working-class organizations, a detailed glimpse of the underside of labour-reform movements. Yet in Hamilton, and quite possibly in other cities prominent in the history of the Knights of Labor, this kind of disruption could easily seep into the fissures created by dissent and factional fighting.[158] In the midst of Morgan's indictment and trial, for instance, his Local Assembly 2225 was engaged in a battle with the Gardner sewing machine factory, a strike initiated when the firm fired six members of the Order in May 1884. "The opinion prevailed in L.A. 2225," wrote E. S. Gilbert to Powderly, "... that their discharge was due to the prominent part they had taken in a previous trouble in the same shop and that although the previous trouble had been settled these six men had been marked for discharge. ... The result was that the D.A. acting on the belief that the men had been victimized declared war on the Company by calling out of the factory all members of the Order."[159] A number of LA 2225's members, however, balked at this directive, an indication of an important breach of solidarity. This refusal to strike resulted in a rash of expulsions from the Order, and LA 2225 was to be embroiled in factional dispute for much of the autumn of 1884.[160] Shoemakers' Assembly 2132, led by the opinionated Robert Coulter, heightened this kind of division by continuing to refuse payment of the assessment levied in the interests of the Montreal strikers, an act which led to their brief suspension from the district assembly.[161] "Nothing on compulsion," it seemed, could be turned to many purposes, and the early months of 1885 saw mass expulsions in many Hamilton assemblies.[162]

Morgan and Harvey had played a considerable role in much of this internal bickering, but their most forceful intervention in the factional strife of DA 61 came when they issued a "little advertising sheet" in Hamilton towards the end of March 1885.[163] Under the banner *Justice*, they proclaimed the paper "the official organ of the Universal Brotherhood of United Labor." In the issue of 18 April 1885, *Justice* editorialized against the cigarmakers, then embroiled in a bitter struggle with their employers. To strike now was unwise, declared the paper, as the trade was slack, and manufacturers were not in need of the workers' skills. The editorial aroused the ire of Cigar Makers' International Union No. 55, which issued a statement advising Morgan and Harvey to "mind their own affairs, and leave the discussion of our questions to ourselves, as we are the proper persons to handle our affairs."[164] What prompted *Justice* to intervene in the cigarmakers' affairs is not known. Perhaps it was to curry favour with the manufacturers, men who could obviously keep such a newspaper afloat with advertising revenue. Or the reason may have turned on a more vindictive purpose. Charles Smith, a member of the Cigarmakers' Assembly of the Knights of Labor, and formerly a Camden, New Jersey, resident, had originally denounced the two adventurers, securing their expulsion from the Knights of Labor. He was certainly no friend of Morgan and Harvey, and it may have been their purpose to antagonize him. Whatever the reason, *Justice* won few working-class adherents by such a stand, and the paper soon lapsed. With this final defeat, Morgan and Harvey bid the Hamilton Knights of Labor farewell.

But there was one legacy of the Morgan-Harvey affair which would persist. In the midst of the factional fighting of 1884-85, many Hamilton Knights had been won away from their leaders: William J. Vale, 1883 representative to the Knights General Assembly, coordinator of the Morgan-Harvey prosecutions, and member of the organization's international cooperative board; George Collis, 1884 representative to the General Assembly, chairman of the local publishing committee, and prominent in the trials and expulsions of LA 2225; Thomas Towers, recording secretary of District Assembly 61 in 1885; and David R. Gibson, delegate to the 1885 General Assembly, and a prominent witness in the Co-operative Store court case.[165] Ill-feeling had been directed against these men, and many charges must have been made in the privacy of homes or the safety of groups. While most Knights seemed to have come to regard Morgan and Harvey with appropriate disdain by the early spring of 1885, many remained suspicious of the group at the helm of DA 61. These antagonisms would die hard in future months. It was perhaps ironic that Hamilton's leading Knights of Labor, who had pursued Morgan and Harvey with such vigilance, would be toppled from their positions of prominence and find themselves thrust into an affair, that of the Home Club, as reprehensible to most members as the Morgan-Harvey episode. Nor does the irony end here, for it was Morgan and Harvey, as editors of *Justice*, who introduced the issue leading to the decline of DA 61's major spokesmen. As the cigarmakers' strike of 1885 dragged into 1886, Collis, Vale, Gibson, and Towers would be drawn into the tragic conflict of the Cigarmakers' Progressive Union No. 34 and the Cigar Makers' International Union No. 55.[166] This dispute, which turned on the Knights' relationship to trade unionism, and to which Hamilton's Charles Smith had provided an introductory statement in his 1884 letter to T. V. Powderly, created strains in Hamilton's Knights of Labor which split the Order at the seams. The events of 1884-86 thus stand as something of a reversal of Marx's extension of Hegel's maxim, "that all facts and personages of great importance in world history occur, as it were, twice . . . the first time as tragedy, the second as farce."[167] For in Hamilton, if the appearance of Morgan and Harvey was the farce, the events of 1886, with Collis, Gibson, Vale, and Towers at their centre, would be the tragedy.

Hamilton's Cigar Makers' International Union had, throughout the 1880's, been a bastion of the craft workers' culture of control. In 1883 they had joined with a host of other skilled trades in a strike wave articulating some of the basic tenets of the nineteenth-century "autonomous workman's" conception of control. Commencing 13 April 1883, the cigarmakers' strike hinged on the central issue of apprenticeship regulation. The conflict raged for a month and a half, the manufacturers apparently going outside the city to secure workmen. Eventually, however, these imported cigarmakers proved unsatisfactory, and the Cigar Manufacturers' Association and the International Union submitted the case to a board of arbitration, composed of Edward Williams, William Vale, and George Tuckett. With a board consisting of a liberal manufacturer and two prominent Knights of Labor, it is not surprising that the union was victorious. On 1 June 1883 the strike was terminated, "the men hav[ing] gained the day in all respects." The manufacturers, undoubtedly harbouring deep resentment, would bide their time until economic downturn provided an opportune moment to reassert themselves against the union.[168]

That moment came in April 1885, when many of the cigar factories in the city closed, some shops being overstocked, others being unable to secure leaf tobacco. During the lay-offs, the Cigar Manufacturers' Association informed the union that "owing to the recent change in the tariff in cigars, and the fact that the manufacturers are unable to realize a sufficient advance on a cigar made of scrap filler, considered by your union as a 'shape' cigar . . . [we] therefore ask you to call a meeting of your union as soon as possible, and give the above matter your careful consideration, and make the bill on scrap shapes the same as on ordinary cigars." The union responded quickly, A. C. Gibb informing the association that "we take no action in the matter, that our prices are low enough now, and that further correspondence in the matter would be useless. It was also resolved that we instruct your body that we consider ourselves out on strike against a lock-out."[169]

The first break in the stalemate occurred in late May 1885, one of the manufacturers, J. S. Lillis, informing the union of his desire to effect a reconciliation. Lillis would eventually break ranks with the Manufacturers' Association, giving in to the cigarmakers and running his shop on union principles. Others, like John Kelly, Blumensteil Brothers, and Z. Pattison, had never made common cause with the larger employers, but continued to hire union men, paying the standard rates and operating within the confines of the union's rules and regulations. The union and the association thus remained locked in battle, each side having a base from which it continued its obstinate stand. As more and more imported cigarmakers drifted into the city, shops began to open, manned by non-union hands. This open defiance of the union led to widespread trade union support for the Cigar Makers' Union and sporadic violence, directed against strikebreaking cigarmakers, was not uncommon. This was the way the matter stood, the community polarized, well into the summer of 1886. By this time, however, the cigarmakers who had taken the places of the strikers had been introduced to the harsh disciplines of their masters. They desired to protect their basic interests through organization, and petitioned No. 55 for admission to their ranks, adding that they would be willing to pay such fines as the organization cared to levy. Their petition was rejected, a decision which could not have surprised them a great deal. As a last resort, according to their secretary, they joined the Cigarmakers' Progressive Union of America, forming a Hamilton local, No. 34.[170]

Meanwhile the rifts in Hamilton's working-class movement, already apparent in the divisions between Knights of Labor and craft unionists, widened. William H. Rowe, editor of the *Palladium of Labor*, launched a relentless attack on Hamilton's International Typographical Union No. 129. Charging the printers with flagrant violations of their union's rules, Rowe labelled the offices of the *Times* and the *Spectator* "rat shops," in which apprentices outnumbered journeymen four to one. "By the Typographical Union of this city allowing such a state of affairs to exist," raged Rowe, "they are simply bringing disgrace on the whole International Typographical Union, and the sooner they make it known to the Organized Labor of the city that they are incompetent to run their Union, the better."[171] In a later rebuke, Rowe linked the printers' deterioration to their absence in the general struggle for the improvement of the lot of the workingman: "The men who are afraid to ask for justice from their own employers, can not be expected to champion the cause of other downtrodden representatives of humanity."[172] Rowe's charges may have had some foundation, for the printers were relatively acquiescent in these years, playing no role in labour's upsurge of the 1880s, but the crusade was intemperate and achieved little of a constructive nature. Moreover, there is a hint that Rowe's attack was rooted in personal malice and the desire for self-betterment. One "Union Printer" accused Rowe of striking out at the union in order to undermine the established dailies, securing the *Palladium of Labor* a permanent situation in the marketplace.

Rowe's critic also thought it suspect that a man with such firm principles would toil "day and night in order to make ends meet, howling constantly during the day for shorter hours, and working half the night to save employing men and paying wages or vice versa."[173] Whatever the reasons behind the dispute, Rowe's assault on the printers could only have alienated the affections of many unionists.

Even more disruptive was Rowe's role in the 1885 municipal campaign, where the renegade manufacturer, J. S. Lillis, was running for alderman. The Central Labor Union resolved to support no candidate, there being no workingmen in the field. Rowe, however, saw Lillis's abandonment of the Manufacturers' Association as an indicator of his progressive orientation, and demanded support for the manufacturer. When the CLU refused, Rowe precipitated a split in the ranks of the body.[174] Clearly, one of the Knights of Labor's difficulties, in times of strain, was keeping a rein on overly opinionated men of Rowe's type.

More telling, however, were the implications of a dispute between the Hamilton Order and the Hat Finishers' Association of America in February and March 1886, a conflict prefaced by Eureka Assembly's discussion of the label question in 1884. The problem was posed when some twenty members of the Hatters' Union boycotted hats made by shops employing members of the Knights of Labor but organized on strict union principles. These shops secured a place for their wares among workingmen through the use of the Order's white label, and the Hatters' Union resented this. "We must and should protect our people," William J. Vale wrote to Powderly. "We have the stamp working in another factory and are we to allow these 20 people to boycott us without resenting the matter." Vale concluded that if the dispute was not immediately settled, "we mean to protect our men first, unions afterwards."[175]

It was in this context that the Home Club affair of 1886 erupted. The coming conflict was prefaced with a note in the *Palladium of Labor*, 5 June 1886: "There reach the *Palladium* from all parts of the States and Canada stirring expressings of opinions, to the effect that the Knights of Labor should not infringe on the rights of trade unions. Considerable feeling was caused in this city by the futile attempts to organize scab cigar-makers into an Assembly of the K. of L." Within three weeks, however, "futile attempts" had been transformed into concrete results, the *Hamilton Spectator* reporting that the Cigarmakers' Progressive Union had been "admitted to the Knights of Labor, which Order has extended its protection by affixing its white label on all their goods."[176]

A mass meeting of the Central Labor Union convened 29 June 1886 to discuss the International Union's charges against the Knights of Labor, charges which would be promiscuously flung at the feet of an obnoxious "clique." On the podium were many prominent Hamilton workingmen, most of whom were jointly affiliated with local assemblies of the Knights of Labor and their respective craft unions. Adolph Strasser, president of the CMIU, set the tone for the proceedings, posing the question as one of "Unionism Versus Anarchy." He applauded the long and vital history of Hamilton's Cigar Makers' Union, said to be the oldest labour organization in the city, dating from 6 December 1851. He noted that, as the immense turnout suggested, the vast majority of workingmen, Knights of Labor as well as unionists, supported the Cigar Makers' in their stand against the Progressive Union, a "scab" organization. Finally, he launched his attack on the pernicious Home Club, a motley crew of "dynamiters, anarchists, and office-seekers," disillusioned with the reasonable policies of Grand Master Workman Powderly. "This mischievous and dangerous element has prominent members right here in Hamilton," thundered Strasser. "I will name them. They are George Collis, William J. Vale, and David R. Gibson. The principal quarters of the Home Club are Washington, Baltimore, Philadelphia, Richmond, and Hamilton. It is a powerful and growing element, as well as an evil element in the Knights of Labor, and threatens the destruction of that grand organization. The Home Club aims to destroy the trades unions all through the country—that is its one great object at present and it seeks to accomplish it by secret underhand means." Hamilton's Knights accepted this assessment, Edward Williams condemning "the greatest mistake that was ever made in Hamilton in connection with the labor movement." Alderman Thomas Brick, ever the opportunist, slandered Collis, Vale, and Gibson, whose efforts to whitewash "scab cigarmakers by chartering them into L.A. 7955 of the Knights of Labor was a disgrace to the Order." He attributed their failure to attend the meeting as proof of their cowardice: "All they were good for was looking around for paid situations in Labor organizations." A resolution, condemning "certain unscrupulous individuals temporarily in control of District Assembly 61," and urging support of the Cigar Makers' International Union and their blue label, ended the proceedings.[177]

In the weeks to follow, Collis, Vale, Gibson, and, additionally, Thomas Towers, continued to be the focus of a hostile harangue. "The great body of the Knights of Labor in this city don't appreciate backdown sneaks and scab whitewashers," noted the *Palladium of Labor*. M. C. Foley of Stratford contended that Vale had attempted to undermine the Stratford Co-operative Cigar Factory, an enterprise run by the Order and employing cigarmakers affiliated with both the Knights of Labor and the International Union.[178] Rumours circulated that the Home Club of Hamilton had granted the Progressive Union a charter when paid to do so by the Cigar Manufacturers' Association.[179] When the Iron Molders' International Union No. 26 passed a resolution condemning the actions of DA 61, and endorsing No. 55's blue label, the *Palladium of Labor* advised others to, "Follow in line, brothers, with the vanguard of unionism in Hamilton— ever watchful I.M.U. No. 26."[180] The feeling continued into September

1886, the CLU eventually boycotting the white label of LA 7955.[181] When District Assembly 61 elected its delegates to the 1886 General Assembly it cast its ballots for J. J. Murphy of Brantford and Alexander B. Holmes of the once suspended Hamilton Shoemakers' assembly. It was a vote against the Home Club, Messrs. Collis, Vale, and Towers being soundly defeated.[182] At the 1886 session of the Canadian Trades and Labor Congress, held in Toronto in September, William Berry (of Shoemakers' Assembly 2132) and James Ripley (a delegate from the IMIU to the CLU) deplored the dissension between Knights and unionists, atttributing it to certain unscrupulous leaders rather than the rank-and-file.[183] By October much of this public clamour had dissipated, and DA 61 was instructed by Powderly to accept delegates from LA 7955.[184] A year later the Progressive Union's Assembly still existed, and not until 1889, when DA 61 finally renounced LA 7955, did the Progressive Cigarmakers withdraw from the Hamilton Knights, affiliating with National Trades Assembly 225 of the Order.[185]

But the Home Club dispute, in the long interval separating the eruption of 1886 and the withdrawal of 1889, continued to flare. Three LA's immediately balked at the general slander of 1886, and remained loyal to Collis, Vale, Gibson, and Towers.[186] John Peebles' assembly, as we have seen, ordered him to withdraw from the Central Labor Union. Collis' own assembly, LA 2586, also remained loyal to the old leadership, and apparently bore Collis no ill will, presenting him with a complete edition of George Eliot's works and an encyclopedia of practical quotations in 1888.[187] James Dore, secretary pro tem. of LA 2586, wrote to Powderly expressing the assembly's anger at the efforts to block a reconciliation of the International Union and the Knights. He further expressed bitterness at the manner in which the Home Club affair had been handled, charging the District Assembly with having committed a serious breach of regulations in its stifling of local autonomy.[188]

George Collis, admittedly not an unbiased observer, outlined the situation in a letter to Powderly. Despite his prejudices, the account testifies to his unwavering allegiance to the Order and serves as witness to the essential purity of his motivation:

> I am somewhat in doubt what course to pursue under the following circumstances. A short time since the Central Labor Union in this city passed a resolution boycotting the Knights of Labor label. This might have been defeated but for the apathy of the members of the K of L coupled with the direct opposition of the Trades Union Element within the K of L. My opinion is that the Local Assemblies must withdraw from the C.L.U. until the obnoxious boycott is removed. I hesitate to rule in that direction until I have your opinion upon the matter for should I so decide and then have my ruling reversed it

would be published all over the country and am sorry to say that those who choose to differ from the District at the present time have very little respect for the sign of obliteration. Our actions are published broadcast. If I am sure that I am right I shall not hesitate one moment. I cannot in a communication like this give you any idea of the trouble which the Kickers are giving us here right now. I have been laid up for two weeks. I cannot go out in the evening for a while yet and the Doctor informs me that it is in consequence of late hours and want of rest. Gibson is working like a Trojan he is a wholesome and hard working fellow with no consideration for self yet he is slandered from one end of the country to the other. I am extremely sorry to bother you when I know that you must have enough to do. But relying upon your giving me council when it is needed I appeal to you knowing full well that you can sympathize with me at this time. I know that you have had your share of abuse. From the articles which appear in the Papers here one would think that I would not dare look you in the face. The public are informed that the votes of A. Holmes and R. R. Murphy will be cast for T. V. Powderly for GMW thanks to the defeat of the Home Clubbers Gibson and Collis. I was not aware that at any time I had expressed any feelings antagonistic to your candidature. But this I will say — that if I attended the G.A. and you were nominated for GMW and some other Brother was nominated and I considered him the best man I should put his name on my card and I should not think that I was doing you an injury or the other man a favor, those are my views and I cannot change them and I know that you would approve of such action.[189]

In the aftermath of the electoral defeats of Hamilton Knights in the provincial and federal elections of 1886-87, this factionalism was heightened.[190] On 9 March 1887 the *Hamilton Spectator* reprinted one unionist's comments on the Knights of Labor, extracted from the *Providence Journal*:

It is despotism instead of democracy, as was supposed. Each assembly is governed by its handful of officers and the members have no voice or vote on important matters. The individual Knight is never anything but a puppet in the hands of the man he elects to office, and often that man is either a knave or a fool. In the trades unions all the members are equal and vote on every important action. The majority rules and every member feels that whether success or failure attends what is done, the members have no one to blame but themselves. Another vital defect of the Knights is that the Order is designed to mind everybody's business. The affairs of any trade, the existence of which may be destroyed, are entrusted to Knights in

other lines of business, who, however able or intelligent they may
be, are not fitted to meddle with technicalities they do not understand.
Other flaws in the constitution are, first, the inability of the order to
compel the payment of assessments, and second, of the members to
force their officers to account for the manner in which funds are
expended.[191]

To many Hamilton unionists, enrolled in the Knights of Labor, this critique struck a chord of sympathy, and many craftsmen must have
resigned from the Order. On 1 November 1887 the Home Club affair
created its last major fracas, the walls of the District Assembly hall vibrat-
ing with dissenting voices as the issue of a reconciliation of the International Union and the Knights was raised once again. The executive board
of DA 61, men who had won their positions in the midst of the condemnation of the Home Club, had raised the prospects of a reconciliation on
terms proposed by No. 55. The cigarmakers suggested that they would be
willing to accept members of the Progressive Union into their ranks upon
payment of appropriate fines, levied against those who had broken the
strike of 1885-86. By this late date, however, only staunch Knights of
Labor remained in the Order, the trade-union element having apparently
retired from District Assembly 61. The result was that the officers were
"subjected to considerable abuse for their action." A small majority carried the day for the cause of the white label, and the officers of DA 61 and
its executive board, disgusted with this obstinate refusal to reconcile trade
union and Knights of Labor interests, resigned to a man. They probably
took what remained of the trade-union element with them. Thomas
Towers was appointed District Master Workman in place of James Hennigan. The Home Club, it seems, had returned to roost.[192]

Even this return to the status quo could not heal the divisions within
many local assemblies. Martin O'Driscoll, District Master Workman, informed Powderly that LA 5329 was torn asunder by a severe factionalism,
in which two camps opposed each other resolutely, grasping at every
opportunity to defeat the other group in all contests.[193] In Musicians'
Assembly 4814, where "one would expect to find everything working
harmoniously," J. P. reported "discord and troubles."[194] Factionalism
even took a secessionist turn, D.A. 61 introducing resolutions at the
1887 General Assembly favouring Canadian autonomy.[195] With the
appointment by Powderly in 1888 of Montreal's Redmond, Hamilton's
Collis, and Toronto's Jury to the Knights of Labor Legislative Committee
for Canada, factional strife began to be reflected back upon the Hamilton
Order, Western Ontario's DA 138 (St. Thomas-London) raising a strong
voice against the appointment of Collis and the despotic control of "Czar
Powderly." In Hamilton, despite the prominence of many Knights antagonistic to Collis, the Order remained loyal, but it was of little conse-

quence.[196] When Thomas Towers resumed the position of District Master Workman in the fall of 1887 he inherited an organization which was but a shadow of its former self. A year later, Hamilton's Knights of Labor had functionally ceased to exist.

There was, of course, no Home Club in Hamilton. The *Palladium of Labor's* declaration that "three or four Home Club appointments" had been made in the city because of its prominence as a centre of organized labour was nothing more than slanderous speculation.[197] Men whom Norman Ware has placed at the centre of the history of the Home Club — W. H. Mullen of Richmond, Virginia, and Victor Drury of New York — did indeed address Hamilton assemblies, but their talks raised the ire of no trade unionists. Rather, they lectured on the eight-hour day, the history of the Order, and labour's rights.[198] As late as April 1886 — a brief two months before the unmasking of the Home Clubbers — Strasser himself had visited the city, and found things to his liking; no vile conspiracy tainted the Knights at that time.[199]

Moreover, none of the Home Clubbers had ever denigrated the accomplishments of trade unionism. Only Collis and Towers are not known to have been members of trade unions. William J. Vale, as we have seen, was a staunch member of Hamilton's International Typographical Union No. 129, and no enemy of trade unionism.[200] David R. Gibson, before and after joining the Knights, was a highly esteemed member of Hamilton's Bricklayers' and Masons' Union.[201] And though the question of Towers's and Collis's union affiliation must remain in abeyance, both men had a long experience of Hamilton's working-class movement, playing some role, apparently, in the 1872 strikes for the nine-hour day. Towers, for instance, had defended *both* Knights of Labor and trade unionists in mid-September 1885, attacking the "drones and non-producers." The prominent Knight of Labor must have flinched in the midst of the Home Club dispute, painfully recalling his poem, "Outcast," published in the *Palladium of Labor* a year earlier.

> Dark lowering clouds are hanging o'er me,
> And vainly I look for the dawn;
> Gloomy is the prospect before me,
> And Shadowy is the path I tread on.[202]

While Towers and Collis, living virtually across the street from one another (at 75 and 76 Markland Street, respectively), must have been on intimate terms, there are indications that their relations with other members of the "ring" were impeded by the neighbourhood divisions of the nineteenth-century city. "I tried my utmost to see Brother Vale in this matter," wrote Collis to Powderly, "but was unable and sent the letter to him by a trusty bearer but he was not at home."[203] This, surely, is not the stuff of which conspiracies are made.

The crime of these men was their devotion to the Order, an allegiance rooted in years of faithful service. It was this attachment which led them to commit a major indiscretion, admitting the Progressive Cigarmakers to the District Assembly. It was a breach of solidarity deserving of stiff rebuttal, but it was bred of no sinister, conspiratorial design. The willingness with which Hamilton's Knights of Labor took up the cudgels against Collis, Vale, Gibson, and Towers, viciously opposing their Home Club affiliations, suggests how deeply embedded the resentments and antagonisms created by the Morgan-Harvey affair must have been. Where unscrupulous adventurers, with an eye only for the easy dollar, had sown, Collis, Vale, Gibson and Towers—honest workingmen all—would reap. The reintegration of the Home Club "clique" into Hamilton's Order—as early as December 1886 Collis was again prominent, directing Hamilton Racey's bid for the Ontario legislature, and in July 1887 he was elected DA 61's delegate to the General Assembly—is confirmation of the fraudulent nature of many of the accusations of the summer of 1886.[204]

If the Home Club, more of a fiction than a conspiratorial clique, was not responsible for the demise of Hamilton's Order, what of the often cited ambivalence of the Knights of Labor towards strikes? Here too the answer must be negative. The record of the District Assembly was blemished only by the chartering of the Progressive Cigar Makers' Union as LA 7955, but this serious mistake had occurred almost a year after the cigarmakers' strike had drifted into an impasse from which there was no exit. While undoubtedly a breach of principle, it was hardly an act of conscious strikebreaking. Hamilton's Order, as we have seen in the cases of the telegraphers' 1883 battle, the shoemakers' struggle of 1884, the Gardner strike in the same year and the bakers' 1886 conflict, broke no craft union conceptions of solidarity. The problematic aspects of strike involvement centred on retaining membership in the midst of conflict and, more emphatically, in the throes of defeat. It was a problem that also faced the craft union, but in the union's case, where allegiance was rooted in adherence to certain key planks—the standard rate, apprenticeship regulation, and set limits on the output of members—and a tradition of union control existed in most shops, it was more easily resolved. With the Noble and Holy Order of the Knights of Labor, whose membership was drawn by a more eclectic, and consequently more nebulous, appeal, solidarity was less secure and deviations from principle more likely to occur.

The very reason for the Knights' rapid growth, the widespread attraction of modern chivalry, thus stands as the central component of the Order's decline. Where men and women banded together on the basis of widely diverging, often individual, principles, those same men and women could discard their unity in times of trouble, when their organizational affiliation posed problems of a social, economic, political, or ideological nature. This is the story of much of the development of faction and rift in Hamilton's Order, a process exacerbated by men of intemperate leanings, such as the *Palladium of Labor*'s W. H. Rowe, and men of unprincipled character, such as Falconer L. Harvey and Enoch P. Morgan. Commenting on the failure of the Order, one local Knight noted the "unfortunate dissensions which were the primary cause of our splitting up." Internal bickering had indeed weakened Hamilton's Knights of Labor.[205]

Beyond this purely local context lies a history of employer resistance, the staying power of industrial-capitalist social relationships, and the growing hostility of trade unions to the Order's entanglements in their supposed jurisdictions.[206] All impinged on Hamilton's Knights of Labor in the years 1885-88, taking their toll in a forceful fashion. By 1889 Hamilton's assemblies had dwindled in number and in membership; in terms of their impact the decline was even greater. Reduced to an adjunct of the budding Trades and Labor Council, District Assembly 61's major contribution was the purchase of an old engine house on Walnut Street, which it planned to renovate and establish as a meeting-place for organized labour.[207] When Terence V. Powderly came to Hamilton in October 1889, his audience, barely filling half of Larkin Hall, attested to the declining fortunes of the organization which he headed.[208]

Yet, despite its early death, the Order of the Knights of Labor left a legacy of much importance to the Hamilton working-class movement. An aged Knight had written to a younger comrade in Hamilton in 1884:

> I can only hope that you and brothers of your cast and temperment will take up the work in all sincerity so that when the younger generations shall be asking for 'Light, more light,' you will pass the luminous torch of knowledge to them and hand it down more bright and more lustrous than you received it at our hands. As ------ told you, we must soon go, and it remains with you to carry on our work. But it must be done without ostentation and without parade, it must be done quietly and without vanity, for love and not for lucre. Yes! We are yet in our infancy, but we will grow to manhood if we have only the patience to pass courageously through our adolescence.[209]

It was an appropriate epitaph for "labor's lordly chivalry." It is also a fitting introduction to the final chapter in the pre-World War I history of Hamilton's skilled workingmen, their efforts to build a "new unionism."

7

The New Unionism

'I see th' sthrike has been called off,' said Mr. Hennessy.
'Which wan?' asked Mr. Dooley. 'I can't keep thrack iv thim.
Somebody is sthrikin' all th' time. Wan day th' horseshoers are
out, an' another day th' teamsters. Th' Brotherhood iv Molas-
ses Candy Pullers sthrikes, an' the' Amalgymated Union iv
Pickle Sorters quits in sympathy.'

Industrial Canada, 10 May 1907

Joseph F. Valentine, president of the Iron Molders' International Union,
provided one of the more succinct interpretations of the "new unionism"
when he noted in 1906 that "amid the startling industrial changes of the
past quarter of a century new problems have arisen that cannot all be
solved by the rules which previously did good service."[1] For the new
unionism defied precise definition outside the context in which it thrived:
the emergence of new industrial sectors; the development of sophisticated techniques of managerial control of the workplace; and the launching after 1904 of a vigorous employers' offensive, the like of which had
never before been experienced by craft unionists.[2] Like other components of the economy and society, unionism too would take a turn towards the new.[3]

To many the new unionism represented a theoretical break with the
past, a progressive leap into social reform guided by radical impulses,
sustained by socialist consciousness.[4] Yet, despite the tendency to regard
it in this light, the reality was somewhat different. As John Herman Randall long ago recognized, the new unionism was a unique blend of past
and present trade union practices, a complex mixture of group advantage
and social idealism:

This new unionism differs from the revolutionary unionism of the
I.W.W. and the radicalism of the socialists in its perfect willingness,
nay, in its conviction, to serve the workers' ultimate interests
through developing to its fullest extent the machinery of collective
agreements with the employers' associations. But it also differs from

business unionism in working with a clear prescience of wither its business tactics are taking it, and with the realization that in the interests of society as a whole, and of the workers as the major part thereof, the policy of group individualism is inadequate and must be superseded.

For Randall the new unionism rested firmly on a bedrock of newly cultivated class solidarity, a consequence of skill dilution and the growing unification of all grades of labour. It manifested itself in efforts to abolish gradually "the wage system itself, with a view to eventually controlling the industries."[5] This stress on practical activity was repeated by André Tridon, whose answer to the question, "What, then, is the New Unionism?," perhaps caught more of the ambiguity of the movement than did Randall's sure assessment:

It is the practice which will enable the workers to assume as the return for their labor the full control of the various industries. It is, mark the word, a practice, not a theory. It is, to quote the word of a former secretary of the French Confederation of Labor, 'the result of much experimenting, and is shaped much more by actual conditions than by any individual in particular. These practical experiments haven't followed a straight line by any means, the movement is characterized by much incoherence, it brims with inconsistency. And it is thus because it is not the result of actions performed in accordance with certain dogmas, but because it is a product of life, modified and renewed from day to day.'[6]

Colin McKay, writing in the *Industrial Banner*, captured much of the new unionism's meaning in southern Ontario in an article entitled, "Industrial Vs. Craft Unionism." Defending the craft form of organization, McKay argued that it offered workers the best chance in the fight "against capitalism." Trade unions, he stressed, were ruled by "a common will, a common purpose." Each union was capable of "autonomous action" and carried into the battle "its own discipline and traditions." Moreover, "the spirit of the corps" was only "developed in comparatively small bodies." For these and other reasons, McKay favoured the craft over the industrial form of organization: where the former was likened to an army composed of disciplined segments and companies, the latter was regarded as a "mob," incapable of concerted action. And it was concerted action that was required of Canadian unionists in the opening decades of the twentieth century, for they faced a new and threatening situation. Whereas trade unions had originally been established "to protect their members in their property rights in the craft," McKay contended, capitalist property had overtaken private property, burying forever "the old notion of property rights in one's craftsmanship or skill": "Questions of property rights in a craft dwindle into insignificance before the recognition of the fact that the real problem of labor is to establish social property rights in the world it has created—its product." Thus a "new form of unionism grows up about the machine which tends to destroy the value of skill." The old, pure and simple unionism had struggled for "a fair day's wage for a fair day's work." The new unionist asked for much more than a living wage. For the new unionist, McKay observed, control was of crucial importance: "The fight assumes the aspect of a struggle not only for the possession of the product but, in addition, for the possession of tools in the hands of the enemy, which tools are in their turn the product of a working group." McKay concluded with the stricture that "More and more trade groups in an industry must make common cause." But for this goal to be realized, "closer organization of the workers" was required.[7]

Even Samuel Gompers could be drawn into the new unionism's embrace. Soliciting an article for the *American Federationist* from Hamilton's Samuel Landers, he felt called upon to stress "The question of organizing the unorganized, instilling a greater spirit of unity and fraternity, agitation and organization, and many other matters."[8]

This orientation toward practical activity, and agitational and organizational work, paid high dividends. "Never since the palmiest days of the Knights of Labor," declared a Toronto reform journal in 1900, "have trade unions taken such a firm hold of the toilers as today." There is no need to detail the national organizational gains of the years 1898-1904 here, for Robert Babcock's study of the American Federation of Labor in Canada in the pre-World War I years conveys the point.[9] As a major Canadian industrial centre, and as the home-base of the AFL's only Canadian organizer, the carpenter John A. Flett, Hamilton would figure prominently in this turn-of-the-century upsurge.[10]

Between 1899-1903, for instance, the city emerged as a stronghold of international craft unionism, trailing only Toronto, Montreal, and Vancouver in the number of organizations affiliated with the AFL.[11] By 1903 the city boasted of fifty-nine labour organizations.[12] Readers of the *American Federationist* soon recognized Hamilton as a prominent centre of working-class organizational activity. "I have been holding meetings nightly," declared Flett, "with this result: We have organized the broom workers, furniture woodworkers, and expect to send for a charter for a federal labour union. We have unions of lathers, coremakers, and bicycle workers under way."[13] Some of these gains would be lost in the post-1904 years of economic downturn and employer opposition, but in 1911 fully forty-nine unions, virtually all of them with international connections, continued to exist in the city.[14] It was among them that the new unionism thrived.

Like its predecessor, the nineteenth-century culture of control, Hamilton's new unionism was most visible in conflict situations, the strike being an essential aspect of its history. Many of these battles were "quickie" strikes, where victory itself was not the important issue: "Statisticians waste their time computing how many strikes were lost and how many won. In many cases a strike from which the workers derive no concrete advantage may constitute a decisive victory from the point of view of future struggles. . . . New Unionist strikes are mere incidents in the class war; they are tests of strength, periodic drills in the course of which workers train themselves for concerted action."[15] In Hamilton such conflicts grew out of five related developments: (1) the continuing craft struggle to preserve restrictive and shop control mechanisms; (2) the emergence of ties among craft unionists and previously unorganized sectors of the local working class, such as street railway workers and municipal labourers, and the adoption of certain control mechanisms by the unskilled; (3) a general working-class offensive resisting the imposition of managerial innovations at the workplace; (4) craft opposition to the employers' open shop drive; and (5) the increasing use of the sympathetic strike as a weapon in the struggle for control.

Among building trades workers, for instance, struggles over traditional realms of craft control figured prominently in the post-1896 years.[16] Bricklayers and stonemasons flexed their muscles in the economic recovery of 1896-97, reestablishing union work rules that had lapsed in the depression of the 1890s.[17] By 1904 they had secured union control of the trade, winning important wage concessions from their employers, the Master Builders' Association.[18] Tested briefly in the summer of the same year in a dispute involving a conflicting assessment of a craftsman's work, the union emerged victorious after a three-week strike-lockout participated in by over 100 union members.[19] In April 1906 the Hamilton union defied the masters and the vice-president of the International Union, Thomas Izzard, to mount a struggle for local autonomy, the closed shop, and a standard rate of 50 cents an hour.[20] Two months later bricklayers struck one job site, securing the dismissal of a foreman who was neither a bricklayer nor a mason and replacing him with a union worker.[21] Six years after their 1906 clash with bosses and bureaucrats, Hamilton's bricklayers again defied the contractors and international union officials. In late April and early May of 1912 they opposed interference in local affairs and were threatened with the revocation of their charter if they struck without the approval of the international organization. One word from their superiors, however, and they did as they pleased, striking on 1 May 1912. International officers were heckled at meetings and "the younger members of the union, almost in a body, lined up behind the committee, which had been negotiating with the contractors and held out for the 55 and 60 cent scale." Only with the intervention of the International Union's president, William J. Bowen, was the strike settled, contractors and men coming to a compromise agreement.[22] But militancy paid dividends. By 1914, with a strong membership of over 400, Hamilton's Bricklayers' and Masons' Union had secured a standard rate of 55 cents an hour, and controlled the trade.[23]

Other building trades workers followed suit. An early dispute in the plumbing trade over apprentice restrictions was followed by a strike in July 1903, when employers refused to pay the union scale. On 1 March 1906, eight plumbers struck A. Rodgers and Company over the employment of a nonunionist. Returning to work on 12 March, after the non-unionist's departure, the plumbers were threatened by the former employee with a civil suit for damages. Thinking the firm responsible for this legal action, the plumbers promptly left work; they were induced to return only upon the firm's assurance that it had no part in the legal proceedings.[24] Carpenters, too, were quick to respond to encroachments on their job control. A two-day walkout at the William Green Company delayed construction at the Bank of Hamilton in January 1907. Twenty-five carpenters struck work, objecting to the employment of nonunion cabinetmakers on carpenter's work.[25] A similar dispute precipitated a strike against the Canadian White Company six months later. Members of both the Amalgamated Association of Carpenters and Joiners and the United Brotherhood of Carpenters and Joiners objected to the hiring of labourers and nonunionists in the dismantling of scaffolding, moulds, and false work (utilized in beam and concrete floor construction), claiming this work for union men.[26] A May 1911 carpenters' and joiners' strike against the Contracting Builders' Association, involving 300 unionists and 35 to 40 contractors, was initiated over wages, union work rules, and apprentice restrictions. Settled 1 June 1911, the month-long dispute secured the carpenters work conditions they had sacrificed in the economic downturn of 1907-1909.[27] Like carpenters, painters clung to their conception of control, defending their union rules and regulations in strikes for the standard rate.[28] Similarly, stonecutters in Hamilton and Thorold staged work stoppages in 1907, demanding the dismissal of a foreman who had discharged a member of the craft's shop committe and obtained "the secrets of the union." They returned to work only after the foreman had been replaced.[29] Six plasterers, members of the International Association of the United States and Canada, No. 298, launched their last job action of the pre-World War I years in late November 1913, leaving the employment of the contractor Arnold Clapham. It was a symbolic desertion. Angered by the men's systematic restriction of output, Clapham had denounced the unionists, charging them with incompetence. The craftsmen calmly demanded a retraction of the slander and a public apology; with neither forthcoming, they boycotted the builders' work sites.[30]

Skilled workers in many other trades rivalled building craftsmen in their efforts to preserve traditional forms of workers' control. Brass polishers at the Hamilton Brass Manufactory struck work over the discharge of two union men.[31] Machinists at the Dundas firm of Bertram and Company left work over the apprentice question in October 1900.[32] The same trade struck work at the Smart-Turner Company in April 1903, demanding the reinstatement of a discharged unionist.[33] One hundred and thirty machinists stopped work at the International Harvester Company in June 1904. "While the trouble was originally over the employment of an apprentice to run two machines instead of one, according to union rules," noted the *Hamilton Spectator*, "there are far deeper principles at stake. The outcome of the strike will determine which is to have the whip hand, the company or the union."[34] Lithographers and stove-mounters struck Hamilton firms in 1905, striving to obtain the control afforded by the closed shop.[35] Tobacco rollers left work in March and April 1902, objecting to the severity of fines levied against them.[36] Tailors and garment workers engaged in similar job actions.[37] Grand Trunk Railway yardmen, Canada Screw Company wire drawers, and coremakers at the Canadian Westinghouse Company all staged brief strikes in 1912-13, objecting to the hiring of strikebreakers and nonunion "foreigners." At the Westinghouse Company the strike erupted when two unionists, with the blatant approval of their shopmates, physically assaulted a nonunionist in the plant. Upon their discharge, fifty coremakers immediately left the factory.[38]

These struggles revealed an important continuity in the skilled worker's attachment to the control mechanisms harboured in his union rules and regulations. The culture of control died hard, and the prewar years saw the persistence of struggles for various forms of the restrictive and shop control so common throughout the later years of the nineteenth century. Once more, however, it was the city's iron molders who exemplified the basic trends in the craft workers' struggle for control.

In the aftermath of the depression of the 1890s, introduced by the 1892-93 defeat of Hamilton's Iron Molders' International Union by the city founders, the molders launched new struggles to regain past shop-floor powers and rights.[39] The first two weeks of April 1899 saw the molders win impressive concessions from the foundrymen, as the city shops once more returned to union principles. Besides a 15 per cent wage increase, the molders demanded, and received, a shop book detailing prices on all goods produced and the founders' acceptance of union shop committees. Moreover, as a victory for the closed shop, the Hamilton molders' struggle had important repercussions, prompting the return to union control in London and Brantford.[40] Further negotiations with employers in 1900 and 1902 earned the union an additional 15 per cent increase, with only minimal resistance from the employers.[41] The 1899-1902 gains, totalling 25 per cent, coupled with the founders' recognition of the union shop, restored the molders to their pre-1892 position of strength.[42] But beyond this point, the city foundrymen would not go.

A modest increase of 5 per cent was reluctantly granted in June 1903, and the founders resisted the demands of six nonunion men employed in a small "scab" shop who staged a one-day walkout two months later, protesting their employer's refusal to grant them a few moments' rest "after pouring off."[43] By November 1905 four foundries had moved against the union, the Moore, Gurney-Tilden, Burrows, Stewart, and Milne, and Bowes, Jamieson and Company concerns being placed on the International Union's "unfair list."[44] During the recession years of 1907-1909 the union was clearly on the retreat. Compromises with the employers were reached in 1908, with wage scales readjusted to the 1904 rates. But even this acquiescence did not satisfy the founders, who closed their shops for months at a stretch, reopening them with nonunion men.[45] On 22 February 1909 the four "unfair" shops precipitated a strike by imposing a 25 per cent reduction in wages. Claiming unfair competition from other Canadian and American foundries, where nonunion rates prevailed, the firms declared their intention to run the foundries without union interference, terminating the employment of 170 men. Moreover, the founders claimed that union restriction of output had figured prominently in their decision to implement the open shop. "We have every reason to believe the output of our Shop formerly was unduly restricted by limitation of the amount of work done by Molders belonging to the Iron Molders' Union," argued a spokesman for D. Moore and Company. The assistant manager of the Gurney-Tilden works concurred, contending that union molders had "unduly restricted" production in the foundry. As if to underline their determination to quash unionism in Hamilton foundries, the four shops proceeded to import groups of nonunionists — known as the Skiboo Molders — and the Gurney-Tilden Company made arrangements to install a compressed air moulding machine and several mechanized squeezers. The molders' situation was obviously not a happy one, the *Hamilton Spectator* commenting: "The memorable strike of 1892, when there was a deadlock between the molders and the manufacturers for thirteen months, is still fresh in the memory of many of the older members of the union, and rather than bring about a recurrence of that trouble they would be willing to consider any reasonable offer."[46]

Yet even in this climate of repression Hamilton foundrymen encountered opposition from an unexpected quarter. The Skiboo Molders, as the *Hamilton Times* pointed out, were capable of an ironic retaliation:

The amusing spectacle of strike-breakers striking was provided by the non-union molders who have been imported by the Gurney-Tilden Company to take the place of the union men who have been shut out. The strikebreakers have three kicks coming: They want a raise from $2.75 a day to $3.50 a day, minimum wage of 25 percent [increase] on board prices for piece work. They also refuse to work with Italians, and they also object to the introduction of the molding machine the firm is contemplating putting in.

James W. Ripley, president of the Hamilton local, informed the Department of Labour that the founders were paying strikebreakers "a Premium above the prices we were willing to work for on purpose to retain them," and Phil Obermeyer, Hamilton correspondent for the *Labour Gazette*, outlined the firm's difficulties in running heats with workmen often judged to be incompetent. Nor were the molders totally passive. Strikers were charged with intimidating nonunionists, although convictions proved difficult to secure; strikebreakers were often beaten in the streets; eight molders opened the Hamilton Foundry Company in defiance of the employers; and the international union, solidly behind the men, sponsored a massive picnic and parade in August 1909, celebrating the Golden Jubilee of the organization. Breaking the union was proving to be a costly and difficult affair.[47]

Bowes, Jamieson, and Company eventually succumbed in May 1910, rehiring union molders.[48] The other nonunion shops, however, held firm, continuing to be operated as open shops. By 1912, Bowes, Jamieson, and Company had returned to their ranks, precipitating a strike with a 20 per cent reduction.[49] Union molders nevertheless retained their grip on some shops, striking successfully to win a wage hike from the Kerr and Coombs foundry, a concern originally started by union molders in the middle of the 1892-93 conflict.[50] In March 1913 the union initiated an aggressive assault against the refusal of three large firms — Canadian Westinghouse Company, Massey-Sawyer, and Dominion Steel Castings — to increase wages to $3.25 a day. Lasting from late March to late August, the strike involved 208 molders/coremakers, 38 machine operators, and 30 apprentices, with over 18,000 working days lost. While failing to gain their objectives, the unionists had shown that employer opposition and prewar recession could not stifle their militancy.[51] The penchant for control still thrived in Hamilton's Iron Molders' Union.

Struggles such as these, of course, were hardly a dramatic departure from nineteenth-century patterns of class conflict. One aspect of the new unionism, however, was the degree to which unskilled workers were drawn into conflicts which had previously attracted only the skilled. Labourers at the Hamilton and Toronto Sewer Pipe Company struck work in April 1897, protesting the "bunglings by the green men," reductions of 10 per cent, and the firing of some "old hands."[52] Often backed by the Bricklayers' and Masons' Union, the Builders' Laborers' Union in Hamilton waged a number of strikes, eliciting important concessions — both in terms of wages and working conditions — from their employers.[53] Pork packers at Lawry and Sons quit work in 1900 when four newly hired men refused to join the union. "The reply," noted the *Hamilton Spectator*, "was that the Company intended to run its own shop, and not to be governed by any union, and that hereafter the union would not be recognized." Three days later the firm capitulated to the men's demands.[54] Within the same framework, labourers at the city smelting works struck work over the discharge of two men, sewer workers opposed the introduction of machines in their construction work, and cotton mill hands left work over the posting of "obnoxious rules."[55] But the most persistently borrowed tactic employed by the unskilled was their demand to control foremen and supervisory personnel.

In June 1899, for instance, ore handlers at the Hamilton Blast Furnace Company balked at a proposed return to the subcontracting system. The men objected violently to the contractor, Peter Peterson, arguing that Peterson was "too liberal in the matter of docking time." Refusing to work for the contractor, the men were ordered off the company's property, retiring to a nearby lot. When Peterson made his appearance at the factory gate, riding a bicycle, he was pelted with mud and stones. Three days after the trouble began, the ore handlers were back at work under the old day system, and Peterson was looking for work.[56] Sewer pipe workers struck work 16 April 1907, demanding the reinstatement of a foreman who had refused to impose more work on his men and had attempted to secure better and safer conditions. They returned the next day, their foreman once more directing their work.[57] Five hundred employees of the Hamilton Steel and Iron Company fought a similar battle in the other direction, securing the dismissal of an irksome foreman in April 1910.[58]

Quarry workers affiliated with the Civic Employes' Union walked off public works sites at the end of August 1900, angered by the replacement of their timekeeper. The trouble commenced when F. P. Franey, president of the union and timekeeper at the city quarry, announced his plans to lay off work for six weeks to cultivate his garden. Robert Nichol, foreman at the quarry, arranged to replace Franey temporarily, agreeing to rehire the timekeeper upon his return to the pits. At that point, however, City Engineer Wingate decided to hire a new timekeeper. "He wanted it understood," explained the *Hamilton Spectator*, "that his department, and not the laborers in the quarry were running that end of the city's big labor bureau." When the men struck, Wingate replied with wholesale dismissals. The strike was eventually lost, but it was the quarry workers' perception of what was at stake that was crucial:

> The men say several things. One of them is that they do not intend
> to have the foreman insulted. The placing of the timekeeper in the
> quarry by the engineer over an appointment by the foreman they
> consider an insult not only to the foreman but to themselves. This
> they resent. Another thing they say is that Mr. Franey simply went

away on a week's holidays, and that the engineer in his mad desire
to throw down the Civic Employes' Union, appointed another man in
his place. This they object to and are determined to stand by their
President. Another thing they say is that the new man is an American,
and that he was appointed by the engineer because he is an old friend.[59]

But perhaps the most forceful demonstration of unskilled labour's cultivation of traditional craft control mechanisms was a brief but unsuccess-
ful strike of labourers on city waterworks construction sites, 18-19 April
1910. Six men employed in laying water mains in the east end of the city
laid down their tools one morning, marching in a body to City Hall, where
they collected their wages. They contended that other employees would
follow suit, claiming a general dissatisfaction with the actions of the city
engineer in appointing Wes Murray foreman of their gang, and reducing
Tom Ambaux, their original foreman, to the status of a day labourer.
"Murray doesn't know anything about laying water mains," said one of
the men. "We were always satisfied with Foreman Ambaux, and would
not stand for him being superseded by Murray, who is a driver." For the
city engineer the conflict raised different issues: "It is just a question of
whether we or the men are running the job. In the past the men have
been accustomed to elect their own foreman and it stands to reason that
he could not get as much work out of his gang by being a hail fellow,
well met, as if he maintained a certain amount of reserve." He closed
his commentary with a condemnation of the labourers' apparent soldiering: "I have heard on all sides that two men could do a job which apparently took four men to perform. I have heard further that one man
would do the digging while the other three would do nothing but smoke
their pipes, taking turn and turn about. You know that sort of thing
could not be allowed to continue." Although lost, the strike was a forceful reminder that the unskilled could also harbour a commitment to job
control.[60]

Also important in the emergence of the new unionism were the widening parameters of trade union activity. Twentieth-century developments
produced new industrial sectors and new skills. The rise of the electrical
engineering industry, for instance, prompted the organization of Hamilton's Brotherhood of Electrical Workers, Union 1058, established as the
first Canadian local of the international union in 1902.[61] In the years
1900-14 electrical workers would lead many struggles for workplace
autonomy, wage increases, and improved conditions.[62] Old trades often
experienced revitalization, as the new unionism sustained organizational
drives in previously depressed trades. Garment workers, largely unorganized and concentrated in "sweated shops" throughout the nineteenth
century, emerged to play a forceful role at the turn of the century.[63]
Almost 1,500 garment workers were affected in a May 1899 Hamilton

strike, as pressers protested the practices of the city's major contractor, John Calder and Company. Grievances included the company's persistent wage cuts, importation of alien labour, and the irksome practice of accepting work, then allowing it to sit in warehouses, necessitating a second, unpaid pressing. Manager Copely of Calder and Company resisted the strikers with all his powers, maintaining that the company must "have complete control of everything." The workers, however, eventually won the day, Copely guaranteeing the strikers that their grievances would be attended to. While their victory was an assertion of newly found strength, the real importance of the strike lay in the consolidation of the Garment Workers' Union No. 134. Its members would remain a force in Hamilton labour circles for many years, playing a vital role in the popularization of the union label.[64]

The most important addition to the ranks of Hamilton's trade union movement, however, was the street railway workers. Across North America, the years 1890-1914 saw the emergence and consolidation of the Amalgamated Association of Street Railway Employees of North America. While some cities, most notably Toronto, first witnessed organizational developments among streetcar workers in the late 1880s, most railway workers were unionized in the post-1893 years. Paralleling this organizational drive was a series of violent confrontations, drawing universal community and craft union support. Antagonistic denunciations of monopolistic privileges and corporate greed often culminated in movements for municipal control of the street railway systems. In Hamilton, as in many other North American cities, trouble on the street railways conformed to a classic pattern.[65]

Street railway workers first clashed with their employer in the fall of 1892. Bitterness prevailed over the company's refusal to bargain with the men, who complained of long hours, forced overtime, and low pay. Fifty-one of the railway's eighty employees organized an association for mutual benefit. Six of the leaders of the organization were promptly discharged, and on 7 September 1892 the workers brought their cars to a halt in front of City Hall, refusing to budge. When Manager T. B. Griffith inquired as to the cause of the tie-up, one of the men replied, "A strike, I guess." Community support quickly gravitated towards the strikers, local aldermen protesting the company's "white slavery" and bemoaning the "lack of British fair play." But the management remained firm. "We will tie up our cars, and keep them tied up, rather than submit to dictation from our men as to how we should manage our business," said B. E. Charlton, president of the company. Eventually settled 10 September 1892, the strike was a victory for neither camp. Though the men gained improved conditions, the company refused to rehire the six discharged "ringleaders," granting them a month's salary and terminating their employment. By mid-October, with services curtailed and business reduced, the company began laying off those workers who had supported the strike. "Naturally," replied Manager Griffith, "we favor those who stood by us during that time." Round one had gone to the company.[66]

Conflict was stifled in the recession of the 1890s, but resumed with economic recovery. Spurred to action by London's striking carmen, the Hamilton workers took steps to affiliate with the international union.[67] In April 1899 a union committee of six workers attempted to meet with Manager Griffith, determined to secure a 60-hour week and a rate of 15 cents per hour. Their consciousness apparently transformed, the new unionists praised the "identity" their organization had produced, and proudly declared that men no longer cowered on the cars, but asserted their rights. By 1 May 1899 the company had granted the men's demands and recognized the union; these concessions, however, had been granted grudgingly.[68]

In the opening years of the twentieth century, Hamilton's Street Railway Company continued to oppose the union. At the same time the workers resisted all encroachments on the limited forms of job control exercised by their union. In 1901 and 1902, for instance, the union resolutely opposed the use of company "spotters" and condemned the discharge of union workers.[69] A February-March 1902 confrontation centred on the company's persistent efforts to thwart the growth of the union.[70] Motormen and conductors opposed shift changes introduced by a new divisional superintendent in October 1903.[71] Three months later the men were organizing resistance to the posting of "obnoxious, objectionable rules" on the company books.[72] Such struggles bred constant antagonism, and growing hostility between the company and the union finally came to a head in 1906.

By that time Hamilton's Amalgamated Association of Street Railway Employees of America, Division 107, had consolidated its ranks.[73] The motormen's and conductors' purpose placed them unmistakably in the ranks of the new unionism. They dedicated themselves:

> To place our occupation upon a high plane of intelligence, efficiency and skill; to encourage the formation in Division Associations of Sick Benefit Funds; to establish schools of instruction and examination for imparting a practical knowledge of modern and improved methods and systems of transportation and trade matters generally. To encourage the settlement of all disputes between employers and employees by arbitration; to secure employment and adequate pay for our work; to reduce the hours of daily labour; and by all legal and proper means to elevate our moral, intellectual, and social condition.[74]

The workers' determination, however, was to be equalled by employer opposition and, following battles in London and Winnipeg, Hamilton's Street Railway Company retaliated in the summer of 1906.[75]

Suburban expansion of the street railway system provided the pretext for the company's assault on the union. With the construction of two commuter lines, the Dundas and the Radial, carmen on these systems joined the union. In late August 1906 the men approached the company demanding pay raises of from 18 to 22 cents an hour, shorter working days, standardization of shifts, and recognition of the union on all three networks. The company balked, Manager Green arguing that "the only obstacle to getting down to real business is that the employees of the street railway want to insist on regulating the terms of employment of the employes on the Radial and Dundas Railway Companies as well as their own." Pointing out that all three lines were owned and operated by the Cataract Power Company, the workmen stood firm, rejecting Green's contention that "the city line men control the suburban line men." Rather, said the workers, "the suburban line men ask for conditions for themselves through the union."[76]

A strike appeared imminent as the company imported strikebreakers and secured the services of detective agencies, threatening to run its cars in defiance of any strike. At the end of August 1906, as the company continued to resist the workmen's wage demands and union recognition of the suburban carmen, the unionists agreed to submit the dispute to a board of arbitration, consisting of three disinterested citizens: Allan Studholme represented the unionists, F. J. Howell the corporation, and County Clerk Jardine served as the third mediator. This trio dragged out proceedings for almost a month, producing an ambiguous compromise highly unsatisfactory to the workmen. The award was eventually released 6 October 1906, after a delay caused by Jardine's insistence on an immediate cash payment for his services. It gave the street railwaymen modest wage increases over a three-year period; the Dundas workers received even less; and the Radial men got nothing. The question of the hours of work was left in abeyance, and the central concern of union recognition of the suburban lines was tabled. Allan Studholme dissented on a number of the major decisions, but the views of the other two arbitrators carried the day for the company.[77]

Resentment on the cars simmered below the surface, but the union agreed to work under the conditions laid down by the board of arbitration. A tense situation was exacerbated as the company circumvented the modest wage increases by means of new schedules intensifying route speeds and cutting the daily hours of labour. By late October 1906 the workmen had had enough; in early November they started a systematic protest, resigning from the company's employment in large numbers. Backed by the Trades and Labor Council, the men struck work 5 November 1906.[78]

For the strikers the real bone of contention was the company's efforts to eliminate unionism on its cars: "The methods of the management of the company antagonised the existence of the employes' association. We were obliged to hang together or we would have hanged separately.... Not only did the management evade the terms of the agreement, but instituted a system of attack upon the organizations by attempting to array classes of employes against one another." At a midnight meeting of the strikers a fund was established to run automobiles alongside the streetcar routes during the strike. "We Walk" ribbons, expressive of a widespread public sympathy for the men, abounded on city streets. With rumours spreading regarding the importation of strikebreakers and with Pinkertons drifting into local hotels, the police prepared for violence.[79] This was not long in coming.

For three days following the declaration of the strike, the city witnessed a number of violent confrontations. On the night of the first day of the strike, "a howling, hooting mob, yelling insulting names at the crews of the Radial cars," bombarded streetcar windows with stones and whiskey bottles. At the Stuart Street barn the company's doors were forced in; roving bands pelted parked cars with stones throughout the city. Cries of "mob the scabs" greeted the arrival of 100 strikebreakers, said to be imported from Buffalo and promised $10 a day. Workers at the International Harvester Works, milling about in crowds of 300 to 400, howled insults at all those boarding the streetcars. As the web of legitimization spread across the city, support for the strikers led to endorsement of such acts. A local constable refused a superior's order to keep a streetcorner crowd moving, to the immense delight of those gathered to harass the strike-breakers. A young lad arrested for smashing a car window was released, quelling a potentially riotous uprising. At a house quartering thirty strike-breakers, a crowd assembled to taunt the imported men. Upon the arrival of eight policemen, the crowd, and not the constables, dispersed their adversaries. Mail cars were derailed by citizens sympathizing with the strikers. Even respectable women and young girls, complained the chief of police, were prominent in the disorder.[80]

Over the course of the next two weeks, community support stiffened, and the pattern of violent confrontation continued. After a labour procession of 300 strikers and sympathizers followed John Theaker, president of the local carmen's union, to the Labor Hall to hear international representative Fred Fay, a group of young boys departed on a stone-throwing spree, smashing numerous car windows. On the suburban Radial line, armed guards were fired upon, thirty or forty rounds being discharged in a brief flurry of gunplay. Local doctors donated their services to the strikers, and shoe dealers promised the men free boots for the duration of the conflict. With the local citizens backing the motormen and conductors openly, the company complained of unfair press coverage, presenting itself as the aggrieved party in the dispute. Traction Manager Green was the recipient of a threatening letter:

To Traction Manager Green:
I know of your dirty work of which you have so much since you had
the management of the street railway here. And as true as I live I swear
to God you will be blown to atoms before Saturday night.

Yours with vengeance.

Superintendent Millar received a similar document, anonymously penned,
adorned with a coffin. Rumours soon circulated that several iron molders
had worked long nights, laying aside a store of huge iron balls, designed to
devastate the cars. Threatening to run its cars in defiance of the strikers, the
company cultivated a fierce opposition, and hundreds of factory hands laid
off work each day "in expectation of giving the streetcars a rousing reception."[81]

Manned by strikebreakers enticed from Toronto, Chicago, Buffalo, and
Winnipeg (where many had seen service in a recent strike), the cars began to move on systematic route runs on 12 November 1906. Crowds
quickly formed to hiss and jeer the drivers; rails were obstructed with
farmers' wagons; large bricks crashed down on the cars from building
construction sites; policemen were attacked and beaten, their horses
forced to jump fires strategically lit in the city streets. Demanding militia
protection, Manager Green reacted belligerently, assuring all concerned
that the union was to be destroyed and that cars would be run even if they
were mobbed or wrecked. To counter his aggressive stance, Toronto
streetcar workers threatened a sympathetic strike if the militia were called
in; local factory operatives dismantled car rails and systematically obstructed traffic; and the Trades and Labor Council began preparations for a
"mammoth concert and monster procession" to aid the strikers. Throughout the city, "We Walk" continued to be a popular slogan.[82]

On 22 November 1906 the strikers' procession wound its way along city
streets, a forceful depiction of the new unionism at work:

To the combined tunes of bagpipes and flutes, the street railway
strikers, accompanied by members of various trade organizations,
pulled off the big parade last evening. It was quite a pretentious
affair and thousands flocked the streets to witness the spectacle. Invitations to every trades organization in the city had been sent out,
and it is estimated that there were between 1,000 and 1,500 men in
line. ... The men formed up at the Trades and Labor Hall at 8
o'clock, and got away promptly on time. Peter Kennedy, on a pranc-
ing charger, made an imposing marshal, and immediately behind
him was a bag pipe organization. Following this came Fred Fay,
President Theaker, Secretary Lamond, President Rollo and representatives of the Trades and Labor Council. Next was a triangular ban-

ner on which was written: 'We want shorter hours and better pay;
we are willing to arbitrate; in union there is strength.' Next came the
labor organizations, including: stonecutters, masons, bartenders,
barbers, electrical workers, carpenters, stove polishers, bricklayers, shoeworkers, machinists, tobacco workers, printers, plasterers, etc.

After returning to the Labor Hall, the strikers heard Fred Fay address
them on the strike and its importance to all workers. "A victory of the
street railway men," he said, "meant a victory for organized labor."[83]

The next evening, Friday 23 November 1906, the conflict escalated,
many undoubtedly taking Fay's words to heart, determined to smash company resistance with a show of force. People had gathered early in the evening outside the City Hall to watch the "scab" cars make their rounds; by 7
o'clock the crowd was unusually large, extending from York Street to Gore
Street. Violent disapproval of the company's refusal to submit union proposals to arbitration was widely voiced. Then, at a critical moment, strikebreakers in a passing vehicle kicked out car windows in an effort to discredit
the crowd which until that time had been orderly. This deliberate action,
however, produced more than the strikebreakers bargained for.

Strikers immediately surged forward, stoning and derailing the car. By
8:30 the crowd had moved well beyond the City Hall area, breaking up
into smaller, more mobile units. Windows of businesses antagonistic to
the strikers' cause were selectively smashed. At the Stanley Mills Company, where employees had been discharged for wearing "We Walk"
badges, the damage was particularly heavy. Police were "utterly power-
less" to halt the rampage, and the crowd repeatedly rescued arrested comrades. Strikebreakers bore the brunt of the attack, often escaping the
angry crowds only with the aid of armed constables. Fearing the worst, the
company withdrew all cars from the streets at 9 o'clock. This did little to
placate the crowd, which followed the cars to the barns, congregating at
the street railway offices to bombard the building with rocks and other
assorted missiles. At a guarded stationhouse, the "vicious temper of the
mob was apparent and those who merely looked on saw a repetition of the
great mobs of the French Revolution. The strikebreakers' door was
broken down by a pine log wielded by strong hands." Well into the early
morning hours the attacks continued; at the Sanford Avenue car barns an
effort was made to dynamite company property. "It was a mob gone wild
or mad — the ascendency, complete and unchecked, of the primeval spirit
of depredation and ferocity over the more temperate sprit of good citizen-
ship caused by law and order," declared the *Hamilton Spectator*. "The
mask of anarchy appeared below the yellow gleam of the street lamps,"
commented another authority. Only the reading of the Riot Act, and the
full-scale involvement of the militia, recruited from London and Toronto
earlier in the week, subdued the uprising.[84]

Friday night's clash was repeated Saturday evening, the Riot Act again being read. Dynamite was discovered on a stretch of track, and assaults on strikebreaking drivers were repeated. J. McConnell, leader of the strike-breaking drivers, stated that the weekend battle was the worst his men had ever faced. Fred Fay was threatened by Police Chief Smith and Wentworth County Sheriff Middleton, but the unionist refused to be intimidated, demanding the protection of the American consulate. "He remains at his own peril," said Smith. "The union thinks that man is the whole cheese, but we will soon cheese him." Yet, even in the context of escalating violence, community support for the strikers never wavered. Troops posted throughout the city were subjected to constant harassment; small stores harboured gangs of rock-clutching youths; a tailor, his windows smashed in the melee, placed a placard on his door—"broken by the strikebreakers." Sunday church services were punctuated by prayers asking that the men be given "a satisfactory wage and have their present difficulties settled." But citizens also turned to more worldly sources of strength, pawnbrokers and hardware stores reporting their stock of guns and ammunition depleted by Saturday night buyers. On Sunday sporadic assertions of the popular temper flared. Harry Hawkins, a printer, told the police, "You're all right now but wait a while and you'll get it." When the militia ordered Fred Fisher of Buffalo off the street, he indignantly replied that he was an American, and "gave them a pressing invitation to migrate to a warmer climate." He was incarcerated for his advice. By Monday morning, with the arrest toll rising, the streets were clear and order restored.[85]

Court dockets, however, were crowded. Between 27 November and 4 December 1906, forty individuals were arraigned before city justices on charges of rioting, disorderly conduct, or assault. Three of the "rioters"—James Morin of Bethel, Arthur King of the Toronto Tammany Football Club, and Fisher of Buffalo—were nonresidents, caught up in the violence of the moment. Of the remaining thirty-seven, one was a woman and a significant number were young boys. Twenty-three of this number could be identified, and they included three printers, two molders, two musicians, two motormen, a labourer, glassblower, heater, operative, boat-builder, cigarmaker, tailor, machinist, blacksmith, florist, and candy-store proprietor, as well as the sons of a labourer, carpenter, and woodworker.[86] It was a representative sample, indicative of the widespread endorsement of the strikers' cause prevailing within the working-class community. As a consequence of this support, the "riot" drew "hundreds of peaceably inclined citizens" into defiance of law and order. The chief of police expressed disappointment that "so many respectable citizens and their wives were seen on the streets."[87] Recognition of the respectability of the "rioters", and their long-established place in the community, saved many of those arrested from imprisonment. George

Phillips, an identified ringleader of a crowd of forty stone-throwers, Joseph Carson, a cigarmaker, and Thomas Camp, a blacksmith, all had their cases dismissed for lack of evidence.[88] When John Seamenes, proprietor of a small candy shop, was convicted for striking a soldier, the *Hamilton Herald* reported: "That storekeeper who struck a soldier on the arm to save one of his employees from being stabbed by the soldier's bayonet, may be technically guilty of a serious offense; but he is no criminal and the *Herald*, for one, thinks he is worthy of admiration, rather than punishment."[89] Four late December convictions brought protests from many quarters, the *Hamilton Spectator* urging judges to issue pardons. On 26 December 1906 Thomas Garritt, a molder sentenced to two years in the Central Prison as the first convicted "rioter," was released through a judge's petition.[90] Those who would see the "rioters" as "hooligans" and "rowdies" miss the mark.[91] In reality, the "riot" and its aftermath served to demonstrate the links between the working-class movement and the community, links which survived in Hamilton much longer than in many other North American cities.[92]

As a result of the events of 23-24 November 1906, both the strikers and the company submitted the dispute to the unconditional arbitration of the Ontario Railway Board. For the company the issue of control was still paramount, Colonel Gibson of the Cataract Power Company asking the board to put some limit "on the interference of the union in the affairs of the ... company." Gibson claimed that "it was intolerable that the company should be taken by the throat and told it must do this and must do that." The strikers stood firm on the central issue of union recognition. In the end both camps received concessions, the strikers gaining union recognition, the company winning all the major hours and wages questions. Moreover, the board decreed that the agreement was to be binding on both parties for three years, until 1909. After the long and bitter conflict, many unionists were understandably ambivalent about the settlement; a good number would quit work in the weeks to follow, annoyed by the company's persistent harassment. Six months later, in June 1907, the management retaliated with the formation of a company union. In a climate of economic recession, the union had no choice but to accept the dual union. Community support and the militancy of the new unionism found corporate opposition a formidable foe.[93]

Another adversary, more subtle and sophisticated than traditional employer obstinacy, plagued the new unionism. In most industrial countries the years 1900-14 saw the introduction of a plethora of managerial innovations aimed at the destruction of the autonomy of the skilled worker. Ranging in scope from the employment of autocratic foremen, pledged to drive men and women harder and faster, to the utilization of complex systems of task simplification, job standardization, time and motion study, cost accountancy, and piece and bonus systems of wage payment, this amalgam of tactics came to be known as "scientific management." This pervasive thrust for efficiency, articulated most forcefully by Frederick Winslow Taylor, constituted a concerted assault upon the control mechanisms and customs of the trade embedded in the consciousness and shop-floor practices of the skilled worker.[94]

Canadian manufacturers lost little time testing the new science of shop management. By 1908 Taylor's hand-picked disciple, Henry L. Gantt, was introducing a sophisticated piece work system on the Canadian Pacific Railroad.[95] In a letter to the Royal Commission on Industrial Training and Education, the Canadian Manufacturers' Association made it quite clear that developments in the United States were not passing them by. They had come to realize that

> The greatest difficulty manufacturers have to face is the securing of competent, well trained mechanical experts to act as foremen, superintendents, managers, etc. Such men must not only be well up in actual trade practices but must also know the theory of their work. The old apprentice system would meet the first requirement, but it would have to undergo important modifications to fulfil the second condition. It is probable that it could be developed so as to provide theoretical training if it were free from restrictions. This has been amply demonstrated by the splendid systems developed by several firms in the United States, notably the Brown & Sharpe Machine Company of Providence, The General Electric Company of Schenectady, The Baldwin Locomotive Works, Philadelphia, The Hoe Press Company, New York, and several others. We would request that the Commission devote special attention to these systems when visiting the United States. They show in a very practical manner how theoretical training can be correlated with shop practice.[96]

Indeed, as early as 1901, the Cramp Steel Company of Collingwood had imported a mechanical engineer to revamp its workplace processes. According to the *Industrial Banner*, the practice was commonplace in the early years of the twentieth century.[97] Gantt, and his mentor, F. W. Taylor, published lengthy articles in *Industrial Canada*, organ of the CMA.[98] Taylor himself spoke before the Canadian Club of Ottawa in 1913, outlining "the principles of scientific management."[99] As Canadian industrialists concerned themselves more and more with the standardization of the work process, *Industrial Canada* could proclaim that the "gravest evil from which this country is now suffering, graver by far than the exaggerated dangers from monopolies or from freight rebates, is the decline in the efficiency of labor."[100] Popularized by men like the educational reformer Albert H. Leake, the efficiency craze captured a growing audience of Canadian zealots.[101]

The showplace of Canadian "efficiency in production methods" was
the Lumen Bearing Company of Toronto. In 1911 *Industrial Canada*
approvingly described the role of experts and the resulting jump in productivity at the foundry:

> Practical assistance to the workmen must be given by an expert. In
> the Lumen Bearing Co.'s shop a man is placed on the floor in an
> advisory capacity to the foreman. His is not the work of administra-
> tion or management. He is there to assist the workmen, to suggest
> short cuts, to evolve economical methods, to save time for the
> workman, and for the manager, to the material advantage of both.

> It is the place of the 'staff boss' the 'expert adviser', to show work-
> men where these minutes may be saved. He is on the floor all the
> time; he is corrective to slovenly practices. The stop watch is his
> gauge. By careful and accurate observations a basis is arrived at for
> piece work prices. In the Lumen Bearing Co.'s foundry a certain
> class of castings was formerly made at the rate of twenty-eight a day.
> That was in the day work era. To-day the average production per
> man of the same castings is sixty-five. The history of the change in
> output from twenty-eight to sixty-five daily is the story in concen-
> trated form of efficiency management. It was accomplished by show-
> ing the moulders how this, that and the other operation could be
> accomplished with greater speed and with less labor. It is the story of
> economy of time and energy; of making the head serve the hand;
> the story of developing more efficient workmen.

The paper then went on to depict the general transformation efficiency-
conscious employers and their managers were attempting to bring about
in many Canadian industries:

> Formerly, as in most shops, the mechanics did a large part of the
> planning how work was to be done. They studied their blue prints
> and decided what operations were necessary, which should come
> first, and how they should be accomplished. They hunted up the
> machine tools they needed, borrowing them with or without permis-
> sion. They drove their planes and lathes at whatever speed or feed
> they thought right. Finishing a job, they left their tools where they
> dropped. The next man who needed them conducted his own search
> for them, lost time putting them into condition again, or used them
> as they were at half efficiency. They 'soldiered' by the hour at times
> on 'fill-in' jobs while waiting for castings or drawings for their princi-
> pal tasks. To list all the wastes would take pages; few manufacturers
> need to be told of them, however. They know.

Today, the workmen do no planning. Every detail of work on every job is thought out for them and put down in unmistakable black and white. Not merely general directions, but the specific instructions indicating operations necessary on each part and the factors bearing on these operations — the character and number of the cuts, the depth of each, the tool to be used, the speed, the feed, the time allowed if a bonus or premium is to be earned, the hourly rate if the bonus time is not attained. Analyzing the drawings and specifications, the planning department reduces each machine or group of machines ordered to its primary elements and prepares an instructions card for each part or lot of similar parts required. Each operation has been standardized; the standards are either carried in the planners brain or in a convenient file: the instructions card carries these to the workman and his gang foreman.[102]

Managerial innovations such as these aimed to restrict the shop-floor autonomy of the skilled workingman.

Much of the zeal for efficiency undoubtedly became transferred to Canadian work settings via the introduction of the branch plant, and the increasing size of corporate holdings, accentuated after 1907 by an accelerating merger movement, lent a logic to the introduction of managers and shop-floor planners.[103] It was perhaps in this context that Hamilton, which by 1912 boasted of forty companies affiliated with American concerns, became a centre of the efficiency movement.[104] "Each manufacturer is confronted with problems concerning the efficiency of his own plant — problems ever varied and ever pressing for solution," concluded the *Hamilton Manufacturer* in 1912. "Much of this efficiency," continued the manufacturer's journal, "has to do with impersonal things — machinery, processes, etc.; but back of it all there is here, as everywhere else, the human personal element, and the efficiency of the workman is a matter at once of individual, local, and national concern."[105] As if to emphasize their concern with efficiency, Hamilton manufacturers gave Albert Leake a rousing welcome when he spoke before the Board of Trade in early 1906.[106] Even more enthusiastic was the reception accorded Frederick Taylor's claims to have doubled the output of skilled workmen in a number of American factories and shops.[107] Frank Jones, head of the Iron and Steel Company of Canada, and often described as the best manager of men in the young Dominion, initiated a common practice when he imported W. R. Cuthbert, an American accountant with specialized experience in steel production, to serve as the new company's comptroller, a post designed to increase efficiency in the corporation's operations. Reminiscing about shop-floor life at the Duncan Lithography Company of Hamilton, Robert T. Armstrong remembered the difficulties involved in running old-fashioned presses. "J. McCarthy did have a job running this old tub," he recalled of one machine. "In those days, as I look back, it was hit and miss. If your job went wrong nobody could tell you a thing." But all of this changed, as "the Company hired a man from the U.S. at $20.00 a week [Armstrong was making $3.50-$6.00 weekly], an expert."[108] The success of Hamilton's factories, claimed one authority, indicated "the presence of studied factory efficiency."[109]

Exemplifying the purpose and practice of this "factory efficiency," was a system of cost accountancy introduced at Hamilton's B. Greening Wire Company by H. L. C. Hall, a member of the International Accountant's Society, in 1906. Involving the transfer of authority from skilled workers to foremen, job standardization, efforts to eliminate all lost time and motion, a record of the minutes required to complete each job, strict tabulation of all materials and tools employed, and the adoption of piece rates and premium plans, Hall's system epitomized the precision introduced on the shop-floor by the new managers. Also characteristic were Hall's goals: "First to induce economy by the elimination of waste and second to induce economy by intensifying production." The successful implementation of such rigorous managerial innovations, of course, sounded the deathknell for nineteenth-century forms of workers' control, just as it had destroyed workers' autonomy at the Lumen Bearing Company in Toronto. The whole issue was further complicated by paternalist practices, consciously employed to siphon off working-class discontent. Hamilton's Frost Wire Fence Company, a firm that had "Solved the Problem of Labor," exemplified the trend:

> Behind the keen judgment and strict business principles of the company's officers is a plant that is generally recognized as being the most complete, and up-to-date establishment of its kind anywhere, while equally important, is a staff of efficient workmen, who receive shares of the firm's profits, according to their merit in following their respective vocations. There is the very best of business foresight in the firm's policy in this respect, for the officers recognize the fact that a man will put more heart into his work and take a keener interest.

For the new unionism, opposition to such systematic efforts to secure managerial control was crucial.[110]

Craft union antagonism to various forms of shop management in the early years of the twentieth century has been well known for some time and requires no elaboration here. In a debate with Frederick W. Taylor, N. P. Alifas of the Metal Trades Department of the AFL succinctly stated the working-class position. "Most people walk to work in the morning, if it isn't too far," he said. "If somebody should discover that they could run to work in one third the time, they might have no objection to have that fact ascertained, but if the man who ascertained that had the power to make them run, they might object to having him find it out."[111] Canadian reform and socialist journals denounced Taylor with a particular vengeance, often adding words of denigration for the most sophisticated Canadian spokesman of managerial reform, William Lyon Mackenzie King.[112] A worker in Alan Sullivan's World War I novel, *The Inner Door*, condemned efficiency engineers as men "who put your immortal soul in a box and say, 'Don't get outside that because it's a waste of energy and a dead loss to the company'." Toronto's Dunlop Tire workers protested the importation of managerial personnel from the United States in 1906. They argued that "American methods" had been introduced, "such as ... no self-respecting and liberty loving Canadian can submit to."[113] Hamilton's *Labor News* struck hard at the introduction of efficiency measures in Canadian machine shops: "The 'one man two machines', the 'Taylor', 'Scientific', 'Premium', 'piece work', and other systems introduced in the metal shops are making of men what men are supposed to make of metal: machines."[114] Such reactions merely reflected the growing discontent at the workplace.

As early as the spring and summer months of 1893, for instance, workers at the Hamilton factory of the Canadian General Electric Company resisted the introduction of a new system of piece payment, put into effect by a new manager. After a series of confrontations, the workers returned to the old method of payment and the manager was fired.[115] Tailors struck work in 1901, angered by their employers' efforts to reclassify work processes.[116] Late in 1902 several hundred female employees of the Eagle Knitting Mill objected to a new system of cutting and work classification. Claiming the innovations would result in wage reductions of $2 a week, they left their benches. The dispute was ultimately "amicably adjusted," a euphemism for workers' defeats, management contending that the cutters would soon be doing more work and collecting larger wages, the promise of all efficiency schemes.[117] One hundred women workers at the Chapman-Holton Knitting Mills struck work in 1910, protesting deductions levelled against spoiled work.[118] In May 1911, 100 coatmakers at the Coppley, Noyes, and Randall Company successfully blocked the introduction of a new piece-work system.[119] Finally, in 1913 workers at the Canadian Westinghouse Company left the plant in opposition to the introduction of time clocks. Like the machinists at the Watertown Arsenal in the United States, these electricians refused to be "put under the clock."[120]

While limited in numbers and extent, such struggles against managerial innovation are highly suggestive. All of the Hamilton confrontations involved workers recently attracted to the new unionism: garment workers, particularly unskilled women, were prominent,[121] and workingmen whose skills rested on new industries, such as electrical engineering, also played a forceful role. The absence of the traditional craft workers from such struggles suggests that the thrust for efficiency exercised little impact in such entrenched Hamilton trades as molding, glassworking, and the various realms of the building trades. There, where union authority still prevailed, and the traditional struggle for workers' autonomy persisted, craftsmen could still thwart such efforts to secure managerial control directly, without recourse to a strike. Or, if confrontation proved inevitable, it would assume the mask of a strike against an irksome foreman or supervisor, conflicts we have seen to have been common during this period. Finally, in trades such as molding, Hamilton founders were a tightly-knit group of self-made men, employers to whom practical experience counted for much. The Hamilton foundrymen would likely have found much to applaud in *Industrial Canada*'s stand on "efficiency quacks":

> Efficiency is a good thing to strive for. Perfect efficiency is never attained, but high degrees of the quality may be secured. Manufacturers are familiar enough with 'efficiency engineers' and 'efficiency' articles in magazines. Some of them are 'efficient', but many are not. When one hears an efficiency engineer instructing an experienced manufacturer how to run his business, one often asks why the advisers efficiency has not secured him the possession of a factory or, at least, the management of one. Similar speculation extends to the apparent inefficiency of the professional writer's efforts to secure for himself more remunerative employment. The manufacturer can learn a great deal about efficiency by talking with other manufacturers or visiting their plants. Still, some efficiency engineers are good men and some efficiency articles are worth filing away; but it is unfortunate that the manufacturer must toss aside so much chaff to find the grains of practical wisdom.[122]

Thus, while various forms of shop management presented a real threat to craft workers, and one that cannot be ignored by the historian, employer ambivalence and union authority probably circumscribed their ability to break the recalcitrance of the autonomous workman in these early years of the twentieth century.[123] Their most potent impact lay in the new industries and callings that came to prominence in the years 1896-1914, and there they were forcefully resisted by the new unionism. But to break the back of craft resistance, Hamilton employers turned to a less complex tactic, the open shop drive. The easiest method of attaining efficiency on the shop floor, in the eyes of many employers, was to eliminate unions.[124]

The CMA launched its assault on unionism with attacks on the most blatant forms of craft workers' "inefficiency," restriction of output. Mr. Dooley articulated the employers' disgust at union practices in a satirical passage: "Hogan injoiced th' hens to jine th' union. But wan iv thim laid an egg two days in succession, an' th' others sthruck, th' rule iv th' union bein' that no hen shall lay more eggs thin th' most reluctant hen in th' bunch." Indeed, industrialists saw union control and limitation of output as twin evils:

> why should organized labor be permitted to control and *limit the output* of our factories? Labor unions in general refuse to 'work by the piece' and the daily output in many lines notwithstanding the introduction of labor saving machinery, is today, not more than two-thirds of what it was a few years ago. No man, nor any body of men have the right to retard so unreasonably the growth of our national trade and commerce.

"Why should organized labor be permitted to *limit the number of apprentices*?" continued *Industrial Canada*. "Young Canadians are every day prohibited from learning the trades for which they are naturally fitted." On these premises, the question, "Why should any body of men be permitted to *unionize the shop* or factory of their employer?," was merely rhetorical.[125] Moving against the "unwarranted aggression of the unions," employers across Southern Ontario formed a united front. "In the great industrial struggles 'twixt capital and labor which are to come," declared the CMA in 1905, "it is to the open shop employers must direct their efforts. The workman must be taught that a better state of individual efficiency will bring a higher standard of remuneration, and that the good workman is worth more to the employer than the indifferent workman."[126] Taking their cue from John Kirby, prominent in the National Association of Manufacturers, and an architect of the American open shop drive, Canadian employers adopted a wide range of tactics to smash unionism: promiscuous use of the injunction, combined with the suit for damages, to stifle the potency of union boycotts and strike pickets; forceful lobbying aimed at securing legislation favourable to the manufacturers' cause; sophisticated use of paternalistic welfare programs and workplace reforms, aimed at softening union criticism of employer negligence; attempts to flood the labour market with skilled workers lured from the British Isles by promises of steady work and high wages; and organized importation of strikebreakers, detectives, and "spotters" in the midst of conflict.[127] Never before had craft unions faced such relentless opposition.

Much of this story should already be clear, for we have seen how strongly many Hamilton employers resisted craft attempts to preserve control mechanisms, striking out at the closed shop. The city founders, for instance, were in the vanguard of the employers' offensive, and their 1909 conflict with Hamilton molders was a classic case of organized resistance to unionism.[128] Employer obstinacy was a well-known and clearly perceived reality among Hamilton's skilled trades, and one that drew constant comment. Discussing labour's upsurge during the years 1899-1903, John Flett noted that "This consolidating of the forces of labor has not been unobserved by our opponents, who have resorted to every plan to disrupt ... the organized workers of this country."[129] The passage of the Industrial Disputes Act, Mackenzie King's corporatist labour legislation of 1907, drew further fire from Flett in the pages of the *American Federationist*.[130] Hamilton's Trades and Labor Council was a vocal opponent of the CMA, which met in the city in 1909 at the height of employer resistance.[131] In the local setting, however, employer hostility was most vehement, and most obvious, within the numerous municipal employers' associations that often backed forceful anti-union campaigns.[132]

Upheavals in the building trades exemplify the case. In May 1907, sixty plumbers successfully resisted the contractors' efforts to impose the open shop in the trade.[133] Carpenters, painters, and stonecutters overcame similar opposition from their employing contractors in the same period.[134] A. M. McKenzie, president of the Hamilton Master Painters' Association, defended his organization's 1905 rules and regulations, which he contrasted with the trade "legislation" of the Painters' Union, stating, "they are not within measurable distance of arbitrariness of some of the union rules I will be delighted to point out to a discerning public, if necessary." But the rules, as both parties well knew, were not what was at issue, as McKenzie explained:

> The union does not object to the rules it objects to the open shop,
> and the master painters of Hamilton are prepared to insist on the
> open shop. It is essential that we have the right to employ any man
> who is capable of doing the work required of him, [ir]respective of
> his standing in the union. It is only right that we the employers,
> should say who we would like to employ, and not an irresponsible
> committee of any labor organization, and it is only right that any
> man should have the privilege of working at his trade without con-
> sulting the union bosses.[135]

Two months after.the employers' stand on the open shop, the painters and contractors clashed, the former emerging victorious, and their union intact.[136]

Victories like those of the building trades' workers were not exceptional. Although employers used the recession of 1907-1909 to great advantage, their stated objective of driving unionism from the city was never achieved. No craft union totally succumbed to the employers' offensive. In some trades, as in printing, the early twentieth century witnessed a resurgence of union strength. During the 1880s Hamilton printers had barely kept their heads above water, apparently demoralized by their employers' flagrant abuse of apprentice regulations and union rules.[137] But by 1906 they had resurfaced, leading struggles for the eight-hour day and consolidating power on the shop-floor.[138] A brief clash over union wage scales, described by Hugh Borthwick, president of the Hamilton local, revealed the newly established strength of the city's printers:

> Did we strike? Well yes, and the members on the three Hamilton news-papers did themselves proud. There was no doubt about their posi-tion. Inside of fifteen minutes from the call of the President every man in the three plants, foremen, proofreaders, operators, and floor-men, and one of the city editors who is a member, were in central labor hall. The strike lasted from 10:45 to 1:45 exactly, and we won. ... Did they want a showdown? They got it. Even the boys wanted to quit. The first strike in the experience of Hamilton Typo-graphical Union and it was a creditable showing.[139]

While few crafts had reason for such jubilation in the early years of the twentieth century, employers' efforts to put an end to union strength were far from successful.[140]

Adding force to trade union resistance was the employment of an essentially new tactic: the sympathetic strike. While the sympathetic strike had attained some degree of prominence in the United States in the post-1886 years of trade union expansion,[141] it gained no real foothold in Canada until the turn of the century. In Hamilton, for instance, the sym-pathetic strike was exceedingly rare in the years 1860-1900, an aberration intruding upon normal patterns of class conflict with the rise of the Knights of Labor or occasionally during the spring offensives of construction workers.[142] But from 1902 on, when a major longshoremen's strike in Halifax engendered sympathetic action by coopers, fish handlers, and coal heavers, involving well over 600 men, the sympathetic strike was to be a powerful weapon in the hands of the new unionism.[143] "The sympathetic strike," declared the *Industrial Banner*, "brings forth the sacred germ of resistance implanted by nature in every man. There is nothing higher or holier in human nature than the impulse which resists oppression and strikes for liberty."[144] The increasing adoption of the sympathetic strike in Hamilton was even more impressive in the context of the AFL's refusal to sanction its use.[145]

Prefaced by early sympathetic strikes involving furnace hands, tin-smiths, and ore handlers in 1900 and 1901, the most dramatic conflict in Hamilton emerged from a strike at the Cataract Power Company in 1902. Electrical workers at the concern struck work in the summer months, demanding union recognition. The central issue, declared the *Hamilton Spectator*, was whether the company "was to be tied up to unionism ex-clusively, and the men demand that it shall be."[146] With the company and the union locked in a stalemate, the dispute was submitted to arbitration, but not before street railway workers threatened sympathetic action. By mid-August 1902 the Trades and Labor Council was discussing the possibility of a general strike, waged by workers in the shops utilizing electricity from the Cataract Power Company. While the strike was never actually enforced (it was settled 28 August 1902), the expressions of solidarity and threats of sympathetic job actions must have strengthened the electrical workers' bargaining position.[147]

In other trades, sympathetic strikes were employed by machinists at the Smart-Turner Company in 1903, protesting the dismissal of a man in another department, and by stonemasons, supporting a bricklayers' walkout at the International Harvester Company, precipitated by a contractor's defiance of union rules.[148] A general wave of sympathetic strikes convulsed the building trades in 1907 as plumbers, painters, carpenters, and stonecutters supported each other against employers' associations' efforts to flood the trades with nonunion labour.[149] In 1911 linemen at the Bell Telephone Company, striking against changes in work scheduling and demanding wage increases, were supported by sympathetic strikes of Bell operatives.[150] And in the midst of the 1912 Eaton's cloakmaker's strike, waged against changes in the work process imposed by a new foreman, Hamilton's garment workers sympathetically refused all Toronto orders.[151]

The struggles of Hamilton's new unionists thus revealed their links with old practices and their recognition of new realities. Restrictive and shop control mechanisms, which we have seen to have been prominent throughout the late nineteenth century, continued to be of importance well into the early years of the twentieth century. Emerging from the depression of the 1890s, Hamilton craft unionists reimposed their limited forms of control in the boom years 1899-1903. At the same time, the emergence of new industrial sectors, and their consequent unionization, as well as organizational gains among the semiskilled and the unskilled, drew labour's ranks together, expanding the context of trade union activity. These developments were followed by a fierce employer offensive, as the Canadian Manufacturers' Association and the municipal employers' organizations sought to break the back of craft resistance. Facing the challenge of the open. shop and the impact of various forms of workplace innovations geared to dilute skill, standardize tasks, and rationalize time, craft unionists continued to struggle for control. For the employer, emboldened by a newly discovered class unity which had become institutionalized at the local level in the employers' associations, the struggle was for workplace control, a power that in his opinion he had been denied long enough. For the skilled workingman, the struggle was waged, as it had been for decades, for workplace autonomy, for the customary control he sought to preserve over his life on the shop-floor. But new conditions bred new responses, and distinctions between skilled and unskilled blurred as they

faced common enemies, and as mechanization, skill dilution, and efficiency engineers attempted to whittle away at craftsman, operative, and
labourer alike. Craft support for the unskilled, the unskilled workers'
adoption of craft control mechanisms, and the growing use of the sympathetic strike all reflected a developing class unity.

This class unity lay behind the impressive electoral victories of Allan
Studholme, who represented Hamilton East workers at Queen's Park
from December 1906 to July 1919. Born near Birmingham, England, in
1846 of respectable working-class parents, Studholme after leaving school
took up the trade of stove-mounting. He was soon active in the Stove-
mounters' and Steel Range Makers' International Union, later serving as
an executive member. In 1870 Studholme emigrated to Canada and for
four years lived in Dundas, where he met and married Priscilla Stearn.
The couple would have three sons (all of whom would reside in the
United States) and one daughter. Scarcity of work in the foundries forced
the stove-mounter to labour at a variety of jobs and travel to a number of
Southern Ontario cities, but he always returned to his home base in the
Hamilton region.

Studholme early involved himself in labour matters, making the trek
from Dundas to the larger centre on 15 May 1872 to march in the nine-
hour parade. By 1874 he had moved to Hamilton and probably played
some role in the secret organization of the Knights of Labor between
1875 and 1880. As early as 1882, for instance, he was recommended to
Powderly as "a fit and proper person to carry on the work of an organizer" in connection with LA 2225; by 1884 he was serving as Master
Workman of the assembly. The stove-mounter first cut his political teeth
on the independent working-class campaigns of the 1880s, being actively
involved in the Knights' Labor Political Association. Victimized by his
employer for his active endorsement of Edward Williams in 1883, Studholme apparently sought work in Toronto. After a brief stint at the
Toronto foundry of Edward Gurney, he returned to Hamilton. There he
supervised the reorganized Knights of Labor cooperative grocery in 1885.
In 1887 he left Canada for reasons of poor health, travelling to Australia,
where he represented a Western Ontario publishing company. He eventually returned to Hamilton and again cast his lot with the working-class
movement. Employed at the Burrow, Stewart, and Milne foundry, he
often served as the Stove Mounters' delegate to the Trades and Labor
Council in the opening years of the twentieth century. Elected to the
Ontario legislature as an independent working-class candidate in 1906,
and thereafter as a member of the Independent Labor Party, Studholme
was the forerunner of many twentieth-century Hamilton labour politicians, elected to the federal and provincial Houses, as well as to the local
city council. Representative of many skilled workingmen of the time,
Studholme was a Methodist, a member of the Ontario Single Tax League,

and a supporter of the Social and Moral Reform Council of Canada. His death, at his Hamilton residence on 28 July 1919, was mourned by many city workers. In his memory, the Trades and Labor Council named their meeting place the Allan Studholme Memorial Temple, Tom Moore presiding over the dedication in 1923.[152]

Studholme's first political success came in the December 1906 provincial election. Well known for his role as an arbitrator during the summer street railway difficulty, the stove-mounter was backed by a coalition of men prominent in the Trades and Labor Council, some of whom would figure in the formation of the Canadian ILP in 1908. Besides the future ILP president, Walter Rollo, labour activist Samuel Landers, and the ex-Knight of Labor John Peebles, Studholme had the public endorsement of John Theaker and Fred Fay, leading men in the escalating autumn conflict on the street railway. Few expected Studholme to effectively challenge John J. Scott, a Conservative lawyer nominated by Studholme's employer, John Milne. The labour candidate lacked previous political experience, and some workingmen feared he would not poll a hundred votes. Nevertheless, in the by-election called to fill the seat vacated by the death of the Conservative member, Henry Carscallen, the stove-mounter emerged victorious, defeating Scott by 854 votes. To the *Hamilton Spectator*, openly an organ of the Tory cause, Studholme and his supporters were merely Grit sympathizers, backed by the Liberal machine.

While this assessment may have rung true in the case of Landers, a notorious opportunist, it hardly applied to Studholme, Rollo, and other Hamilton workers in the cause of independent labour politics. The Grits' failure to nominate a candidate in Hamilton East undoubtedly played some role in labour's electoral victory, as well as contributing to the small voter turnout. But the real force behind the politics of late autumn 1906, sweeping Studholme into office, was the episodic clash on the street railway. Wielding Hamilton East's working-class voters into a united front, it demonstrated the political clout of the aroused new unionists. "Don't let the excitement of the street railway strike keep you out on the street," urged the *Industrial Banner*, "but button up your coat and put in your time to better advantage by boosting the man who is worthy the support of the workers of Hamilton."[153]

Studholme stood as the ILP representative in 1908. Campaigning upon his record in the House, the labour candidate again received the endorsement of Hamilton East. Backed by the temperance forces, Studholme received 2,699 votes, besting the Conservative Scott by 363. Running a dismal third was the Liberal candidate, William Melville McClermont, who received 1,277 votes; the socialist Lockhart M. Gordon drew the support of only 26 Hamilton East residents. The Tory platform, advocating a technical college for Hamilton, free school books, no school fees, antagonism to assisted immigration, and abolition of prison labour contracts, revealed how the Conservatives sought to woo the working-class vote. Again the *Spectator* saw the victory as a function of Liberal strategy: "Mr. Studholme has the Grits to thank for his election. It is pretty safe to say that there were comparatively no Grit votes polled for Mr. McClermont after 3 o'clock. The Grit slogan was—defeat Scott, and at any cost."[154]

Hamilton's ILP also contested the 1908 federal election, nominating Samuel Landers to oppose the two regular party candidates. Landers ran a distant third, polling 1,309 of the total 6,164 votes cast.[155] He apparently lacked the widespread support of Studholme, whose honesty and integrity now commanded respect from all quarters. Landers, however, may well have been marked as a mere office-seeker. It was well known, for instance, that he had been nominated as a labor candidate in Waterloo some years before and had "stumped the country" in the interests of the Laurier government.[156] On the eve of the 1908 election, Landers was courting the favour of Mackenzie King, assuring the rising politician that he endorsed his election and had spoken to delegates at the recent Trades and Labor Congress convention about him. King tried to entice Studholme in a similar manner, asking him to address a Berlin campaign meeting on his behalf. Studholme, although personally attracted to King, declined, informing the future Liberal leader that "labour men have lost all faith in party men and are determined to have their own class on the floor of the house so as to have some say in the making [of] the laws they have to live under."[157]

It was perhaps this kind of principled stand that won the "old stovemounter" continued re-election. His 1911 and 1914 victories were easily accomplished, with majorities of 650 and 900. Upon the completion of his successful 1914 campaign, the *Industrial Banner* declared that the recent political struggle served "effectually to demonstrate that the political machinery of the workers in Hamilton is the best class conscious organization in Ontario." Socialists like Toronto's Jimmy Simpson or Phillips Thompson might disagree, pointing an accusatory finger at Studholme's deficiencies and the ILP's failure to establish a programmatic conception of social change. But Studholme's political success was nevertheless an established reality exceptional in Ontario, demonstrating to the country that Hamilton workers stood capable of unity and independence, defiantly standing against Conservatives and Liberals to send one of their own class to the Ontario legislature.[158]

This dramatic illustration of class unity, in fact, was to be the most significant contribution of the political victories of 1906-14. In the legislature itself Studholme's hands were effectively tied. He backed a number of causes, articulating labour's grievances concerning assisted immigration and prison contract labour; introduced a bill attempting to prohibit telephone girls from working more than five hours a day; pushed for the establishment of institutions of technical education; and argued vehemently over a bill to amend the public health act, attempting to secure "fair play" for Hamilton and its citizens.[159] His efforts to secure eight-hour legislation, a fair wages bill, and a workmen's compensation act helped to popularize reforms which admittedly contributed towards material benefits and securities for Ontario workers. His presence may have pushed some industrialists towards reform, and his utterances were always grist for the newspapers' mill. In March 1909 Studholme actually triumphed in blocking the proposed extension of a purely speculative railway enterprise.[160] But in general Studholme's speeches were lost on empty benches or deaf ears. His was a lone voice in the parliamentary wilderness. Commenting on the 1911 budget, the Hamilton labour representative noted that "not one member, on either side of the House, had put in one word for the wage worker." Praising Colonel Hendrie, Hamilton West's Conservative member, the stove-mounter "experienced the new sensation of hearing the legislative halls ring with hearty applause at his utterances." Studholme's 1910 effort to introduce a woman suffrage bill epitomized his problems as a spokesman for radical causes. When no seconder could be found, the bill died a quick death.[161]

There was something almost sad in the isolated, ritualistic presence of the "little Labor Man" in the Ontario House, periodically pounding the table with an exclamation of discontent: "I care not for your politics. The question is are you honest? Are you square? Can you make good laws? And if you can, will you?" Apparently one of his proudest moments came in April 1909, when he was the recipient of Premier Whitney's praise, words that obviously meant a great deal to the "independent" workingman. His face beaming, Studholme ejaculated across the floor of the House, "Thank you, Mr. Prime minister, thank you."[162]

Labour's political victories were hardly the signal of a fully realized class consciousness, nor did they usher in many significant reforms for the city's workers. Studholme exercised his greatest impact on a local level: in the Trades and Labor Council he was an honoured speaker; his charity work was constantly praised. "It isn't every Trades Council in the province that can claim M.L.A.'s," noted the *Industrial Banner*.[163] This local significance is hardly surprising, for the rise of the ILP was itself a political expression of the various forms of independent or semi-autonomous working-class organization that had been built and consolidated in Hamilton during the previous forty-five years. Studholme himself, a recently arrived immigrant in the area during the uprising of 1872, prominent in the Knights of Labor, and active in the new unionist organizational spurt of the opening decade of the twentieth century, represented this lineage. The ILP's ultimate successes rested firmly on the bedrock of solidarity conditioned by the class conflict that had dominated life in the working-class community for decades; defining much of the experience of the new unionism, this continuity in the history of confrontation cultivated class feelings that emerged most visibly in the street railway strike of 1906. And it was as a symbolic expression of this class unity that the stove-mounter served as labour's representative from 1906 to 1919.[164]

There were, to be sure, significant cracks appearing in the wall of class unity. The most significant fissure was opened with the influx of unskilled and skilled immigrant labour into the city in the post-1896 years. Labour, of course, consistently opposed this phenomenon, especially when it was assisted by government aid, employers, or the Salvation Army.[165] Labour's resentment flared in 1908-1909, years of severe economic dislocation. Samuel Landers attacked British immigrants as "raw meat" enticed to the city to strengthen the employers' hand; and the Trades and Labor Council condemned the actions of English emigration societies, which were openly advertising in British newspapers, "stating that there was an opening in the Hamilton factories for a large number of workers and general labourers." One recently arrived immigrant noted that "we were told that a thousand men were wanted in Hamilton at once, so I came."[166] While the Hamilton workers' anger grew in the face of this deluge, labour unity suffered a setback. "An Undesirable Pauper," himself a victim of false promises, chastised Landers for blaming those who often suffered most. The real problem, he argued, was not pauper immigration, but employer subterfuges and the lack of work.[167]

More telling was the growing rift between skilled English-speaking workers and the unorganized "horde" of "foreign unskilled labour" pouring into Hamilton's large industrial plants.[168] In many factories foreign workers were merely numbered, the impersonality of the capitalistic labour market denying these workers the individuality of a name. When some of the newcomers suffered fatal injuries on the job, their relatives remained ignorant of their deaths, notification being impossible because of the enforced anonymity of the labourer. As foreign workmen sought to remedy this "evil," they were left to struggle alone, the skilled workers affiliated with the Trades Council taking little interest in the grievances of the immigrant community.[169]

Absent too was any significant support for the series of spontaneous, often violent, strikes waged by ethnic workers, usually Italians.[170] In fact, as we have seen, skilled workers often refused to work with foreign-speaking labourers, striking to preserve specific jobs as the exclusive terrain of the English-speaking. As the *Hamilton Spectator* published sensationalist, front-page accounts of the violence of immigrant life and the emergence of the Black Hand Society in the city, skilled workers increasingly viewed the ethnic community with disdain.[171] This attitude surfaced in a conflict at the Hamilton Iron and Steel Company. Between 500 and 1,000 immigrants walked off the job 1 April 1910, demanding a four-cent-an-hour wage increase. Fearing violence, the company called in the police, but a number of old trade unionists laughed at the prospect of a struggle. To them, the foreign element lacked the "nerve" and staying power to stand up to authority. Led by agitators and unscrupulous "interpreters," the ethnic workers were likened to sheep, an unthinking "mob" following blindly the utterings of demagogues. The skilled would have nodded knowingly when the strikers returned to work in defeat four days later.[172]

In another area, also, the skilled tended to isolate themselves from class brothers. Between 1908 and 1914 many workers were thrown out of work in periodic crises and recessions. These workers built mass movements of the unemployed, three hundred to six hundred strong, composed of English and foreign-speaking labourers. In 1908 over six hundred petitioned the city for work. Disturbances were often feared, and a 1914 headline tells of the tactics employed: "Workless Men Besieged Mayor— Bombarded His House This Morning Early." But the skilled workers, despite their own job insecurity and enforced idleness, conspicuously avoided involvement. Instead, the movement developed in a leadership vacuum. Robert Roadhouse and Lockhart M. Gordon sought to redirect the men, moving them towards an understanding "that nothing would result from such ... demonstration [s] and advised them that ... the principles of socialism would cover their case." But the out-of-work labourers were hardly receptive to this message, and were quick to point out that they wanted work, not theory. The Industrial Workers of the World, in town in 1914 to agitate among the unemployed, likely faced similar resistance.[173]

Skilled workers and the new unionism which they led thus remained isolated from important developments among segments of the labouring poor. This was one of the chief differences between the British and North American experiences. For in England it was unskilled London dockers, led by socialists like John Burns, Tom Mann, and Ben Tillett, who served notice that "the lower ranks of labour ... can organize themselves at least as well and be at least as true to their class, as the aristocracy of labour."[174] In Hamilton, however, the new unionism was essentially a continuation of the craft experience, drawing elements of the unskilled and semiskilled into its ranks around specific community or workplace issues. The record of achievement, on the shop-floor and in the political realm, rested firmly upon a bedrock of class unity. We cannot comprehend the widespread support freely given to the street railway strikers and the exceptional successes of Allan Studholme if we ignore this class unity. Nevertheless, this solidarity had its blind spots, particularly in the case of the immigrant workers, and the full realization of class unity was thwarted in these years. Distinctions between skilled and unskilled, foreign and English, had meant little in the history of working-class organization in nineteenth-century Hamilton, a city which was ethnically relatively homogenous, where the unskilled followed the forceful leadership of the skilled in 1872 and united with them in the Knights of Labor in the 1880s. But the

1890-1914 years saw a changed context. At the same time that industrial capitalism was levelling distinctions among workers, reducing the importance of skill, cultivating a similarity of experience that pushed workers towards class unity, the influx of "alien" labour introduced yet another division in class ranks. As the new unionism groped towards embracing all workers, it simultaneously retreated from the immigrant and the chronically unemployed, many of whom were foreign-speaking. These years of the new unionism thus highlight something of the ambivalence of the craft experience, its limitations as well as its impressive accomplishments.

The new unionism would not bear real fruit until the World War I years, when Hamilton workers, insulated from reprisal by wartime needs, would experience a transformation of consciousness, realizing their power in a series of work stoppages.[175] "If the machinists of the world were to strike today," said the oldest member of Hamilton's International Association of Machinists, "this war, large as it is, would immediately cease, the world would stand still, because this is a war of machines and an age of the same."[176] During the post-reconstruction years, however, in the aftermath of the upheavals of 1919, forces at work in the prewar years began to take their toll.[177] By the mid-1920s unionism in North America had been stopped in its tracks, the victim of a new, reinvigorated open shop drive and the blending of the principles of scientific management with the practices of personnel management and paternalistic welfare programs.[178] When Roetheisberger and Dickson conducted their experiments at Western Electric's Hawthorne Works, they found the worker "at the bottom level of a highly stratified organization," his "established routines of work, his cultural traditions of craftsmanship, [and] his personal interrelations" all "at the mercy of technical specialists."[179] The situation was likely very much the same in Hamilton's plants; after more than sixty years of struggle, capitalist control of the workplace had finally been attained. What is remarkable is not that this development occurred, but rather that Hamilton's workers resisted for so long, retaining much of their power in the pre-World War I years.

Part IV

CONCLUSION

Social life is essentially practical. All mysteries which mislead theory to mysticism find their rational solution in human practice and in the comprehension of this practice.

Karl Marx (1845)

Strikes, trusts, taxes, socialism, tariffs, and banking bulk a good deal larger in the public mind than the authenticity of John's gospel or the wherefore of the shyness of Hegel.

O. D. Skelton to Adam Shortt (1907)

8

Dimensions of Continuity and Change

> All continuity of history means is after all perpetual change, and it is not hard to see that we have changed with a vengeance, and thereby established our claim to be the continuers of history.
>
> William Morris (1889)

Hamilton changed greatly—one could almost say with a vengeance—in the years from 1860 to 1914. The contrast between the earlier and later periods is conveyed visually in depictions of the city in 1853 and 1908. Robert Whale's landscape, the *General View of Hamilton*, shows a sleepy town nestled between an escarpment and a lake. Fifty-five years later, etchings and photographs reveal the stark, angular contours of a setting dominated by factories, mills, and smoke stacks. As early as 1873 the city's destiny, purpose, and place had been recorded in verse.

> The busy hum of industry upon her streets is heard,
> And Science vies with Art, and Toil brings home a Fair reward,
> Her artizans have earned a place upon the scroll of fame,
> And Europe's sons have learned to pay respect unto her name.

The industrial city had arrived.[1]

It was in the context of this great change that continuities in certain realms of the lives of skilled workers assumed an importance. What does this study of the years 1860-1914 tell us about skilled workingmen in Hamilton? Answering this question demands, at the outset, a recapitulation of the aims and purposes of this book.

A glance at the preceding pages might suggest that they have inadvertently demonstrated the truth of G. M. Trevelyan's often-quoted aphorism. Social history, claimed Trevelyan, was little more than "history with the politics left out."[2] And it is true that politics have figured only peripherally in this study. There are other obvious gaps. The family, for instance, has been systematically ignored, as has working-class involvement in Hamilton's churches. These omissions, however, do not flow from any conception of the proper terrain of social history, but rather from the interpretive, evidential, and organizational problems that the inclusion of such subjects would have posed for this particular study.

Treatment of Hamilton working-class politics would have necessitated an exploration of early involvement in the Conservative or Tory party; a discussion of the attraction of Liberal or Grit reformism throughout the Victorian and Edwardian periods; and an attempt to chronicle the rise of independent working-class political activity, initially strong in the 1880s and then resurfacing in the early years of the twentieth century.[3] The detailed examination of local campaigns, coupled with the complex interaction of community concerns and national issues, would have demanded a lengthy study that would have effectively limited the inquiry to a discussion of traditional political activity. It therefore seemed appropriate to relegate political involvement to the margins of the work, introducing working-class politics only when it drew close to the processes of culture and conflict.

A discussion of the family, similarly, seemed outside the realm of the feasible. Family history, to be done effectively, demands painstaking structural analysis, resting upon elaborate statistical data illustrating the composition, size, ethnic makeup, and wealth distribution of a community's households. It must also consider marital and fertility patterns, stages in the life cycle, and the meaning of such complex human activities as boarding. This, indeed, is what most family history, as it presently stands, has concentrated upon; Michael B. Katz's lengthy treatment of the Hamilton family is cast unambiguously within this mould.[4] But Katz's analysis, set within the confines of the 1851-71 census poles, is frozen in time, illustrating one of the central problems of a method demanding laborious utilization of manuscript census material. For family history is nothing if it is not probed over time, where the life processes of several generations lend meaning to the interpretation of the role and importance of the family.[5] Finally, family history should be informed by a sensitivity to the wider cultural framework within which it evolves. A history of the family that neglects to place the institution within the context of a larger social history leaves important questions unanswered and ignores crucial social processes. Family history, in short, is an enterprise unto itself, and is best left to those skilled in the art.[6]

Also missing is any effort to deal with the religious life of Hamilton's workers. This, of course, could ultimately prove to be a major deficiency of this study, for the church may have served as a central institution breeding passivity, acquiescence, and accommodation. Or, looking in another direction, it may have lent force to an emerging critique of the social order and buttressed the workingman's developing sense of injustice in the world of the industrial-capitalist city. For the late nineteenth century, when the Knights of Labor assembly to some extent served as the workingman's church, there is abundant evidence to sustain the argument that Hamilton's workers avoided the established churches, patronizing those institutions that catered to their class needs with "labour sermons". But by the early years of the twentieth century all this may have changed, and one source suggests that the church played an important role in integrating British workers into the social structure of pre-World War I Hamilton.[7] More research may tell us much, but even the most diligent of historians will likely be forced to admit that this sphere of working-class life is shrouded in obscurity and ambivalence.

Enough, then, about what this book has not tried to do. What it has attempted is to use the experience of Hamilton's skilled workers in the years 1860-1914 as a prism through which to view the processes of working-class culture and working-class protest, or class conflict. Within this general purpose an effort has been made to retain a precarious balance between "a sense of place" (the specific community focus of Hamilton)[8] and a wider context. While it is a difficult task, the preservation of this balance is essential if the community study is to retain force as a detailed historical inquiry, transcending the narrow boundaries of antiquarianism. The results can tell us a great deal about culture and conflict in the nineteenth-century city.

The Hamilton experience, for instance, sheds some light on questions associated with the notion of the labour aristocracy: a conception of the skilled worker emphasizing his privileged status and sectional consciousness; a judgement of the craft worker's inability to contribute to the revolutionary struggles of the proletariat.[9] H. M. Hyndman, doctrinaire leader of the Social-Democratic Federation in Britain, echoed the sentiments of such prominent revolutionaries as Friedrich Engels and V. I. Lenin: "Trade Unionists are, all told," he said, "but a small fraction of the total working population. They constitute, in fact, an aristocracy of labour who, in view of the bitter struggle now drawing nearer and nearer, cannot be said to be other than a hindrance to that complete organization of the proletariat which alone can obtain for the workers their proper control over their own labour."[10] And yet among the skilled workers of Hamilton one would be hard-pressed to isolate a particular stratum that conformed to the requirements of this pejorative conception. Indeed, the Hamilton craft experience seems to indicate that Rev. Charles Stelzle's advice to the city's workers in 1912 had a long history of popular endorsement:

> Talk about the 'aristocracy of labor'. There's a sense in which labor has a right to be proud, because it is producing something worthwhile, instead of grafting on the rest of the world. But this is the

only reason it has for counting itself of better stuff than the parasite who lives on the labor of others. Any sort of aristocracy that causes one workingman to look down upon another workingman because he happens to wear a different kind of working clothes, or because he earns a few cents less a day, or because he has a job which compels him to do some things which most of us don't like to do — such aristocracy is a curse to labor and the workers should be heartily ashamed of it.[11]

There is no denying the distinct social and cultural place of skilled workers in working-class communities of the late nineteenth and early twentieth centuries.[12] Nor can the existence of a hierarchical arrangement of trades and job classifications, buttressed by wage differentials, be written out of the picture of the world of work.[13] Nevertheless, cultural separation, often expressed in terms of the skilled worker's attachment to respectability, self-help, and social improvement, coupled with preferential wage rates, do not a labour aristocracy make. Nor, it needs to be stressed, do contempt, however reprehensible, for the foreign-born, and isolation from the most insecure, impoverished sections of the working class. The defining characteristic of the labour aristocracy, as John Foster has made abundantly clear, and as Marxists since Lenin have always stressed, is the integration of a stratum of workers into "the structure of authority" of capitalist social relations. In Oldham, Lancashire, the process worked itself out by the 1860s in these terms: "about one-third of all male workers in cotton were acting as pacemakers and taskmasters over the rest; and in doing so made a decisive break with all previous traditions of skilled activity." Of central importance in this development was the breaking of the "restrictionist" workplace psychology of craft workers.[14]

Foster's work raises serious problems of approach, method, and conception,[15] but his study does clarify the issues involved in an understanding of the labour aristocracy. No longer can the hierarchical place and privilege of skill be judged defining characteristics of the labour aristocracy. If they could, we would locate an aristocracy among the unskilled, where carters and teamsters stood a rank above the municipal labourers and sewer workers (and often looked down their noses at them). In the shoemaking trade, the lasters, hanging on to their skilled status into the 1890s, might well appear as an aristocracy of one craft.[16] But if we see the critical and determining feature of the labour aristocracy as its integration into the system of capitalist authority, its role as pacesetter and taskmaster on the shop-floor, and its explicit place in stifling labour militancy, we will come closer to a true understanding of what Hyndman, Lenin, and Engels may have meant by the term.

In this sense, there was no labour aristocracy in Hamilton. Some Hamilton crafts, primarily printers and bricklayers, did tend to adopt a more conservative stance than others, remaining on the fringes of the working-class movement's oppositional culture. Even they, however, were necessarily thrust into the arena of class conflict by modern developments. Both trades were well represented in the early Central Labor Union and Trades and Labor Council; both crafts contributed important personnel to the Knights of Labor and the new unionism. The continuing tradition of craft control, the persistent restriction of output practised by all trades, and the threat of seasonal unemployment, short time, or economic downturn meant that conflict, not collaboration, was the rule in Hamilton. Moreover, this experience blurred the distinctions between skilled and unskilled over time, the craft experience becoming "less self-contained than it had been."[17]

Though the cultural experience was undoubtedly ambivalent, drawing Hamilton craftsmen into contact with petty shopkeepers, clerks, professionals, merchants, and subcontracting masters in the friendly society hall, the mechanics' institute, or the engine house, there is little evidence to indicate that this experience cultivated accommodation with the emerging bourgeois order. And on the baseball diamond and in the craft union there was certainly more than a hint of a semi-autonomous workingman's culture, relatively immune to the class manipulation of the city's elite. Subcontracting was practised in the Great Western Railway shops and other manufacturing concerns from the 1860s, but there is *no* suggestion that skilled workers ever developed as pacesetters or taskmasters on any significant scale. Individuals did, of course, climb out of the working class; often it was those workers who were potential leaders of class actions. Henry B. Witton was able to take the political route; the president of the Trades Assembly in 1872, the printer Cornelius Donovan, ended his days as a school inspector, elevated to the position through experience gained in supervising separate schools for the Catholic community. Thomas Towers, William Bews, William Vale, and Edward Williams — skilled workers who had helped to direct the Knights of Labor upsurge of the 1880s — all settled into comfortable patronage positions at the municipal or provincial level. This process of upward mobility was openly acknowledged to be a stumbling block inhibiting labour's political success. While a mainstay of capitalist stability, it hardly demonstrates the existence of a section of the working class actively functioning in the interests of capital. In short, one must look long and hard to find anything resembling the fully accommodated labour aristocrat in Hamilton, integrated into the structure of industrial-capitalist authority.[18]

It was, above all else, the persistent involvement of Hamilton's skilled workers in the class struggle that ill-suited them for the role of the labour aristocrat. Polemicizing against Sidney Webb and the Fabians in 1889, William Morris wrote: "This is the barrier that they will not be able to pass, so long as they are in their present minds, *the acknowledgement of the class war. . . .* It is most important that young socialists should have this fact of the class-war always before them. It explains pre-history, and in the present gives us the only solid hope for the future."[19] Morris could have been speaking to modern historians, who all too quickly push aside the respectable working class of the late nineteenth and early twentieth centuries, assuming that this stratum had rather painlessly adapted to the social relations of industrial capitalism. It was never quite that simple.

Hamilton craft workers' involvement in class conflict also illuminates other questions of interest to the historian. The issue of control, we have seen, was of central importance in the history of nineteenth- and early twentieth-century workplace confrontations. A recent polemic, penned under the pseudonym Jean Monds, attacks two historians, David Montgomery and James Hinton, whose work has centred on the practice of workers' control. Monds's critique takes Montgomery and Hinton to task for their imprecise terminology, arguing that what they have referred to as workers' control was in fact nothing more than job control. Workers' control, contends Monds, involves the full realization of revolutionary class consciousness and has a limited historical experience, confined to the rising of industrial workers in Russia in the 1917-21 years. What Montgomery and Hinton have termed workers' control, however, was but "one of the many aspects of the development of class consciousness" and "is really equivalent to the defensive devices built up by workers through years of struggle at the point of production." By refusing to explore the political context within which workers' control existed, claims Monds, Montgomery and Hinton have succumbed to the "workerist illusion"; the result has been a nostalgic and romantic version of working-class history filtered through the lens of syndicalism. By implying that "the struggle for power at the point of production leads to advances in class consciousness in and of itself and without the intervention of political organization in the working class," the historians have given birth to a "new economism." The real question, and one which they ignore, claims Monds, is: "How does the workers' ability to 'control' what takes place in the factory lead to political power for the working class?" As a conscious attempt to reassert basic Leninist conceptions of trade union and Bolshevik party, this assessment of the limitations of workers' control, and of the historians' depiction of that phenomenon, vindicates the classic polemic, *What Is To Be Done?*.[20] It is as though Monds desires to remind all concerned that "Class political consciousness can be brought to the workers' *only from without*, that is, only from outside the economic struggle, from outside the sphere of relations between workers and employers."[21]

Monds's attack on the "new economism" clarifies a number of issues. His differentiation between workers' control and job control, for instance, is little more than semantical hair-splitting, but it does raise the question of the relationship between workplace control and political struggle. As our discussion of Hamilton workingmen suggests, the practice of nine-teenth-century workers' control was far from revolutionary. As a culture of the shop-floor, workers' control demanded no explicit opposition to the status quo of industrial-capitalist society, and survived well into the twentieth century in the absence of any revolutionary working-class movement.[22] Indeed, there was much in the tradition of nineteenth-century variants of workers' control that was essentially conservative, including the emergence of bureaucratized *union* control of strikes, a development of obvious importance in terms of its institutionalized ability to stifle militancy.[23]

With the development of the new unionism in the early years of the twentieth century, the conservative aspects of the long-standing practices of workplace control seemed to be given a new stimulus. Antirevolution-ary labour spokesmen — Gompers, Green, Hutcheson, and others — came to positions of power and authority, exercising their influence in the upper echelons of the American Federation of Labor. This development had its local manifestations, as men like Samuel Landers assumed leader-ship roles, proclaiming: "Hamilton, although one of the best organized, is one of the most conservative labor cities in America. While organized labor in Hamilton would never think of relinquishing the right to strike, yet strikes are rarely resorted to. The men In whose hands the trade unions of the city are in are wise and careful leaders. This fact is known everywhere, and for years Hamilton has had a reputation as a conserva-tive labor, or 'no strike' city, and this has perhaps been one of the prime reasons for so many large industries locating here during the last few years."[24] This kind of statement has often been cited as proof of the con-servative tendencies of the labour movement and as an indication of the social and political views of labour's aristocracy; for some historians it is an indication of the essentially corporatist outlook of twentieth-century workers.[25] In fact, however, such statements were often purely rhetorical, the expression of an ideological fantasy or a misplaced optimism concern-ing labour's pragmatic and reasonable approach to the relationships of the workplace.

Landers's statement, of course, flies directly in the face of the Hamil-ton experience. A city that experienced at least ninety-two strikes and lockouts in the brief period 1901-14, including the dramatic 1906 con-frontation between street railway workers and their employer, was hardly a "no strike" city. And the struggle for control figured prominently in these industrial conflicts, just as it had in the last decades of the nine-teenth century.[26] To ignore this persistent practice of workplace control is thus to close one's eyes to one of the major forces propelling workers into battle with employers. The issue of control — all questions of economism aside, and all arguments about its nonrevolutionary character tabled — can be seen as the critical determinant in many Victorian and Edwardian class struggles. Without these struggles, the working-class movement would have been deprived of valuable lessons on the nature of class relationships in a capitalist society, lessons that had to be learned if revolutionary class consciousness and political organization were to develop. The reality of workers' control must be confronted, and it is the task of both revolutionary and historian to understand its significance.[27]

In coming to grips with the nature of workers' control, the historian is challenged by the delicate balance between continuity and change, for the revolutionary variant of workers' control would first appear in the war and postwar years, 1919 witnessing minor uprisings across the country, culminating in the Winnipeg General Strike.[28] Out of the nonrevolutionary practices of the past would emerge a consciousness of the potential of workers' control. A machinist tells the story well:

> In the machine shop we have a lot of belts ... and sometimes these belts break, but we've got fasteners there, and you join them up again, and this running around especially — pupupup, pupup ... comes to this part where it's joined up, you know ... and you make up a little ditty to this particular thing. It presses on your mind so much you know, you can't avoid it ... and its just like — 'The boss is — robbing me,' 'The boss is — robbing me' — and this is exactly the noise ... and you make up a little saying to whatever noise it is ... And I think this is why so many machinists are involved in what you might call the revolutionary movement, because you know darn well you're being robbed. I mean, very often the boss — a customer will walk in and I'm standing with the boss and — 'How much is this?', and the boss says 'Thirty dollars,' and you know darned well that you made this in about three hours and you probably got about seven or eight dollars for it, and the boss pockets the rest, and you've done all the work. ... And that is my outlook, ... what we've got to get away from is the ownership of the means of production by a small number of people.[29]

This was a consciousness nurtured in the mundane context of workplace control; but the ultimate realization was far from commonplace, a testimony of how change emerged from basic continuities in the practices of workers' control.

Finally, the essential importance of continuity and change in the history of workers' control is underlined by developments of the mid-1970s, as Stelco workers battled contracts stipulating that "The Management of the plant and the direction of the working forces including the right to direct, plan and control plant operations, and to schedule working hours, and the right to hire, promote, demote, transfer, suspend or discharge employees for just cause, or to release employees because of lack of work or for other legitimate reasons, or the right to introduce new and improved methods or facilities and to manage the plant in the traditional manner is vested exclusively in the Company, subject to the express provisions of the agreement.''[30] Working-class discontents under industrial capitalism have exhibited a fundamental continuity, for the resentments of the 1970s bear a striking resemblance to the grievances of the 1870s.

These dimensions of continuity and change pervade much of our discussion of the skilled workers of Hamilton. Against the background of economic change, the associational life of the community exhibited a fundamental continuity, a process adding stability to working-class lives disrupted by harsh change. On the basis of this coherence skilled workers adapted to the changed rules of the game in the wake of industrial capitalist development, defining a conception of workplace control that allowed them a measure of autonomy in the "dark satanic mills" of early Canadian capitalism. Working-class thought, too, adapted to the capitalist transformation of the nineteenth century, moving away from the producer ideology and its manufacturer-mechanic alliance towards visions of the world that recognized class polarization and social inequality. The process of class conflict also reflected basic continuities, as well as change. While working-class resistance to the disciplines and development of industrial capitalism provided the continuous foundation, new patterns of conflict emerged, developing through struggles over time, building on the organizational gains achieved by the Knights of Labor and the new unionism of the prewar years.

It is appropriate to conclude with a brief note on one Hamilton workingman whose life reflected these processes of continuity and change. John Stephen McDonough was born in Hamilton in the year 1857. A blacksmith by training, he was apparently displaced from his trade and found work in a dairy. His ties to the community were likely complex: as a practising Catholic he must have been part of a cultural milieu structured around the church and buttressed by the experience of ethnicity; as a father of five children his family was certainly of some significance to him; and as a member of the Knights of Labor he probably had strong ties to the working-class community, a community that had been moving slowly but steadily against its employers since McDonough's birth. The forces tending to root McDonough in Hamilton, acquiescent and passive, resigned to a life of respectable toil, cannot be underestimated. Yet on 27 October 1891 John Stephen McDonough, professing his belief in cooperation, applied for entrance to the Kaweah Co-operative Commonwealth in the United States. Willing to pay the entrance fee of $100 and move his family to California, McDonough, a man of middle-age, must have been thoroughly disillusioned with life in a late nineteenth-century industrial-capitalist city. He admitted to reading Edward Bellamy's *Looking Backward*, implying that it was this text that moved him to such a course of action. But it was not likely the printed word that prodded this displaced craftsman to apply for admission to a "new world utopia." John Stephen McDonough had simply looked backward over thirty-four years of his life in Hamilton, Ontario. He apparently did not like what he saw.[31]

Notes

ABBREVIATIONS
HS	*Hamilton Spectator*
HT	*Hamilton Times*
PAC	Public Archives of Canada
POL	*Palladium of Labor*

PREFACE

1. Here one can consult no better introduction than the works of E. P. Thompson and David Montgomery. See especially Thompson, *The Making of the English Working Class* (Harmondsworth, Middlesex: Pelican, 1968); Montgomery, *Beyond Equality: Labor and the Radical Republicans, 1862-1872* (New York: Knopf, 1967); Montgomery, "The 'New Unionism' and the Transformation of Workers' Consciousness, 1909-1922," *Journal of Social History* 7 (Summer 1974): 509-29; Montgomery, "Workers' Control of Machine Production in the Nineteenth Century," *Labor History* 17 (Fall 1976): 485-509.

2. Bryan D. Palmer, "Most Uncommon Common Men: Craft and Culture in Historical Perspective," *Labour/Le Travailleur* 1 (1976): 5-31. Cf. Palmer, "Class, Conception, and Conflict: The Thrust for Efficiency, Managerial Views of Labor, and Working Class Rebellion, 1903-1922," *Review of Radical Political Economics* 7 (Summer 1975): 31-49; Craig Heron and Bryan D. Palmer, "Through the Prism of the Strike: Industrial Conflict in Southern Ontario, 1901-1914," *Canadian Historical Review* 58 (December 1977): 423-58.

3. Note the discussion in Harry Braverman, *Labor and Monopoly Capital: The Degradation of Work in the Twentieth Century* (New York: Monthly Review, 1974). Chap. 7, focusing on these developments, is thus not meant to be a definitive treatment of the 1890-1914 period. Rather, it is intended to highlight the processes of continuity and change. A full discussion awaits Craig Heron's forthcoming Dalhousie dissertation on Hamilton workers in the years 1896 to 1929.

4. An introduction to the Katz enterprise is provided in Michael B. Katz, *The People of Hamilton, Canada West: Family and Class in a Mid-Nineteenth Century City* (Cambridge, Mass.: Harvard University Press, 1975).

5. Mr. Katz and I have had our differences. See my review, "Modernizing History," *Bulletin of the Committee on Canadian Labour History* 2 (Autumn 1976): 16-25, and the following exchange, pp. 25-31.

6. For the kind of structuralist approach I am drawn to see Peter Friedlander, *The Emergence of UAW Local 229, Hamtramck, Michigan: A Study in Class and Culture* (Pittsburgh: University of Pittsburgh Press, 1975). The nonspecialist will find Jean Piaget, *Structuralism* (New York: Basic Books, 1970), a useful introduction. Claude Lévi-Strauss, *Structural Anthropology* (New York: Basic Books, 1963), is perhaps the best collection for the historian. A piercing critique of structuralism is found in Raol Makarius, "Structuralism — Science or Ideology," in Ralph Milliband and John Saville, eds., *The Socialist Register, 1974* (London:

Merlin Press, 1974), pp. 189-225. For a rejection of Althusserian structuralism see Leszek Kolakowski, "Althusser's Marx," in *The Socialist Register, 1971* (London: Merlin Press, 1971), pp. 111-28.

7. On Lévi-Strauss's historical approach see "History and Anthropology," *Structural Anthropology*, pp. 1-30. For Althusser's antihistorical approach see Louis Althusser and Etienne Balibar, *Reading Capital* (New York: Pantheon, 1970), p. 110. E. P. Thompson, "The Poverty of Theory: or An Orrery of Errors," in *The Poverty of Theory and Other Essays* (London: Merlin Press, 1978), pp. 193-397, came to my attention too late to influence these pages. As a relentless and devastating assault upon Althusserian structuralism, it suggests the need for a nuanced appreciation of the above, as well as the importance of what follows.

8. Richard Cobb, "History by Numbers," *Tour de France* (London: Duckworth, 1976), p. 8.

9. Elizabeth Fox-Genovese and Eugene D. Genovese, "The Political Crisis of Social History: A Marxian Perspective," *Journal of Social History* 10 (Winter 1976): 205-20.

10. E. P. Thompson, "The Long Revolution I," *New Left Review* 9 (May-June 1961): 30.

11. "An Interview with E. P. Thompson," *Radical History Review* 3 (Fall 1976): 16.

12. Thompson, "The Long Revolution I," p. 33. Cf. Thompson, "The Long Revolution II," *New Left Review* 10 (July-August 1961): 34-39.

13. See the writings of E. P. Thompson, as follows: "The Peculiarities of the English," in John Saville and Ralph Milliband, eds., *The Socialist Register, 1965* (London: Merlin Press, 1965), pp. 311-62; *Making of the English Working Class*; "The Moral Economy of the English Crowd in the Eighteenth Century," *Past & Present* 50 (February 1971): 76-136; "Time, Work-Discipline, and Industrial Capitalism," *Past & Present* 38 (December 1967): 56-97; "Patrician Society, Plebeian Culture," *Journal of Social History* 7 (Summer 1974): 382-405; *Whigs and Hunters: The Origin of the Black Act* (New York: Pantheon, 1975). See also Douglas Hay et al., *Albion's Fatal Tree: Crime and Society in Eighteenth-Century England* (New York: Pantheon 1975). For brief discussions of the importance of Thompson's work see Tim Patterson, "Notes on the Historical Application of Marxist Cultural Theory," *Science & Society* 39 (Fall 1975): 258-60; Harold Perkin, "Social History in Britain," *Journal of Social History* 10 (Winter 1976): 129-43. I have attempted a brief assessment of Thompson, relating his historical writing to his political convictions and his break from Stalinism in the 1950s in Palmer, "E. P. Thompson: Marxism, Humanism, and History," paper presented at New York State Association of European Historians, 28th Annual Meeting, 6-7 Oct. 1978. The quotation is from Thompson, "An Open Letter to Leszek Kolakowski," in Milliband and Saville, eds., *The Socialist Register, 1973* (London: Merlin Press, 1973), p. 25. This polemic introduces themes fully developed in Thompson, "The Poverty of Theory."

14. See Thompson, "Open Letter," pp. 21, 27, 29; Thompson, *Making of the English Working Class*, esp. pp. 9-11; Thompson, "Peculiarities of the English," pp. 319, 321, 359; and Thompson, "Romanticism, Utopianism and Moralism: the Case of William Morris," *New Left Review* 99 (September-October 1976): 83-111.

15. See Michelle Perrot, "The Strengths and Weaknesses of French Social History," *Journal of Social History* 10 (Winter 1976): 167; James R. Green, "Be-

havioralism and Class Analysis: A Review Essay on Methodology and Ideology," *Labor History* 13 (Winter 1972): 89-106; Herbert G. Gutman, *Work, Culture, and Society in Industrializing America* (New York: Knopf, 1976), pp. xi-xiv; E. J. Hobsbawm, "From Social History to the History of Society," *Daedalus* 100 (Winter 1971): 20-45; and Hobsbawm's remarks in his review of Zygmunt Bauman, *Between Class and Elite: The Evolution of the British Labour Movement; A Sociological Study* (Manchester: Manchester University Press, 1972), in *The Guardian*, 28 December 1972.

16. The most explicit statement remains Neil J. Smelser, "Sociological History: The Industrial Revolution and the British Working-Class Family," *Journal of Social History* 1 (Fall 1967): 17-35. Cf. Peter Laslett, *The World We Have Lost* (London: Methuen, 1971), pp. 242-253; Clifford Geertz, *The Social History of An Indonesian Town* (Cambridge, Mass.: M.I.T. Press, 1965), esp. p. 2; Bauman, *Between Class and Elite*, p. ix; Tom Nairn, "The English Working Class," *New Left Review* 24 (March-April 1964): 43-57; Martin Blumer, "Sociology and History: Some Recent Trends," *Sociology* 8 (January 1974): 138-50; Gilbert Shapiro, "Prospects for a Scientific Social History," *Journal of Social History* 10 (Winter 1976): 196-204; Fernand Braudel, *Capitalism and Material Life, 1400-1800* (New York: Harper and Row, 1973). A study exemplifying the approach of sociological history is Immanuel Wallerstein, *The Modern World System: Capitalist Agriculture and the Origins of the World Economy in the Sixteenth Century* (New York: Academic Press, 1974).

17. On the blurring of distinction between sociological and social history see Mario S. De Pillis, "Trends in American Social History and the Possibilities of Behavioral Approaches," *Journal of Social History* 1 (Fall 1967): 37-60. Sociological history has been practised by both Marxists and non-Marxists. See Althusser and Balibar, *Reading Capital*, pp. 110, 282; Herbert Blumer, "Early Industrialization and the Laboring Class," *The Sociological Quarterly* (January 1960), reprinted as Institute for Industrial Relations Reprint No. 150 (Berkeley, 1960).

18. See for instance the recent attempt toward a Marxist synthesis in Perry Anderson, *Passages from Antiquity to Feudalism* (London: New Left Books, 1974); Anderson, *Lineages of the Absolutist State* (London: New Left Books, 1974). Other important works within this tradition include Barrington Moore, *Social Origins of Dictatorship and Democracy: Lord and Peasant in the Making of the Modern World* (Boston: Beacon Press, 1966); Karl Polanyi, *The Great Transformation* (Boston: Beacon Press, 1957); V. I. Lenin, *The Development of Capitalism in Russia* (Moscow: Progress Publishers, 1964). An impressive recent effort is Robert Brenner, "Agrarian Class Structure and Economic Development in Pre-Industrial Europe," *Past & Present* 70 (February 1976): 30-74.

19. Note the discussion in Zygmunt Bauman, "Marxism and the Contemporary Theory of Culture," *Co-Existence* 5 (July 1968): 161-73. Influenced by nineteenth-century German conceptions of culture, Marx's work reflected a preoccupation with the arts. For an excellent account of one aspect of Marx's work in this context see S. S. Prawer, *Karl Marx and World Literature* (London: Oxford University Press, 1976).

20. Raymond Williams, "Base and Superstructure in Marxist Cultural Theory," *New Left Review* 82 (November-December 1973): 8.

21. This, obviously, is not the place for an extensive discussion of the literature on class. These two paragraphs have drawn on E. P. Thompson, "Eighteenth-Century English Society: Class struggle without Class?" *Social History* 3

(May 1978): 146-50. The importance of class relations and class conflict, *within* a generally structuralist analysis, is stressed in Brenner, "Agrarian Class Structure," pp. 30-74; Brenner, "The Origins of Capitalist Development: a Critique of neo-Smithian Marxism," *New Left Review* 104 (July-August 1977): 25-92, esp. pp. 27, 78.

22. The contribution of social history to Marxist thought is generally ignored. See for instance Pierre Vilar, "Marxist History, a History in the Making: Towards a Dialogue with Althusser," *New Left Review* 80 (July-August 1973): 65-106.

23. R. H. Tawney, *Social History and Literature* (Leicester: Leicester University Press, 1958), p. 12.

24. See the comments in Christopher Hill, *Change and Continuity in 17th Century England* (London: Weidenfeld and Nicholson, 1974), esp. pp. 278-84; Pedro Cavalcanti and Paul Piccone, eds., *History, Philosophy and Culture in the Young Gramsci* (St. Louis: Telos Books, 1975), pp. 36-37; E. P. Thompson, "A Nice Place to Visit," *New York Review of Books* 22 (6 Feb. 1975): 34-37; Thompson, "A Special Case," *New Society* 24 (February 1972): 402-4.

CHAPTER 1

1. See the brief excerpts from a carpenter's diary in "100th Anniversary: 1846-1946," *HS*, 15 July 1946.

2. "Saturday Musings," ibid., 7 Mar. 1908.

3. H. C. Pentland, "The Development of a Capitalistic Labour Market in Canada," *Canadian Journal of Economics and Political Science* 25 (November 1959): 450-61; Pentland, "Labour and the Development of Industrial Capitalism in Canada" (Ph.D. diss., University of Toronto, 1960); Leo A. Johnson, *A History of the County of Ontario, 1615-1875* (Whitby, Ont.: County of Whitby, 1973); Jacob Spelt, *Urban Development in South-Central Ontario* (Toronto: McClelland and Stewart, 1972); James Rinehart, *The Tyranny of Work* (Toronto: Longman, 1975), pp. 23-53.

4. H. C. Pentland, "The Lachine Strike of 1843," *Canadian Historical Review* 29 (September 1949): 256; C. M. Johnson, *The Head of the Lake: A History of Wentworth County* (Hamilton: Wentworth County, 1958), pp. 182-201.

5. Pentland, "Labour and Industrial Capitalism," pp. 208-81; Wilson Benson, *Life and Adventures of Wilson Benson written by himself* (Toronto: n.p., 1876), p. 27; Gustavus Myers, *A History of Canadian Wealth* (Toronto: James Lewis and Samuel, 1972), p. 181; Michael B. Katz, *The People of Hamilton, Canada West: Family and Class in a Mid-Nineteenth Century City* (Cambridge, Mass.: Harvard University Press, 1975), pp. 176-77; Robert Storey, "Industrialization in Canada: The Emergence of the Hamilton Working Class, 1850-1870s" (M.A. thesis, Dalhousie, 1975), pp. 34, 86-96.

6. Pentland, "Lachine Strike," p. 277; Stanley B. Ryerson, *Unequal Union: Roots of Crisis in the Canadas, 1815-1873* (Toronto: Progress Books, 1973), p. 37.

7. *Census of the Canadas, 1851-1852* (Quebec: Lovell and Lamoureaux, 1853), II, 42.

8. On the depression of the late 1850s see Katz, *People of Hamilton*, pp. 5, 46, 75-77, 127, 199, 273; Douglas McCalla, "The Commercial Politics of the Toronto Board of Trade, 1850-1860," *Canadian Historical Review* 50 (March

1969): 64; *Hamilton Weekly Times*, 20 Feb. 1858; *HS*, 25 Sept., 31 Oct. 1861, 19 Jan., 3 June 1863.

9. Cited in Steven Langdon, *The Emergence of the Canadian Working Class Movement* (Toronto: New Hogtown Press, 1975), p. 3.

10. On the impact of the Civil War see *HS*, 26 Aug. 1863; William J. McCulloch, "Hamilton, Canada West, the Civil War Years," Bailey Memorial Lecture, Head-of-the-Lake Historical Society, 9 Feb. 1962, Hamilton Collection, Hamilton Public Library. On the impact of Confederation see Ryerson, *Unequal Union*, pp. 309-26; Isaac Buchanan-Joseph Howe correspondence, 1845-72, Buchanan Papers, MG 24 D 16, vol. 34, pp. 28082-156, PAC. Charles Lipton, *The Trade Union Movement of Canada, 1827-1959* (Montreal: Canadian Social Publications, 1968), pp. 26-27.

11. Langdon, *Emergence of Working Class Movement*, pp. 3-5; Langdon, "The Political Economy of Capitalist Transformation: Central Canada from the 1840s to the 1870s" (M.A. thesis, Carleton University, 1972), pp. 70-122; H. Beaumont Small, *The Products and Manufactures of the New Dominion* (Ottawa: G. E. Desbartes, 1868), pp. 136-54; *The Journal of the Board of Arts and Manufactures for Upper Canada* 7 (1867): 220; 4 (1864): 1-3; 3 (1863): 84-85, 248, 265-66.

12. Peter Warrian, "The Challenge of the One Big Union Movement in Canada, 1919-1921" (M.A. thesis, University of Waterloo, 1971), p. 11.

13. Myers, *Canadian Wealth*, pp. xxxi-xxxvi, dates the period of concentration from 1879 with the Grand Trunk's absorption of a number of smaller railway lines. The process would accelerate in the late 1880s, with the rise of Massey-Harris in Toronto, and continue in the 1890s. The post-1907 merger wave gave this development new stimulus in the early years of the twentieth century. See Tom Naylor, *The History of Canadian Business, 1867-1914*, II (Toronto: Lorimer, 1975), 186-93; H. G. Stapells, "The Recent Consolidation Movement in Canadian Industry" (M.A. thesis, University of Toronto, 1922).

14. See William Kilbourn, *The Elements Combined: A History of the Steel Company of Canada* (Toronto: Clarke, Irwin, 1960), pp. 48-95; H. V. Nelles, *The Politics of Development: Forests, Mines & Hydro Electric Power in Ontario, 1849-1941* (Toronto: Macmillan, 1974), pp. 108-53, 215-55; Alan Sullivan, *The Rapids* (Toronto: University of Toronto Press, 1974); Margaret Van Every, "Francis H. Clergue and the Rise of Sault Ste. Marie as an Industrial Centre," *Ontario History* 56 (September 1964): 191-202.

15. See Katz, *People of Hamilton*, p. 316; S. R. Mealing, "The Concept of Social Class and the Interpretation of Canadian History," *Canadian Historical Review* 46 (September 1965): 201-18.

16. Marx's theory is outlined in David Levine, "The Theory of the Growth of the Capitalist Economy" (typescript, Yale University, 1973).

17. David S. Landes, *The Unbound Prometheus: Technological Change and Industrial Development in Western Europe from 1750 to the Present* (London: Cambridge University Press, 1970), p. 78. On Landes's error see John Saville, "Primitive Accumulation and Early Industrialization in Britain," in Ralph Milliband and John Saville, eds., *The Socialist Register, 1969* (London: Merlin Press, 1969), p. 265.

18. On primitive accumulation the basic source is Karl Marx, *Capital*, I (New York: International, 1967), 713-74. Cf. Saville, "Primitive Accumulation," pp. 247-71; Alfred Evenitsky, "Preobrazenhsky and the Political Economy of

Backwardness," *Science & Society* 30 (Winter 1966): 50-62; E. Preobrazenhsky, *The New Economics* (Oxford: Clarendon University Press, 1965), pp. 77-146; Alexander Erlich, *The Soviet Industrialization Debate, 1924-1928* (Cambridge, Mass.: Harvard University Press, 1960), pp. 42-43; Adam Smith, *An Inquiry into the Nature and Causes of the Wealth of Nations* (New York: Everyman's Library, 1937), pp. 47-48, 64, 313-42, 523-606; Jairus Banjai, "Backward Capitalism, Primitive Accumulation and Modes of Production," *Journal of Contemporary Asia* 3 (1973): 393-413; Rose Luxembourg, *The Accumulation of Capital* (New York: Monthly Review, 1968), pp. 368-418; Stephan Hymer, "Robinson Crusoe and Primitive Accumulation," *Monthly Review* 23 (September 1971): 11-36; Maurice Dobb, *Studies in the Development of Capitalism* (New York: International, 1947), pp. 177-254; Jon S. Cohen and Martin L. Weitzman, "Enclosures and Depopulation: A Marxian Analysis," in William N. Parker and Eric Jones, eds., *European Peasants and Their Markets: Essays in Agrarian Economic History* (Princeton, N.J.: Princeton University Press, 1975), pp. 161-77; Philip McMichael, "The Concept of Primitive Accumulation: Lenin's Contribution," *Journal of Contemporary Asia* 7 (1977): 497-512; Alan R. Richards, "Primitive Accumulation in Egypt, 1798-1882," *Review* 1 (Fall 1977): 3-50.

    19. Marx, *Capital*, I, 714.

    20. Karl Marx, *Grundrisse: Foundations of the Critique of Political Economy* (Harmondsworth, Middlesex: Pelican, 1973), p. 502.

    21. Saville, "Primitive Accumulation," pp. 267-68. Cf. Wakefield's discussion of the need to foster a wage-labour class in the colonies in Marx, *Capital*, I, 765-74.

    22. Richard Garret, "On Primitive Accumulation" (typescript, New School for Social Research, 1975); Philip McMichael, "Primitive Accumulation," and "Pastoralism and Capital Accumulation: A Study of the Development of Capitalism in Australia in the Nineteenth Century," (typescripts, SUNY at Binghamton, 1976).

    23. Eric J. Hobsbawm, "The Crisis of the Seventeenth Century," in Trevor Ashton, ed., *Crisis in Europe, 1560-1660* (Garden City, N.Y.: Doubleday, 1967), pp. 5-62. Cf. Karl Marx, *Pre-Capitalist Economic Formations* (New York: International, 1955), pp. 9-65; Eugene D. Genovese, *The World the Slaveholders Made* (New York: Vintage, 1969), pp. 1-20; and, despite its efforts in the direction of model-building, Immanuel Wallerstein, *The Modern World System: Capitalist Agriculture and the Origins of the European World Economy in the Sixteenth Century* (New York: Academic Press, 1974).

    24. Marx, *Capital*, I, 338.

    25. Ibid., p. 330.

    26. The argument is well made in Paul Sweezy, "Karl Marx and the Industrial Revolution in England," in R. Eagly, ed., *Events, Ideology and Economic Theory* (Detroit: Wayne State University Press, 1968), pp. 107-26.

    27. Marx, *Capital*, I, 383-84.

    28. Marx's analysis of technical change is outlined in David Levine, "Accumulation and Technical Change in Marxian Economics" (Ph.D. diss., Yale, 1973), esp. pp. 119-59, 160-81, 248-87. I have also found the following useful: Nathan Rosenberg, "The Direction of Technological Change: Inducement Mechanisms and Focusing Devices," *Economic Development and Cultural Change* 18 (October 1969): 1-24; Rosenberg, "Technological Change in the Machine

Tool Industry, 1840-1910," *Journal of Economic History* 23 (December 1963): 414-46; Francois Crouzet, "England and France in the Eighteenth Century: A Comparative Analysis of Two Economic Growths," in Hartwell, ed., *The Causes of the Industrial Revolution* (London: Methuen, 1967), pp. 139-74. The impact of technical change on labour is discussed in Edward Young, *Labor in Europe and America: A Special Report on the rate of wages, the cost of subsistence, and the condition of the working classes, in Great Britain, France, Belgium, Germany and other countries of Europe, also in the United States and British America* (Philadelphia: S. A. George & Co., 1875), pp. 176-95.

    29. Johnson, *History of Ontario County*, pp. 20-195; Johnson, "Land Policy, Population Growth, and Social Structure in the Home District," *Ontario History* 63 (March 1971): 41-60; Gary Teeple, "Land, Labour, and Capital in Pre-Confederation Canada," in Teeple, ed., *Capitalism and the National Question in Canada* (Toronto: University of Toronto Press, 1972), pp. 43-66; Pentland, "Labour and the Development of Industrial Capitalism," pp. 384-434.

    30. Langdon, *Emergence of Working Class Movement*, p. 4; Langdon, "Political Economy of Capitalist Transformation," pp. 51-69; J. K. Johnson, "The Businessman as Hero: The Case of William Warren Street," *Ontario History* 65 (September 1973): 125-32; McCalla, "Commercial Politics of the Toronto Board of Trade," pp. 51-67.

    31. Langdon, "Political Economy of Capitalist Transformation," pp. 71-122; Pentland, "Labour and Industrial Capitalism," p. 283. Note the discussion of the Toronto economy in Gregory S. Kealey, "The Working-Class Response to Industrial Capitalism in Toronto, 1867-1892" (Ph.D. diss., University of Rochester, 1977), pp. 13-93.

    32. Adam Hope to his father, 1 Mar. 1837, Hope Letters, Hamilton Collection, Hamilton Public Library.

    33. On land speculation see Katz, *People of Hamilton*, pp. 192-93; Marjorie Freeman Campbell, *A Mountain and a City: The Story of Hamilton* (Toronto: McClelland and Stewart, 1966), p. 141. On land speculation in London see Johnson, "The Businessman as Hero," pp. 125-32.

    34. See Adam Hope to his father, 26 Feb. 1837, Hope Letters.

    35. On the Buchanan businesses see P. Douglas McCalla, "The Buchanan Businesses, 1834-1872: A Study in the Organization and Development of Canadian Trade" (Ph.D. diss., Oxford, 1972), esp. pp. 126-34. Cf. Douglas McCalla, "The Decline of Hamilton as a Wholesale Centre," *Ontario History* 65 (September 1973): 247-54; and, on the importance of the Buchanan businesses in the city's credit structure, R. G. Dun and Company, Wentworth County Records, Canada West, p. 144, Dun and Bradstreet Collection, Baker Library, Harvard Business School. I am indebted to Michael Katz, and the Canadian Social History Project of York University, for allowing me access to the latter source.

    36. On the "York State Molders" see *HS*, 21 Nov., 1 Dec. 1884, 20 May 1908; Kilbourn, *Elements Combined*, pp. 33-35; *Report of the Royal Commission on the Relations of Labor and Capital in Canada*, "Ontario Evidence," II (Ottawa: Queen's Printer, 1889), 834-35; and, on Edward Jackson, Katz, *People of Hamilton*, pp. 179, 187, 195, 205. Cf. Johnson, *Head of the Lake*, p. 192; *Monetary Times* 20 (7 Jan. 1887): 789.

    37. Marx, *Capital*, III, 334.

    38. Ibid., p. 333.

39. On Wakefield see Marx, *Capital*, I, 765-74.

40. *Hamilton Gazette*, 23 Feb. 1852. Cf. Robert McVicar, *Letters on Emigration from the British Isles and the Settlement of the Waste Lands in the Province of Canada* (Hamilton: S. Hewson, 1853), pp. 20-21, 47-48, for a detailed description of land practices forcing immigrants to turn to wage labour to sustain themselves. Less pessimistic is John Newton, *The Emigrant and Other Pieces* (Hamilton: J. Robertson, 1846), a collection of poems dealing with the emigration of a radical Chartist to Canada, and his subsequent conversion to "toryism" after the acquisition of a farm.

41 On the Irish see Pentland, "Labour and Industrial Capitalism," pp. 208-81; Katz, *People of Hamilton*.

42. *Hamilton Gazette*, 2 Sept., 7 Oct. 1852.

43. Ibid., 22 and 25 Mar. 1852.

44. Ibid., 28 June 1852.

45. See for instance the reminiscent treatment of the period in *HS*, 31 July 1871; and the discussion of periodization in Marx, *Capital*, I, 371.

46. On the importance of the railways, and the year 1853, see "Through the Lens of 1853," and "Hamilton of Today Justifies Faith of City Fathers," in *HS*, 15 July 1946; William Kilbourn, "Hamilton, A City Shaped by Industry," *Royal Architectural Institute of Canada Journal* 40 (1963): 52.

47. "Through the Lens of 1853," *HS*, 15 July 1946. The year also saw one of the first Canadian strikes against mechanization, as Lawson's tailors resisted the introduction of the sewing machine. See Lloyd Atkinson and Eugene Forsey, "The Labour Movement in Hamilton, 1827-1888," Canadian Labour Congress Collection, MG 28 I 103, vol. 249, p. 2, PAC. An introduction to class struggle in Hamilton in the period 1850-60, years not systematically explored in this study, is found in Paul Campbell Appleton, "The Sunshine and the Shade: Labour Activism in Central Canada, 1850-1860" (M.A. thesis, University of Calgary, 1974).

48. "Hamilton of Today Justifies Faith of City Fathers," in *HS*, 15 July 1946; R. G. Dun, Wentworth County Records, p. 165.

49. *Hamilton Gazette*, 22 Sept. 1853.

50. Michael Katz, "The Entrepreneurial Class in a Canadian City: The Mid-Nineteenth Century," *Journal of Social History* 8 (Winter 1975): 1-29, reprinted in Katz, *People of Hamilton*, pp. 176-208. Katz now prefers the term capitalist class, using it in his recent unpublished study of Hamilton and Buffalo, which Katz and his collaborators kindly let me read. See Michael B. Katz, Michael Doucet, and Mark Stern, "The Social Organization of Early Industrial Capitalism: Aspects of the North American Experience" (typescript, York University, 1978). This study argues that the class structure of nineteenth-century cities conformed to a two-class model, dominated by employers and workers.

51. McCalla, "The Buchanan Businesses," pp. 353-54. It needs to be stressed that Katz, Doucet, and Stern have, in their forthcoming study, placed some significance upon the demise of the independent commodity producer, a factor Katz's previous work had not confronted. In a working paper, "Occupation and Class," Katz notes that "By the mid-nineteenth century independent artisans as a social class largely had disappeared from North American cities." See Katz, *York Social History Project: Third Report—February 1978*, Working Paper no. 24, p. 236.

52. McCalla, "The Buchanan Businesses," pp. 440-67; *HS*, 1 Oct. 1867; Johnson, "The Businessman as Hero," pp. 125-32. McCalla's stress on the per-

sonal shortcomings of Isaac Buchanan as a prime cause of the failure of the businesses differs from my own analysis of the firm's fall. Again, while Johnson stresses the tragic nature of one merchant's fall, occasioned by his speculative use of funds earmarked for other purposes, the case can be seen as representative of larger trends at work in the economy.

53. R. G. Dun, Wentworth County Records, pp. 91, 100g, 105, 107, 125, 160, 160c, 183. This source, it should be stressed, was biased toward the more well-to-do independent producers and merchants. Thus among less prosperous men the process of decline would be even more severe.

54. Ibid., p. 165. Gunn's case should serve as an adequate reminder that it was likely not moral laxity — primarily an attachment to drink — that precipitated these men downwards. The Dun ratings tend to imply this, and Katz has followed the source a little too uncritically for my tastes. Moral laxities may well have been a consequence of decline rather than a cause, and a careful reading of the source provides grounds for such an interpretation.

55. *Journal of the Board of Arts and Manufactures for Upper Canada* 5 (1865): 305. On the problem of capital shortage see H. C. Pentland, "The Role of Capital in Canadian Economic Development before 1875," *Canadian Journal of Economics and Political Science* 16 (November 1950): 457-74; *Journal of the Board of Arts and Manufactures for Upper Canada* 3 (1863): 18, 97-98.

56. On the GWR shops see *HS*, 10 Feb. 1860; Campbell, *A Mountain and a City*, p. 139; James Herbert Bartlett, *The Manufacture, Consumption, and Production of Iron, Steel, and Coal in the Dominion of Canada* (Montreal: Dawson Brothers, 1885), p. 36; Kilbourn, *Elements Combined*, pp. 36-38.

57. GWR Pay List, February 1863, Hamilton Collection, Hamilton Public Library. Subcontracting obviously played a role in these early factories: one boilermaker, I. McIntyre, earned a total of $261.30 ($36.00 + $225.30 on piece work) for a two-week period, indicating that he must have paid out considerable to a "gang" under his direction.

58. *HS*, 10 Feb. 1860.

59. Langdon, *Emergence of the Working Class Movement*, p. 4; Langdon, "Political Economy of Capitalist Transformation," pp. 82, 92-95; Pentland, "Labour and Industrial Capitalism," p. 291; Campbell, *A Mountain and a City*, pp. 141-42; *Journal of the Board of Arts and Manufactures for Upper Canada* 7 (1867): 220. Descriptions and depictions of some leading Hamilton shops are found in *Canadian Illustrated News*, 14 Feb., 26 Sept., 21 Nov. 1863.

60. *Journal of the Board of Arts and Manufactures for Upper Canada* 6 (1866): 123-26.

61. Hamilton is first referred to as "the Birmingham of Canada" in an article on the city's industrial progress, *HS*, 13 Sept. 1871. Cf. Johnson, *Head of the Lake*, pp. 239-48.

62. *HS*, 22 Dec. 1870.

63. Ibid., 1 May 1871. On Wanzer's cf. "Saturday Musings," ibid., 27 June 1914; *Canadian Illustrated News* (January-June 1871), pp. 354, 357.

64. *HS*, 3 Sept. 1870. Cf. Hamilton, Ontario, Mss. Census Returns, 1871, Supp. Schedules, pp. 2, 3, and 6, PAC.

65. Langdon, *Emergence of the Working Class Movement*, p. 4.

66. Katz, Doucet, and Stern, "Social Organization of Early Industrial Capitalism." Because pagination had not been coordinated in this study, it was impossible to cite exact page references.

67. Mss. Census, 1871, Schedule no. 6. Other discussions of the presence of large and small firms are found in Katz, Doucet, and Stern, "Social Organization of Early Industrial Capitalism," and in Harold Bernard Ward, "Hamilton, Ontario, as a Manufacturing Center" (Ph.D. diss., University of Chicago, 1934), pp. 27-48.

68. On the National Policy and industrial development in Hamilton see *HS*, 26 Nov. 1878, 22 Mar., 16, 19, and 25 Apr., 15 May 1879, 16 Feb., 24 Dec. 1880, 9 May, 7, 15, and 16 July 1881, 12 Mar. 1882; A. J. Bray, *Canada Under the National Policy, Arts and Manufactures, 1883* (Montreal: Industrial Publishing, 1883), pp. 109, 126-28; J. Beaufort Hurlbert, *Protection and Free Trade with special reference to Canada and newly settled countries* (Ottawa: A. S. Woodburn, 1882), pp. 181-82, 189-90; Kilbourn, *Elements Combined*, p. 43. The quotations are from *Monetary Times* 20 (7 Jan. 1887): 789; *Hamilton, the Birmingham of Canada* (Hamilton: *Times* Publishing, 1892), n.p.

69. On the iron and steel industry and bonuses see Naylor, *History of Business*, II, 138-40, 182-84; Kilbourn, *Elements Combined*, p. 48; *HS*, 18 Apr. 1899, 20 Apr., 18 June 1900; Ward, "Hamilton," pp. 135-39.

70. "Hamilton of Today Justifies Faith of City Founders," *HS*, 15 July 1946; Herbert Lister, *Hamilton, Canada, Its History, Commerce, Industries and Resources* (Hamilton: *Spectator* Publishing, 1913), pp. 37-43; Ward, "Hamilton," pp. 48-60.

71. Fernand Braudel, *The Mediterranean and the Mediterranean World in the Age of Philip II*, I (New York: Harper and Row, 1972), 353.

72. *HS*, 31 July 1871.

73. *Relations of Labor and Capital*, "Ontario Evidence," II, 826-28. Cf. "Red-Ink," *'Pi': A Compilation of Odds and Ends Relating to Workers in Sanctum and Newsroom, Culled From a Scrap-Book of a Compositor* (Hamilton: Griffin and Kidner, 1890), pp. 215-16.

74. On the craft response to mechanization see chaps. 3 and 7 below and, more generally, Irwin Yellowitz, *Industrialization and the American Labor Movement, 1850-1900* (Port Washington, N.Y.: Kennikat Press, 1977).

75. See an iron molder's repudiation of capitalists in *HS*, 7 Mar. 1892.

76. The problem goes far beyond that of factory discipline. With the emergence of labour as a commodity, a vital aspect of capitalist development, all work came under a more rigorous discipline. Thus the terms industrial, labour, or work discipline can be used interchangeably to connote an important component of capitalist social relationships affecting work in the factory, on the shop-floor, or in the fields of an increasingly commercialized agriculture. On the importance of the emergence of labour as a commodity, and its relationship to capitalist development, see C. B. Macpherson, *The Political Theory of Possessive Individualism* (New York: Oxford University Press, 1962), esp. pp. 48-59. On the question of work discipline see E. P. Thompson, "Time, Work Discipline and Industrial Capitalism," *Past & Present* 38 (December 1967): 56-97; Sidney Pollard, *The Genesis of Modern Management* (Cambridge, Mass.: Harvard University Press, 1965); Pollard, "Factory Discipline in the Industrial Revolution," *Economic History Review* 16 (1963): 254-71; Herbert G. Gutman, "Work, Culture and Society in Industrializing America, 1815-1919," *American Historical Review* 78 (June 1973): 531-88; Daniel Creamer, "Recruiting Laborers for Amoskeag Mills," *Journal of Economic History* 1 (May 1941): 42-48; Neil McKendrick, "Josiah Wedgwood and Factory Discipline," *The Historical Journal* 4 (1961): 30-56; and Joseph Walker, *Hopewell*

Village: The Dynamics of a Nineteenth Century Iron-Making Community (Philadelphia: University of Pennsylvania Press, 1966). In Canada the question has been hastily, and wrongly, passed over on the assumption that the skilled British craftsman was totally adapted to the disciplines of the industrial society which he had left, and so required little prodding to acclimatize to the work disciplines of the Canadian setting. This perspective, resting on assertion only, forms an important argument in Pentland, "Labour and Industrial Capitalism," pp. 390-92, 403-6; Pentland, "Development of a Capitalistic Labour Market," pp. 460-61; Martin Robin, *Radical Politics and Canadian Labour, 1880-1930* (Kingston, Ont.: Industrial Relations Centre, 1968), pp. 10-13; Robin, "The Working Class and the Transition to Capitalist Democracy in Canada," *Dalhousie Review* 47 (1967-68): 326-43. The argument has recently been resurrected, with a new twist, in Michael B. Katz, Michael Doucet, and Mark Stern, "Migration and the Social Order in Erie County, New York: 1855," *Journal of Interdisciplinary History* 7 (Spring 1978): 700, and will likely figure in the forthcoming work of Katz et al., "The Social Organization of Early Industrial Capitalism."

77. Bartlett, *Manufacture ... of Iron, Steel, and Coal*, p. 27.

78. *Coburg Sentinel*, 4 May 1872.

79. James Rose Diary, 1873-75, MG 55 29, no. 89, PAC.

80. Malcolm MacLeod, *Practical Guide for Emigrants to the United States and Canada* (Manchester: A. Ireland, 1870), p. 8.

81. On employers' perceptions of the problems associated with English artisans see *Relations of Labor and Capital*, "Quebec Evidence," III, 354; Rowland Tappan Berthoff, *British Immigrants in Industrial America, 1790-1950* (Cambridge, Mass.: Harvard University Press, 1953). The Hamilton manager is quoted in Department of Labour Strikes and Lockouts Records, RG 27, vol. 299, Strike no. 3475, PAC.

82. *Relations of Labor and Capital*, "Ontario Evidence," II, 252; "Quebec Evidence," III, 254, 319; "Nova Scotia Evidence," VI, 373, 417; Greg Kealey, ed., *Canada Investigates Industrialism: The Royal Commission on the Relations of Labor and Capital, 1889* (Toronto: University of Toronto Press, 1973), pp. 133-35.

83. See *HS*, 19 Jan. 1867, 17 Aug. 1869, 27 Aug. 1881. Saint Monday is discussed in Thomas Wright, *Some Habits and Customs of the Working Class* (London: Tinsley Brothers, 1867), pp. 108-30; Gutman, "Work, Culture, Society," pp. 558-60; Thompson, "Time, Work-Discipline," pp. 72-76; and Douglas A. Reid, "The Decline of Saint Monday, 1766-1876," *Past & Present* 71 (May 1976): 76-101. On opposition see Robert Malcolmson, *Popular Recreations in English Society, 1700-1850* (London: Cambridge University Press, 1973), pp. 94-99. On craft drinking practices see John Dunlop, *Artificial Drinking Usages of North Britain* (Greenock: K. Johnson, 1836); *Workingman's Advocate*, 23 Mar. 1872; and Eliphalit Nott, *Lectures on Temperance* (Hamilton: A. M. Moffat, 1858), esp. pp. 329-30, 348.

84. "Saturday Musings," *HS*, 6 June, 6 Mar. 1908.

85. *Relations of Labor and Capital*, "Quebec Evidence," III, 1310. Cf. Michael Bliss, *A Living Profit: Studies in the Social History of Canadian Business, 1883-1911* (Toronto: McClelland and Stewart, 1974), p. 58.

86. Kealey, ed., *Canada Investigates Industrialism*, p. 389; *Relations of Labor and Capital*, "Quebec Evidence," III, 30-34; Bliss, *Living Profit*, pp. 58-59.

87. On child labour in early factories see Langdon, "Political Economy of Capitalist Transformation," pp. 239-49.

88. On Fortier's see *Relations of Labor and Capital*, "Quebec Evidence," III, 31-34; *Cigar Makers' Official Journal*, March 1888.

89. *Relations of Labor and Capital*, "Quebec Evidence," III, 134, 399, 1243-1246. Other examples of these kinds of workplace rules are found in Toronto Street Railway Company, *Rules and Regulations for Drivers and Conductors on the Toronto Street Railway Company* (Toronto: n.p., 1880); Frost and Wood Company, *Factory Rules* (Smith Falls: n.p., n.d.); *Industrial Banner*, October 1905, August 1911; *Journal of United Labor*, 21 May 1887; *Ontario Workman*, 28 Aug. 1873.

90. See *Industrial Banner*, September, October, November 1905, April 1906.

91. What follows introduces themes to be developed more fully in chaps. 3 and 7 below.

92. See the rules drawn up to discipline these children while in the asylum. "Rules for Hamilton Orphans' Home," in Hamilton Aged Women's Home, *Minutes, 1881*, vol. 5, pp. 1-7, Hamilton Collection, Hamilton Public Library. Other parentless children had been introduced into Hamilton through the assisted immigration schemes of the early 1870s and 1880s. See *HS*, 21 and 30 May, 2 and 4 June, 11 Nov. 1870, 11 May 1881.

93. Record of Orphan's Apprenticeships, Hamilton Orphan Asylum, pp. 1-9a, Hamilton Collection, Hamilton Public Library.

94. Ibid., pp. 10-20, 21, 24, 30, and passim.

95. Ibid., p. 34.

96. Ibid., p. 23.

97. Ibid., William Williams to Mrs. Dagsmith, 12 Apr. 1898, Guelph (loose letter).

98. Ibid., pp. 23, 25.

99. R. G. Dun, Wentworth County Records, p. 131.

100. *HS*, 24 May 1869. Cf. *HT*, 21 Aug. 1865.

101. *HS*, 29 May 1872.

102. Ibid., 8 Dec. 1888; *POL*, 20 Sept. 1884, 3 and 6 Sept. 1881.

103. *POL*, 17 Apr. 1886; *HS*, 14 and 15 Apr. 1886.

104. *HS*, 22 Dec. 1870.

105. Ibid., 16 Feb. 1872.

106. Ibid., 22 Apr. 1875.

107. See Terry Copp, *The Anatomy of Poverty: The Condition of the Working Class in Montreal, 1897-1929* (Toronto: McClelland and Stewart, 1974); Langdon, "Political Economy of Capitalist Transformation," pp. 224-68. On nineteenth-century poverty in Hamilton see *Relations of Labor and Capital*, "Ontario Evidence," II, 759, 819.

108. On the differences in wage rates see "A Workman's View of Canada and Its Trades," *HS*, 23 Mar. 1871; MacLeod, *Practical Guide*, p. 31; "Testimony of William Weir before the Hamilton Water Works, 1858," Buchanan Papers, vol. 58, pp. 46616-24; Edward Young, *Labor in Europe and America*, discussed at length in Katz et al., "Social Organization of Early Industrial Capitalism."

109. This, certainly, was the case with the 1873-74 depression and the downturn of the early 1880s. See *HS*, 10 Dec. 1873, 2 and 21 Feb., 19 Mar. 1874, 23 Feb. 1875, 15 Feb., 10 Apr. 1876, 18 Dec. 1877, 21 and 25 Dec. 1880; *Iron Molders' International Journal*, October 1873, November 1873, December 1873,

February 1874, 10 Sept. 1877, December 1883; Charles Brian Williams, "Canadian American Trade Union Relations — A Study of the Development of Binational Unionism" (Ph.D. diss., Cornell, 1964), pp. 131-40.

110. *HS*, 25 Aug. 1877.

111. *Proceedings of the U.G.G. Workers Association of the United States and Canada, Composed of Glass Bottle Makers, 17th Annual Session, Milwaukee, 10-19 July 1893* (Lockport, N.Y.: James Murphy, 1893), p. 147, where glass workers' death lists indicate an average age of death of about forty years. The youngest glass worker to die was twenty-four, the oldest sixty-five. Christian Apple, a Hamilton blower, was representative, passing on at the age of thirty-three. On the molders see *Iron Molders' International Journal*, 10 Sept. 1875.

112. *Typographical Journal*, 1 Aug. 1901, April 1909; W. L. Davis, "A History of the Early Labor Movement in London, Ontario" (M.A. thesis, University of Western Ontario, 1930), pp. 6, 127-31; *HS*, 28 Aug. 1895.

113. Hospital Records, pp. 6-7, Marjorie Freeman Campbell Papers, Special Collections, McMaster University.

114. Ibid., pp. 16-17, 24, 30.

115. Ibid., p. 75. On the *grippe* see Ian Davey, "Educational Reform and the Working Class: School Attendance in Hamilton, Ontario, 1851-1891" (Ph.D. diss., University of Toronto, 1975), pp. 246-47; *HS*, 4, 15, and 21 Jan. 1890.

116. Hospital Records, pp. 37, 39-40, 42, 107-8, 117, 125-26, 84, 109-10, 153-54, 177-79, 187-90, 222-25, Campbell Papers.

117. Ibid., pp. 9-10.

118. Davey, "Educational Reform," pp. 223-69. Other forces, including the children's own resistance, must also have limited the effectiveness of the school. See *HT*, 4 Nov. 1863.

119. *Relations of Labor and Capital*, "Ontario Evidence," II, 774-75. On Tuckett's paternalism cf. *Iron Molders' International Journal*, January 1883; *HS*, 24 Dec. 1894, 24 Dec. 1895. Despite his innovations at the workplace, Tuckett drew working-class criticism for his attempts to influence municipal politics. See *POL*, 15 and 29 Nov., 6 Dec. 1884.

120. *Relations of Labor and Capital*, "Ontario Evidence," II, 296.

121. Katz, *People of Hamilton*, pp. 176-77; Pentland, "Labour and Industrial Capitalism," pp. 416-17.

122. *HS*, 18 Feb., 11 Dec. 1895.

123. Department of Labour, Strikes and Lockouts Records, vol. 297, Strike no. 3231.

124. Gutman, "Work, Culture, and Society," pp. 531-88; Donald Howard Avery, "Canadian Immigration Policy and the Alien Question, 1896-1919: The Anglo-Canadian Perspective" (Ph.D. diss., University of Western Ontario, 1973); Avery, "Immigrant Workers and Labour Radicalism" (typescript, University of Western Ontario, 1976). Cf. Jean Morrison, "Ethnicity and Violence: The Lakehead Freight Handlers Before World War I," in Gregory S. Kealey and Peter Warrian, eds., *Essays in Canadian Working Class History* (Toronto: McClelland and Stewart, 1976), pp. 143-60.

125. Note the accounts of violent confrontations at the workplace, led by immigrant workers, in *HS*, 15 Oct. 1890, 7 Oct., 12 Dec. 1895, 11 Jan. 1896, 1, 2, and 4 Apr. 1910; Department of Labour, Strikes and Lockouts Records, vol. 294, Strike nos. 1868, 2857, 2890; vol. 296, Strike no. 3153; vol. 303, Strike no. 111A; *Labour Gazette* 10 (1909-10): 1327-30.

126. See Craig Heron and Bryan D. Palmer, "Through the Prism of the Strike: Industrial Conflict in Southern Ontario, 1901-1914," *Canadian Historical Review* 58 (December 1977): 423-58. Cf. Wayne Roberts, "Metal Workers and the Second Industrial Revolution, Toronto, 1896-1914" (typescript, University of Toronto, 1976).

127. See David Montgomery, "The 'New Unionism' and the Transformation of Workers' Consciousness, 1909-1922," *Journal of Social History* 7 (Summer 1974): 509-29; Bryan D. Palmer, "Class, Conception and Conflict: The Thrust for Efficiency, Managerial Views of Labor, and Working-Class Rebellion, 1903-1922," *Review of Radical Political Economics* 7 (Summer 1975): 31-49; Bruno Ramirez, *When Workers Fight: The Politics of Industrial Relations in the Progressive Era, 1898-1916* (Westport, Conn.: Greewood, 1978).

128. *POL*, 11 Aug. 1883.

CHAPTER 2

1. *HS*, 7 Apr. 1904.

2. *POL*, 5 Dec. 1885; *Cigar Makers' Official Journal*, October 1885.

3. Note the vivid accounts of funeral processions in London and Ottawa in *Ontario Workman*, 11 Dec., 24 Apr. 1873.

4. *POL*, 15 Nov. 1884.

5. On funerals of Hamilton fire company officials and members, many of whom were skilled workingmen, see *HT*, 20 Apr. 1863; *HS*, 18 and 19 Nov. 1865, 25 Mar. 1867, 29 Apr. 1872.

6. James Shuttleworth, a shoemaker and co-founder of the Maple Leaf Base Ball Club, was followed to his grave by his working-class teammates. See *HS*, 27 Aug. 1869.

7. See ibid., 15 Oct. 1873, 26 May 1882, 19 Feb. 1883, 11 Oct. 1890, 29 June 1906; *Typographical Journal*, November 1911.

8. A deceased Hamilton glass worker, Ephraim McHenry, received a resolution of condolence from his union and from his American currency reform club, the National League. See *Labor Union*, 27 Jan. 1883.

9. Printers were perhaps the strongest supporters. See *HS*, 28 Nov. 1861, 29 Sept. 1891, 8 June 1893, 28 Aug., 26 Oct. 1895, 12 Feb. 1898; *Typographical Journal*, November 1911. Funerals of cigarmakers, glassworkers, molders, and rail workers are noted in *HS*, 26 May 1882, 19 Feb. 1883, 11 Oct. 1890; *POL*, 24 Oct. 1885; *Iron Molders' International Journal*, May 1882, July 1882; *Proceedings of the U.G.G. Workers' Association of the United States and Canada . . ., 1893* (Lockport, N.Y.: James Murphy, 1893), p. 147. For Knights of Labor funerals see *POL*, 8 and 15 May 1886; *HS*, 25 June, 7 Sept. 1887. On funeral policy in the Knights of St. Crispin, see *Constitution, By-Laws and Rules of Order of London Lodge No. 242, K.O.S.C.* (London: K.O.S.C., 1872), p. 23.

10. On the general importance of working-class funerals see Gregory S. Kealey, "The Orange Order in Toronto: Religious Riot and the Working Class," in Kealey and Warrian, eds., *Essays in Canadian Working Class History* (Toronto: McClelland and Stewart, 1976), pp. 23-24; Wayne Roberts, "The Last Artisans: Toronto Printers, 1896-1914," in ibid., pp. 132-33; Kealey, "Artisans Respond to Industrialism: Shoemakers, Shoe Factories, and the Knights of St. Crispin in Toronto," Canadian Historical Association, *Historical Papers* (1973), pp. 137-58. Cf. *Iron Molders' International Journal*, 4 Apr. 1904; *Canadian Labor Reformer*, 19 June 1886; *The Craftsman*, 20 Nov. 1886, 5 Mar. 1887; "Memorial Service of the Knights of Labor," Powderly Papers, Catholic University, Washington, D.C. Par-

ticular instances of importance are recorded for Hamilton molders, carpenters, and nailmakers in *HS*, 26 Mar. 1880, 1 Oct. 1890; *POL*, 23 Feb. 1884, 7 Feb. 1885.

11. *John Swinton's Paper*, 1 Feb. 1885.

12. *Iron Molders' International Journal*, June 1904, Cf. *Hamilton Gazette*, 8 July 1852.

13. One recent attempt to categorize working-class cultural types is Alan Dawley and Paul Faler, "Working-Class Culture and Politics in the Industrial Revolution: Sources of Loyalism and Rebellion," *Journal of Social History* 9 (June 1976): 466-80. The Dawley-Faler argument, positing traditionalist, modernist, loyalist, and rebel dichotomies, fractures the complexity and subtlety of continuities in the working-class cultural experience. It draws upon Paul Faler, "Cultural Aspects of the Industrial Revolution: Lynn, Massachusetts Shoemakers and Industrial Morality, 1826-1860," *Labor History* 15 (Summer 1974): 367-94. For a more sophisticated conception of working-class culture, resting on the basic premise that cultural forms are a complex fusion of residual (old) and emergent (new) forms see Raymond Williams, "Base and Superstructure in Marxist Cultural Theory," *New Left Review* 82 (November-December 1973): 3-16; Williams, *Marxism and Literature* (London: Oxford University Press, 1977), esp. pp. 11-20, 75-144. Williams's concepts have been fruitfully employed in Gregory S. Kealey, "The Honest Workingman and Workers' Control: The Experience of Toronto Skilled Workers, 1860-1892," *Labour/Le Travailleur* 1 (1976): 33; Leon Fink, "Class Conflict in the Gilded Age: The Figure and the Phantom," *Radical History Review* 3 (Fall-Winter 1975): 56-73. For another critique of the Dawley-Faler article see Daniel J. Walkowitz, "Working Class Political Culture," *Newsletter on European Labor and Working Class History* 7 (May 1975): 13-18.

14. *HS*, 12 Feb. 1898.

15. Herbert Gutman's work remains the most extended discussion of this phenomenon. See his essays in Gutman, *Work, Culture, and Society in Industrializing America* (New York: Knopf, 1976); and, especially, his discussion of the family in *The Black Family in Slavery and Freedom, 1750-1925* (New York: Pantheon, 1976). For an attack on Gutman's orientation see Elizabeth Fox-Genovese and Eugene D. Genovese, "The Political Crisis of Social History: A Marxian Perspective," *Journal of Social History* 10 (Winter 1976): 205-21. More confusing is the attack in Michael B. Katz, Michael Doucet, and Mark Stern, "Migration and the Social Order in Erie County, New York: 1855," *Journal of Interdisciplinary History* 8 (Spring 1977): 700.

16. See Bryan D. Palmer, "Most Uncommon Common Men: Craft and Culture in Historical Perspective," *Labour/Le Travailleur* 1 (1976): 5-32. Important theoretical statements on culture are found in Brian Stock, "The Visible and Invisible Cultures," *Canadian Forum* 52 (March 1973): 30-31; Sidney W. Mintz, "History and Anthropology: A Brief Reprise," in Stanley L. Engerman and Eugene D. Genovese, eds., *Race and Slavery in the Western Hemisphere: Quantitative Studies* (Princeton, N.J.: Princeton University Press, 1975), pp. 477-94; Zygmunt Bauman, "Marxism and the Contemporary Theory of Culture," *Co-Existence* 5 (July 1968): 161-73; and Clifford Geertz, "Thick Description: Toward an Interpretive Theory of Culture," in Geertz, *The Interpretation of Cultures* (New York: Basic Books, 1973), pp. 3-30.

17. Henri Lefebvre, *Everyday Life in the Modern World* (New York: Harper, 1971), p. 14.

18. This, I fear, is a major flaw in Michael B. Katz, *The People of Hamilton, Canada West: Family and Class in a Mid-Nineteenth-Century City* (Cambridge, Mass.: Harvard University Press, 1976), esp. p. 6. It appears to survive in Katz's more recent work. See Katz et al., "Migration and the Social Order," p. 700.

19. Katz, *People of Hamilton*, pp. 183-85; Walter S. Glazer, "Participation and Power: Voluntary Associations and the Functional Organization of Cincinnati in 1840," *Historical Methods Newsletter* 5 (September 1972): 151-68.

20. Kealey, "The Orange Order," pp. 13-34; Bryan D. Palmer, "'Give us the road and we will run it': The Social and Cultural Matrix of an Emerging Labour Movement," in Kealey and Warrian, eds., *Essays*, pp. 106-24; Brian Harrison, "For Church, Queen and Family: The Girl's Friendly Society, 1874-1920," *Past & Present* 61 (November 1973): 107-38.

21. *The Book of Constitution of the Grand Lodge of Ancient, Free and Accepted Masons* (Hamilton: *Spectator*, 1866), pp. 10-11.

22. See *Constitution of the St. Andrew's Benevolent Society of Hamilton, Ontario, with a list of Office Bearers* (Hamilton: Lawson, 1882), p. 5; *Constitution of the Hamilton St. George's Benevolent Society* (Hamilton: J. Robertson, 1844), n.p.; *Constitution of the St. Andrew's Benevolent Society of Hamilton* (Hamilton: Gillespy and Robertson, 1860), p. 3; "Cornelius Donovan," *Cathedral Magazine*, reprinted in *Papers and Records of the Wentworth Historical Society* 11 (1924): 43-45; *Constitution and Laws of the Orange Association of British America* (Toronto: Sentinel, 1892), p. 4.

23. See Palmer, "'Give us the road'," pp. 111-12; Kealey, "The Orange Order," pp. 16-17; Kealey, "Artisans Respond to Industrialism," pp. 137-58; Henry T. Smith, *Introduction of Royal Arch Masonry Into Toronto* (n.p., n.d.), pp. cxxi-cxxii; Captain William Morgan, *The Mysteries of Free Masonry* (New York: Wilson and Company, n.d.), pp. 1-9; *POL*, 13 Oct. 1883. Possibly the most explicit working-class endorsement of secrecy and ritual is found in the *Labor Standard*, 16 Nov. 1878. For a discussion of the importance and place of ritual in the Knights of Labor see chap. 6 below.

24. See John S. King, *Early History of the Sons of England Benevolent Society* (Toronto: Thomas Moore, 1891), pp. 10-13; *HT*, 16 Jan. 1866. Note also the role of the Hamilton societies in providing aid for the unemployed cotton operatives in Lancashire amidst the disruption of the American Civil War. See ibid., 2 Oct., 4 and 13 Nov. 1862.

25. Ancient Order of United Workmen, *Ritual* (n.p., n.d.), p. 29.

26. James L. Ridgely, *The Odd Fellows Pocket Companion: A Correct Guide to All Matters Relating to Odd-Fellowship* (Cincinnati: Odd Fellows, 1867), pp. 44-45.

27. Rev. A. B. Gosh, *The Odd Fellows Improved Pocket Manual* (Philadelphia: Odd Fellows, 1869), p. 1.

28. *Rules of the Independent Order of Oddfellows, Manchester Unity Friendly Society* (Chorlton-upon-Medlock, England: n.p., 1879), p. 3. Cf. *Ontario Workman*, 24 Apr. 1873.

29. *HS*, 1 Dec. 1872.

30. *Labor Advocate*, 30 Jan. 1891.

31. *Labor News*, 19 Jan. 1912.

32. "Cornelius Donovan," pp. 43-45. Cf. *Hamilton Herald*, 6 Jan. 1895.

33. Freed, a staunch Tory and eventual editor of the *Hamilton Spectator*, was the Hamilton representative on the Royal Commission on the Relations of

Labor and Capital, and came under attack by organized labour for his views. See Greg Kealey, ed., *Canada Investigates Industrialism* (Toronto: University of Toronto Press, 1973), pp. ix-xxvii. For his central place in Hamilton Conservative Party politics see Freed to Macdonald, 6 Sept. 1884, Sir John A. Macdonald Papers, MG 26 A, vol. 318, pp. 144008-14, PAC; Freed to Macdonald, 23 Oct. 1888, vol. 465, pp. 231552-53; Freed to Macdonald, 11 June 1889, vol. 63, pp. 25728-31; Macdonald to Freed, 10 Dec. 1889, vol. 527, p. 343; Freed to Macdonald, 1890, vol. 332, pp. 150046-50. On Freed's prominence in Masonic circles see Freed to Macdonald, 25 June 1886, ibid., vol. 427, pp. 208867-68; David Hastings, *Historical Sketch of Acacia Lodge, No. 61, G.R.C., Ancient, Free and Accepted Masons* (Hamilton: Spectator, 1905), p. 16. On Hastings see *HS*, 5 Sept. 1896; *Typographical Journal*, 1 Sept. 1896.

34. *HS*, 9 May 1892; *Labor Advocate*, 8 Jan., 6 Feb. 1891; *Ye lyttle Home booke of ye revelles of Sanct George . . .* (Hamilton: Times, 1893), n.p., notes Vale's role in a St. George's Society carnival.

35. *HS*, 19 Feb. 1895.

36. Cf. *Industrial Banner*, April 1907; *POL*, 1 Sept., 13 Oct., 15 Dec. 1883, 7 June, 19 July, 9 Aug. 1884, 31 Oct. 1885; *Labor Union*, 14 July 1883; *Bobcaygeon Independent*, 5 June 1896; *The Lance*, 26 Nov. 1910; *Labor Advocate*, 27 Feb., 12 June 1891; *Labor News*, 19 Jan. 1912; *HS*, 21 July 1904.

37. Many problems are posed by occupational classification. See Michael B. Katz, "Occupational Classification in History," *Journal of Interdisciplinary History* 3 (Summer 1972): 63-88; Katz, *People of Hamilton*, pp. 343-48; Thomas Smith, "Reconstructing Occupational Structures: The Case of the Ambiguous Artisans," *Historical Methods Newsletter* 8 (June 1975): 134-46. Despite these warnings, however, it is not clear that quantitative methods can overcome problems in the original data; it is entirely possible that sophisticated technological methods may simply mask fundamental ambivalences. Given these shortcomings socioeconomic rankings are probably not needed. There is no problem, for instance, in differentiating the merchant tailor of the 1880s from the working tailor, or the contractor from the carpenter, and most of Katz's classifications are of real importance in the earlier years of industrial-capitalist development, when lines between master and journeyman were blurred. There is very little to be mistaken in the cases of molders, boilermakers, blacksmiths, machinists, or labourers. They were, in fact, what they said they were. True, many would understate their occupational classification, but a knowledge of the inhabitants of a city, in which men of wealth and substance generally stand out, is the safest means of guarding against this problem. Katz, Doucet, and Stern have, however, made considerable progress in their efforts to distinguish master craftsmen from journeymen. See "Social Organization of Early Industrial Capitalism."

38. See for instance St. George's Benevolent Society of Hamilton, *Collections of Programs, Invitations, Announcements, Etc.*, Hamilton Collection, Hamilton Public Library, on the prominence of non-working-class elements. St. George's Society officers were listed in *HT*, 15 Jan. 1862, 16 Jan. 1866; *HS*, 17 Jan. 1865. Checking the occupations of these officials in the city directories revealed few workingmen. A similar procedure was followed in the case of the Masonic Lodges, whose officials were listed in *HT*, 25 June 1861, 29 Dec. 1863, 15 Feb. 1866. Cf. listings of officials of both societies in *City of Hamilton Directory, 1895*, pp. 325-29; *Vernon's City of Hamilton Directory, 1911*, pp. 767-74. Most lodges or chapters were dominated by merchants and proprietors, with the exception of St.

John's Lodge, A.F. & A.M., in which a jeweller, boilermaker, fitter, watchmaker, and carpenter held positions of prominence.

39. The listing is in Hastings, *Historical Sketch of Acacia Lodge, No. 61*, pp. 39-54. Occupations were determined by checking names in city directories. Some of the Masons simply did not appear in the directories, while others, often those with common names (William Brown, Charles Frank, Richard McKay, etc.), could not be identified because of multiple listings.

40. Some of this group may well have had some ties to the working-class community for it included professional firemen, foremen-superintendents, and grocers. I also considered any craftsman prefacing his trade with merchant or proprietor in this group.

41. The others: seven each of engineers, printers, hatters, blacksmiths, and butchers; six tailors; five bricklayers and five bakers; four from each of the trades of harness-making/saddliery, watchmaking, cabinetmaking, fitting, molding, shoemaking, tinsmithing; four from each of the railway occupations of engineer, brakesman, and conductor; three upholsterers, three dyers, and three electricians; two each of jewellers, tanners, stonecutters, plumbers, cigarmakers; and a single furrier, finisher, street railway conductor, cutter, plasterer, foundryman, ironworker, stove-mounter, bookbinder, mason, hammersmith, ornamental japaner, painter, carver, slater, glass engraver, boilermaker, picture framer, lino-type operator, and locksmith.

42. See Norman MacDonald, *The Barton Lodge, A.F. & A.M., No. 6, G.R.C., 1795-1945* (Toronto: Ryerson, 1945), pp. 234-39. Skilled workers included seven engineers, six molders, five cutters and five carpenters, three cabinet makers, blacksmiths, machinists, and tailors, two painters, plasterers, telegraphers and tinsmiths, and one each of the following: iron melter, engine driver, iron worker, coremaker, lithographer, jeweller, brakesman, boat builder, electrician, shoemaker, brickmaker, broommaker, conductor, tobacco roller, and stonecutter.

43. Jas. Henigan to Powderly, 26 Jan. 1884, Powderly Papers.

44. *Report of the Royal Commission on the Relations of Labor and Capital in Canada*, "Ontario Evidence," II (Ottawa: Queen's Printer, 1889), 813.

45. Officers were cited in *HS*, 25 Dec. 1880, 24 Dec. 1881. Occupations were culled from the 1880-81 and 1881-82 city directories. The Workmen had a membership of 79 in 1880. See ibid., 20 Mar. 1880. On the confusion prevailing throughout the 1880s regarding the Knights and the Workmen see *Canadian Workman*, June 1886.

46. Ancient Order of United Workmen, Lodge No. 49, *Minute Book*, Hamilton Collection, Hamilton Public Library, esp. pp. 25, 181, 211, 231, 238, 244, 277, 286, 290, 293. Membership stood at 357 in 1904 (86). Cf. *City of Hamilton Directory, 1895*, pp. 325-29; *Vernon's Directory, 1911*, pp. 767-74, for more listings of officials of the AOUW, many of whom were skilled workingmen.

47. Officials cited in *HT*, 28 Sept. 1863, and occupations checked in city directories. On Black see ibid., 16 Aug. 1875.

48. Officials cited in *POL*, 22 Dec. 1883, and occupations checked in city directories.

49. Officials were listed in *HT*, 6 Nov. 1863, 6 Nov. 1866, 19 Feb. 1867, 18 Feb. 1868; *HS*, 19 Feb. 1868, 15 Dec. 1869, 13 Dec. 1872, 12 Dec. 1877; *City of Hamilton Directory, 1874*, pp. 12-13. I was able to identify 63 of these officials occupationally: 39 were skilled workers; 15 belonged to unskilled categories; and 9 were non-working-class elements (salesmen, proprietors, clerks, and grocers).

50. *City of Hamilton Directory, 1895*, pp. 325-29.

51. *Vernon's Hamilton Directory, 1911*, pp. 767-74.

52. On the problems associated with interpreting friendly society involvement see the recent discussion in John Foster, *Class Struggle and the Industrial Revolution: Early Industrial Capitalism in Three English Towns* (London: Weidenfeld and Nicholson, 1974), esp. pp. 216-18.

53. *Labor Advocate*, 6 Feb. 1891. For evidence of the validity of Vale's argument see *HS*, 23 July 1883, where the AOUW supports striking telegraphers. Note the widespread friendly society endorsement of street railway strikers documented in my "Give Us the Road," pp. 106-24. It was not uncommon for Orange Lodge Bands to participate in processions of craft unions or parades of the Knights of Labor. See ibid., 4 Aug. 1884; *Industrial Banner*, January 1899, September 1899; *Labor Standard*, 16 Dec. 1877, 4 Oct. 1879, 5 June 1880, for other instances of friendly society ties to the working-class movement. On Flett see Robert H. Babcock, *Gompers in Canada: A Study in American Continentalism Before the First World War* (Toronto: University of Toronto Press, 1974).

54. A general introduction to Orangeism, of limited utility, is Hereward Senior, *Orangeism: The Canadian Phase* (Toronto: McGraw-Hill, 1972). In treating the Order as an adjunct of the Tory Party, and in stressing the leadership of propertied elements, Senior misses much of the importance of the Orange Lodges, including their community context. See his "Orangeism in Ontario Politics," in Donald Swainson, ed., *Oliver Mowat's Ontario* (Toronto: Macmillan, 1972), pp. 136-53. On Toronto conflict see Kealey, "The Orange Order in Toronto," pp. 13-24. For a comment on Orange violence see Michael S. Cross, "Stony Monday, 1849: The Rebellion Losses Riots in Bytown," *Ontario History* 63 (September 1971): 177-90.

55. Martin Gavin, "The Jubilee Riots in Toronto," Canadian Catholic Historical Association, *Annual Report* (1959), pp. 93-107; *The National*, 30 Sept., 7 Oct. 1875.

56. *Hamilton Gazette*, 17 Jan. 1853. Cf. ibid., 19 and 26 Jan. 1852, 25 July, 4 Aug., 7 Nov. 1853, on Hamilton's Orange Lodge in the 1850s and its efforts to consolidate local autonomy.

57. *The Orange Herald and Protestant Intelligencer*, 27 Sept. 1860. Note the general discussion in Sean Gerard Conway, "Upper Canadian Orangeism in the Nineteenth Century: Aspects of a Pattern of Disruption" (M.A. thesis, Queen's University, 1977).

58. *HS*, 16 Aug. 1887.

59. The above account is based on the detailed and graphic account, "Orange and Green: Disgraceful Rowdyism in the City Last Night," ibid., 7 Aug. 1878.

60. See the pathbreaking overview in Douglas Hay, "Property, Authority, and the Criminal Law," in Hay, ed., *Albion's Fatal Tree: Crime and Society in Eighteenth Century England* (New York: Pantheon, 1975), pp. 17-64.

61. *HS*, 8 Aug. 1878. For a representative case of Brick's clashes with the local police see *HT*, 4 Nov. 1863.

62. It is interesting to note that the affair occurred in 1878, a time of severe recession. It is thus worthy of comparison with David Montgomery's analysis of ethnic and cultural conflict in Philadelphia in another period of economic downturn. See Montgomery, "The Shuttle and the Cross: Weavers and Artisans in the Kensington Riots of 1844," *Journal of Social History* 5 (Summer 1972): 411-46.

63. See my discussion of London, where Orange-Green conflict was virtually nonexistent, in "Give us the Road," pp. 106-24. On the Protestant ethnic structure of Hamilton see Katz, *People of Hamilton*, p. 41.

64. Trevellick to Powderly, 8 Dec. 1883, Powderly Papers. Trevellick's comments were coloured by a disappointing speaking engagement in Toronto, where he may have been influenced by D. J. O'Donoghue.

65. *POL*, 27 Mar., 27 Nov. 1886, 18 July, 15 Aug. 1885; *HT*, 24 Oct. 1863.

66. On fire companies see Bruce Laurie, "'Nothing on Compulsion': Life Styles of Philadelphia Artisans, 1820-1850," *Labor History* 15 (Summer 1974): 836-67; Laurie, "Fire Companies and Gangs in Southwark: The 1840s," in Davis and Haller, eds., *The Peoples of Philadelphia* (Philadelphia: Temple University Press, 1973), pp. 71-88; Joel Schwartz, "Morissania's Volunteer Firemen, 1848-1874: The Limits of Local Institutions in a Metropolitan Age," *New York History* 55 (April 1974): 159-78; Andrew Neilly, "The Violent Volunteers: A History of the Volunteer Fire Department of Philadelphia, 1736-1871" (Ph.D. diss., University of Pennsylvania, 1959); E. L. Doctorow, *Ragtime* (New York: Bantam, 1975).

67. This overview is based on Fireman's Benefit Fund, *History of the Hamilton Fire Department* (Hamilton: n.p., 1920); Marjorie Freeman Campbell, *A Mountain and a City: The Story of Hamilton* (Toronto: McClelland and Stewart, 1966), pp. 148-51; D. A. Jehan, *A Century of Service: Hamilton Fire Department, 1867-1967* (Hamilton: Spectator, n.d.), p. 3; *Sutherland's City of Hamilton Directory, 1862-1863*, pp. 21-22; ibid., 1867-1868, pp. 21-22; as well as the many references in *HS* and *HT*. The companies of the 1860s were the Hook and Ladder Company, the Neptune Hose Company, Phoenix Engine Company No. 1, Cataract Engine Company No. 2, and Rescue Engine Company No. 3. The Great Western Railway also had its own brigade, organized by the mechanics in 1862, composed of a hose company, a steam engine company, and two hand engine companies, with a total membership of 300 in 1867.

68. On Amor see Campbell, *A Mountain and a City*, p. 151; *HS*, 18 Sept. 1871, 13 Mar. 1893. The verse is from William Haley, "More Remarks from Old Timer," ibid., 17 Nov. 1906. Cf. Alex. H. Wingfield, *Poems and Songs in Scotch and English* (Hamilton: Times, 1873), pp. 190-91.

69. Officials were listed in *Hutchinson's Directory, 1862-1863*, pp. 21-22, and their occupations obtained from the same source.

70. *Sutherland's Directory, 1867-1868*, pp. 21-22. Of the twenty-five officials, only eight were not skilled workers, and these included two foremen.

71. Ibid.

72. Officials were listed in *HT*, 14 Feb. 1863, 12 and 17 Feb. 1864, 13, 15, and 26 Feb. 1866, 14 and 15 Feb., 6 and 7 Nov. 1867; *HS*, 10 Feb. 1860, 9 Feb. 1864, 18 Nov. 1865, 3 Mar. 1868, 9 and 10 Feb. 1872. Occupations were then traced in directories and, among the skilled, included seven carpenters; six blacksmiths; four each of machinists, hatters, tailors, and shoemakers; three printers and three engineers; two painters, bakers, tinsmiths, watchmakers, boilermakers, molders, scalemakers, and masons; and one of each of the following: bookbinder, piler, plasterer, whipmaker, cooper, collarmaker, brushmaker, jeweller, harness-maker, fitter, cleaner, coppersmith, gunsmith, and turner.

73. *HT*, 26 Dec. 1863. Cf. ibid., 18 and 29 July 1863, 10 Mar. 1864, 29 Nov. 1866, 12 Jan., 1 June 1867; *HS*, 15 Sept. 1863, 10 Mar. 1864, 1 June, 14 July 1867. On the importance of fires in nineteenth-century cities see John C.

Weaver and Peter de Lottinville, "The Conflagration and the City: Disaster and Progress in British North America During the Nineteenth Century," paper presented at the Canadian Historical Association meetings, London, 1978; Thomas Cowherd, *The Emigrant Mechanic and other tales in verse, together with numerous songs upon Canadian subjects . . . by the Brantford tinsmith rhymer* (Brantford: published by author, 1884), pp. 287-88.

74. Campbell, *A Mountain and a City*, pp. 149-50; *HT*, 2 Mar. 1866, 12 Feb., 8 June 1867. On violence among competing brigades cf. Laurie, "Fire Companies and Gangs in Southwark," pp. 71-88; and Neilly, "The Violent Volunteers."

75. Campbell, *A Mountain and a City*, p. 149; *HT*, 16 Feb., 1 May 1866, 25 May 1869; *HS*, 8 Aug. 1868, 25 May 1869, 21 Aug. 1875. A prize broom, symbolic of the superiority of a company, was presented to the most efficient company, and was an honoured possession. Superiority was determined by periodic match contests. On fireman's parades and dinners in London and Hamilton see *Canadian Illustrated News* (July-December 1872), p. 274; (July-December 1874), p. 120.

76. The Butler recollections are from *History of the Hamilton Fire Department*, n.p. Butler was a printer, and his place in the Hamilton fire brigade is outlined in *HS*, 18 Dec. 1879. On Charles Smith see *HT*, 4 Jan. 1866.

77. On this process see E. P. Hennock, *Fit and Proper Persons: Ideal and Reality in Nineteenth Century Urban Government* (Montreal: McGill-Queen's University Press, 1973), pp. 118-20; and Schwartz, "Morissania's Volunteer Firemen," pp. 159-78.

78. *History of Hamilton Fire Department*, n.p.; Campbell, *A Mountain and a City*, pp. 149-50. Cf. "Saturday Musings," *HS*, 19 Dec. 1908.

79. *HT*, 11 July 1864, 30 July 1867; *HS*, 3 Aug. 1860, 11 Aug. 1865, 19 Mar. 1868, 18 Dec. 1872.

80. *HS*, 1 Mar. 1878; *History of Hamilton Fire Department*, n.p. On opposition to professionalization see the letters by "Hoseman" and "Mechanic" in *HS*, 1 May 1862, 29 Nov. 1879.

81. On Clark see *Industrial Banner*, September 1908. On an outing of firemen and workers to Brantford see *POL*, 23 May 1885.

82. See the overview of the Hamilton and Gore Mechanics' Institute's history in *HS*, 28 May 1881; Foster Vernon, "The Development of Adult Education in Ontario, 1790-1900" (Ph.D. diss., University of Toronto, 1969), pp. 242-45.

83. Vernon, "Development of Adult Education," p. 520. Similar perspectives can be found in J. Donald Wilson, "Adult Education in Upper Canada Before 1850," *The Journal of Education* 19 (1973): 43-54; Harvey J. Graff, "Respected and Profitable Labor: Jobs, Literacy and the Working Class," in Kealey and Warrian, *Essays*, pp. 58-82, esp. n. 16; and the more subtle treatment in Patrick Keane, "A Study in Problems and Policies in Adult Education: the Halifax Mechanics' Institute," *Histoire Sociale/Social History* 8 (November 1975): 255-74. For the best study of educational reform in Hamilton, illuminating the case of the hegemony of non-working-class elements, see Ian E. Davey, "Educational Reform and the Working Class: School Attendance in Hamilton, Ontario, 1851-1891" (Ph.D. diss., University of Toronto, 1975).

84. See the excellent discussion in E. Royle, "Mechanics' Institutes and the Working Classes, 1840-1860," *The Historical Journal* 14 (1971): 305-21. Cf. Palmer, " 'Give us the road'," pp. 112-13; and Keane, "Halifax Mechanics' Institute," pp. 263, 267.

85. Directors and officials were listed in *HT*, 27 Feb., 2 Mar. 1863; *HS*, 2 Mar., 8 Jan. 1863; 1 Mar. 1869; *Hamilton Gazette*, 27 Feb. 1852; Hamilton and Gore Mechanics' Institute, *Act of Incorporation, Rules and Regulations* (Hamilton: Lawson, 1867), pp. 3-4. Occupations were culled from city directories. On the class character of the directors see *HS*, 28 May 1881; *Journal of the Board of Arts and Manufactures for Upper Canada* 4 (1864): 77. On individual directors (Craigie, Macallum, McIlwraith, Meakins, and McNab) see Davey, "Educational Reform and the Working Class," p. 30; *Journal of the Board of Arts and Manufactures for Upper Canada* 3 (1863): 236; J. H. Smith, *The Central School Jubilee Reunion, August 1903: A Historical Sketch* (Hamilton: Spectator, 1903); Katz, *People of Hamilton*, pp. 176-208; *HS*, 9 Aug. 1862.

86. *Journal of the Board of Arts and Manufactures* 1 (1861): 105-7.

87. *HT*, 1 Mar. 1862, 7 Feb. 1863, 25 Feb. 1865; *HS*, 1 Mar. 1869, 28 May, 27 July, 10 Aug., 1881; Hamilton and Gore Mechanics' Institute, *Minute Book, Proceedings of the Management Committee, 1839-1851*, 7th anniversary meeting, February 1846, Hamilton Collection.

88. See *HT*, 12 Dec. 1862, 20 Jan., 12 and 20 Feb., 18 Apr., 2 May, 25 Sept. 1863; *HS*, 25 Feb. 1860, 9 Dec. 1863; Hamilton Mutual Improvement Social and Literary Society, *Declaration of Incorporation*, 15 Feb. 1876, Hamilton Collection; Hamilton Association for the Advancement of Literature, *Members Book, 1857-1911*, Hamilton Collection; *Constitution and By-Laws of the Hamilton Mercantile Library Association and General News Room, 1845* (Hamilton: Journal and Express, 1845), pp. 5-6, 18-19.

89. Mechanics' Institute, *Minute Book, 1839-1851*, annual report, 1850.

90. *Les Miserables*, which the library possessed, was one of the most popular books in Victorian Hamilton. See *HT*, 11 Oct. 1862. Lists of books held by the institute are recorded in ibid., 19 Feb. 1864; *HS*, 14 Dec. 1868, 13 Oct. 1869, 21 Dec. 1872; Hamilton and Gore Mechanics' Institute, *Act of Incorporation*, p. 26.

91. *HT*, 20 Jan. 1866.

92. *HS*, 24 Jan. 1860, 7 Mar. 1862, 3 Mar. 1863, 18 Apr. 1864, 17 Feb., 8 Mar. 1865, 7 Nov. 1878, 7 Nov. 1879; *HT*, 9 Jan. 1858, 17 Feb., 24 May 1859, 28 May, 25 June 1861, 20 Feb., 13 Sept. 1862, 18 Mar., 5 Nov. 1863, 10 and 24 Mar., 26 Sept., 5 and 23 Nov. 1864, 14 Feb., 25 May 1866, 3 Sept. 1867; Hamilton Mechanics' Institute, *Exhibition of Fine Arts, Manufactures, Machines, Natural History, Curiosities, Etc.* (Hamilton: Spectator, 1865), esp. pp. 4, 9. Cf. the positive assessments of the institute in *HS*, 6 Dec. 1871; and *HT*, 11 May 1864.

93. *HT*, 27 Feb. 1863.

94. Ibid., 24 June 1862.

95. *HS*, 20, 21, and 24 Feb. 1860.

96. *HT*, 29 Jan. 1866.

97. Ibid., 23 Feb. 1866. Nineteen years later "Watchman" was still penning letters to the press, this time condemning wage-payment practices. See *POL*, 2 May 1885.

98. *HS*, 31 Mar. 1883, quoted in Vernon, "The Development of Adult Education," p. 245.

99. *HS*, 31 Oct. 1881.

100. *POL*, 23 Aug. 1884.

101. On the struggle for a free library, led by the organized section of Hamilton's working class, see *HS*, 31 Mar. 1883, 2 and 7 May 1885, 10 June 1887, 16 and 26 Feb., 15 Apr. 1889; *POL*, 1 Sept. 1883, 25 Apr., 2 May 1885, 13

Nov., 4 Dec. 1886; H. B. Witton to Macdonald, 23 Mar. 1889, Macdonald Papers, vol. 471, pp. 234404-7; A. T. Freed to Macdonald, 11 June 1889, vol. 63, pp. 25728-31; *Minute Book of the Trades and Labor Council, 1888-1896*, pp. 7, 9, 20, 121, Hamilton Trades and Labor Council; *Labor Union*, 27 Jan. 1883. Hamilton's Knights of Labor DA 61 established a reading room/library in 1886. See *Annual Reports of the Bureau of Industries for the Province of Ontario, 1888*, pt. iv, p. 46; *1889*, pt. iv, p. 18.

102. On the importance of baseball see *Cigar Makers' Official Journal*, September 1884, December 1902, 15 Aug. 1907; *Labor Leaf*, 17 Feb. 1886; *Craftsman*, 12 Mar., 11 June, 1887; *Typographical Journal*, 15 Aug. 1901, 15 Jan. 1902, March 1906, September 1911, October 1912; *Iron Molders' International Journal*, March 1906; *Labor Standard*, 5 June 1880; *Workingman's Advocate*, 3 Aug. 1867, 3 and 10 June 1871, 18 May 1872; Laurie, "Fire Companies and Gangs in Southwark," p. 88.

103. See the pathbreaking essay on the dominance of "the middle class" in the historical evolution of sport in Ontario and Quebec: S. F. Wise, "Sport and Class Values in Old Ontario and Quebec," in W. H. Heick and Roger Graham, eds., *His Own Man; Essays in Honour of A. R. M. Lower* (Montreal: McGill-Queen's University Press, 1974), pp. 93-118. Wise considers curling, lacrosse, rowing, and football, but unfortunately neglects baseball, which could have altered his argument. On the particularly working-class nature of baseball see Irving Howe, *World of Our Fathers: The Journey of the East European Jews to America and the Life They Found and Made* (New York: Harcourt, Brace, Jovanovitch, 1976), pp. 181-82. Contradicting Wise's thesis is the case of the Hamilton Mechanic's Curling Club, in *HS*, 12 Feb. 1873. Buttressing his position is the case of the Leander Rowing Club, which "decided to admit *no mechanic* to membership, nor allow such to take part in any of their competition matches"; see ibid., 23 Sept. 1879. The Hamilton Football Club was composed entirely of young clerks. Officers and members were listed in ibid., 4 Nov. 1869, and their occupations checked in city directories. A similar situation prevailed in the Hamilton Cricket Team, where clerks and young professionals dominated the membership. See *HT*, 1 Aug. 1864. The first case of university football players being hired to protect strikebreakers is recorded in *The Typographical Journal*, May 1906. Note the illustration and discussion of the GWR employees' Queen's Birthday celebration in 1863, where sport figured prominently, in *Canadian Illustrated News*, 30 May 1863.

104. On professionalization see Frank Cosentino, "A History of the Concept of Professionalism in Canadian Sport," *Canadian Journal of Sport and Physical Education* 6 (December 1975): 75-81. The development of professional teams in Hamilton is outlined in *HS*, 3 Mar. 1887, 4 May 1889; C. M. Johnson, *The Head of the Lake: A History of Wentworth County* (Hamilton: Wentworth County, 1958), p. 258.

105. *Hamilton Evening Journal*, 14 July 1870.

106. Officials, players, and information on the Maple Leaf Club are found in *HS*, 4 July, 27 Aug., 11 Sept. 1863; *HT*, 4 and 17 Apr. 1863, 30 July 1864, 5 Apr., 6 May 1865, 7 July 1866, 23 and 24 Feb. 1867. A brief history of the club, founded in 1854, appeared in *HS*, 2 Dec. 1865. Occupations were found in city directories.

107. Lists of players for each of these clubs were found in *HS*, 26 Aug. 1868, 26 July 1869, 24 May 1881; *HT*, 25 Apr. 1866, 31 May, 20 July, 30 Sept.

1867. Occupations were checked in city directories. Note also the case of the Hop Bitters Club in *Labor Union*, 17 Mar. 1883.

108. *HS*, 22, 30, and 31 July 1869, 10 and 23 May 1870, 15 Sept. 1871, 30 Aug. 1875; *HT*, 18 Aug. 1866; *POL*, 27 June, 18 July 1885.

109. On the Hamilton printers' penchant for baseball see *HS*, 1, 2, and 4 Sept. 1871, 22 July, 15 Aug. 1881, 31 Aug. 1885, 11 Aug. 1890; *POL*, 9 Apr. 1884, 11 Sept. 1886; *Typographical Journal*, July 1911, September 1911. The printers were also drawn to other sporting activities, establishing a fishing club and a bowling league.

110. *HS*, 5 Aug. 1884; *POL*, 3 May 1884.

111. For condemnations of professionalism and the gambling and commercialism following in its wake see *POL*, 26 July 1884, 1 Aug. 1885, 12 Apr. 1886.

112. For a working-class defence of the game see *POL*, 1 May and 19 June 1886.

113. *HS*, 4 Aug. 1883, 5 Aug. 1884.

114. Ibid., 5 Dec. 1884. The Primroses, a semiprofessional team, tendered a benefit for an unemployed comrade. See ibid., 3 Mar. 1885.

115. *POL*, 17 Apr. 1886. In the spring of 1889 the employees of John MacPherson and Company met to organize a baseball club, the Hamilton Shoemakers. A leading participant in the formation of this team was William Berry, an activist in the Knights of Labor. See *HS*, 9 Apr. 1889, 6 June 1904.

116. *HS*, 29 Aug. 1881.

117. The printers' picnic, known as the wayzgoose, is especially noteworthy. See the engaging discussion in Anglo-American's "The Wayzgoose and Other Printer's Customs," *Typographical Journal*, 15 June 1899; "Red-Ink," *'Pi': A Compilation of Odds and Ends Relating to Workers in Sanctum and Newsroom, Culled from the Scrap-Book of a Compositor* (Hamilton: Griffin and Kidner, 1890), pp. 19-20. For the general importance of picnics to the crafts see *Typographical Journal*, 1 Aug. 1899; *American Workman*, 5 July 1869; *The Craftsman*, 3 Sept. 1887; *Iron Molders' International Journal*, May 1881; *John Swinton's Paper*, 12 Sept. 1886; *Labor Standard*, 14 Sept. 1878; *POL*, 6 Sept. 1884.

118. On balls, suppers, festivals, and smokers see *Typographical Journal*, 15 Feb. 1902; *The Craftsman*, 29 Jan., 25 June 1887, 25 Feb. 1888; *Industrial Banner*, May 1902; *Labor Standard*, 2 Sept. 1877; *Labor Advocate*, 2 and 16 Jan. 1891; *Labor Union*, 17 Mar. 1883.

119. See the accounts of parades in *Typographical Journal*, October 1908, *The Carpenter*, 15 Aug. 1889; *Labor Leaf*, 7 Oct. 1885; *Iron Molders' International Journal*, May 1881, June 1881; *Ontario Workman*, 18 Apr., 2 Sept. 1872; *Industrial Banner*, September 1903, September 1905; *POL*, 18 Aug. 1883, 6 Sept. 1884, 22 Aug. 1885; Palmer, "Give us the Road," p. 117; and Herbert Gutman, "Work, Culture, and Society in Industrializing America, 1815-1919," *American Historical Review* 78 (June 1973): 531-88.

120. *HS*, 16 Aug. 1886.

121. See *The Craftsman*, 28 Aug. 1886; *POL*, 5 and 12 Sept. 1885, 28 Aug. 1886; *HS*, 4, 6, and 7 Sept. 1869, 10 Sept. 1881, 30 Aug. 1886.

122. *HS*, 17 Dec. 1874.

123. Ibid., 23 Jan. 1860. The verse in the above paragraph is from "A Call to the Soiree," in Cowherd, *The Emigrant Mechanic*, p. 266.

124. On these gatherings see *The Carpenter*, March 1904; *Labor Union*, 27 Jan., 17 Mar. 1883; *Labor News*, 12 Apr. 1912; *POL*, 20 Oct., 10 Nov., 10 Dec. 1883, 12 and 19 Jan., 2 Feb., 19 Apr. 1884, 28 Mar., 11 Apr., 9 May, 1 Aug., 3 Oct. 1885; *HT*, 19 Jan. 1858, 15 and 22 Nov. 1866; *HS*, 23 Jan., 10 Feb. 1860, 1 Jan. 1864, 12 Dec. 1867, 16 and 21 Jan. 1869, 17 Feb. 1872, 1 Jan. 1878, 8 July 1881, 7 Jan. 1882, 11 Dec. 1883, 19 Feb. 1887, 6 and 27 Dec. 1890, 28 Oct. 1893.

125. See *Labor News*, 20 Mar. 1914; *Typographical Journal*, April 1914, p. 533. On the organization of the printers' union see *Hamilton Gazette*, 2 Aug. 1852; Lloyd Atkinson and Eugene Forsey, "The Labour Movement in Hamilton," typescript, Canadian Labour Congress Collection, MG 28 I 103, vol. 249, p. 1, PAC.

126. As a brief introduction to this phenomenon, as yet unstudied in any systematic fashion, see "Labour History: Notes and Articles," Eugene Forsey Papers, MG 30 D 84, vol. 12, PAC, esp. the quotations from *Halifax Weekly Citizen*, 22 June 1867, and *Montreal Witness*, n.d. Cf. Katz, *People of Hamilton*, pp. 3-4, 316; *Canadian Labor Reformer*, 18 Sept. 1886; *HS*, 25 and 26 May 1860.

127. *HT*, 25 May 1867.

128. Ibid., 25, 26, 28, and 29 June 1867; *HS*, 1 July 1867.

129. *HS*, 2 July 1867.

130. *POL*, 11 Aug. 1883; *HS*, 31 July, 4 Aug. 1883.

131. On the parades in honour of "labour's holiday" and, later, Labour Day, see *POL*, 19 July, 9 Aug. 1884; *HS*, 19 July, 9 Aug. 1884, 29 Aug. 1894, 5, 8, and 31 Aug., 3 Sept. 1895, 7 Aug. 1896, 7 Sept. 1897, 4 Sept. 1900, 5 Sept. 1904; *Labor Advocate*, 25 Sept. 1891; *Cigar Makers' Official Journal*, August 1894; *Minute Book, Trades and Labor Council, 1888-1896*, pp. 55-56, 315-19, 390-95.

132. On the early vigour of Labour Day parades and the workingmen's recognition of their importance see *HS*, 4 Sept. 1900, 21 Aug. 1903, 6 Sept. 1904; *Official Programme and Souvenir of the Labor Day Demonstration Held at Dundurn Park, Hamilton, Ontario, 1897, 6th September, Held Under the Auspices of the Trades and Labor Council* (Hamilton: Spectator, 1897). Representative of Labour Day's degeneration is Supplement to the *Labor News, Labor Day, 1914, Annual Review* (Hamilton: Labor News, 1914). See *Labor News*, 30 Aug. 1912 for regret at this deterioration.

133. *POL*, 12 July 1884.

134. *Industrial Banner*, October 1901.

135. *Cigar Makers' Official Journal*, September 1884, December 1902, 15 Aug. 1907.

136. *Industrial Banner*, April 1906.

137. *POL*, 10 Apr. 1886.

138. *HS*, 24 Dec. 1863.

139. *HT*, 12 Jan. 1867; *HS*, 4, 6, and 7 Sept. 1869. Atkinson and Forsey, "The Labor Movement in Hamilton," p. 5 and n. 27, note the importance of Dan Black's in early union organization. Note also "Amalgamated Society of Carpenters & Joiners, Canada, 1871-1924, Statistical Notes," and "Amalgamated Society of Engineers, Canada, 1853-1920, Statistical Notes," Forsey Papers, vol. 11, on the Fountain Saloon and Dan Black's Club House as meeting places of early unions. On Black's Club House and the nine-hour movement see chap. 5 below.

140. *POL*, 14 Feb. 1884, 30 May, 6 and 13 June 1885, 28 Aug. 1886; *Cigar Makers' Official Journal*, 10 Feb. 1878.

141. *POL*, 15 Dec. 1883.

142. *Labor Advocate*, 2 Jan. 1891.

143. *Ontario Workman*, 27 Mar. 1873, commenting on a gathering of Hamilton molders at Victoria Hall, honouring a visit of their International's president.

144. On Hamilton see *POL*, 30 May, 6 and 13 June, 5 and 12 Sept. 1885; *The Carpenter*, September 1883; *Labor Union*, 14 July 1883.

145. *POL*, 15 Aug. 1885.

146. *Industrial Banner*, September 1905, October 1905, November 1905, January 1906, and esp. August 1909.

147. *HS*, 24 Aug. 1867; *HT*, 21 Sept. 1867. Cf. Kealey, "Artisans Respond to Industrialism," pp. 137-58.

148. Ed Williams, "Labor Day," in *Programme of the Labor Day Celebration*, pp. 3-5. Cf. *Trades Union Advocate*, 20 and 29 July 1882.

149. This is a central theme in Robert W. Malcolmson, *Popular Recreations in English Society, 1700-1850* (London: Cambridge University Press, 1973), a source with obvious relevance to our earlier discussion of sport, picnics, parades, and festive balls and suppers. It is also forcefully presented in Natalie Zemon Davis, "The Reasons of Misrule," and "The Rites of Violence," in *Society and Culture in Early Modern France* (Stanford: Stanford University Press, 1975), pp. 97-123 and 152-88. Cf. Mary Thale, ed., *The Autobiography of Francis Place, 1771-1854* (London: Cambridge University Press, 1972), pp. 65-68; Alfred Young, "Pope's Day, Tar and Feathering, and Cornet Joyce, jun.: From Ritual to Rebellion in Boston, 1745-1775," paper delivered to the Anglo-American Conference of Labor Historians, April 1973; Samuel Bamford, *Bamford's Passages in the Life of a Radical in Two Volumes*, (London: Fisher Unwin, 1905), I, 126, 140; Thomas Wright, *Some Habits and Customs of the Working Classes*, (London: Tinsley Brothers, 1867), p. 81; E. P. Thompson, "Patrician Society, Plebian Culture," *Journal of Social History* 7 (Summer 1974): 382-405.

150. *HT*, 3 July 1863. Note the case of the Hellfriar's Club in London, Ontario, a similar body active in the period, composed of soldiers, cabinetmakers, and printers. See Orlo Miller, *A Century of Western Ontario: The Story of London, The "Free Press", and Western Ontario* (Toronto: Ryerson, 1949), pp. 169-74.

151. *HS*, 26 May 1868.

152. *HT*, 26 and 29 June 1867, 15 and 26 May 1868. The Kalithumpians often met in friendly society halls or engine houses. The last recorded instance of a gathering was in June 1870. See *HS*, 3 June 1870; *Hamilton Evening Journal*, 21 June 1870. For a wider discussion of the Kalithumpian Klan, as well as an introduction to charivaris and whitecapping, both to be dealt with below, see my "Discordant Music: Charivaris and Whitecapping in Nineteenth-Century North America," *Labour/Le Travailleur* 3 (1978): 5-63.

153. *The Workingman's Journal*, 18 June 1864, supported the club movement in England. On Victorian workingmen's clubs see Gareth Stedman Jones, "Working-Class Culture and Working-Class Politics in London, 1870-1900: Notes on the Remaking of a Working Class," *Journal of Social History*, 7 (Summer 1974), esp. p. 44; John Taylor, *From Self-Help to Glamour: The Working Man's Club, 1860-1972* (Oxford: History Workshop, 1971); Stan Shipley, *Club Life and Socialism in Mid-Victorian London* (Oxford: History Workshop, 1972).

154. *HS*, 22 Jan. 1876.

155. Ibid., 19 Nov. 1878, 20 Oct. 1884; *POL*, 10 Dec. 1883, 12 June 1886.

156. See *POL*, 3 and 10 Nov. 1883, 6 Dec. 1884, 28 Mar. 1885; and the fictionalized accounts of "Our Social Club," an association of working-class intellectuals debating aspects of popular political economy in ibid., 8, 15, 22, and 29 Sept., 13 Oct. 1883. Cf. *HS*, 19 Mar. 1885, on a tradesmen's club meeting in a local tavern; and the case of the Burlington Quoiting Club, whose officers included a tinsmith, a painter, and a cabinetmaker, listed in the *City of Hamilton Directory, 1872-1873*.

157. *POL*, 18 Oct. 1884; *HS*, 14, 16, and 20 Oct. 1884. Officers of the club were listed in *POL*, 28 Mar. 1885, and their occupations checked in city directories.

158. On the East and West End Clubs see *HS*, 4 and 11 Nov., 23 Dec. 1897, 14 Jan., 3 Feb., 17 Nov. 1898; 20 Jan., 15 Feb., 17 Mar. 1899, 7 June 1904. The only case found of a club similar to those of the 1880s existing in the 1890s was that of an association of young boys, ages 13-17, who worked during the day. See *HS*, 28 Mar. 1893.

159. *Minute Book, Hamilton Trades and Labor Council, 1910-1914*, pp. 51-52, Hamilton Collection; *Cotton's Weekly*, 4 Mar. 1909, 22 June 1911.

160. On the charivari see Edward Shorter, *The Making of the Modern Family* (New York: Basic Books, 1975), pp. 46, 64, 217-18; Violet Alford, "Rough Music or Charivari," *Folklore* 70 (1959): 505-18; Davis, "The Reasons of Misrule," pp. 97-123. The best treatment, combining rich detail and subtle analysis, is E. P. Thompson, "'Rough Music': The Charivari anglaise," *Annales, E.S.C.* 27 (1972): 285-312.

161. On the nuclear family in Hamilton see Katz, *People of Hamilton*, pp. 209-308.

162. Data on Hamilton and district charivaris were culled from the local press, where accounts ranged from brief passages in the police and court dockets to extraordinarily detailed descriptive articles on specific events. See *HT*, 7 Aug. 1867, 13 Jan. 1868, 16 July 1875; *HS*, 9 Sept. 1879, 30 Jan. 1880, 1 Nov., 29 Oct. 1881, 24 Feb. 1883, 17 Mar. 1884, 16 June 1885, 15 May 1886, 4, 5, and 9 June, 10 July 1890, 24 Feb. 1892, 14 Aug. 1894.

163. See *Hamilton Charivari, An Election Fly Sheet Edited on this Occasion Only by Canadian Sepoys! Dulce et Decorum est Pro Hamiltonia Vivere, Vitat! Regina!* (Hamilton: n.p., 1857), in the National Library, Ottawa. I am grateful to Robert Storey for making this source available to me. It is possible that the circular drew its name from the British periodical, *Punch, or the London Charivari*, which in turn borrowed from the earlier French satirical journal of the 1830s.

164. Susanna Moodie, *Roughing It in the Bush* (Toronto: McClelland and Stewart, 1962), pp. 145-46.

165. *HT*, 7 Aug. 1867, 13 Jan. 1868, *HS*, 1 Nov. 1881.

166. *HS*, 10 July 1890.

167. Ibid., 14 Aug. 1894.

168. Ibid., 29 Apr., 3 June 1890; *Minute Book, Trades and Labor Council, 1888-1896*, pp. 99, 102-4.

169. *HS*, 10, 4, and 5 June 1890.

170. Ibid., 9 June 1890.

171. Thompson, "Rough Music," esp. p. 297.

172. A brief but useful introduction to the White Caps is found in Hugh Graham and Ted Robert Gurr, eds., *Violence in America: Historical and Comparative Perspectives* (Washington: Bantam, 1969), pp. 70-71, 806.

173. B. F. De Costa, *The White Cross: Its Origins and Progress* (Chicago: Sanitary Publishing, 1887); Ellice Hopkins, *The White Cross Army* (London: Baines, 188?).

174. See William F. Holmes, "Whitecapping: Agrarian Violence in Mississippi, 1902-1906," *Journal of Southern History* 25 (May 1969): 165-85. On the Georgia White Caps, and the lynching of two blacks who "had run away from contract labor after having got into debt," see *HS*, 1 Mar. 1901. On the regalia of the White Caps see Nettie H. Pelham, *The White Caps* (Chicago: T. S. Denison, 1891), p. 2; E. W. Crozier, *The White Caps: A History of the Organization in Sevier County* (Knoxville, Tenn.: Bean, Warters, and Baut, 1899), p. 31.

175. See Crozier, *The White Caps*, pp. 12-13; C. M. Graham, "Have You Ever Heard of the White Caps?" *New Mexico Genealogist* 6 (December 1967): 3-8; Charles A. Siringo, *Cow-Boy Detective: An Autobiography* (New York: J. S. Ogilvie, 1912), pp. 120-22.

176. The only scholarly treatment is Madelein M. Noble, "The White Caps of Harrison and Crawford County, Indiana: A Study in the Violent Enforcement of Morality" (Ph.D. diss., University of Michigan, 1973). Indiana was apparently the birthplace of whitecapping and Booth Tarkington used the phenomenon as a major theme in his novel, *The Gentleman from Indiana* (New York: Doubleday, 1899).

177. *HS*, 10 June 1896, 11 Jan. 1901; Graham, "Have You Heard of White Caps," pp. 3-8; Andrew Bancroft Schlesinger, "Los Gorros Blancas, 1889-1891," *Journal of Mexican American History* 1 (Spring 1971): 87-143; Robert W. Larson, "The White Caps of New Mexico: A Study of Ethnic Militancy in the Southwest," *Pacific Historical Review* 44 (May 1975): 171-85.

178. Crozier, *White Caps*, pp. 7-24.

179. Holmes, "Whitecapping," pp. 165-85.

180. Graham, "Have You Heard of White Caps," pp. 3-8; Siringo, *Cow-Boy Detective*, pp. 120-22; Schlesinger, "Los Gorros Blancas," pp. 87-143.

181. *POL*, 21 June 1884.

182. On the Hamilton White Caps' defiance of authority see *HS*, 2 May, 19 June 1900.

183. The Ollman brothers were cited in ibid., 19 June 1900, and their occupations culled from city directories.

184. On the importance of the strike, which will be discussed in more detail in chap. 3 below, see Kealey, "Honest Workingman," pp. 45-46 and n. 80.

185. *HS*, 11 Apr. 1892. For other anonymous, threatening letters see chaps. 5 and 7 below, and *London Free Press*, 1 Nov. 1898; *Globe*, 1 Jan. 1881 (my thanks to Gregory S. Kealey for bringing the latter source to my attention).

186. One attempt to transcend this tendency to ignore continuities in working-class life is Gutman, "Work, Culture and Society in Industrializing America, 1815-1919," pp. 531-88. A brief but illuminating discussion of cultural continuity is found in E. P. Thompson, "A Special Case," *New Society* 24 (February 1972): 404.

187. *Labor Union*, 10 Feb. 1883.

CHAPTER 3

1. See for instance James Hinton, *The First Shop Stewards' Movement* (London: George Allen and Unwin, 1973); Branko Pribicevic, *The Shop Stewards' Movement and Workers' Control, 1910-1922* (Oxford: Basil Blackwell, 1959);

Arthur Gleason, "The Shop Stewards and Their Significance," *Survey* 41 (4 Jan. 1919): 417-22; Gleason, "British Labor Breaks the Truce," *Survey* 40 (27 July 1918): 467-72; Peter Warrian, "The Challenge of the One Big Union Movement in Canada, 1919-1921" (M.A. thesis, University of Waterloo, 1971), pp. 52-60. Cf. the important discussion of the situation in the United States in David Montgomery, "The 'New Unionism' and the Transformation of Workers' Consciousness, 1909-1922," *Journal of Social History* 7 (Summer 1974): 509-22. The quote is from Carter Goodrich, *The Frontier of Control: A Study of British Workshop Practices* (New York: Harcourt, Brace, and Howe, 1920), p. 31.

2. See the recent studies: David Montgomery, "Workers' Control of Machine Production in the Nineteenth Century," *Labor History* 17 (Fall 1976): 485-509: Gregory S. Kealey, "The 'Honest Workingman' and Workers' Control: The Experience of Toronto Skilled Workers, 1860-1892," *Labour/Le Travailleur* 1 (1976): 32-68; Bob Gilding, *The Journeymen Coopers of East London: Workers' Control in an Old London Trade* (Oxford: History Workshop, 1972).

3. Quoted in Dale Chisamore et al., *Brockville: A Social History, 1890-1930* (Brockville, Ont.: Waterway Press), p. 87.

4. *HS*, 5 May 1883.

5. *John Swinton's Paper*, 8 and 15 June 1884.

6. *Workingman's Advocate*, 25 Mar. 1876.

7. *Trades Union Advocate*, 4 May 1882.

8. *POL*, 17 Nov. 1883.

9. *Labor Union*, 10 Mar. 1883.

10. *Cigar Makers' Official Journal*, 15 Oct. 1882.

11. *HS*, 18 May 1876.

12. *POL*, 1 May 1886.

13. *Labor Union*, 27 Jan. 1883.

14. *POL*, 25 Aug. 1883.

15. See the accounts of the Hamilton glass factory and the work process in glassblowing in *HS*, 12 Sept. 1864, 29 Mar., 24 June 1867, 29 Aug. 1871, 15 Apr. 1874. On nailmaking in the Hamilton rolling mill see *HS*, 27 Sept. 1879. On molding at the Gartshore foundry see *The National*, 17 Oct. 1878. On hand cigar-making, prior to the introduction of the mold, see *Workingman's Advocate*, 11 May 1872. On the limitations of technological innovation in some important trades see Daniel J. Walkowitz, "Worker City, Company Town: Adaptation and Protest Within the Troy Iron Worker and Cohoes Cotton Worker Communities, 1855-1884" (typescript, Rutgers, 1976), chap. 2; Lee W. Minton, *Flame and Heart: A History of the Glass Bottle Blowers Association of the United States and Canada* (New York: Merkle Press, 1961), pp. 3, 23-24; Margaret Loomis Stecker, "The Founders, The Molders and the Molding Machine," in John R. Commons, ed., *Trade Unionism and Labor Problems*, 2nd ser. (New York: Ginn and Co., 1921), pp. 433-57; Wayne Roberts, "Metal Workers and the Second Industrial Revolution: Toronto, 1896-1914" (typescript, University of Toronto, 1976), esp. p. 5, n. 3.

16. See the excellent discussion in Benson Soffer, "A Theory of Trade Union Development: The Role of the 'Autonomous' Workman," *Labor History* 1 (Spring 1960): 141-63.

17. See George Barnett, "The Printers: A Study in American Trade Unionism," *American Economic Association Quarterly* 3rd ser., 10, no. 3 (1909): 182-208, 243-56; Barnett, *Chapters on Machinery and Labor* (Carbondale, Ill.:

Southern Illinois University Press, 1969); Wayne Roberts, "The Last Artisans: Toronto Printers, 1896-1914," in Gregory S. Kealey and Peter Warrian, eds., *Essays in Canadian Working Class History* (Toronto: McClelland and Stewart, 1976), pp. 125-42; *Proceedings of the 24th Annual Session, Glass Bottle Blowers Association of the United States and Canada, Detroit, 9-16 July 1900* (Camden, N.J.: C. S. McGrath, 1900), pp. 40-41; *Proceedings of 26th Session, Glass Blowers Association, 1902* (Camden, N.J.: C. S. McGrath, 1902), p. 51; Minton, *Flame and Heart*, pp. 19-22, 30; *The Craftsman*, 29 Oct. 1887.

18. *Labor Advocate*, 5 Dec. 1890. See the early statements on controlling the machine in *The Socialist*, 6 May 1876; *Iron Molders' International Journal*, 10 Oct. 1875.

19. Carter L. Goodrich, "Problems of Workers' Control," *Locomotive Engineers' Journal* 57 (May 1923): 356-65, 415; Goodrich, *The Frontier of Control*, pp. 41-42, 137-38, 260, 264-65.

20. On Canada see *Report of the Royal Commission on the Relations of Labor and Capital in Canada*, "Quebec Evidence," III (Ottawa: Queen's Printer, 1889), 55, 457; "Quebec Evidence," IV, 900; "New Brunswick Evidence," V, 131; "Nova Scotia Evidence," VI, 61, 371, 401, 411. On the United States practices see the monumental Carrol D. Wright et al., "Regulation and Restriction of Output," *Eleventh Special Report of the Commissioner of Labor* (Washington: Government Printing, 1904); and the abbreviated discussion in Wright, "The Restriction of Output," *North American Review* 183 (2 Nov. 1906): 887-96.

21. On the foreman see Benson Soffer, "The Role of Union Foremen in the Evolution of the International Typographical Union," *Labor History* 2 (Winter 1961): 62-81; *Canadian Labor Reformer*, 16 Oct. 1886. On shop committees see the discussions in Kealey, "Honest Workingman," pp. 40-42; Frank T. Stockton, *The International Iron Molders' Union of North America* (Baltimore: John Hopkins, 1921), p. 40; *Iron Molders' International Journal*, 10 Dec. 1875.

22. *POL*, 19 July 1884, reported an interesting case of restriction of output by a gang of labourers: "A gang of Italian labourers near Saratoga was recently cut down ten cents a day. Instead of striking they cut an inch off their shovel blades at night. The boss asked what it meant and one of the men replied: 'Not so much pay, not so much dirt left; all right, job last the more long. Italian no fool like Irishman; he no strike.'" On the persistence of output restriction in unorganized trades see S. B. Mathewson, *Restriction of Output Among Unorganized Workers* (Carbondale, Ill.: Southern Illinois University Press, 1969).

23. "What One Trade Has Done," *John Swinton's Paper*, 23 Mar. 1884; Montgomery, "Workers' Control," pp. 493-94; Irwin Yellowitz, *Industrialization and the American Labor Movement, 1850-1900* (Port Washington, N.Y.: Kennikat Press, 1977), p. 59. Other assessments of glass workers' power are found in *HS*, 6 and 9 Jan. 1879; *Relations of Labor and Capital*, "Nova Scotia Evidence," VI, 371; *Proceedings of the U.G.G. Workers' Association of the United States and Canada, Composed of Glass Bottle Makers, 18th Annual Session, Atlantic City, 9-19 July 1894* (Lockport, N.Y.: Democrat, 1894), pp. 90-93; *Proceedings of the National Trade Assembly of No. 143, Knights of Labor of America, Composed of Glass Bottle Workers in the United States and Canada, 15th Annual Session, St. Louis, 13-24 July 1891* (Lockport, N.Y.: James Murphy, 1891), pp. 367-69; *The Carpenter*, March 1884; *POL*, 10 Jan. 1885. Cf. the discussion of French glass workers' strength prior to 1895 in Joan Wallach Scott, *The Glassworkers of Carmaux: French Craftsmen and*

Political Action in a Nineteenth Century City (Cambridge, Mass.: Harvard University Press, 1974), pp. 19-52.

24. See *HS*, 24 June 1867; *POL*, 16 Aug. 1884, 5 and 22 Aug. 1885, 16 Oct. 1886. On the esteem in which glass workers were held see the coverage of the 1886 convention, and the reception afforded a group of Steubenville glass blowers, camping at Burlington Beach over one summer stop, in *HS*, 15 July 1886, 10 and 17 July, 5 Aug. 1890; *POL*, 17 July 1886.

25. *HS*, 8 Apr. 1886.

26. Exceptional conflicts are mentioned in *HS*, 5 and 7 May 1881; *Minute Book of the Trades and Labor Council, 1888-1896*, p. 28, Hamilton Trades and Labor Council. Note the endorsement of the Pittsburgh glass workers' 48-box limit in *POL*, 19 Apr. 1884.

27. M. A. Pigott to Adam Brown, MP, 8 May 1888, Macdonald Papers, MG 26 A, vol. 155, pp. 63160-64, PAC; "Combinations Restricting the Amount of Work," *POL*, 22 Dec. 1883.

28. On depreciation of the "hog" see *Relations of Labor and Capital*, "Ontario Evidence," II, 821-22; *POL*, 12 Apr. 1884, 7 Feb., 25 July 1885, 10 Apr. 1886. Attacks on "rushing" were widespread. See *The Carpenter*, November 1885, 15 Jan. 1889; *Iron Molders' International Journal*, 31 Oct. 1870, 10 Sept. 1875, April 1884, November 1885, December 1885; Wright, *Eleventh Special Report*, "Regulation and Restriction of Output," pp. 18, 26-30. Note the religious critique in *POL*, 27 Mar. 1886.

29. Montgomery, "Workers' Control," p. 491; Kealey, "Honest Workingman," p. 37; *Iron Molders' International Journal*, November 1887; *Workingman's Advocate*, 5 Nov. 1864; *POL*, 26 Jan., 20 Sept. 1884. The quotation is from *Industrial Banner*, September 1908.

30. *Industrial Banner*, December 1899.

31. *POL*, 9 Oct. 1886. On union discipline see Iron Molders' International Collection, Box I, Archives of Labor History and Urban Affairs, Wayne State University, *Minute Book, Molders' Union of New York, 1860-1868*, p. 26; International Iron Molders' Union No. 191 (Peterborough), *Minute Book, 1882-1892*, 4 Sept. 1882, Gainey Collection, Trent University Archives. Cf. Solomon Blum, "Trade Union Rules in the Building Trades," in Jacob H. Hollander and George C. Barnett, eds., *Studies in American Trade Unionism* (New York: Henry Holt, 1907), pp. 295-319.

32. The most detailed study of the standard rate is David A. McCabe, *The Standard Rate in American Trade Unions* (Baltimore: John Hopkins, 1912). Cf. Stockton, *International Molders' Union*, pp. 137-58.

33. The strike is mentioned in 'Hamilton Early Stronghold in Organized Labor Cause," *HS*, 15 July 1946; *The Hamilton and District Trades and Labor Council, 60th Anniversary, Diamond Jubilee, 1888-1848* (Hamilton:Spectator, 1948), p. 3. Both of these sources, however, mistakenly date the conflict in 1859. Contemporary accounts are found in *HS*, 8 Nov. 1856; *Windsor Herald*, 7 and 14 Nov. 1856.

34. Lloyd Atkinson and Eugene Forsey, "The Labour Movement in Hamilton, 1827-1888," typescript, Canadian Labour Congress Collection, MG 28 I 103, vol. 249, p. 4, PAC.

35. *HT*, 1 June 1864; *HS*, 31 May 1864.

36. *Iron Molders' International Journal*, 15 Dec. 1864; *HS*, 13 Dec. 1864.

37. *HT*, 23 Feb. 1866.

38. Ibid., 23 Mar. 1866.

39. On the Troy molders' struggle see Walkowitz, "Worker City, Company Town," chaps. 1-2; *Iron Molders' International Journal*, April 1866, May 1866; *HT*, 5 May 1866; *Workingman's Advocate*, 21 Apr. 1866.

40. *HT*, 5 May 1866; *Iron Molders' International Journal*, May 1866, June 1866, July 1866, August 1866, October 1866, January 1867; Charles Brian Williams, "Canadian American Trade Union Relations — A Study of the Development of Binational Unionism" (Ph.D. diss., Cornell University, 1964), p. 122.

41. Atkinson and Forsey, "Hamilton Labor Movement," p. 7. Hamilton's Molders' Union was organizationally inactive for some of the period. See *Iron Molders' International Journal*, 31 Oct. 1871.

42. Williams, "Canadian American Trade Union Relations," pp. 126-27; *Ontario Workman*, 23 May 1872; *Dumfries Reformer*, 22 May 1872. For detail on the molders and the 1872 upheaval see chap. 5 below. On the reorganization of IMIU No. 26 see *Iron Molders' International Journal*, January 1872.

43. *Iron Molders' International Journal*, October 1872.

44. Ibid., December 1872.

45. Williams, "Canadian American Trade Union Relations," pp. 131-40; *Iron Molders' International Journal*, 30 June 1873, October 1873, February 1874, 30 Apr. 1874.

46. *Iron Molders' International Journal*, 10 Sept. 1874; Robert H. Storey, "Industrialization in Canada: The Emergence of the Hamilton Working Class, 1850-1870s" (M.A. thesis, Dalhousie, 1975), pp. 179-80.

47. *Iron Molders' International Journal*, April 1874.

48. *HS*, 27 Aug. 1874.

49. On the beginnings of the struggle see *HS*, 27 and 28 Aug., 4 and 11 Sept. 1874; *Iron Molders' International Journal*, 10 Sept., 10 Oct., 10 Dec. 1874; Storey, "Industrialization in Canada," pp. 179-80; *Minutes of the Proceedings of the Toronto Trades Assembly, 1871-1878*, typescript, p. 211, PAC. This period was one of a general assault on the molders. See *Iron Molders' International Journal*, 10 Oct. 1875; Kealey, "Honest Workingman," pp. 43-44.

50. *Iron Molders' International Journal*, 10 Feb. 1875.

51. On the tailors' struggle see *HS*, 15 and 19 Aug., 24 and 30 Oct. 1873; *Ontario Workman*, 21 Aug., 30 Oct. 1873.

52. *HS*, 21 Nov. 1879.

53. Ibid., 17 and 19 Feb. 1881.

54. Ibid., 21 and 25 Apr. 1881.

55. Ibid., 6 and 9 May 1881.

56. Ibid., 5 May 1879, 25-30 Apr. 1881.

57. Ibid., 9 July 1881.

58. Ibid., 9 and 13 July 1881.

59. Ibid., 2, 5, and 6 May 1881.

60. Ibid., 5 May 1881.

61. Ibid., 10 May 1881.

62. Ibid., 7 May 1881. Note the editorial in ibid., 9 May 1881.

63. Ibid., 27 May, 1 and 2 June 1881.

64. Ibid., 4, 6, and 16 Mar. 1882.

65. Ibid., 9 Mar.–3 Apr. 1882.

66. Ibid., 28 and 29 Mar. 1882.

67. Ibid., 10 and 14 Apr. 1882.

68. Ibid., 5 Apr.–1 June 1882.

69. Ibid., 8, 10, 12, and 17 June 1882.

70. Ibid., 27 Mar., 10 and 15 Apr. 1882; Eugene Forsey, "The Canadian Labour Movement, 1812-1902," Canadian Historical Association, *Historical Booklet No. 27* (1974), p. 9.

71. *HS*, 15 Apr. 1882.

72. See chap. 6 below for detail.

73. *HS*, 18 and 20 Apr., 1 and 5 May 1883.

74. Ibid., 1-26 May 1883.

75. *Relations of Labor and Capital*, "Ontario Evidence," II, 795; *HS*, 4, 10, and 13 Dec. 1883; *POL*, 15 Dec. 1883.

76. *HS*, 12, 13, 17, and 20 Jan. 1885; *The Craftsman*, 21 March 1885; *POL*, 17 Jan., 2 May 1885.

77. *Relations of Labor and Capital*, "Ontario Evidence," II, 790-91.

78. *POL*, 4 and 11 Apr. 1885. On the coopers' demise see Kealey, "Honest Workingman," pp. 34-40.

79. On the shoemakers' experience see Gregory S. Kealey, "Artisans Respond to Industrialism: Shoemakers, Shoe Factories and the Knights of St. Crispin in Toronto," Canadian Historical Association, *Historical Papers* (1973), pp. 137-57.

80. *POL*, 7 Nov. 1885. The poem, from an 1875 issue of *The National*, is quoted in N. Brian Davis, *The Poetry of the Canadian People, 1720-1920: Two hundred years of hard work* (Toronto: NC Press, 1976), p. 148.

81. *HS*, 5 Mar. 1888.

82. Ibid., 23, 24, and 26 Mar. 1888.

83. Ibid., 26 Mar. 1888. For Hamilton bricklayers' apprenticeship regulations see *The Carpenter*, March 1887.

84. *HS*, 28 Mar. 1888.

85. Ibid., 30 Mar. 1888.

86. Ibid., 2 Apr. 1888.

87. Ibid., 25 Apr. 1888.

88. Ibid., 27 Apr., 1 and 8 May 1888.

89. Ibid., 30 Apr., 21 June, 28 Nov. 1888, 5 and 6 Feb., 10 May 1889.

90. Ibid., 20 and 16 Aug. 1888. Cf. clippings in R. R. Elliot to Sir John A. Macdonald, 11 Mar. 1889, Macdonald Papers, vol. 332, pp. 150045-46.

91. *HS*, 5 July 1888.

92. Ibid., 6 Apr., 21 May 1891; *Labor Advocate*, 10 Apr., 29 May 1891.

93. *HS*, 5 July 1892, 20 and 27 Sept., 7 and 10 Oct. 1895.

94. *Relations of Labor and Capital*, "Ontario Evidence," II, 796; *HS*, 4, 6, 8, and 9 June, 18, 19, and 27 July 1887, 21 and 22 Feb., 12 and 13 Mar. 1888; *Iron Molders' International Journal*, June 1887, July 1887. On the molders and control see *POL*, 6 Feb. 1886.

95. Between 1888 and 1892 only one brief skirmish occurred. See *Iron Molders' International Journal*, November 1890, on a strike in one foundry.

96. *HS*, 11–29 Jan. 1892; *Iron Molders' International Journal*, January 1892, February 1892.

97. *HS*, 1 Feb. 1892.

98. Similar conflicts had been precipitated in Toronto in 1891 and in Kingston, Ontario, in 1892. See Kealey, "Honest Workingman," p. 46; *HS*, 6 Feb. 1892.

99. *HS*, 5–10 Feb. 1892.

100. On the progress of the strike and the increasing use of violence see *HS*, 11 Feb. – 11 May 1892.

101. John Jennings to Mr. Parkes, Hamilton, 20 Mar. 1892, Iron Molders' International Union No. 191, "Canadian Correspondence," Gainey Collection, vol. 10, file 3, Trent University Archives. Cf. M. Basquil and Fred Walters to No. 191, Hamilton, 8 Feb. 1892, ibid.; *Minute Book, Hamilton Trades and Labor Council, 1888-1896*, p. 224.

102. "Labor Struggle Against Capital," Molders' Union No. 191, "Miscellaneous," Gainey Collection, vol. 10, file 6.

103. *HS*, 1 and 3 Aug. 1892.

104. Ibid., 5 and 10 Aug. 1892.

105. Ibid., 17 and 27 Feb. 1893, and *Iron Molders' International Journal*, March 1893, document the continuing struggle.

106. On this practice in Hamilton see *HS*, 25 Apr. 1879, 14 June 1882. The phenomenon was common among skilled workers. See *Labor Standard*, 2 Sept. 1877; *Workingman's Advocate*, 11 May 1872; *Toronto Tribune*, 23 Sept. 1905; Samuel Gompers, *Seventy Years of Life and Labor: An Autobiography* (New York: E. P. Dutton, 1925), pp. 80-81; Herbert G. Gutman, "Work, Culture, and Society in Industrializing America, 1815-1919," *American Historical Review* 78 (June 1973): 558.

107. *Relations of Labor and Capital*, "Ontario Evidence," II, 791; Robert T. Armstrong, "Memoir of Duncan Lithographing Company, 1882-1978," n.p. John Weaver provided a xerox of this interesting document, currently in the archives of the Duncan Lithographing Company of Hamilton. "Red Ink's" recollections are in *'Pi': A Compilation of Odds and Ends Relating to Workers in Sanctum and Newsroom, Culled From the Scrap-Book of a Compositor* (Hamilton: Griffin and Kidner, 1890), pp. 5-7, 186, drawing upon an article by Bob Burdett and a poem by Jimmy Platt.

108. See GWR Pay List, Locomotive Department, 18-31 Jan., 1-14 Feb., 1863, files 1-18 and 19-22, Hamilton Collection, Hamilton Public Library; *HS*, 22 Feb. 1881, 23 Feb. 1882; *Relations of Labor and Capital*, "Ontario Evidence," II, 743-44, 761.

109. On the molders opposition to "bucks" see *Iron Molders' International Journal*, October 1873, 10 Nov. 1875, December 1866, Stockton, *Molders' International Union*, pp. 170-85; Joseph A. Barford, "Reminiscences of the Early Days of Stove Plate Molding and the Union," *International Molders' and Foundry Workers' Journal* 94 (July 1958): 8-12; Kealey, "Honest Workingman," pp. 45-46; *Labor Leaf*, 16 June 1886.

110. *HS*, 29 Feb. 1892.

111. The question of helpers is discussed in Montgomery, "Workers' Control," p. 488; John H. Ashworth, *The Helper and the American Trade Unions* (Baltimore: Johns Hopkins, 1915).

112. *The Carpenter*, November 1885; *POL*, 22 Dec. 1883.

113. *Iron Molders' International Journal*, October 1883.

114. On Hamilton apprenticeship conditions and their importance to the crafts see *POL*, 20 Sept. 1884; *Relations of Labor and Capital*, "Ontario Evidence," II, 296, 797.

115. Harriet Annie Wilkins, *Victor Roy: A Masonic Poem* (Hamilton: Spectator, 1882), pp. 99-100. Cf. *Journal of the Board of Arts and Manufactures for Upper Canada* 5 (1864): 305.

116. See Kealey, "Honest Workingman," pp. 43-44; *HS*, 20 Sept. 1892, 12 Apr. 1893; Craig Heron and Bryan D. Palmer, "Through the Prism of the Strike: Industrial Conflict in Southern Ontario, 1901-1914," *Canadian Historical Review* 58 (December 1977): 423-58.

117. As an introduction to nineteenth-century cooperation see John F. C. Harrison, *Quest for the New Moral World: Robert Owen and the Owenites in Britain and America* (London: Routledge and Kegan Paul, 1969); Sidney Pollard, "Nineteenth Century Co-operation: From Community Building to Shopkeeping," in Asa Briggs and John Saville, eds., *Essays in Labour History* (London: Macmillan, 1960), pp. 74-112. The relationship between cooperation and control is outlined in Kealey, "Honest Workingman and Workers' Control," pp. 58-61.

118. *Fincher's Trade Review*, 15 Aug. 1863. My thanks to Gregory S. Kealey for making this source available to me.

119. *HT*, 26 Nov. 1864.

120. *Constitution and By-Laws of the Hamilton Co-operative Association, Constituted December 1864* (Hamilton: Times, 1864), p. 3. Cf. *HS*, 5 and 13 Dec. 1864.

121. On the rise and fall of the association see *HS*, 17 Jan., 18 Apr., 16 Aug., 22 Oct. 1867, 16 Jan. 1868, 9 Mar., 28 Oct. 1870; *HT*, 5 July, 28 Dec. 1865, 18 Jan., 9 Feb., 4 Apr., 20 July 1866, 29 May 1867.

122. *HS*, 29 Nov., 12 Dec. 1865, 26 and 29 June 1878; *Labor Union*, 10 Feb. 1883.

123. *Workingman's Advocate*, 25 May 1872.

124. *HS*, 13 Feb. 1892.

125. Ibid., 14 Apr. 1882, 13 Apr. 1883; *POL*, 20 June 1885.

126. Minute Book, *Hamilton Trades and Labor Council, 1888-1896*, p. 28.

127. *HS*, 10 and 16 May, 4 and 7 Apr. 1888.

128. See chap. 6 below.

129. *Relations of Labor and Capital*, "Report," I, 112.

130. Henry L. Gantt, *Work, Wages and Profits* (New York: Engineering Magazine, 1913), p. 186.

CHAPTER 4

1. The poem, originally dedicated to the political economist W. E. Sumner of Yale University, appeared in a number of labour-reform newspapers including *The National*, 17 Oct. 1878; *Labor Standard*, 14 Dec. 1878; *The Craftsman*, 26 Mar. 1887. It is reproduced in Ramsay Cook, "The Professor and the Prophet of Unrest," *Transactions of the Royal Society of Canada*, 4th ser., 13 (1975): 249-50.

2. See R. V. Clement, "British Trade Unions and Popular Political Economy," *Economic History Review* 2nd ser., 14 (1961-62): 93-104; and the socialist classic, Robert Tressell, *The Ragged Trousered Philanthropists* (London: Lawrence and Wishart, 1955). For North American labour's attack on classical political economy see *Labor Union*, 20 Jan., 3 Feb. 1883; *Canadian Labor Reformer*, 28 Aug. 1886; *Cigar Makers' Official Journal*, January 1877; *The Craftsman*, 12 Dec. 1885, 23 Jan. 1886; *POL*, 7 June, 5 July 1884; *Journal of United Labor*, December-November 1881, December 1883, 25 May 1884, 10 June 1885, 25 Sept. 1890; *HS*, 20 Mar. 1885.

3. John McCormick, *The Conditions of Labour and Modern Civilization* (Toronto: Bell, 1880), p. 5; *HS*, 10 Mar. 1871; *POL*, 15 May 1886. Cf. F. P.

Mackelcan, *Labor and Capital; How to Unite Them and Produce Universal Industry and Prosperity* (Montreal: Gazette, 1872), pp. 22-23, 32-43.

4. For an important discussion of the continuity and impact of this ideology see L. R. Macdonald, "Merchants Against Industry: An Idea and its Origins," *Canadian Historical Review* 56 (September 1975): 263-81.

5. On the language of class see Asa Briggs, "The Language of 'Class' in Early Nineteenth Century England," in Briggs and Saville, eds., *Essays in Labour History* (London: Macmillan, 1960), pp. 43-73.

6. On the National Policy see O. J. McDiarmid, *Commercial Policy in the Canadian Economy* (Cambridge, Mass.: Harvard University Press, 1946); Vernon C. Fowke, "The National Policy — Old and New," *Canadian Journal of Economics and Political Science* 18 (1952): 271-86; F. W. Watt, "The National Policy, the Workingman and Proletarian Ideas in Victorian Canada," *Canadian Historical Review* 40 (March 1959): 1-26; and the idiosyncratic argument in R. T. Naylor, "The Rise and Fall of the Third Commercial Empire of the St. Lawrence," in Gary Teeple, ed., *Capitalism and the National Question in Canada* (Toronto: University of Toronto Press, 1972), pp. 1-41.

7. The contours of economic development are outlined in Jacob Spelt, *Urban Development in South-Central Ontario* (Toronto: McClelland and Stewart, 1972), pp. 101-86; O. J. Firestone, *Canada's Economic Development, 1867-1953* (London: Bowes and Bowes, 1958), pp. 31-39, 203-10; Firestone, "Development of Canada's Economy, 1850-1900," in Report of the National Bureau of Economic Research, *Trends in the American Economy in the Nineteenth Century* (Princeton: Princeton University Press, 1960), pp. 217-52.

8. Steven Langdon, *The Emergence of the Canadian Working Class Movement* (Toronto: New Hogtown Press, 1975), pp. 13-23; Bernard Ostry, "Conservatives, Liberals and Labour in the 1870s," *Canadian Historical Review* 41 (June 1960): 93-127; Leo A. Johnson, *History of the County of Ontario, 1615-1875* (Whitby, Ont.: County of Ontario, 1975), p. 334. For Hamilton detail see chap. 5 below.

9. Victor Oscar Chan, "Canadian Knights of Labor with Special Reference to the 1880's" (M.A. thesis, McGill University, 1949); Douglas R. Kennedy, *The Knights of Labor in Canada* (London: University of Western Ontario, 1956); and Greg Kealey, ed., *Canada Investigates Industrialism* (Toronto: University of Toronto Press, 1973), pp. ix-xxvii. Cf. chap. 6 below for fuller treatment.

10. This argument parallels an important theme — the role of class conflict in the demise of Radical Republicanism in the United States — in David Montgomery's insightful *Beyond Equality: Labor and the Radical Republicans, 1862-1872* (New York: Knopf, 1967). Cf. the as yet unappreciated Frank William Watt, "Radicalism in English Canadian Literature Since Confederation" (Ph.D. diss., University of Toronto, 1957).

11. Useful for comparative purposes is Norman Pollack, *The Populist Response to Industrial America* (New York: Norton, 1966). This chapter can be seen as a prologue to Norman Penner's recently published, *The Canadian Left: A Critical Analysis* (Scarborough, Ont.: Prentice-Hall, 1977). Whereas Penner contends that socialism in Canada was originally Marxist and working-class in character, becoming infused with social-democratic or reformist tendencies only with the increasing role of intellectuals and farmers in the opposition movements of the twentieth century, this discussion takes a different approach. Instead, it stresses the input of intellectuals and non-working-class elements from the outset, and

argues that Canadian working-class thought, rather than being Marxist, was populist in its origins. This is not to dismiss the populist critique, which was often
quite cogent, but simply to lend more analytical precision to our understanding of
the working-class experience, which stopped short of a revolutionary assault on
Canadian capitalism.

12. *Hamilton Herald*, 19 Jan. 1895.

13. On early protectionist sentiment see Samuel Thompson, *Reminiscences
of a Canadian Pioneer for the last Fifty Years (1833-1883): An Autobiography*
(Toronto: McClelland and Stewart, 1968), pp. 251-60; Craufurd D. W. Goodwin,
*Canadian Economic Thought: The Political Economy of a Developing Nation, 1814-
1914* (Durham, N.C.: Duke University Press, 1961), esp. pp. 42-49; *Hamilton
Gazette*, 25 Mar., 1 and 15 Apr. 1852. Cf. Gregory S. Kealey, "The Working-Class
Response to Industrial Capitalism in Toronto, 1867-1892" (Ph.D. diss., Univer-
sity of Rochester, 1977), pp. 18-22.

14. Buchanan's failures as a merchant have recently been dissected in P.
Douglas McCalla, "The Buchanan Businesses, 1834-1872: A Study in the Organization and Development of Canadian Trade" (Ph.D. diss., Oxford University,
1972). McCalla broadens his treatment of Buchanan in his "Buchanan, Isaac,
merchant, politician, and pamphleteer," *Dictionary of Canadian Biography*, 11,
1881-90, forthcoming.

15. Langdon, *Emergence of the Canadian Working Class Movement*, p. 4;
and, in more detail, Langdon, "The Political Economy of Capitalist Transformation: Central Canada from the 1840s to the 1870s" (M.A. thesis, Carleton University, 1972), pp. 173-80. Buchanan is also discussed, in a more critical fashion,
in Goodwin, *Canadian Economic Thought*, pp. 49-54, 82-83, 111, 200; and
McCalla, "Buchanan, Isaac," in *Dictionary of Canadian Biography*, 11, forthcoming. Cf. the contemporary assessment in *Canadian Illustrated News*, 30 May
1863, pp. 25-29.

16. "The Iron and the Fire," respectfully inscribed to Isaac Buchanan, 1
Nov. 1853, Buchanan Papers, MG 24 D 16, vol. 47, p. 37702, PAC. Cf. Thomas
Cowherd, "Stanzas," in *The Emigrant Mechanic and other tales in verse, together
with numerous songs upon Canadian subjects . . . by the Brantford tinsmith rhymer*
(Brantford: published by author, 1884), pp. 137-38.

17. *The Daily Spectator and Journal of Commerce* (Hamilton), 14 Feb. 1860.

18. See the forceful discussion of the 1858-59 tariff schedule in D. F. Barnett, "The Galt Tariff: incidental or effective protection?" *Canadian Journal of
Economics* 9 (August 1976): 389-407. The argument, stressing the "incidental
protection" of the revisions in the tariff, is found in Tom Naylor, *The History of
Canadian Business, 1867-1914*, I (Toronto: James Lorimer, 1975), 28-30.

19. Isaac Buchanan, memorandum, 15 Aug. 1874, Buchanan Papers, vol.
58, p. 46706.

20. *Hamilton Evening Times*, 15 Mar. 1859.

21. Ibid., 16 Mar. 1859; Naylor, *History of Canadian Business*, I, 29; Weir-
Buchanan correspondence relating to the Association for the Promotion of Canadian Industry, scattered dates, Buchanan Papers, vol. 58, pp. 46606-46744; *Report
of the Public Meeting of Delegates from Various Parts of Canada, Held in St. Lawrence
Hall, Toronto, 14 April 1858* (Toronto: APCI, 1858), pp. 4-10. On Buchanan's
reputation in protectionist circles see R. Coleman to Buchanan, 13 July 1858,
Buchanan Papers, vol. 21, p. 18182; Wm. Barber & Brother to Buchanan, 11 May
1860, vol. 2, pp. 1262-68; Buchanan to the Chairman of the Dominion Board of

Trade, 8 July 1874, vol. 34, pp. 28170-76. On Buchanan, the Galt tariff, and the APCI see also the recent discussion in Kealey, "Working-Class Response," pp. 26-28.

22. Isaac Buchanan to Charles Lindsay, 8 Mar. 1856, Charles Lindsay Papers, Public Archives of Ontario; *HT*, 9 Jan. 1858; *Greenlock Advertiser*, 5 Mar. 1850.

23. J. B. Burns to Buchanan, 14 Dec. 1857, Buchanan Papers, vol. 18, p. 14889, on $5 bribe for a vote; *Hamilton Evening Times*, 4 and 26 June 1861, on Buchanan's use of drink during elections (the paper was strongly anti-Buchanan); and Buchanan to Campbell, 12 Dec. 1879, Alex Campbell Papers, Public Archives of Ontario, on Buchanan's role as dispenser of patronage.

24. Buchanan to U. S. Grant, 23 Nov. 1870, Buchanan Papers, vol. 28, pp. 23892-93; Buchanan to Joseph Hickson, 4 Jan. 1877, vol. 31, pp. 25600-2.

25. "To the Workingmen of Hamilton," *The Hamilton Charivari: Election Fly-Sheet, Edited on This Occasion Only By Canadian Sepoys* (Hamilton: n.p., 1857), p. 4.

26. Buchanan to Grant, 23 Nov. 1870, Buchanan Papers, vol. 28, pp. 23892-93, on support for the ten-hour movement; Buchanan to Hickson, 4 Jan. 1877, vol. 31, pp. 25600-1, on the trainmen; Robert H. Storey, "Industrialization in Canada: The Emergence of the Hamilton Working Class, 1850-1870s" (M.A. thesis, Dalhousie University, 1975), pp. 166-80, on the election of Witton.

27. "Isaac Buchanan and the Mechanics," letter from "A Free Mechanic," 7 Sept. 1867, Buchanan Papers, 1697-1896, pp. 321-23, Hamilton Collection, Hamilton Public Library. Cf., *Hamilton Evening Times*, 1 and 20 Apr., 13 July 1864; *HS*, 5, 9, and 11 Apr. 1864.

28. Buchanan, *A Home Market for the Farmer, Our Best Reciprocity: Britain the Country versus Britain the Empire* (Hamilton: Spectator, 1860), pp. 10-11. The inconsistencies and confusions of Buchanan's writings can be all too easily stressed. Yet these logical deficiencies did not necessarily undermine the force of Buchanan's concerns, which addressed central interests of "the producing classes."

29. Buchanan, "An Address to the Free and Independent Electors of the City of Hamilton," in ibid., p. vii.

30. Buchanan, *A Home Market for the Farmer*, p. 13. Cf. Buchanan, "Speech at Toronto, 1864," cited in Naylor, *History of Canadian Business*, I, 29.

31. On Buchanan's horror of the 1837 uprising, which he referred to as "the irreligious and dangerous gulf of Revolutionary Republicanism that *we saw* yawning to embrace us," see Buchanan, *First Series of Five Letters Against the Baldwin Faction, by an advocate of Responsible Government and the New College Bill* (Toronto: British Colonist, 1844), pp. 3, 8, 13.

32. Buchanan, "Can the British Monarchy be Preserved?", letter to George Bentinck, M.P., 25 Mar. 1848, Pamphlet Collection, PAC.

33. Buchanan, *The British American Federation a Necessity, Its Industrial Policy Also a Necessity* (Hamilton: Spectator, 1865), p. 45.

34. Buchanan, *The Patriotic Party Versus the Cosmopolite Party* (Toronto: Scobie and Balfour, 1848), p. 32. For later writings expressive of the same position see Buchanan, *National Uplift: or the Cup of British Prosperity as It Unfortunately Is* (Hamilton: Spectator, 1860), pp. 11, 46, 181.

35. Buchanan, *Letters Illustrative of the Present Position of Politics in Canada* (Hamilton: Spectator, 1859), p. 5. For comparative purposes, and a work Buchanan borrowed liberally from, see Horace Greeley, *Labor's Political Economy; or the Tariff Question Considered* (Toronto: APCI, 1858).

36. Buchanan, "An Address to the Free and Independent Electors of Hamilton," in *Home Market for the Farmer*, pp. xvi-xvii.

37. Buchanan, *Letters Illustrative of Politics in Canada*, p. 6; Buchanan, *Home Market for the Farmer*, pp. 11-12; Buchanan, *British American Federation a Necessity*, pp. 22-23.

38. Buchanan, "National Vitalities: Or Britain the Country Versus Britain the Empire: The Vital Politics for the Hustings — A Home Market for the Farmer," in *Home Market for the Farmer*, pp. xci-xcii.

39. Buchanan, "The Money Power of England versus the Labor Power of England and of the World," in ibid., p. 75.

40. Buchanan, "An Address to Independent Electors," in ibid., p. xxiv; Buchanan, *British American Federation a Necessity*, pp. 22-23, 27, 29-30. Buchanan's views must be considered in the context of the period. Canada had no currency until the end of the 1850s, and then opted for private bank issues. This policy created innumerable problems when the Bank of Upper Canada found itself in severe financial trouble during the economic downturn of the 1850s.

41. Buchanan, *Letters Illustrative of Politics in Canada*, p. 8; H. J. Morgan, ed., *Buchanan on Industrial Politics of America* (Montreal: Lovell, 1864), pp. 19-21. Cf. Wm. Barber, Georgetown, C.W., to Buchanan, and memorandum, "The Success of Canadian Manufacturing No Longer Doubtful," 11 May 1860, Macdonald Papers, MG 26 A, vol. 297, pp. 136159-62, PAC.

42. On the exodus of skilled labour from Hamilton to the United States see "Testimony of William Weir before the Hamilton Water Works, 1858," Buchanan Papers, vol. 58, p. 46618. On the problem nationally see Dominion National League, *Country Before Party* (Hamilton: n.p., 1878), pp. 6, 24; Malcolm MacLeod, *Practical Guide for Emigrants to the United States and Canada* (Manchester: A. Ireland, 1870), pp. 31-34; *HS*, 21 Dec. 1868.

43. Morgan, ed., *Buchanan on Industrial Politics*, p. 20; Buchanan, "Speech to Pioneers of Western Canada at London, C.W., 1863," p. 20, Pamphlet Collection, PAC. Cf. Naylor, *History of Canadian Business*, I, 29.

44. Morgan, ed., *Buchanan on Industrial Politics*, p. 41.

45. Buchanan, "Speech to Western Pioneers," p. 22.

46. *HS*, 15 Aug. 1860.

47. Ibid., 12 Apr. 1864.

48. *Workingman's Journal*, 18 June 1864. On the importance of the paper locally see *HT*, 1 and 20 Apr. 1864. Commencing publication 16 April 1864, the *Journal* had lapsed by mid-June. Its significance was noted in *Finchers' Trade Review*, 25 June 1864. My thanks to Gregory S. Kealey for bringing the latter source to my attention.

49. *Workingman's Journal*, 18 June 1864.

50. Ibid.

51. Morgan enticed the *Journal* to review his collection. His secretary, John O'Neil, later wrote to Buchanan to complain of the exorbitant charges of Mr. Howie, a Hamilton printer active in the establishment of the local Co-operative Society and undoubtedly involved in the establishment of the *Workingman's Journal*. See O'Neill to Buchanan, 20 Sept. 1864, Buchanan Papers, vol. 49, pp. 40090-93. On the Buchanan-Morgan relationship see Buchanan to Macdonald, 7 Feb. 1864, Macdonald Papers, vol. 338, pt. III, pp. 154476-77.

52. *Workingman's Journal*, 18 June 1864; *HS*, 3 Apr. 1865.

53. *People's Journal*, 18 Dec. 1869. On McLean see *HS*, 4 July 1885; Buchanan to McLean, 26 Dec. 1871, Buchanan Papers, vol. 46, pp. 36750-52;

McLean to Buchanan, 1 Apr. 1879, ibid., pp. 36770-71; *Industrial Canada*, 30 Nov. 1901. On the paper cf. *HS*, 25 and 26 Oct. 1869, 13 July 1871; Kealey, "Working-Class Response," pp. 363-65.

54. *People's Journal*, 18 Dec. 1869; "Prospectus," Buchanan Papers, vol. 46, p. 36749. Buchanan's influence is illustrated in his article on "emblematic currency" in the *People's Journal*, 20 Nov. 1869.

55. *People's Journal*, 18 Dec. 1869, 12 Feb. 1870.

56. Ibid., 18 Dec. 1869, 26 Feb. 1870, 4 Dec. 1869, 15 Jan. 1870. This kind of reasoning left the paper dangerously close to a critique of imperialism which would surface in later years. See *Bobcaygeon Independent*, 5 Nov. 1880, 2 Aug. 1895.

57. *People's Journal*, 5 Feb. 1870.

58. Ibid., 12 Feb. 1870.

59. Ibid., 8 Jan. 1870.

60. Ibid., 17 Apr. 1870, expounding on a theme central to Buchanan's argument in *A Home Market For the Farmer*.

61. *People's Journal*, 8 Jan. 1870.

62. Ibid., 7 May 1870.

63. Ibid., 26 June, 2 July 1870; *Hamilton Evening Journal*, 23 and 28 June 1870.

64. See Langdon, *Emergence of Canadian Working Class Movement*, pp. 8-13; Charles Lipton, *The Trade Union Movement of Canada, 1827-1958* (Montreal: Canadian Social Publications, 1968), pp. 20-28; Charles Brian Williams, "Canadian American Trade Union Relations: A Study of Binational Unionism" (Ph.D. diss., Cornell University, 1964), pp. 100-22; Storey, "Industrialization in Canada," pp. 85-196. See chaps. 3 and 5 for Hamilton detail.

65. On the rise of the Crispins see Gregory S. Kealey, "Artisans Respond to Industrialism: Shoemakers, Shoe Factories, and the Knights of St. Crispin in Toronto," Canadian Historical Association, *Papers* (1973), pp. 137-57; Langdon, *Emergence of Canadian Working Class Movement*, pp. 15-17; *Workingman's Advocate*, 22 Mar. 1873; Don D. Lescohier, "The Knights of St. Crispin, 1867-1874," *Bulletin of the University of Wisconsin, Economics and Political Science Series* 7 (1910): 1-102; John R. Commons, "American Shoemakers, 1648-1895: A Sketch of Industrial Evolution," *Quarterly Journal of Economics* 24 (1909): 72-75. For Hamilton developments see Lloyd Atkinson and Eugene Forsey, "The Labour Movement in Hamilton, 1827-1886," typescript, Canadian Labor Congress Collection, MG 28 I 103, vol. 248, p. 6, PAC.

66. "Preamble," *Constitution, By-Laws, and Rules of the Order of London Lodge No. 242, Knights of St. Crispin* (London: KOSC, 1872), p. 3. The most recent study of the Crispins stresses that in Lynn, Mass., they were factory hands and not master craftsmen. See Allan Dawley, *Class and Community: The Industrial Revolution in Lynn* (Cambridge, Mass.: Harvard University Press, 1976), pp. 143-48.

67. *People's Journal*, 2 Apr. 1870, and the early attack on the Cigar Makers' Union in ibid., 22 Jan. 1870.

68. Wilmot to Buchanan, 2 July 1870, Buchanan Papers, vol. 62, pp. 49389-98; Buchanan to U. S. Grant, 23 Nov. 1870, vol. 28, pp. 23892-93.

69. *People's Journal*, 22 Apr. 1871.

70. On the emergence of the nine-hour movement see the discussion in chap. 5 below and the recent treatment in John Battye, "The 'Nine Hour Pio-

neers': Genesis of the Canadian Labour Movement," paper presented at the Canadian Historical Association meetings, London, 1978.

71. *Ontario Workman*, 18 Apr. 1872.

72. Ibid., 25 Apr. 1872.

73. Ibid., 18 Apr. 1872.

74. Ibid.

75. Ibid.

76. Morgan, ed., *Buchanan on Industrial Politics*, pp. 237-38.

77. *Ontario Workman*, 18 Apr. 1872.

78. This argument is sustained in Montgomery, *Beyond Equality*, pp. 230-60.

79. *Ontario Workman*, 18 Apr. 1872. This excerpt appeared fourteen years before the first English edition of *Capital*. See Lipton, *Trade Union Movement of Canada*, pp. 31-32; Stanley B. Ryerson, *Unequal Union: Roots of Crisis in the Canadas, 1815-1873* (Toronto: Progress Publishers, 1973), p. 420. Ryerson argues that Mark Szalatnay, a revolutionary socialist, employed in Toronto as a cigarmaker in 1872, played some role in the publication of the excerpt. See Ryerson, "Mark Szalatnay, trade unionist and revolutionary socialist," *Dictionary of Canadian Biography*, 10 *1871-1880*, 670-71. Ryerson probably overstates Szalatnay's role in this development. A more likely candidate would have been John Hewitt, major spokesman of the nine-hour cause, and a former associate of William Jessup of the International Workingman's Association in New York. As a cooper, Hewitt would have been familiar with the excerpt from *Capital*, for it had appeared in *The Coopers' Journal*, November 1871. On ties between the Toronto Trades Assembly, of which Hewitt was an active member, and the London and New York branches of the International Workingman's Association see *Minutes of the Proceedings of the Toronto Trades Assembly*, esp. pp. 1, 28. *The Ontario Workman* often reprinted material from *The Coopers' Journal*, including Martin Foran's (president of the Coopers' Union) serialized novel, *The Other Side*. Hewitt's role is outlined in Battye, "Nine Hour Pioneers." Cf. Philip Foner, "Marx's *Capital* in the United States," *Science & Society* 31 (Fall 1967): 461-66. My thanks to Gregory S. Kealey for enlightening me on some of this material.

80. On Steward see Montgomery, *Beyond Equality*, pp. 249-60; *Iron Molders' International Journal*, April 1866.

81. "Letter to the Editor," *New York Star*, n.d., reprinted in *Ontario Workman*, 11 June 1872.

82. Montgomery, *Beyond Equality*, pp. 254-56; Karl Marx, *Capital*, I (New York: International, 1967), 235.

83. *Ontario Workman*, 18 Apr. 1872.

84. Ibid., 11 June 1872.

85. On the limited victories of the nine-hour movement in Hamilton see *Labor News*, 10 Apr. 1914, and the argument in chap. 5 below. The deterioration of the movement in Toronto is outlined in Kealey, "Working-Class Response," pp. 311-44.

86. On the impact of the depression see *Iron Molders' International Journal*, October 1873, February 1874, 10 Sept., 10 Oct. 1874, 10 Feb., 10 May 1875; Williams, "Canadian American Trade Union Relations," pp. 131-40, all of which chronicle the disintegration of molders' longstanding power in Hamilton shops and foundries. Cf. the discussion in chap. 3 above.

87. Buchanan to W. H. Howland, 2 Oct. 1878, Buchanan Papers, vol. 34, p. 28192.

88. Langdon, "The Political Economy of Capitalist Transformation," p. 185. The Canadian Manufacturers' Association would, however, pay tribute to Buchanan in future years. See *Industrial Canada*, 30 Nov. 1901. On the 1878 election in Toronto see Kealey, "Working-Class Response," pp. 367-74.

89. For a discussion of these phenomena in Hamilton in the late 1870s see *HS*, 15 Feb., 13 Mar. 1876, 18 Dec. 1877.

90. Ibid., 23 Apr. 1875.

91. Buchanan to A. W. Wright, 8 Mar. 1879, 30 Aug. 1880, Buchanan Papers; A. W. Wright to Buchanan, 26 May 1880, all in vol. 63, pp. 49718-26.

92. Wm. B. Anderson to Buchanan, 15 Dec. 1874, ibid., vol. 1, pp. 459-60; Buchanan to Anderson, 19 Dec. 1874, vol. 1, pp. 461-64; Buchanan to Henry Carey Baird, 14 Nov. 1871, vol. 2, p. 658; Buchanan to Baird, 30 Oct. 1873, vol. 2, pp. 676-82; Buchanan to Baird, 26 Jan. 1874, vol. 2, p. 700; Baird to Buchanan, 15 Apr. 1874, vol. 2, p. 728; Buchanan to Baird, 24 Apr. 1876, vol. 2, pp. 805-6; Buchanan to Baird, 4 Apr. 1874, vol. 2, p. 744; Eugene Beeble, Secretary, New York U.S. Legal Tender Club, to Buchanan, 5 Jan. 1875, vol. 3, pp. 1488-89; Beeble to Buchanan, 22 Oct. 1875, vol. 3, pp. 1495-96; Buchanan to E. G. Dyer, 6 Feb. 1875, vol. 25, pp. 21346-52; R. M. Wilmot to Buchanan, 22 May 1879, vol. 62, pp. 49409-12.

93. On the continued influence of Buchanan see "Prospectus of the *Canadian Tribune*, an Advocate of Home Industry, A New Weekly Journal," n.d., ibid., vol. 58, p. 46615; A. W. Wright to Buchanan, 5 Nov. 1878, vol. 63, pp. 49716-17; *HS*, 8 Nov. 1878, 27 Nov., 6 Dec. 1879.

94. *The National*, 22 and 29 Jan. 1874, 21 Jan., 13 May 1875, 11 Apr. 1878, 4 Mar. 1882. On the "Canada First Movement" see Ryerson, *Unequal Union*, pp. 413-16, 420; W. H. Foster, *Canada First; or, Our New Nationality* (Toronto: Adam, Stevenson, and Co., 1871).

95. See *The National*, 18 Feb., 13 May, 17 June, 12 and 19 Aug. 1875, 15 and 22 Aug. 1878, 1 Nov. 1879. For the paper's attack on the "Canada First" advocates see ibid., 8 Apr. 1875.

96. See ibid., 8 and 22 Apr. 1875, 11 Apr., 2 Aug., 26 Sept., 10, 17, 24, and 31 Oct. 1878, 29 Nov. 1879, 4 Mar. 1882. The paper's significance is discussed in Kealey, "Working-Class Response," pp. 363-65; Cook, "The Professor and the Prophet of Unrest," pp. 228-50.

97. *The National*, 7 Nov. 1878.

98. *The Commonwealth*, 29 July 1880.

99. Ibid. On the emergence of the Beaverback cause see the discussions of the "Rag Baby," sometimes referred to as "Buchanan's Baby," in *The National*, 26 Aug. 1875, 26 Sept. 1878, 17 Apr., 11 Oct., 29 Nov., 13 and 27 Dec. 1879.

100. I am indebted to Russell Hann for information on Brooks. Hann's forthcoming Harvard dissertation on labour-reform journalism in nineteenth-century Canada should fill a prominent void in our intellectual and cultural history, telling us much about little-known men like Brooks. Cf. *The National*, 14 Nov. 1878, 8 Nov. 1879, on Brooks's involvement with Wright and Buchanan in the National Currency League.

101. *The Commonwealth*, 5 and 26 Aug. 1880; *The National*, 27 Dec. 1879.

102. *The Commonwealth*, 5 Aug. 1880. Cf. Montgomery, *Beyond Equality*, pp. 425-27.

103. *The National*, 22 Apr. 1875. The phrase, of course, derives from Francis Bacon's famous aphorism, "Money is like muck, not good except it be spread." See Brian Pullen, *Rich and Poor in Renaissance Venice: The Social Institu-*

tions of a Catholic State, to 1620 (Oxford: Oxford University Press, 1971), p. 132. Buchanan, always capable of rooting his argument in a social context, argued that if the circulating medium could be increased to three times the 1877 level, it would put an end to strikes and labour-capital conflict. See Buchanan to Hickson, 4 Jan. 1877, Buchanan Papers, vol. 31, pp. 25600-2.

104. *The National*, 31 Oct. 1878; *HS*, 8 Nov. 1878.

105. This period, well known for the corruption and scandal linking business and government, is outlined in Gustavus Myers, *A History of Canadian Wealth* (Toronto: James Lewis and Samuel, 1972), pp. 264-377; Naylor, *History of Canadian Business*, I, 260-90; II, 2-98; Martin Robin, *The Rush for Spoils: The Company Province, 1871-1933* (Toronto: McClelland and Stewart, 1972), pp. 49-86.

106. *HS*, 1 Oct. 1883.

107. See *HS*, 19 July 1883–21 Aug. 1883; *POL*, 11 and 25 Aug. 1883; Eugene Forsey, "The Telegraphers' Strike of 1883," *Transactions of the Royal Society of Canada*, 4th ser., 10 (1971): 245-60; and the discussion in chap. 6 below. For brief acknowledgements of Buchanan's death and his contribution to working-class thought see *POL*, 6 and 12 Oct. 1883.

108. On Thompson see Jay Atherton, "An Introduction," in T. Phillips Thompson, *The Politics of Labor* (Toronto: University of Toronto Press, 1975), pp. vii-xxiv. Atherton's assessment of Thompson, treating him as a precursor of the welfare state, understates his importance in the evolution of Canadian working-class thought, and distorts the continuities in nineteenth-century popular political economy. Fortunately other work, most notably that of Russell Hann, is currently under way, promising to establish Thompson as a figure of central importance. For a preliminary report on Hann's work see his "Brainworkers and the Knights of Labor: E. E. Sheppard, Phillips Thompson, and the Toronto *News*, 1883-1887," in Gregory S. Kealey and Peter Warrian, eds., *Essays in Canadian Working Class History* (Toronto: McClelland and Stewart, 1976), pp. 35-57; and Hann's review of Thompson's book and Atherton's introduction, "An Early Canadian Labour Theorist," *Bulletin of the Committee on Canadian Labour History* 4 (Autumn 1977): 38-43. Cf. Watt, "Radicalism in English Canadian Literature," pp. 117-21; Cook, "The Professor and the Prophet of Unrest," pp. 228-50; John David Bell, "The Social and Political Thought of the *Labor Advocate*" (M.A. thesis, Queen's University, 1975).

109. T. Phillips Thompson, *The Future Government of Canada; being Arguments in Favor of a British American Republic* (St. Catharines: Herald Press, 1864), p. 24.

110. Phillips Thompson, *The Political Experiences of Jimuel Briggs* (Toronto: Flint, Morton and Company, 1873); *The Commonwealth*, 26 Aug. 1880; "Complimentary Banquet to Mr. Phillips Thompson, Albert Hall, Toronto, 17 January 1882," Phillips Thompson Papers, Correspondence file, 1907-23, PAC.

111. *POL*, 22 Dec. 1883–6 Feb. 1886, for only a sampling of the topics discussed by "Enjolras." Atherton's edited version of *The Politics of Labor* contains an appendix (pp. 213-30) reprinting four of the "Enjolras" articles, although hardly the most important of the lot. This source also misplaces the *Palladium of Labor*, referring to it as a Toronto journal.

112. T. Phillips Thompson, *The Politics of Labor* (New York: Belford, Clarke, and Company, 1887). On the importance of the work in international labour-reform circles see P. Kropotkin to Thompson, 16 Mar. 1888, Thompson Papers, PAC; R. W. Belford to Thompson, 17 Nov. 1888; Henry George-Thompson

correspondence, 4 Nov. 1885, 20 Mar., 8 and 24 May, 6 Aug. 1886, 26 Apr., 18 June 1887. Other Thompson-George correspondence is found in the Phillips Thompson Papers, 1889-1933, file 1, Correspondence, Public Archives of Ontario.

113. Thompson, *Politics of Labor*, pp. 10, 22, 39, 51-52, 153.

114. Ibid., 6-7.

115. Ibid., 40.

116. The most explicit statement of George's argument, of course, is *Progress and Poverty* (New York: Lovell, 1883). Cf. David M. Ricci, "Fabian Socialism: A Theory of Rent as Exploitation," *Journal of British Studies* 9 (1969): 108-21; John L. Thomas, "Utopia for an Urban Age: Henry George, Henry Demarest Lloyd, Edward Bellamy," *Perspectives in American History* 6 (1972): 135-63. The appeal of George's writings can be surmised from the voluminous newspaper treatment. See the Henry George Scrapbooks, New York Public Library. Specific Hamilton references to George's work can be found in *HT*, 29 Oct. 1884, in Scrapbook 8, NYPL; *POL*, 9 Aug. 1884, 20 Dec. 1886; *Labor Union*, 13 and 20 Jan., 24 Mar. 1883; *Henry George in Canada* (London, 1884); Hamilton and District Trades and Labor Council, *30th Anniversary Complimentary Souvenir, Presented to Delegates, Trades and Labor Congress of Canada, Hamilton, Ontario, 1919* (Hamilton: Spectator, 1919), n.p. On the working-class perception of the barriers inhibiting home ownership see *Report of the Royal Commission on the Relations of Labor and Capital*, "Ontario Evidence," II (Ottawa: Queen's Printer, 1889), 861-65, where members of the Hamilton Land Tax Club testified. A recent discussion of the impact of George on Canadian thought is Ramsay Cook, "Henry George and the Poverty of Canadian Progress," Canadian Historical Association, *Papers* (1977), pp. 142-57.

117. Thompson could thus write against capitalism, while reserving a positive role for capital in its many-faceted employments. See *Politics of Labor*, pp. 9-10. On Thompson's attraction to the Single Tax, and his relationship with George, who was largely responsible for the publication of *The Politics of Labor*, see the two collections of George-Thompson correspondence cited in note 112 above.

118. *Report of the Royal Commission on the Relations of Labor and Capital*, II, 98.

119. Ibid., p. 100; *The Week*, 1 Feb. 1889, where Thompson discussed the Single Tax Movement and its relationship to social and labour reform in Canada, Britain, and the United States. My thanks to Russell Hann for bringing this latter source to my attention. For an assessment of George's work and its relationship to the international working-class movement see Karl Marx and Friedrich Engels, *Correspondence, 1846-1895* (New York: International, 1935), pp. 394-97, 448-53.

120. See Hann, "Brainworkers and the Knights of Labor," pp. 35-57.

121. *Canadian Labor Reformer*, 15 May 1886. On Wright's continued attachment to currency reform see his "Spokeshave" articles on usury in *Journal of United Labor*, 20 Sept. 1888; *Journal of the Knights of Labor*, 19 Sept. 1889, 30 Oct. 1890, 22 Sept. 1892.

122. See Kealey, "Working-Class Response," pp. 241-307.

123. On this transformation see Bernard Ostry, "Conservatives, Liberals, and Labour in the 1880s," *Canadian Journal of Economics and Political Science* 27 (May 1961): 111-61.

124. Note the discussion of the Knights of Labor in chap. 6 below.

125. *Labor Advocate*, 27 Mar. 1891. This abandonment of Georgism had been developing since the late 1880s. See Phillips Thompson, "Thoughts and

Suggestions on the Social Problem and Things in General," manuscript, Oxton, 1888, n.p., in Thompson Papers, file 3, Public Archives of Ontario.

126. *Labor Advocate*, 11 Sept. 1891.

127. *Citizen and Country*, 11 Nov. 1899.

128. On his socialist activity see Atherton, "An Introduction," pp. vii-xxiv; Thompson to Goldwin Smith, 28 Sept. 1906 (?), Thompson Papers, PAC; "Manifesto of the Local Toronto, Socialist Party," n.d., ibid.; *Citizen and Country*, 13 July 1900. Thompson, who derived much of his income from writing for various government publications allied with the Labour Department, was constantly under attack for his socialist activities. See Attorney General to Thompson, 22 Mar. 1901, Thompson Papers, PAC; A. B. Aylesworth (Office of Postmaster General) to Thompson, 28 Apr. 1906; Office of Postmaster General to Thompson, 7 June, 12 Oct. 1906; Wilfrid Laurier to Thompson, 12 Oct. 1906.

129. *Labor Advocate*, 18 Sept. 1891. See the discussion of the debate in Bell, "Thought of the *Labor Advocate*," pp. 178-82.

130. *Labor Advocate*, 25 Sept. 1891.

131. See for instance *Canadian Labor Reformer*, 15 May 1886; *Iron Molders' International Journal*, January 1887; *The Craftsman*, 23 Apr., 31 Dec. 1887; *Citizen and Country*, 11 Mar. 1889; *Industrial Banner*, December 1897.

132. See the Wright-Thompson exchange in *The Lance*, 18 and 25 Sept. 1909.

133. *HS*, 15 and 29 Jan. 1898, 27 Feb. 1897; *Proceedings of the Eleventh Annual Session of the Trades and Labor Congress, London, 1895* (Ottawa: Free Lance, 1895), p. 4. Marks played a critical role in the formation of the Labor Educational Association which, in turn, championed the cause of the Industrial Brotherhood. See *Industrial Banner*, May 1903, June 1903, September 1903, May 1905, February 1906, June 1907, June 1909. On the origins of the Brotherhood see Jacqueline Flint Cahan, "A Survey of Political Activities in the Ontario Labour Movement, 1850-1935" (M.A. thesis, University of Toronto, 1935), pp. 10-11.

134. *Labour Gazette* 4 (1904): 24; ibid., 9 (1909): 993; *Industrial Banner*, August 1905; and, on a cooperative venture drawing international recognition, the toy factory of the London Experiment, *Typographical Journal*, March 1909; *Industrial Banner*, February 1909, March 1909, April 1909, May 1909; *HS*, 27 Feb. 1897.

135. On the Patrons see Russell Hann, *Farmers Confront Industrialism: Some Historical Perspectives on Ontario Agrarian Movements* (Toronto: New Hogtown Press, 1975), esp. p. i, on Thompson's involvement. Cf. the different orientation in S. E. D. Shortt, "Social Change and Political Crisis in Rural Ontario: The Patrons of Industry, 1889-1896," in D. Swainson, ed., *Oliver Mowat's Ontario* (Toronto: Macmillan, 1972), pp. 211-35.

136. *Citizen and Country*, 11 Mar., 6 May 1899, 15 June 1900.

137. On Ashplant, an early London delegate to the Trades and Labor Congress of Canada from the Retail Clerks Association, and once prominent in the London YMCA, Congregational Sunday Schools, and the Methodist Church, see *Citizen and Country*, 25 Mar. 1899; *The Tribune*, 24 Mar. 1906. Ashplant was considered the principal spokesman of the Canadian Socialist Labor Party.

138. On these developments see *HS*, 5 Dec. 1896, 4 and 11 Nov., 23 Dec. 1897, 14 and 29 Jan., 28 Feb., 7 May 1898, 17 and 23 March 1899; *Citizen and Country*, 15 Apr. 1899, 9 Mar. 1900.

139. *HS*, 17 June, 13 and 15 Dec. 1902.

140. *Citizen and Country*, 13 Apr. 1900.

141. *Cotton's Weekly*, 4 Mar. 1909, 12 June 1911, 7 Nov. 1912, 11 Dec. 1913. Cf. *Minute Book, Hamilton Trades and Labor Council, 1910-1914*, pp. 51-52, Hamilton Collection, Hamilton Public Library.

142. *Citizen and Country*, 4 May 1900.

143. "A good liberal voter" to Sir Wilfrid Laurier, 7 Oct. 1904, Hamilton, Laurier Papers, RG 26 1 (a), vol. 339, pp. 90559-60, PAC.

144. *HS*, 29 Jan. 1872.

145. Ibid., 9 Apr., 2 and 20 June, 19 July, 26 and 31 Aug., 18 Sept. 1878.

146. See the movement away from protection in *Canadian Labor Reformer*, 15 May 1886; *POL*, 8 and 22 Sept., 13 Oct. 1883, 19 Jan., 2 Feb., 31 May, 6 Sept. 1884.

147. See, for instance, *Citizen and Country*, 29 Apr. 1899; *Bobcaygeon Independent*, 12 July 1895; *Industrial Banner*, November 1903; *Cotton's Weekly*, 26 Nov., 17 Dec. 1908, 29 Dec. 1910.

148. *The Observer*, 17 and 24 Sept. 1908.

149. Such ideas formed an important component of the thought of Toronto's labour leadership in the years 1896-1914. See Wayne Roberts, "The Evolution of Toronto Labour Leadership, 1896-1914," paper presented at the Canadian Historical Association meetings, Quebec City, 1976; Gene Howard Homel, "'Fading Beams of the Nineteenth Century': Radicalism and Early Socialism in Late Victorian Toronto," paper presented at the Canadian Historical Association meetings, London, 1978.

CHAPTER 5

1. See E. P. Thompson, "Time, Work-Discipline, and Industrial Capitalism," *Past & Present* 38 (December 1968): 56-97; Herbert G. Gutman, "Work, Culture, and Society in Industrializing America, 1815-1919," *American Historical Review* 78 (June 1973): 531-88.

2. "Labor Reminiscences," *Workingman's Advocate*, 23 Mar. 1872.

3. Frank Thistlethwaite, "Atlantic Migration of the Pottery Industry," *Economic History Review* 11 (1958): 4.

4. Gregory S. Kealey, "The 'Honest Workingman' and Workers' Control: The Experience of Toronto Skilled Workers, 1860-1892," *Labour/Le Travailleur* 1 (1976): 34-40; Gutman, "Work, Culture, Society," pp. 558-59; Melvyn Dubofsky, *Industrialism and the American Worker, 1865-1920* (New York: Crowell, 1975), pp. 7-8.

5. Barford, "Reminiscences of the Early Days of Stove Plate Molding and the Union," *International Molders' and Foundry Workers' Journal* 94 (July 1958): 8-12. The account was written in 1902 by a 73-year old molder, whose father had taught him the trade in the 1840s and 1850s.

6. Thompson, "Time, Work-Discipline," esp. p. 85; E. J. Hobsbawm, "Custom, Wages, and Workload in the Nineteenth Century," in *Labouring Men: Studies in the History of Labour* (New York: Basic Books, 1964), pp. 344-70. The quotation is from George McNeill, *The Labor Movement: The Problem of Today* (New York: M. W. Hazen, 1892), p. 470.

7. Thomas Hood, "The Workhouse Clock," *Canadian Labor Reformer*, 16 Apr. 1887.

8 *The Craftsman*, 26 Mar. 1887.

9. *POL*, 9 Aug. 1884.

10. *Journal of United Labor*, 29 Jan. 1887.

11. *POL*, 21 Feb. 1885. Cf. McNeil, *Labor Movement*, p. 477; *Progress: Official Organ of the Cigarmakers Progressive Union of America*, 21 Aug. 1885; *POL*, 14 Mar. 1885.

12. *POL*, 21 Feb. 1885. For a useful discussion of the concept of the reserve army see Harry Braverman, *Labor and Monopoly Capital: The Degradation of Work in the Twentieth Century* (New York: Monthly Review, 1974), pp. 377-402. The concept was developed by Marx, and suggests Thompson's familiarity with Marxist terms at an early date. See Karl Marx, *Capital*, I (New York: International, 1967), esp. pp. 628-40.

13. *John Swinton's Paper*, 22 June 1884.

14. *Iron Molders' International Journal*, 10 Sept. 1875, pp. 434-35.

15. On the connection between the struggle for shorter hours and workers' control see David Montgomery, "Workers' Control of Machine Production in the Nineteenth Century" (typescript, University of Pittsburgh, 1976).

16. Montgomery, "Workers' Control," citing John D. Lawson, ed., *American State Trials*, 10 (1919), 99. On the aftermath of the eight-hour struggle see *Record of the Proceedings of the Special Session of the General Assembly, Knights of Labor, Cleveland, Ohio, 1886*, p. 39.

17. W. H. Foster, "To the Officers and Members of all Trade and Labor Unions," January 1886, quoted in Wisconsin Bureau of Labor Statistics, *Second Biennial Report* (1885-86), pp. 315-16; *POL*, 16 May, 18 July 1885.

18. *Labor Standard*, 24 Mar. 1877.

19. *Labor Advocate*, 10 July 1891.

20. Edward R. Place, "Eight Hours," *The Socialist*, 8 July 1876.

21. See *Canadian Labor Reformer*, 27 Nov. 1886; *Journal of United Labor*, 25 Feb. 1885; N. Brian Davis, *The Poetry of the Canadian People, 1720-1920: Two Hundred Years of Hard Work* (Toronto: NC Press, 1976), pp. 264-65.

22. *HT*, 30 June, 1 July 1862.

23. Ibid., 24 July 1862.

24. Ibid., 12 and 27 Aug. 1862.

25. Ibid., 27 Aug. 1862.

26. Ibid., 29 Aug. 1862.

27. Ibid., 11 Sept. 1862.

28. Ibid., 5 and 9 Sept. 1862.

29. Ibid., 5 Sept. 1862.

30. Ibid., 15 Sept. 1862.

31. *HS*, 24 and 27 Apr. 1869.

32. Ibid., 5 and 7 May 1869.

33. *Canadian Labor Reformer*, 15 May 1886; *POL*, 12 Apr. 1886; *HS*, 19 and 22 Apr. 1886.

34. See *HT*, 8 July 1862, 10 July 1863. Cf. my comments in " 'Give us the road and we will run it': The Social and Cultural Matrix of an Emerging Labour Movement," in Kealey and Warrian, eds., *Essays in Canadian Working Class History* (Toronto: McClelland and Stewart, 1976), p. 109.

35. See *HT*, 2 Apr. 1866; *HS*, 28 Aug. 1871. The best brief discussion of the American movement for shorter hours in the 1860s is David Montgomery, *Beyond Equality: Labor and the Radical Republicans, 1862-1872* (New York: Knopf, 1967), pp. 296-334.

36. *HT*, 10 Oct. 1862.

37. On the nine-hour movement see Charles Lipton, *The Trade Union Movement of Canada, 1827-1959* (Montreal: Canadian Social Publications, 1968), pp. 28-37; H. A. Logan, *Trade Unions in Canada: Their Development and Functioning* (Toronto: Macmillan, 1948), pp. 38-43; Bernard Ostry, "Conservatives, Liberals, and Labour in the 1870s," *Canadian Historical Review* 41 (1960): 93-104; Sally Friedberg Zerker, "A History of the Toronto Typographical Union, 1832-1925" (Ph.D. diss., University of Toronto, 1972), pp. 420-40; Zerker, "George Brown and the Printers Union," *Journal of Canadian Studies* 10 (1975): 42-49; Gregory S. Kealey, "The Working-Class Response to Industrial Capitalism in Toronto, 1860-1892" (Ph.D. diss., University of Rochester, 1977), pp. 311-44. All of these studies focus on the Toronto experience. Contemporaries certainly recognized the importance of the Hamilton workingmen. See *Ontario Workman*, 18 Apr. 1872. John H. Battye, "The 'Nine Hour Pioneers': Genesis of the Canadian Labour Movement," paper presented at the Canadian Historical Association meetings, London, 1978, reestablishes Hamilton's importance. On the relationship of the nine-hour movement to an emerging class consciousness see Frank William Watt, "Radicalism in English Canadian Literature since Confederation" (Ph.D. diss., University of Toronto, 1957), p. 83; Watt, "The National Policy, the Workingman, and Proletarian Ideas in Victorian Canada," *Canadian Historical Review* 40 (1959): 2-4; Steven Langdon, *The Emergence of the Canadian Working Class Movement* (Toronto: New Hogtown Press, 1975), pp. 14-15. It is important to note that Watt considers this only a beginning in the formation of class consciousness, Langdon arguing that it marks the establishment of that consciousness. As our earlier discussion of working-class thought, in chap. 4 above, suggests, such perspectives ignore basic continuities which circumscribed the development of class consciousness.

38. *HS*, 19 Jan. 1872. Logan, *Trade Unions in Canada*, p. 39, mistakenly asserts, with no evidence, that Hamilton possessed a Nine Hours League in the spring of 1871. More likely correct is the *Ontario Workman*, 23 Jan. 1873, which dates the birth of the league twelve months earlier, in January 1872.

39. *Minutes of the Proceedings of the Toronto Trades Assembly, 1871-1878*, cited in Lipton, *Trade Union Movement of Canada*, p. 29.

40. *HS*, 20 Jan. 1872.

41. Ibid., 25 Jan. 1872.

42. Ibid., 26 Jan. 1872.

43. Ibid., 29 Jan. 1872. Little is known of Cole and Scarth. Parker would assume a presence in the political struggles of 1872-73, surrounding the formation of the Canadian Labor Union, discussed below in this chapter. James Ryan is perhaps the best-known figure. See Bernard Ostry, "Ryan, James, labour leader; fl. 1872," *Dictionary of Canadian Biography*, 10, *1871-1880*, 637-38. Beyond his activity in the Nine Hours League, little is known of his life. He was a native of County Clare, Ireland, and died in Hamilton in 1896, after more than twenty years' service on the Grand Trunk Railway. See *HS*, 17 Dec. 1896, for his obituary. A brief description of Ryan is found in *Labor News*, 10 Apr. 1914. Pryke certainly had the longest, and most visible, presence in the city. See *HT*, 20 July, 21 Sept. 1867; *HS*, 24 Aug. 1867, 1 Dec. 1872. He remained active in the Hamilton labour movement as late as 1914.

44. *HS*, 29 Jan. 1872. On Watkins see *Labor News*, 10 Apr. 1914; *Ontario Workman*, 26 Dec. 1872.

45. *HS*, 29 Jan. 1872.

46. *Lightning Express*, quoted in *HS*, 8 June 1872, cited in Battye, "Nine Hour Pioneers," p. 3.

47. *HS*, 31 Jan. 1872.

48. Ibid., 31 Jan., 2, 5, 6, 8, and 14 Feb. 1872.

49. The above paragraphs draw upon ibid., 1-23 Feb. 1872.

50. Ibid., 23 and 27 Feb. 1872; Ostry, "Ryan," pp. 637-38. Battye, "Nine Hour Pioneers," p. 13, points out that the foreman Webster and forty others remained out of work.

51. *HS*, 22 and 23 Feb. 1872.

52. See ibid., 23 Feb. 1872. McGiverin apparently had attempted to curry favour with both workers and employers during the development of the nine-hour movement. He ended by antagonizing both groups. John A. Macdonald wrote to a supporter that, "McGiverin is reaping the just reward of his double dealing." See Macdonald to W. Gillespy, 29 Feb. 1872, Macdonald Papers, Letter-book 17, PAC, quoted in Battye, "Nine Hour Pioneers," p. 34.

53. *HS*, 24 Feb. 1872.

54. See ibid., 22 Feb.–4 Apr. 1872.

55. On the parameters of the upsurge see *Ontario Workman*, 9 May 1872, documenting the existence of support in a number of Canadian communities.

56. *HS*, 26 Feb. 1872; *Minutes of the Proceedings of the Toronto Trades Assembly, 1871-1878*, p. 39, PAC.

57. *Minutes, Toronto Assembly*, pp. 39, 40-43, 46, 52-53; *Ontario Workman*, 2 May 1872.

58. *HS*, 1 Mar. 1872. Note too the meeting of Ontario manufacturers in Toronto. See *Globe*, 24 Apr. 1872; Langdon, *Emergence of Canadian Working Class Movement*, p. 19.

59. See sources cited in note 38 above. Cf. *Ontario Workman*, 18 and 25 Apr., 2 and 9 May 1872; *Coburg Sentinel*, 4 May 1872; *Globe*, 25 Apr., 8 May 1872; *American Workman*, 27 Apr. 1872; *Workingman's Advocate*, 20 Apr. 1872.

60. Lipton, *Trade Union Movement of Canada*, p. 29; *Ontario Workman*, 25 Apr., 30 May 1872; *Minutes, Toronto Assembly*, p. 78.

61. *Ontario Workman*, 2 May 1872; *Minutes, Toronto Assembly*, pp. 61-62; *The Dumfries Reformer and Waterloo County Commercial and General Advertiser*, 22 May 1872; *Globe*, 20 May 1872; *St. Catharines Evening Journal*, 15 May 1872; Acton Burrows, *Annals of the Town of Guelph* (1877), p. 151, quoted in Leo A. Johnson, *A History of Guelph, 1827-1927* (Guelph: Guelph Historical Society, 1977), p. 309.

62. *Mail*, 14 May 1872; *Ontario Workman*, 16 May 1872.

63. *Ontario Workman*, 18 May, 13 June 1872.

64. Ibid., 25 April 1872; *Sarnia Observer and Lambton Advertiser*, 23 Feb., 29 Mar., 5 Apr. 1872.

65. *Woodstock Review*, quoted in *Sarnia Observer and Lambton Advertiser*, 5 Apr. 1872. "Justice" is quoted in *Montreal Evening Star*, 16 May 1872. On John Hewitt and internationalism see *Ontario Workman*, 25 Apr. 1872. Resistance to the nine-hour movement is also documented in C. Henry Stephens, "The Nine Hours Movement," *Canadian Monthly and National Review* 1 (May 1872): 430, quoted in Allan Smith, "The Myth of the Self-Made Man in English Canada, 1850-1914," *Canadian Historical Review* 59 (June 1978): 204.

66. *HS*, 12 Apr., 1 May 1872; *Labor News*, 10 Apr. 1914; *Ontario Workman*, 18 Apr., 9 May 1872; and, on the GWR mechanics' celebration following the winning of the shorter working day, *HS*, 13 Apr. 1872.

67. *Ontario Workman*, 25 Apr. 1872.

68. *Minutes, Toronto Assembly*, pp. 57-60; *Ontario Workman*, 9 May 1872.

69. *Ontario Workman*, 9 May 1872; *HS*, 4 May 1872; *Minutes, Toronto Assembly*, pp. 57-58; Lipton, *Trade Union Movement of Canada*, p. 35; Logan, *Trade Unions in Canada*, p. 42; Langdon, *Emergence of Canadian Working Class Movement*, pp. 19-20.

70. *HS*, 9 May 1872; *Ontario Workman*, 16 May 1872. On Tarbox, an American machinist who would prove to be one of the most vigorous opponents of the nine-hour men see *HS*, 27 June 1914; J. A. Bryce, "Patterns of Profit and Power: Business, Community, and Industrialization in a Nineteenth-Century City," Working Paper No. 28 in Michael Katz, ed., *York Social History Project: Third Report — February 1978*, pp. 369-412.

71. *HS*, 10 May 1872.

72. Ibid., 11 and 13 May 1872; *Ontario Workman*, 23 May 1872. On the lock-out see *Coburg Sentinel*, 18 May 1872; *Dumfries Reformer and Waterloo Advertiser*, 22 May 1872; *Globe*, 13 and 15 May 1872; *Mail*, 13 and 14 May 1872; *London Advertiser*, 14 May 1872; *St. Catharines Journal*, 13 May 1872.

73. *Mail*, 14 May 1872; *HS*, 13 May 1872.

74. *Mail*, 14 May 1872; *HS*, 13 May 1872; *London Advertiser*, 14 May 1872. The termination of the Kraft strike is recorded in the *Globe*, 15 May 1872.

75. See *Labor News*, 10 Apr. 1914. Written by Sam Landers to commemorate the events of 1872, this account romanticizes the willingness of employers to grant concessions, but conveys well the degree of spontaneous solidarity generated in the midst of the struggle.

76. See accounts of the procession in *Mail*, 16 May 1872; *Globe*, 16 May 1872; *HS*, 15 May 1872; *Minutes, Toronto Assembly*, p. 61; *Workingman's Advocate*, 25 May 1872; *Ontario Workman*, 23 May 1872. After coming across the account in the Chicago *Workingman's Advocate*, reprinted from an account in the *Ontario Workman* which I could not locate, I was directed by Peter Warrian to an undated "Supplement to the *Ontario Workman*," inserted in the bound volume of the *Workman*, Regional Collection, University of Western Ontario, between the issues of 18 and 25 Apr. 1872. Undoubtedly circulated with the 16 May 1872 issue of the *Workman*, this supplement is one of the most illuminating accounts of the parade, and is unavailable in any of the microfilmed reproductions of the paper. A striking depiction of the parade is found in *Canadian Illustrated News* (January-June 1872), p. 353.

77. *Mail*, 16 May 1872; *Globe*, 16 May 1872; *Workingman's Advocate*, 25 May 1872.

78. Alex Wingfield, "The Nine Hour Pioneers," *Ontario Workman*, 23 May 1872.

79. Cited in Robert Storey, "Industrialization in Canada: The Emergence of the Hamilton Working Class, 1850's-1870's" (M.A. thesis, Dalhousie University, 1975), p. 165.

80. *Mail*, 17 May 1872.

81. *HS*, 20 May 1872.

82. Ibid., 22-30 May 1872; *Ontario Workman*, 30 May 1872.

83. *HS*, 28 and 29 May 1872.

84. Ibid., 10 June 1872.

85. Ibid., 11, 12, and 15 June 1872. The only sustained victory rested with the GWR mechanics, who continued to work the nine-hour day, achieved during the early months of the struggle. Yet this cannot be seen as a major victory, for the men won relatively little. The workingmen's demand had been for a 54-hour week. In the winter they had been working a 53½-hour week already, while in summer months their week consisted of 56 hours. The company thus gave in to the men, losing, on an average, three-quarters of an hour a week throughout the whole year. Despite this minor gain, the GWR men's triumph probably had wider repercussions, for they played the central role in the development of the movement as a whole. See *HS*, 12 Apr. 1872.

86. *Hamilton Standard*, reprinted in *Ontario Workman*, 13 June 1872.

87. On the Canadian Labor Union see *Ontario Workman*, 18 and 25 Sept. 1873; Langdon, *Emergence of the Canadian Working Class Movement*, pp. 21-25; Lipton, *Trade Union Movement of Canada*, pp. 35-37; Logan, *Trade Unions in Canada*, pp. 43-45. Hamilton's nine-hour men certainly played an important role in the formation of the CLU. The boilermaker, Robert Parker, affiliated with a Hamilton-based group, Canadian Labour Unity, launched an early attack on the Mechanics' Lien Law, a favourite target of the CLU. See *Ontario Workman*, 13 and 20 Feb. 1873. Fred Walters and Ralph Ingledew, prominent in Hamilton's nine-hour movement, and associated with the Molders' Union and the Amalgamated Society of Carpenters and Joiners, also contributed to the emergence of the CLU. Hamilton delegates to the CLU convention included Isaac Hodgins of the Machinists and Blacksmiths Lodge No. 2, John Calvart of the Crispin's Lodge No. 212, and D. Craig and William McDougal, of the Amalgamated Society of Engineers, all certainly involved in the 1872 struggle. Finally, another delegate, Thomas McGregor, of Hamilton's IMIU No. 26, may well have been the financial Secretary of the Hamilton League. See *Ontario Workman*, 25 Sept. 1873.

88. *Ontario Workman*, 6 Mar. 1873.

89. Ibid., 13 June 1872.

90. This is the argument in Langdon, *Emergence of the Canadian Working Class Movement*, pp. 21-23.

91. D. G. Creighton, "George Brown, Sir John A. Macdonald, and the 'Workingman'," *Canadian Historical Review* 24 (1943): 362-76; Ostry, "Conservatives, Liberals, and Labour in the 1870s," pp. 93-127. The process in Hamilton is documented in Macdonald to I. Buchanan, 29 June 1872, Macdonald Papers, Letterbook 18, pt. I, vol. 521, pp. 52-54; Macdonald to Fred Walter, 1872, Letterbook 18, pt. II, vol. 521, p. 263; Macdonald to Rt. Rev. Lord Bishop of Hamilton, 17 May 1872, Letterbook 17, pt. III, vol. 520, p. 605; F. Walter to Macdonald, 1 Aug. 1872, vol. 344, pp. 157748-49. On the Trades Union Bill see Langdon, *Emergence of the Canadian Working Class Movement*, p. 22; Lipton, *Trade Union Movement of Canada*, pp. 46-49; Macdonald Papers, vol. 66, pp. 26863-85.

92. For Toronto see Kealey, "Working-Class Response," pp. 308-402.

93. *HS*, 14 July 1872. The following section on Witton has benefited greatly from a close reading of an excellent account in Storey, "Industrialization in Canada," pp. 166-96.

94. Macdonald to Buchanan, 29 June 1872, Macdonald Papers, Letterbook 18, pt. 1, vol. 521, pp. 52-54; Donald Swainson, "The Personnel of Politics: A

Study of the Ontario Members of the Second Federal Parliament" (Ph.D. diss., University of Toronto, 1968), p. 151. Cf. Kealey, "Working-Class Response," p. 331.

95. On Chisholm and Witton see *HS*, 18 July 1872; Storey, "Industrialization in Canada," pp. 168-69; Swainson, "Personnel of Politics," pp. 150-57; Martin Robin, *Radical Politics and Canadian Labour* (Kingston, Ont.: Industrial Relations Centre, 1968), p. 8; *Workingman's Advocate*, 14 Sept. 1872; *Ontario Workman*, 25 July, 1 Aug. 1872.

96. Herbert Fairbain Gardiner, *Nothing But Names* (1899), p. 515, quoted in Swainson, "Personnel of Politics," p. 151.

97. *HS*, 20 and 22 July 1872; *Ontario Workman*, 25 July 1872; Robin, *Radical Politics*, p. 8. On Buchanan's involvement in the campaign see Buchanan to Macdonald, 8 and 22 July 1872, Buchanan Papers, vol. 33, pp. 649-52, cited in Swainson, "Personnel of Politics," pp. 152-53. On the activity of the nine-hour militants—Pryke and Parker—see Storey, "Industrialization in Canada," p. 172; Kealey, "Working-Class Response," p. 331; *HS*, 20 July 1872.

98. Buchanan to Macdonald, 22 July 1872, Buchanan Papers, vol. 33, pp. 651-52, quoted in Swainson, "Personnel of Politics," p. 153.

99. *HS*, 8 and 6 Aug. 1872, quoted in Storey, "Industrialization in Canada," p. 173.

100. *HS*, 13 Aug. 1872. See the illustration in *Canadian Illustrated News* (July-December 1872), p. 140.

101. *HS*, 14 and 19 Aug. 1872; Macdonald to Buchanan, 21 Sept. 1872, Buchanan Papers, vol. 33, pp. 655-56.

102. *Globe*, 17 Sept. 1872, quoted in Langdon, *Emergence of the Canadian Working Class Movement*, p. 22.

103. See Macdonald to Witton, 15 Oct. 1872, Macdonald Papers, Letterbook 20, pt. 3, vol. 523, p. 863; Witton to Macdonald, 22 Nov. 1879, vol. 362, pp. 167826-29.

104. Swainson, "Personnel of Politics," p. 152, quoting *Journals of the House of Commons of the Dominion of Canada*, 6, 7 May 1873, p. 291; Canadian Legislative Assembly, *Debates*, 2 Apr., 27 Oct. 1873; Marchioness of Dufferin and Ava, *My Canadian Journal, Extracts from my Letters Home Written while Lord Dufferin was Governor General* (1891).

105. *Proceedings of the Second Session of the Trades and Labor Congress of Canada* (1886), pp. 21-22, cited in Robin, *Radical Politics*, p. 25.

106. These two paragraphs on Witton's 1874 defeat draw upon Storey, "Industrialization in Canada," pp. 181-86; Swainson, "Personnel of Politics," pp. 152-54; "Saturday Musings," *HS*, 26 Sept. 1908. Witton often addressed the Hamilton Association, speaking on subjects as varied as early printers, Indian fables, and ballad literature.

107. *Hamilton Evening Times*, 13 May 1875, quoted in Davis, *Poetry of Canadian People*, p. 155.

108. *Ontario Workman*, 11 July 1872.

109. Ibid., 2 Oct. 1873; *Workingman's Advocate*, 11 Oct. 1873.

110. *HS*, 2 Sept. 1872.

111. *Ontario Workman*, 16 Jan. 1873.

112. *Labor News*, 10 Apr. 1914. Cf. Mercer's statement quoted earlier in this chapter, indicating that the movement degenerated into a struggle for wages.

113. *Ontario Workman*, 13 June 1872.

114. Ibid.

115. Ibid., 23 Jan. 1873.

116. Ibid., 13 June 1872. On the devastating effects of the 1873-78 depression see *Iron Molders' International Journal*, October 1873, p. 154; February 1874, p. 267; 10 Sept. 1874, pp. 54-56; 10 Oct. 1874, pp. 66-67, 89; 10 Feb. 1875, p. 198; 10 May 1875, p. 308; Storey, "Industrialization in Canada," pp. 179-80; Charles Brian Williams, "Canadian-American Trade Union Relations — A Study of the Development of Binational Unionism" (Ph.D. diss., Cornell University, 1964), pp. 131-40; *HS*, 2 Feb., 10 Dec. 1873, 21 Feb. 1874; 15 Feb. 1876; 18 Dec. 1877. Fred Walters, a molder with strong allegiances to craft union principles, was forced to break ranks and work in a "scab" shop in these years, an indication of just how disruptive the economic downturn was. See *HS*, 17 and 21 Feb. 1887.

117. *HS*, 6, 9, 13 Sept. 1881, 18 Jan. 1882, 28 June 1883, 15 Apr. 1884.

118. Ibid., 8 Apr. 1885, 26 and 29 Apr., 3, 11, and 13 May, 26 June 1886; *POL*, 15 Dec. 1883, 2 and 23 Feb., 26 Apr., 1 Nov., 20 Dec. 1884, 14 Feb., 2, 9, 16, and 23 May, 18 July, 17 and 31 Oct., 21 Nov. 1885; 20 Mar., 8 May, 19 June 1886; *Journal of United Labor*, 4 June 1887; 30 June 1888; *Canadian Labor Reformer*, 16 Oct. 1886.

119. *HS*, 12 Oct., 23 Sept. 1903; *Typographical Journal*, January 1906, p. 113; *Industrial Banner*, December 1897, December 1907; Department of Labour Strikes and Lockouts Records, RG 27, vol. 294, Strike no. 3019, PAC; vol. 297, Strike no. 3275; vol. 294, Strike no. 2854; vol. 299, Strike no. 3422A; vol. 299, Strike no. 3450A; vol. 301, Strike no. 35; vol. 304, Strike no. 27A; vol. 304, Strike no. 28; *Labour Gazette* 3 (1903-4): 757-58; 4 (1904-5): 1104-5; 8 (1908-9): 729; 11 (1911-12): 123-26; *Hamilton Evening Times Scrapbook*, compiled by Brian Henley, "Labour," pt. I, pp. 4, 47; pt. II, pp. 52-59, Hamilton Collection, Hamilton Public Library; *Minute Book of the Trades and Labor Council, Organized 3 December 1888*, Trades and Labor Council, Hamilton, p. 156; *OFFICIAL Programme and Souvenir of the Labor Day Demonstration Held at Dundurn Park, Hamilton, Ontario, 1897* (Hamilton: Spectator, 1897), p. 3.

120. *POL*, 12 Apr., 2 Aug. 1884. Its author was David R. Gibson, prominent in the Bricklayers' Union and the Knights of Labor.

121. Ibid., 24 May 1884, Cf. *HS*, 20 May 1884; *Report of the Royal Commission on the Relations of Labor and Capital in Canada*, "Ontario Evidence," II (Ottawa: Queen's Printer, 1889), 762-63.

122. On the strike, which commenced 12 June 1916, see the clippings from *HT*, 2 May, 7 and 19 Aug. 1916; *HS*, 8 Aug. 1916; *Hamilton Herald*, 22 and 31 July, 10, 12, and 25 Aug. 1916, all found in Department of Labour Strikes and Lockouts Records, vol. 304, Strike no. 27A. Cf. the clippings from *HT*, 9, 10, and 12 June 1916, in *Hamilton Evening Times Scrapbook*, "Labour," pt. I, pp. 41, 44-49; pt. II, pp. 52-63. The strike has recently been treated in Myer Siemiatycki, "Munitions and Labour Militancy: The Hamilton Machinists' Strike of 1916," *Labour/Le Travailleur* 3 (1978): 131-51.

CHAPTER 6

1. "Recollections of John Peebles, Mayor of Hamilton, 1930-1933," 7 Feb. 1946, Hamilton Collection, Hamilton Public Library.

2. *HS*, 16 Oct. 1885, 26 Aug. 1886, 21 Jan. 1888; *Report of the Commission on the Relations of Labor and Capital in Canada*, "Ontario Evidence," II (Ottawa: Queen's Printer, 1889), 861-65; "Register of the Knights of Labor Organizers,"

Terence V. Powderly Papers, Catholic University, Washington, D.C. Peebles was praised as "an affable young man," his wares advertised in *POL*, 5 Sept. 1885. Peebles was listed as a shoemaker in the Royal Commission report, but this must have been an error. In *POL* he was identified as a jeweller, and city directories refer to him as a labourer (1883-84) and a watchmaker, jeweller, optician (1885-90).

3. On the beginnings of the Order in Canada, with reference to the first Hamilton assembly, see Douglas R. Kennedy, *The Knights of Labor in Canada* (London: University of Western Ontario, 1956), p. 35; Victor Oscar Chan, "Canadian Knights of Labor with special reference to the 1880's" (M.A. thesis, McGill University, 1949), pp. 1-45; D. J. O'Donoghue, "The Labor Movement in Canada," in George E. McNeill, ed., *The Labor Movement; The Problem of Today* (New York: M. W. Hazen, 1892), p. 594; H. A. Logan, *Trade Unions in Canada* (Toronto: Macmillan, 1946), p. 50; Martin Robin, *Radical Politics and Canadian Labour* (Kingston, Ont.: Industrial Relations Centre, 1968), p. 20; "Hamilton Early Stronghold in Organized Labour Cause," *HS*, 15 July 1946. None of these sources dates the establishment of LA 1852, and it is likely that they all rely upon O'Donoghue's account, or reprints of it. My dating follows Fred A. Fenton to T. V. Powderly, 7 Dec. 1882, Powderly Papers. Eugene Forsey, "The Canadian Labour Movement, 1812-1902," Canadian Historical Association *Booklet No. 27* (1974), p. 7, notes that the Order was present in Hamilton as early as 1875 on a secret basis. On the secret assembly cf. Jonathon Garlock, *Knights of Labor Data Bank* (Ann Arbor, Mich.: Inter-University Consortium for Social and Political Research, 1978); *Journal of United Labor*, 15 May 1880.

4. *Record of the Proceedings of the Seventh Regular Session of the General Assembly of the Knights of Labor, Cincinnati, 1883*, pp. 528, 545, 549.

5. *Record of the Proceedings of the Eighth Regular Session of the General Assembly of the Knights of Labor, Philadelphia, 1884*, p. 796. Cf. *POL*, 11 Aug., 8 Sept. 1883.

6. On the impact of the depression in Hamilton see the correspondence in *The Craftsman*, 18 and 25 Oct., 1 and 22 Nov., 13 and 20 Dec. 1884, 10 and 17 Jan., 7 Feb. 1885; *John Swinton's Paper*, 28 Sept., 19 Oct. 1884, 22 Feb. 1885. Cf. *POL*, 20 Sept., 1 and 8 Nov. 1884; Bernard Ostry, "Conservatives, Liberals, and Labour in the 1880s," *Canadian Journal of Economics and Political Science* 27 (May 1961): 143.

7. *Record of the Proceedings of the Ninth Regular Session of the General Assembly of the Knights of Labor, Hamilton, 1885*, pp. 173, 192.

8. *Record of the Proceedings of the General Assembly of the Knights of Labor, Eleventh Regular Session, Minneapolis, 1887*, p. 1847.

9. *Proceedings of the General Assembly of the Knights of Labor of America, 12th Regular Session, Indianapolis, 1888*, "Report of the Secretary," p. 2. This source chronicles Canadian decline generally, although only DA 138 (St. Thomas) appears to have rivalled Hamilton in terms of the severity of the demise.

10. *Labour Gazette* 1 (1901-2): 560-61.

11. On the eclectic appeal of the Knights see Gregory S. Kealey, "The Working-Class Response to Industrial Capitalism in Toronto, 1860-1892" (Ph.D. diss., University of Rochester, 1977), pp. 241-307; Leon Fink, "Workingmen's Democracy: The Knights of Labor in Local Politics, 1886-1896" (Ph.D. diss., University of Rochester, 1977). The widespread appeal of the Knights forms an important component of an early but still valuable discussion. See Norman J.

Ware, *The Labor Movement in the United States, 1860-1890: A Study in Democracy* (New York: Vintage, 1964), esp. pp. xi-xviii.

12. See chap. 3 above and, for a general discussion of the phenomenon, Benson Soffer, "A Theory of Trade Union Development: The Role of the Autonomous Workman," *Labor History* 1 (Spring 1960): 141-63.

13. On the relationship of the Knights of Labor to the practices of workers' control in the nineteenth century see David Montgomery, "Workers' Control of Machine Production in the Nineteenth Century," *Labor History* 17 (Fall 1976): 498-501.

14. This struggle has been ably chronicled, in terms of the Canadian case, in Eugene Forsey, "The Telegraphers' Strike of 1883," *Transactions of the Royal Society of Canada*, 4th ser., 9 (sec. 2, 1971): 245-60. Cf. T. V. Powderly, *The Path I Trod: The Autobiography of Terence V. Powderly*, (New York: Columbia University Press, 1940), pp. 101-13. On Hamilton detail see this chapter, below.

15. Quoted in *HS*, 30 July 1883.

16. See for instance *Journal of United Labor*, 2 Apr., 21 May 1887, 14 Mar. 1889, 23 Mar., 24 July 1890; *Labor Leaf*, 16 June 1886.

17. The Knights' attachment to cooperation is well known. See *POL*, 23 Feb. 1884; *Journal of United Labor*, 10 May 1884, 25 Feb. 1886, 7 Apr. 1888; *Canadian Labor Reformer*, 21 Aug., 4 Dec. 1886, 15 Jan. 1887.

18. *Journal of United Labor*, 25 Nov. 1885.

19. *Proceedings, General Assembly, 1887*, pp. 1286-87.

20. Ibid., pp. 1875-76.

21. *Canadian Labor Reformer*, 31 July 1886.

22. *HS*, 19 Apr. 1886.

23. Ibid., 22 and 29 Apr., 3, 11, and 13 May 1886; *Canadian Labor Reformer*, 15 May 1886.

24. *Proceedings of the Third Session of the Trades & Labor Congress of Canada, Hamilton, 1887* (Toronto: Labor Record, 1887), p. 11.

25. On the Gardner strike see *POL*, 8 Nov. 1884; Powderly to F. M. Wilson, 29 Oct. 1884, Powderly Papers; E. S. Gilbert to Powderly, 31 Oct. 1884; Wilson to Powderly, 5 Nov. 1884; Gilbert to Powderly, 8 Nov. 1884; and this chapter, below.

26. *Labor Advocate*, 23 Jan. 1891.

27. *POL*, 18 July 1885.

28. On the Hamilton struggle for the eight-hour day see *POL*, 14 Mar., 4 and 18 Apr., 12 Dec. 1885, 20 and 27 Mar., 1 and 15 May 1886; *HS*, 22 Mar., 8 and 12 Apr. 1886.

29. *HS*, 22 Mar. 1886.

30. Ibid., 8 Apr. 1886.

31. *Journal of United Labor*, 16 May 1889.

32. This forms an integral component of the discussion of the Knights in Ware, *Labor Movement in the United States*, esp. p. xviii; Philip S. Foner, *History of the Labor Movement in the United States*, II (New York: International, 1955), 55-74; Charles Lipton, *The Trade Union Movement of Canada, 1827-1959* (Montreal: Canadian Social Publications, 1968), pp. 71-72, makes the point for Canada.

33. Powderly, *The Path I Trod*, p. 42.

34. Quoted in Foner, *History of the Labor Movement*, II, 55.

35. *Journal of United Labor*, 25 Dec. 1890. Cf. *POL*, 3 Oct. 1885; *Proceedings, General Assembly, 1886*, pp. 38-39.

36. *POL*, 3 July 1886; *HS*, 24 Aug. 1882.

37. On "Enjolras" and internationalism see *POL*, 17 Jan. 1885. For Towers' statement see *Report, Royal Commission, 1889*, "Ontario Evidence," II, 874.

38. *Canadian Labor Reformer*, 22 May 1886.

39. See Foner, *History of the Labor Movement*, II, 56-74; Foner, *Organized Labor and the Black Worker, 1619-1973* (New York: Pantheon, 1974), pp. 47-63; Sidney H. Kessler, "The Negro and the Knights of Labor" (M.A. thesis, Columbia University, 1950). The most recent treatment, stressing the barriers inhibiting the Knights of Labor's approach to the race question in the American South, is Melton A. McLaurin, "The Racial Policies of the Knights of Labor and the Organization of Southern Black Workers," *Labor History* 17 (Fall 1976): 568-85.

40. George N. Havens to Powderly, 30 Jan. 1883, Powderly Papers.

41. *POL*, 3 Oct. 1885.

42. Ibid., 9 Aug. 1884.

43. Ibid., 19 July 1884, 25 Apr., 25 May 1885, 6 Feb., 20 Mar. 1886; *The Wage Worker*, 24 Apr. 1883; *Journal of United Labor*, 25 Sept. 1885, 25 Apr. 1886, 8 and 15 Jan. 1887; *Canadian Labor Reformer*, 3 July 1886; Ware, *Labor Movement in the United States*, pp. 346-49; *Proceedings, General Assembly, 1888*, "Report of the General Investigation of Woman's Work and Wages," esp. pp. 3-4; Foner, *History of the Labor Movement*, II, 56-74. Recent treatments include Kealey, "Working-Class Response," pp. 241-307; Susan Levine, "'The Best Men in the Order': Women and the Knights of Labor," paper presented at the Canadian Historical Association meetings, London, 1978.

44. *POL*, 20 Mar. 1886.

45. See for instance *Proceedings, General Assembly, 1888*, "Report of the General Investigation of Woman's Work and Wages," pp. 3-4, on women and the Order in Thorold, Merriton, Waterloo, and St. Catharines; *POL* (Toronto edition), 24 Apr. 1886.

46. *Canadian Labor Reformer*, 26 June 1886. On the first stirrings of women's organization in Hamilton see Fred. A. Fenton to Powderly, 7 Dec. 1882, Powderly Papers. The following paragraphs draw upon Gregory S. Kealey, "McVicar, Katie, shoeworker and union leader," *Dictionary of Canadian Biography*, 11, *1881-1890*, forthcoming.

47. *POL*, 6 and 13 Oct., 8 Sept., 10 Nov. 1883. It is possible that McVicar penned a series of letters signed "Sewing Girl," appearing in *HS*, 28 Mar. – 5 Apr. 1882.

48. *POL*, 3 Nov. 1883.

49. Powderly to Miss Annie Gillespie, 29 Jan. 1887, Powderly Papers; Powderly to Miss Maggie Wilkes, 30 Aug. 1887; Powderly to Miss Margaret Wilkes, 27 Dec. 1887; Powderly to Lydia Salisbury, 3 Dec. 1888.

50. Given the apparent absence of any woman willing to serve as directress of LA 3179, it is possible that McVicar was "the lady member of L.A. 3040" referred to in *Canadian Labor Reformer*, 15 May 1886, as responsible for the growth of the Order in Dundas.

51. See Gerald N. Grob, *Workers and Utopia: A Study of Ideological Conflict in the Labor Movement, 1865-1900* (Chicago: Quadrangle, 1961); Grob, "The Knights of Labor and the Trade Unions, 1878-1886," *Journal of Economic History* 18 (June 1958): 176-92. The general contours of Grob's argument are accepted in Melton Alonza McLaurin, *Paternalism and Protest: Southern Cotton Mill Workers*

and Organized Labor, 1875-1905 (Westport, Conn.: Greenwood, 1971), esp. pp. 114-16.

52. See for instance Charles A. Scrontas, *Organized Labor and Labor Politics in Maine, 1880-1890* (Orono, Maine: University of Maine Press, 1966). Impressive recent discussions of the political activities of the Knights of Labor include Kealey, "Working-Class Response," pp. 403-503; Fink, "Workingmen's Democracy."

53. On the Royal Commission see Greg Kealey, ed., *Canada Investigates Industrialism: The Royal Commission on the Relations of Labor and Capital, 1889* (Toronto: University of Toronto Press, 1973), esp. pp. ix-xxvii.

54. See Martin Robin, *Radical Politics and Canadian Labor*, pp. 86, 91, 115, 123-25; "Labor Owes Much to Fighting Quality of Allan Studholme," in *The Hamilton and District Trades and Labor Council, 60th Anniversary, Diamond Jubilee, 1888-1948* (Hamilton: Spectator, 1948), p. 13; *Industrial Banner*, December 1906, January 1907, June 1908.

55. "Peebles Recollections," Hamilton Public Library; *POL*, 27 Oct., 3 and 24 Nov. 1883, 31 May 1884; *HS*, 21 June 1884; William Bews to Powderly, 28 Dec. 1882, Powderly Papers.

56. See for instance the attack on a Toronto Knight standing as a Conservative candidate in *Canadian Labor Reformer*, 16 Oct. 1886.

57. "Peebles Recollections," Hamilton Public Library; *Labor Union*, 3, 10, 17, and 24 Feb., 3 Mar. 1883; *HS*, 20, 24, and 27 Nov., 14 Dec. 1886, 7 Jan. 1887; *POL*, 4 and 7 Dec. 1886; *Canadian Labor Reformer*, 4 and 11 Dec. 1886; Jacqueline Flint Cahan, "A Survey of Political Activities in the Ontario Labor Movement, 1850-1935" (M.A. thesis, University of Toronto, 1936), pp. 7-9.

58. See *POL*, 5 Jan. 1884; George N. Havens to Powderly, 4 Jan. 1883, Powderly Papers; *Journal of United Labor*, April 1884; *Report, Royal Commission, 1889*, "Ontario Evidence," II, 818.

59. *POL*, 22 Aug. 1885. Another St. Thomas correspondent, possibly the same individual, reiterated this defence of independent political activity in ibid., 19 Sept. 1885.

60. See ibid., 20 Oct., 3 Nov. 1883, 7 June 1884.

61. See *Labor Union*, 3, 17, and 24 Feb. 1883; *POL*, 8 Dec. 1883, 12 Apr. 1884.

62. Note the discussion in Ostry, "Conservatives, Liberals, and Labour in the 1880s," pp. 141-61. The lure of the traditional party remained forceful, of course, but the extent to which Liberals and Conservatives inaugurated ingenious methods to stifle defection from the ranks of their working-class supporters suggests strongly the crisis engendered by independent working-class action. See Russell Hann, "Brainworkers and the Knights of Labor: E. E. Sheppard, Phillips Thompson, and the Toronto *News*, 1883-1887," in Gregory S. Kealey and Peter Warrian, eds., *Essays in Canadian Working Class History* (Toronto: McClelland and Stewart, 1976), pp. 51-53.

63. See Ware, *Labor Movement in the United States*, pp. 21, 28, 35, 38; Warren Van Tine, *The Making of the Labor Bureaucrat: Union Leadership in the United States, 1870-1920* (Amherst, Mass.: University of Massachusetts Press, 1973), pp. 1-31.

64. See Carrol D. Wright, "An Historical Sketch of the Knights of Labor," *Quarterly Journal of Economics* 1 (January 1887): 142-43. On ritual see the discussions in E. J. Hobsbawm, *Primitive Rebels: Studies in Archaic Forms of Social Move-*

ment in the 19th and 20th Centuries (Manchester: University of Manchester Press, 1959), pp. 150-74; Natalie Zemon Davis, "The Rites of Violence," in *Society and Culture in Early Modern France* (Stanford: Stanford University Press, 1975), pp. 152-88.

65. McNeill, *The Labor Movement*, pp. 124-25.

66. On the Order's growth and its relationship to the supposed demise of secrecy see Foner, *History of the Labor Movement*, II, 47. More subtle, and more convincing, is the discussion in Ware, *Labor Movement in the United States*, p. 93.

67. "General Assembly, Noble and Holy Order, Knights of Labor of North America, Charter of the Knights of Hope Assembly, Port Hope, Ontario," 20 Nov. 1882, MG 28 I 54, PAC.

68. Ezra A. Cook, ed., *Knights of Labor Illustrated. "Adelphon Kruptos." Full Illustrated Ritual including the "Unwritten Work" and an Historical Sketch of the Order* (Chicago: Cook, 1886), pp. 36-37. A Hamilton sign calling a meeting of LA 2225 is found in *POL*, 3 Nov. 1883.

69. John G. Gibson to Powderly, 4 Feb. 1883, Powderly Papers; Powderly to Gibson, 9 Feb. 1883.

70. John W. Goodson to Powderly, 11 Dec. 1882, ibid.; Powderly to Goodson, 14 Dec. 1882.

71. J. M. Brady to W. H. Rowe, 22 Aug. 1884, ibid.

72. Cook, ed., *Adelphon Kruptos*, pp. 32-37. Cf. Powderly, *Path I Trod*, pp. 431-33; Henry Joseph Browne, *The Catholic Church and the Knights of Labor* (Washington: Catholic University, 1949), pp. 359-62; *Journal of United Labor*, November 1882. Hamilton assemblies often heard lectures on the "secret work." See *POL*, 28 Feb. 1885; *HS*, 23 Feb. 1885.

73. See the discussion in Herbert G. Gutman, "Protestantism and the American Labor Movement: The Christian Spirit in the Gilded Age," in *Work, Culture, and Society in Industrializing America* (New York: Knopf, 1976), pp. 79-117; Carl Warren Griffiths, "Some Protestant Attitudes on the Labor Question in 1886," *Church History* 11 (June 1942): 138-48. On pietism and its relationship to activism see Paul Kleppner, *The Cross of Culture: A Social Analysis of Midwestern Politics, 1850-1900* (New York: Free Press, 1970); William G. McLoughlin, "The Role of Religion in the Revolution: Liberty of Conscience and Cultural Cohesion in the New Nation," in Stephen G. Kurtz and James H. Hutson, eds., *Essays on the American Revolution* (New York: Norton, 1973), pp. 197-255.

74. *Journal of United Labour*, 10 May 1884.

75. McNeill, *Labor Movement*, p. 468.

76. *Labor: Its Rights and Wrongs, Sentiments and Comments by the Leading Men of Our Nation on the Labor Question of Today* (Washington: Labor Publishing, 1886), p. 321.

77. *Journal of United Labor*, 10 Oct., January, 25 May 1884, 28 May 1887, 5 July 1888; Ware, *Labor Movement in the United States*, esp. p. xvi.

78. *HS*, 17 Sept. 1888.

79. *POL*, 20 Mar. 1886. Cf. H. Francis Perry, "The Workingman's Alienation from the Church," *American Journal of Sociology* 4 (March 1899): 626.

80. *POL*, 29 Aug. 1885. Cf. ibid., 7 Nov. 1885.

81. Ibid., 12 Sept. 1885.

82. Cf. the account of Powderly's speech in the city in *HS*, 30 Nov. 1882; and an account of a delegate's speech at the 1885 General Assembly held in Hamilton, in *POL*, 17 Oct. 1885. Note also the number of labour sermons

preached by ministers sympathetic to the Knights' cause, chronicled in *HS*, 25 Oct. 1883; *POL*, 20 and 27 Mar. 1886; *Journal of United Labor*, 28 May 1887.

83. *Trade Union Advocate*, 4 May 1882.

84. *POL*, 28 Nov. 1885.

85. *Trade Union Advocate*, 15 June 1882.

86. *HS*, 13 Oct. 1885; *POL*, 17 Oct. 1885. On Foster see Ware, *Labor Movement in the United States*, pp. 115, 177, 181, 250, 254, 267, and passim.

87. On the importance of this, the first international strike, see Forsey, "Telegraphers' Strike," pp. 245-60. For an assessment of the role of this conflict in stimulating the Order's growth in Canada see Kealey, "Working-Class Response," pp. 241-307.

88. *HS*, 19 July 1883. Cf. Powderly, *The Path I Trod*, pp. 101-13.

89. *HS*, 19 July 1883; Forsey, "Telegraphers' Strike," pp. 257-58.

90. *HS*, 20 July 1883. On street railway struggles, strikingly similar in terms of the tactics and the language of opposition to a monopolistic service, see David Frank, "Trouble in Toronto: The Street Railway Lockout and Strike of 1886" (typescript, University of Toronto, 1970); Bryan D. Palmer, " 'Give us the road and we will run it': The Social and Cultural Matrix of an Emerging Labour Movement," in Kealey and Warrian, eds., *Essays in Canadian Working Class History*, pp. 106-24; and chap. 7 below.

91. *HS*, 23 and 26 July 1883.

92. Ibid., 23 July 1882; *POL*, 11 Aug. 1883.

93. *HS*, 26 July 1883.

94. Ibid., 19 July 1883.

95. Ibid., 10, 15, 18, and 21 Aug. 1883.

96. Ibid., 10 and 17 Sept. 1883; Forsey, "Telegraphers' Strike," p. 259.

97. See Ware, *Labor Movement in the United States*, pp. 117-54.

98. *POL*, 18 Aug. 1883. Cf. "Enjolras" in ibid., 19 Apr. 1884.

99. On blacklisting of Hamilton's Brotherhood see *HS*, 21 Aug. 1883.

100. Ibid., 14 Feb. 1884.

101. Ibid., 16 and 21 Feb. 1884; *POL*, 15 and 23 Feb. 1884.

102. *HS*, 21 and 16 Feb. 1884.

103. Ibid., 18, 21, and 22 Feb. 1884. The radicalization of shoeworkers, occasioned by the presence of women in the struggle, is outlined in David Montgomery, "Workers' Control of Machine Production," p. 500; G. S. Kealey, "Artisans Respond to Industrialism: Shoemakers, Shoe Factories, and the Knights of St. Crispin in Toronto," Canadian Historical Association, *Historical Papers* (1973), pp. 145-47; Augusta E. Galster, *The Labor Movement in the Shoe Industry, with Special Reference to Philadelphia* (New York: Columbia University Press, 1924), pp. 55-57.

104. *HS*, 16 Feb. 1884.

105. *POL*, 23 Feb. 1884; *HS*, 21 Feb. 1884.

106. *HS*, 8 Mar. 1884.

107. Ibid., 10 and 12 Mar. 1884.

108. See chap. 3 above.

109. For a general introduction to the importance of the anti-Chinese agitations see McNeill, *The Labor Movement*, pp. 429-54; Grob, *Workers and Utopia*, pp. 57-58. Note also the discussion of labour's response to the Chinese in the early 1870s, in chap. 4 above. Cf. Isabella Black, "American Labor and Chinese Immigration," *Past & Present* 25 (July 1963): 59-76.

110. Some of "Ah Sin's" letters can be found in *Labor Union*, 17 Mar. 1883; *POL*, 12 Apr., 24 May, 20 Sept. 1884. Cf. "Hung Wah's" letter in *Labor Union*, 24 Mar. 1883; and the discussions in *POL*, 12 Apr., 31 May, 16 Aug. 1884, 13 and 20 June 1885.

111. *POL*, 12 Apr. 1884.

112. Efforts to go beyond the racist contours of the exclusion argument can be found in *The National*, 29 Jan. 1874; *POL*, 6 Sept. 1884; and in Robert Coulter's speech before the CLU, recorded in *HS*, 26 Mar. 1885.

113. Accounts of Hamilton's anti-Chinese demonstration, the efforts to prepare for it, and its impact, can be found in *POL*, 27 Sept., 4 Oct. 1884; *HS*, 2 and 3 Oct. 1884; *The Craftsman*, 7 Oct., 1 Nov. 1884. On Sheppard and Thompson see Hann, "Brainworkers and the Knights of Labor," pp. 33-57.

114. *HS*, 3 Oct. 1884.

115. *The Craftsman*, 1 Nov. 1884.

116. Note the interesting comments in Arthur Mann, "Gompers and the Irony of Racism," *Antioch Review* 13 (Spring 1953): 203-14.

117. On the Knights' endorsement of temperance see *Journal of United Labor*, 24 Sept. 1887, 19 Sept. 1889; Griffiths, "Protestant Attitudes in 1886," pp. 146-47; *Report of the Proceedings of the General Assembly of the Knights of Labor, 1882*, p. 284; *Proceedings, General Assembly, 1885*, p. 20; Ware, *Labor Movement in the United States*, pp. 89, 107, 223-27, 365.

118. *Workingman's Journal*, 18 Apr. 1864. Cf. my brief comments in " 'Give us the road'," pp. 109-10, relating to London, Ontario, in the same period.

119. Officers of the Hamilton Temple No. 9, IOGT were located in *HT*, 13 Aug. 1862. Of the thirteen officers, only nine could be located in city directories: a tailor, a merchant, a turner, a printer, and a carpenter, and the daughter of a carpenter, and the wives of a carriagemaker, a printer, and a carpenter. Officers of the St. Patrick's Young Men's Temperance Society, located in *HT*, 1 Oct. 1868, included two printers and a molder. On Donovan see "Cornelius Donovan," from *Cathedral Magazine*, reprinted in *Papers and Records of the Wentworth Historical Society* 2 (1924): 43-45.

120. See the argument in Joseph R. Gusfield, *Symbolic Crusade: Status Politics and the American Temperance Movement* (Urbana, Ill.: University of Illinois Press, 1963), which views temperance as a mechanism of social control.

121. See *Report, Royal Commission, 1889*, "New Brunswick Evidence," v, 11, 121; "Nova Scotia Evidence," VI, 373, 417-18; "Quebec Evidence," III, 254; Kealey, ed., *Canada Investigates Industrialism*, pp. 19, 35, 135.

122. *The Temperance Journal and New Brunswick Reporter*, 31 Mar. 1888.

123. *HS*, 13 Jan. 1879.

124. J. W. Bengough, *The Gin Mill Primer* (Toronto: William Briggs, 1898), n.p.

125. *HS*, 14 Apr. 1881.

126. Attempts to attract workingmen to the temperance cause are chronicled in *The Temperance Journal and New Brunswick Reporter*, 17, 24, and 31 Mar., 14 Apr., 5 May 1888; *Royal Templar Platform; A Collection of Readings and Recitations for Council and Lodge, Social Entertainments and Public Meetings* (Hamilton, 1892), p. 64. On the non-working-class character of the movement and its leadership see "Men of the Movement," Supplement to *The Templar*, 1 June 1894; Eliphalet Nott, *Lectures on Temperance* (Hamilton: Royal Templar, 1858); F. H. L. Sims, *Drink and Drugery: Two Social Sins* (Toronto: n.p., 1900).

127. Bruce Laurie, " 'Nothing on Compulsion': Life Styles of Philadelphia Artisans," *Labor History* 15 (Summer 1974): 337-66; *HS*, 14 Apr. 1881.

128. *Report, Royal Commission, 1889*, "Ontario Evidence," II, 889-90.

129. *Canadian Labor Reformer*, 19 Nov. 1886.

130. *Industrial Banner*, November 1905.

131. This kind of autonomous working-class temperance activity has received little treatment in North America. In terms of sophistication, the English study, Brian Harrison, *Drink and the Victorians: The Temperance Question in England, 1815-1872* (Pittsburgh: University of Pittsburgh Press, 1971), surpasses all others.

132. See Powderly, *Thirty Years of Labor, 1859-1889* (Columbus, Ohio: Excelsior, 1889), pp. 580-626; David Montgomery, *Beyond Equality: Labor and the Radical Republicans, 1862-1872* (New York: Knopf, 1967), pp. 171, 187-97, 202-6, and passim; on some prominent Knights and their temperance views, Samuel Walker, "Terence V. Powderly, the Knights of Labor and the Temperance Issue," *Societas* 5 (Autumn 1975): 279-94.

133. *Temperance Journal and New Brunswick Reporter*, 11 Aug. 1888.

134. *POL*, 10 Oct. 1885. Cf. *Labor Union*, 13 Jan. 1883; *HS*, 24 Aug. 1882, 30 Nov. 1883.

135. See accounts of speeches in *POL*, 15 Dec. 1883, 5 Sept. 1885; *HS*, 27 June, 10 Dec. 1883, 13 Oct., 5 Dec. 1885. Cf. the account of another lecture, by the well-known Knight, Victor Drury, in ibid., 22 Apr. 1886.

136. On "Enjolras" and temperance see *POL*, 12 Jan. 1884.

137. Ibid., 21 June 1884. Cf. *Labor Union*, 17 Feb. 1883, on a wife's support for temperance.

138. *POL*, 31 May 1884.

139. *Canadian Labor Reformer*, 19 June 1886.

140. W. W. Buchanan, Dominion secretary, Royal Templars of Temperance, to Powderly, 10 May 1886, Powderly Papers. For accounts of this temperance gathering see *POL*, 9 and 10 Aug. 1886; *POL*, 24 and 31 July 1886.

141. *POL*, 8 Aug. 1885.

142. Ibid., 7 Aug. 1886.

143. On the temperance movement's endorsement of Racey see *POL*, 7 Dec. 1886; *Evening Palladium*, 13 Dec. 1886.

144. See for instance *Minute Book, Hamilton Trades and Labor Council, 1910-1914*, p. 34, Hamilton Collection, Hamilton Public Library.

145. *POL*, 16 May 1885.

146. Ibid.

147. Ibid., 2 May 1885.

148. Ibid., 2 and 9 Aug. 1884; *HS*, 4 Aug. 1884.

149. *HS*, 4 Aug. 1884.

150. R. McDougall to Powderly, 6 Jan. 1883, Powderly Papers.

151. Powderly to McDougall, 26 Jan. 1883, ibid.

152. Charles Smith to Powderly, 3 Mar. 1884, ibid.

153. Fred A. Jones to Powderly, 11 Aug. 1884, ibid.

154. E. S. Gilbert to Powderly, 20 Oct. 1884, ibid.

155. Powderly to Gilbert, 20 Oct. 1884, ibid.

156. On Wright see sketches in *Journal of United Labor*, 16 Aug., 20 Sept., 27 Nov. 1890. On his schemes see Wright to Eugene V. Debs, 23 Jan. 1893, Alexander W. Wright Papers, MG 29 A 15, Letterbook II, pp. 25-29, PAC;

Wright to Powderly, 18 Oct. 1893, Letterbook II, pp. 309-11; Wright to Mr. Wiman, 24 Apr. 1891, Letterbook II, pp. 468-69; Wright to H. S. Pingree, 24 Mar. 1894, Letterbook III, p. 94; Wright to Devlin, 10 Apr. 1894, Letterbook II, p. 114; Wright to George McCaddin, 30 May, 2 June 1893, vol. 4, Miscellaneous Letters.

157. This episode is treated in greater detail in my "The Underside of the Knights of Labor: The Morgan-Harvey Affair," in a forthcoming study of the Knights of Labor in Ontario by Gregory S. Kealey and myself.

158. See Thomas R. Hines, *The Anarchist's Conspiracy; or the Blight of 3770, A True History of the Experience of Daniel Hines as a Knight of Labor* (Boston: published by author, 1887).

159. Gilbert to Powderly, 8 Nov. 1884, Powderly Papers. On the Gardner strike see the sources cited in note 25 above.

160. See *POL*, 23 Aug. 1884; *Journal of United Labor*, 10 Nov. 1884; Herman Klinger to Powderly, 3 Nov. 1884, Powderly Papers; Gilbert to Powderly, 8 Nov. 1884; Committee appointed by LA 2225 in Klinger Case to Powderly, 15 Nov. 1884; Powderly to Fred. Aldridge, 19 Nov. 1884.

161. D. B. Skelly to Powderly, 15 Dec. 1884, Powderly Papers.

162. *Journal of United Labor*, 25 Feb., 10 and 25 May 1885; *HS*, 24 Feb. 1885.

163. *POL*, 4 Apr. 1885.

164. *HS*, 23 Apr. 1885.

165. On these men see *Proceedings, General Assembly, 1883*, pp. 394, 485-86; *Proceedings, General Assembly, 1884*, p. 790; *Proceedings, General Assembly, 1885*, p. 174; *Journal of United Labor*, August 1883, 31 Mar. 1884; *HS*, 24 Feb. 1885; Powderly to Smith, 7 Oct. 1884, Powderly Papers; George Collis to Powderly, 23 Nov. 1884; W. H. Bews to Powderly, 14 Jan. 1885.

166. As an introduction to this dispute see Ware, *Labor Movement in the United States*, pp. 103-12, 258-79; *POL*, 31 July 1886; *Journal of United Labor*, December 1883.

167. Karl Marx, "The Eighteenth Brumaire of Louis Bonaparte," in Marx and Engels, *Selected Works* (Moscow: Progress Publishers, 1968), p. 97.

168. On the 1883 strike see *Labor Union*, 24 Mar. 1883; *HS*, 6 Apr. 1883-1 June 1883.

169. *HS*, 14 Apr. 1885.

170. On the evolution of the dispute of 1885-86 see *POL*, 2 Apr.-2 May 1885; *Cigar Makers' Official Journal*, October 1885; *The Craftsman*, 28 Apr., 16 May, 11 July, 15 Aug. 1885; *John Swinton's Paper*, 19 Apr., 7 June 1885; *HS*, 17 Apr.-29 July 1885. On the Progressive Cigarmakers' Union see Ware, *Labor Movement in the United States*, pp. 262-79; *Progress: The Official Organ of the Cigarmakers' Progressive Union of America*, 20 Sept. 1882, 28 Sept. 1883, 21 Aug. 1885; William Kirk, "The Knights of Labor and the American Federation of Labor," in Jacob H. Hollander and George E. Barnett, eds., *Studies in American Trade Unionism* (New York: Henry Holt, 1907), pp. 363-65. On the Hamilton local of the Progressive Union see *HS*, 9 July 1886; *POL*, 17 July 1886.

171. See *POL*, 19 Sept. 1885, 27 Mar. 1886.

172. Ibid., 12 Apr. 1885.

173. Ibid.

174. Ibid., 12 Dec. 1885.

175. Will. J. Vale to Powderly, 8 Mar. 1886, Powderly Papers.

176. *HS*, 24 June 1886.

177. Ibid., 30 June 1886; *POL*, 3 July 1886; *Cigar Makers' Official Journal*, July 1886.

178. *POL*, 10 July 1886. On Cigar Makers' Union and Knights of Labor unity cf. Dennis East, "Union Labels and Boycotts: Co-operation of the Knights of Labor and the Cigar Makers' International Union, 1885-1886," *Labor History* 16 (Spring 1975): 266-71; Cigar Makers' Union No. 130, Saginaw, Mich., *Minute Book*, pp. 20-21, 26-27, 88, Archives of Labor History and Urban Affairs, Wayne State University, Detroit, Mich.

179. *POL*, 17 July 1886.

180. Ibid., 31 July 1886.

181. See *Cigar Makers' Official Journal*, August 1886; *The Craftsman*, 3 July 1886; *POL*, 31 July, 14 Aug., 4 and 25 Sept. 1886; *HS*, 12 Aug. 1886.

182. *HS*, 31 Aug. 1886; *John Swinton's Paper*, 5 Sept. 1886.

183. *Proceedings of the Second Session of the Canadian Trades and Labor Congress, 1886* (Toronto: Labor Reformer, 1886), p. 40.

184. Powderly to Jas. Hennigan, 3 Sept. 1886, Powderly Papers.

185. *HS*, 29 Sept. 1887; *Record of the Proceedings of the General Assembly of the Knights of Labor, 1888*, p. 49; *Proceedings, General Assembly, 1889*, p. 16.

186. *The Craftsman*, 2 Oct. 1886.

187. *HS*, 25 Aug. 1888.

188. James Dore to Powderly, 1 Oct. 1886, Powderly Papers; George Collis to Powderly, 1 Oct. 1886.

189. George Collis to Powderly, 9 Sept. 1886, ibid.

190. See *HS*, 28 Jan., 8, 9, 14, and 17 Feb. 1887.

191. Ibid., 9 Mar. 1887.

192. Ibid., 2 Nov. 1887.

193. Martin O'Driscoll to Powderly, 31 July 1888, Powderly Papers.

194. *Journal of United Labor*, 3 Dec. 1887.

195. *Proceedings, General Assembly, 1887*, pp. 1729-30. Cf. Jas. Hennigan to Powderly, 21 Aug. 1887, Powderly Papers.

196. George Collis to Powderly, 4 Feb. and 20 Feb. 1888, Powderly Papers; Powderly to George Collis, 14 Feb. 1888; Thomas Towers to Powderly, n.d. (February 1888?).

197. *POL*, 21 Aug. 1886.

198. See Ware, *Labor Movement in the United States*, pp. 111, 290, which also identifies D. R. Gibson as a member of the Home Club. On speeches of Mullen and Drury see *POL*, 17 Oct. 1885, 24 Apr., 1 May 1886; *HS*, 21, 22, and 26 Apr. 1886.

199. *POL*, 2 Apr. 1886.

200. *Labor Advocate*, 23 Jan. 1891.

201. *HS*, 16 Jan. 1882.

202. George Collis to Powderly, 23 Nov. 1884, Powderly Papers; *Labor News*, 12 Apr. 1914; *POL*, 12 Sept. 1885.

203. Collis to Powderly, 23 Nov. 1884, Powderly Papers.

204. *POL*, 4 Dec. 1886; *HS*, 28 July, 2 Nov. 1887; *Proceedings, General Assembly, 1887*, p. 1831.

205. E. S. Gilbert to John W. Hayes, 24 Feb. 1892, Hayes Papers, Catholic University, Washington, D.C.

206. See Melvyn Dubofsky, *Industrialism and the American Worker, 1865-1920* (New York: Crowell, 1975), pp. 59-60.

207. *HS*, 12 Mar. 1889.

208. Ibid., 8 Oct. 1889.
209. *POL*, 17 Oct. 1884.

CHAPTER 7
1. Quoted in *Industrial Banner*, November 1906.
2. For an introduction to this context of social and economic development in South-Central Ontario see Craig Heron and Bryan D. Palmer, "Through the Prism of the Strike: Industrial Conflict in Southern Ontario, 1901-1914," *Canadian Historical Review* 58 (December 1977): 423-58.
3. The term "new unionism" has generally referred to the rise of British labour in the 1880-1900 period, particularly to the participation of the unskilled. See Henry Pelling, *A History of British Trade Unionism* (Harmondsworth, Middlesex: Penguin, 1971), pp. 93-122; E. J. Hobsbawm, "General Labour Unions in Britain, 1889-1914," in *Labouring Men: Studies in the History of Labour* (New York: Basic Books, 1964), pp. 179-203. But the term had an international application and, as David Montgomery has stressed, denoted an important shift in consciousness among skilled workers affiliated with the AFL. See the pioneering overview of the 1903-22 years in Montgomery, "The 'New Unionism' and the Transformation of Workers' Consciousness, 1903-1922," *Journal of Social History* 7 (Summer 1974): 509-29. Note too the discussion in Bruno Ramirez, *When Workers Fight: The Politics of Industrial Relations in the Progressive Era, 1898-1916* (Westport, Conn.: Greenwood, 1978).
4. *The Lance*, 4 Mar. 1911; *Typographical Journal*, 15 Nov. 1898.
5. John Herman Randall, Jr., "The Growth of Class Solidarity and the New Unionism," in *The Problem of Group Responsibility to Society* (New York: Arno Reprint, 1969), pp. 220-21. Cf. J. Potofsky, "The New Unionism in America," *Labour Monthly* 1 (July 1922), pp. 73-82.
6. André Tridon, *The New Unionism* (New York: B. W. Heubsch, 1913), p. 17; Montgomery, "The 'New Unionism'," p. 509.
7. *Industrial Banner*, 5 June 1914.
8. Gompers to Landers, 16 June 1908, Samuel Gompers Letterbooks, 1883-1924, vol. 137, pp. 502-3, Library of Congress, Washington, D.C.
9. *Citizen and Country*, 4 May 1900; Robert H. Babcock, *Gompers in Canada: A Study in American Continentalism Before the First World War* (Toronto: University of Toronto Press, 1974), pp. 38-58; Eugene Forsey, "The Canadian Labour Movement, 1812-1902," Canadian Historical Association, *Booklet No. 26* (1974), pp. 11-13; *Labor News*, 12 Jan. 1912.
10. On Flett see *Labor News*, 30 Aug. 1912; Babcock, *Gompers in Canada*, pp. 38-58; and virtually every volume of the post-1899 Gompers Letterbooks.
11. Babcock, *Gompers in Canada*, p. 58; *American Federationist* 10 (September 1903): 821; *HS*, 1 Aug. 1900. At the end of the period under study Hamilton continued to be a centre of union activity. See *HS*, 23 June 1914.
12. *Labour Gazette* 4 (1904): 1065-66.
13. *American Federationist* 7 (June 1900): 175.
14. *Labour Gazette* 11 (1911): 1313-14.
15. Tridon, *The New Unionism*, pp. 31-32.
16. For an overview of building trades activity in Toronto in the same period see Wayne Roberts, "Artisans, Aristocrats and Handymen: Politics and Unionism Among Toronto Skilled Building Trades Workers, 1896-1914," *Labour/Le Travailleur* 1 (1976): 92-121.

17. *HS*, 27 July 1896, 6 Mar. 1897.

18. Ibid., 17 Feb., 1 and 15 Mar. 1904.

19. *Labour Gazette* 5 (1905): 296.

20. *HS*, 2-18 Apr. 1906; *Labour Gazette* 6 (1906): 1267-68.

21. *HS*, 11 June 1906.

22. Ibid., 25 Apr. – 8 May 1912.

23. Department of Labour Strikes and Lockouts Records, RG 27, vol. 297, Strike no. 3241, PAC; vol. 299, Strike no. 3483. Cf. *Labour Gazette* 14 (1915): 202, on a dispute involving a nonunionist.

24. *HS*, 10 May 1900; *Labour Gazette* 4 (1904): 161; 6 (1906): 1157, 1214-15.

25. *Labour Gazette* 7 (1907): 921.

26. Strikes and Lockouts Records, vol. 295, Strike no. 2926; *Labour Gazette* 8 (1908): 104-5, 106, 230.

27. Strikes and Lockouts Records, vol. 298, Strike no. 3343; *Labour Gazette* 11 (1911): 1430-35; 12 (1912): 78. On other brief carpenters' struggles see Strikes and Lockouts Records, vol. 298, Strike no. 3357; vol. 302, Strike no. 66.

28. Strikes and Lockouts Records, vol. 294, Strike no. 2282; *Labour Gazette* 13 (1913): 1303-4; 8 (1908): 99.

29. *Labour Gazette* 7 (1907): 1440; 8 (1908): 99.

30. *HS*, 27 Nov. 1913; *Hamilton Herald* clipping, 26 Nov. 1913, in Strikes and Lockouts Records, vol. 303, Strike no. 117A.

31. *HS*, 10-24 Aug. 1900; *Labour Gazette* 1 (1901): 118.

32. *Labour Gazette* 1 (1901): 287; *HS*, 9 and 10 Oct. 1900.

33. *HS*, 22 and 23 Apr. 1903.

34. Ibid., 3 and 10 June, 3 Aug. 1904; *Labour Gazette* 5 (1905): 188, 296; Gompers to Flett, 19 July 1904, Gompers Letterbooks, vol. 91, p. 71; Gompers to Flett, 22 Aug. 1904, vol. 92, p. 190.

35. *Labour Gazette* 6 (1906): 337, 462-63, 581-83, 803; 7 (1907): 133.

36. *HS*, 26 and 31 Mar., 3 Apr. 1902; *Labour Gazette* 2 (1902): 613, 675.

37. *HS*, 22 Oct. 1906; *Labor News*, 23 Feb. 1912; *Hamilton Evening Times*, 15 May 1911, clipping in Brian Henley, compiler, *Hamilton Evening Times Scrapbook*, "Labour," pt. II, p. vii, Hamilton Collection, Hamilton Public Library; Strikes and Lockouts Records, vol. 297, Strike no. 3246; *Industrial Banner*, March 1899; *Labour Gazette* 5 (1905): 636, 753.

38. *Labour Gazette* 12 (1912): 357, 1110-11; 13 (1913): 1000, 1059-61, 1139; Strikes and Lockouts Records, vol. 297, Strike no. 3457; vol. 301, Strike no. 15.

39. For a brief discussion of a parallel situation in Toronto foundries in the years 1899-1904 see Gregory S. Kealey, "The 'Honest Workingman' and Workers' Control: The Experience of Toronto Skilled Workers, 1860-1892," *Labour/Le Travailleur* 1 (1976): 46-47.

40. *HS*, 30 Mar. – 3 July 1899.

41. Ibid., 2 May, 12 June 1900, 10, 11, 20, and 27 Mar. 1902.

42. *Labour Gazette* 2 (1902): 577, 612-15; 6 (1906): 302-3.

43. Ibid., 3 (1903): 957-58; 4 (1904): 116, 160; *HS*, 17 Mar., 3 and 6 Apr., 28 May 1903.

44. *Industrial Banner*, November 1905. On a conflict at the Sawyer-Massey foundry see *Labour Gazette* 5 (1905): 899, 1070, 1199-1200.

45. The key period of struggle was between February and May 1908. See *HS*, 17 Feb. – 20 May 1908. A brief conflict in 1908, involving forty-five molders, was terminated by the International Union, which deemed the men's protests over differential payment for two types of molding outside the jurisdiction of the trade/shop regulations. See *Labour Gazette* 9 (1909): 339. On a brief struggle at the Kerr-Coombs foundry for the closed shop see ibid., 7 (1907): 299-302, 1361-62.

46. *HS*, 15 Feb. – 1 Mar., 24 Mar. 1909; *Labour Gazette* 9 (1909): 436, 1058-59, 1145-46, 1193-94, 1257, 1374; 10 (1910): 125, 305, 436, 654-55. The most detailed source, from which the quotations on union restriction of output are taken, is Strikes and Lockouts Records, vol. 296, Strike no. 3124.

47. This paragraph draws on material in Strikes and Lockouts Records, vol. 296, Strike no. 3148. Cf. *HS*, 13-26 May, 6 and 14 Aug., 23 Oct. 1909.

48. *HS*, 11 Apr., 6 May 1910; *Labour Gazette* 10 (1910): 1371-72; *Industrial Banner*, July 1910.

49. Strikes and Lockouts Records, vol. 299, Strike no. 3460; *Labor News*, 8 and 15 Mar. 1912; *Industrial Banner*, April 1912; *Labour Gazette* 12 (1912): 996, 1110-11, 1173, 1176-78; 13 (1913): 80, 273-75; *Minute Book, Hamilton Trades and Labor Council, 1910-1914*, pp. 150-51, Hamilton Collection, Hamilton Public Library.

50. Strikes and Lockouts Records, vol. 299, Strike no. 3492.

51. Ibid., vol. 300, Strike no. 27; *Labour Gazette* 13 (1913): 1059-61, 1139, 1302; 14 (1915): 88-89, 355. Cf. ibid., 13 (1913): 273-75; *HS*, 17 Apr. 1912, for other molders' conflicts.

52. *HS*, 12 and 17 Apr. 1897.

53. See for instance Strikes and Lockouts Records, vol. 294, Strike nos. 2854, 2876; *HS*, 26 and 28 May 1906.

54. *HS*, 25 and 28 May 1900.

55. *Labour Gazette* 1 (1901): 402-3, 437, 516-17; 2 (1902): 503-4, 577.

56. *HS*, 16, 17, and 19 June 1899.

57. Strikes and Lockouts Records, vol. 294, Strike no. 2856.

58. *HS*, 28, 29, 30, 31 Aug. 1900.

59. *Labour Gazette* 10 (1910): 1327-30.

60. The quotations are taken from clippings and reports in Strikes and Lockouts Records, vol. 297, Strike no. 3238. Cf. *Labour Gazette* 10 (1910): 1327-30; *Hamilton Evening Times*, 16 Jan. 1914, in *Hamilton Evening Times Scrapbook*, p. xv. For another attack on the soldiering of unskilled municipal workers see *HS*, 17 May 1913.

61. On the emergence of the electrical engineering industry in Hamilton see "Hamilton – The Electric City of Canada," Souvenir Edition, *Magazine of Industry and Daily Times* (December 1910). On the organization of the electrical workers see Hamilton and District Trades and Labor Council, *60th Anniversary, Diamond Jubilee, 1888-1948* (Hamilton: Spectator, 1948), p. 49.

62. See for instance *HS*, 27 and 29 Aug. 1900, 17 June – 28 Aug. 1902; *Labour Gazette* 3 (1903): 50, 53; 13 (1913): 1000; Strikes and Lockouts Records, vol. 301, Strike no. 11.

63. See J. M. Budish and George Soule, *The New Unionism in the Clothing Industry* (New York: Russell and Russell, 1920); Potofsky, "The New Unionism," pp. 78-82; Melvyn Dubofsky, *When Workers Organize: New York City in the Progressive Era* (Amherst, Mass.: University of Massachusetts Press, 1968).

64. *HS*, 30 Jan., 3 Feb., 6 Apr. 1897, 1 May–5 June 1899; *Industrial Banner*, March 1899. On the union label in the city see *Industrial Banner*, February 1911. Note too the large garment workers' strike outlined in *HS*, 15 Apr. 1913.

65. For discussions of relations on the street railways see Frederic W. Spiers, *The Street Railway System of Philadelphia, Its History and Present Condition* (Baltimore: Johns Hopkins, 1897); Gurdon W. Wattles, *A Crime Against Labor: A Brief History of the Omaha & Council Bluffs Street Railway Strike, 1909* (Omaha: published by author, n.d.); David Frank, "Trouble in Toronto: The Street Railway Lockout and Strike, 1886" (typescript, University of Toronto, 1971); Edward S. Mason, *The Street Railway in Massachusetts: The Rise and Decline of an Industry* (Cambridge, Mass.: Harvard University Press, 1932); Emerson P. Schmidt, *Industrial Relations in Urban Transportation* (Minneapolis: University of Minnesota Press, 1937); Sam Bass Warner, *Streetcar Suburbs: The Process of Growth in Urban Boston, 1879-1900* (New York: Atheneum, 1973). On major early strikes see *Motorman and Conductor*, 1895-1910. For a discussion of the streetcar strike in Brooklyn, N.Y., and its place in Dreiser's *Sister Carrie*, see Fay M. Blake, *The Strike in the American Novel* (Metuchen, N.J.: Scarecrow Press, 1972), pp. 83-84. The expansion of the Amalgamated in Canada is outlined in *Motorman and Conductor*, February 1900. Struggles on Canadian street railways are discussed in *Labour Gazette* 3 (1903): 48, 706, 1029; 6 (1906): 174, 1155-56, 1265-66; 7 (1907): 174; 14 (1915): 90; *Motorman and Conductor*, November 1898, March 1899, July 1899, August 1899, September 1899, April 1906. See my discussion of the 1898-99 London strike in " 'Give us the road and we will run it': The Social and Cultural Matrix of an Emerging Labour Movement," in Gregory S. Kealey and Peter Warrian, eds., *Essays in Canadian Working Class History* (Toronto: McClelland and Stewart, 1976), pp. 106-24. Recent discussions include H. V. Nelles and Christopher Armstrong, *The Revenge of the Methodist Bicycle Company* (Toronto: Hakkert, 1978); M. J. Doucet, "Mass Transit and the Failure of Private Ownership: The Case of Toronto," *Urban History Review* 3 (1977): 3-33.

66. *HS*, 1, 6, and 7 Sept., 18 Oct. 1892.

67. The London strike was a topic of much discussion in Hamilton. Using the strike as a means of popularizing the new unionism, London's Joseph Marks spoke before the Hamilton Trades and Labor Council on a number of occasions, outlining the development of the 1898-99 conflict and urging the organization of the unskilled and unorganized. See *HS*, 27 Feb. 1897, 29 Jan., 4 Nov. 1898, 8 June 1899, 3 May 1900; Gompers to Flett, 14 May 1900, Gompers Letterbooks, vol. 34, p. 125.

68. *HS*, 28 Mar., 20, 21, 28 Apr., 1 May 1899; *Motorman and Conductor*, February 1900.

69. *HS*, 22 Oct. 1901, 29 Jan. 1902.

70. Ibid., 30 Jan., 11, 14, and 17 Mar. 1992.

71. Ibid., 30 Oct. 1903.

72. Ibid., 6 Feb. 1904.

73. See *Motorman and Conductor*, February 1906, May 1906, August 1906.

74. Ibid., March 1895.

75. On the London and Winnipeg 1906 strikes see *Industrial Banner*, May 1906, July 1906, August 1906, September 1906; *Motorman and Conductor*, April 1906.

76. *HS*, 16, 20, 21, and 22 Aug. 1906; *Industrial Banner*, September 1906; *Labour Gazette* 7 (1907): 616, 686, 689; *Motorman and Conductor*, September 1906.

77. *HS*, 31 Aug.–6 Oct. 1906.

78. Ibid., 23 Oct.–5 Nov. 1906.

79. Ibid., 5 Nov. 1906.

80. Ibid., 6, 7, and 8 Nov. 1906. For an important discussion of the notion of the legitimacy of community violence in an earlier period see E. P. Thompson, "The Moral Economy of the English Crowd in the Eighteenth Century," *Past & Present* 50 (February 1971): 76-136.

81. *HS*, 9-15 Nov. 1906; *Motorman and Conductor*, November 1906; *Industrial Banner*, November 1906.

82. *HS*, 12-21 Nov. 1906.

83. Ibid., 23 Nov. 1906.

84. Ibid., 24 Nov. 1906; *Industrial Banner*, December 1906; Frank L. Jones, compiler, "Reading of the Riot Act Ended Black Period of Hamilton History: Cavalry Had to Charge Mob on James Street North," *Historical Articles from the Hamilton Spectator*, pp. 25-29, Hamilton Collection, Hamilton Public Library. The militia's role in the strike was outlined by Karl Liebknecht, who used it as the sole Canadian example in his *Militarism* (Toronto: William Briggs, 1917), pp. 146-47. My thanks to Wayne Roberts for bringing this source to my attention.

85. *HS*, 26 Nov. 1906.

86. Rioters were named in ibid., 19, 24, 26, and 28 Nov., 4 Dec. 1906. Their occupations were checked in *Vernon's City of Hamilton Directory* for 1905 and 1906.

87. *HS*, 24 Nov. 1906.

88. Ibid., 28 Nov., 17 Dec. 1906.

89. *Hamilton Herald*, n.d., cited in *HS*, 18 Dec. 1906.

90. *HS*, 20, 24, and 26 Dec. 1906; *Motorman and Conductor*, December 1906.

91. See "Reading of the Riot Act," in *Historical Articles from the Hamilton Spectator*.

92. The most forceful introduction to the phenomenon is the work of Herbert G. Gutman, recently assembled in Gutman, *Work, Culture, and Society in Industrializing America* (New York: Knopf, 1976). Cf. Gutman's pioneering essay, "The Workers' Search for Power: Labor in the Gilded Age," in H. Wayne Morgan, ed., *The Gilded Age: A Reappraisal* (Syracuse, N.Y.: Syracuse University Press, 1963), pp. 38-68; and Gutman's discussion of the 1873-74 depression in Gutman, "Social and Economic Structure and Depression: American Labor in 1873 and 1874" (Ph.D. diss., University of Wisconsin, 1959). The erosion of the link between the working-class community and the wider community was part and parcel of the rise of the industrial-capitalist class, and its emergence as a national force, transcending the power of local institutions. See John T. Cumbler, "Labor, Capital, and Community: The Struggle for Power," *Labor History* 15 (Summer 1974): 395-415; Melvyn Dubofsky, *Industrialism and the American Worker, 1865-1920* (New York: Crowell, 1975); Daniel J. Walkowitz, "Worker City, Company Town: Adaptation and Protest within the Troy Iron Worker and Cohoes Cotton Worker Communities, 1855-1884" (typescript, Rutgers University, 1976). Perhaps because of the strength of the Hamilton working-class movement, these links retained some—albeit weakened—force well into the twentieth century, and community endorsement of the strikers' cause reflected this important reality. Note the discussion in Wayne Roberts, "Class, State, and Community: Unskilled Male Workers and the Toronto Labour Movement, 1896-1914" (typescript, Uni-

versity of Toronto, 1978). Fay contended community support for the Hamilton strike was exceptional. See *Motorman and Conductor*, December 1906. In London, where similar rioting took place in 1899, public sentiment moved immediately and forcefully against the strikers. See "'Give us the road'," pp. 106-24.

93. *HS*, 30 Nov.–20 Dec. 1906; *Industrial Banner*, March 1907, June 1907, July 1907, June 1908, February 1908. In July 1908 the company and the union again clashed, with the firm emerging the victor. The union's president, John Theaker, was dismissed, workers grew angered by the company's use of "spotters," factions developed within the union, and a board of arbitration ultimately favoured the company. See *HS*, 4 Feb.–23 Apr. 1908.

94. The study of the scientific management movement has recently produced a number of important works. On its impact in the United States see Harry Braverman, *Labor and Monopoly Capital: The Degradation of Work in the Twentieth Century* (New York: Monthly Review, 1974), esp. pp. 45-152; Montgomery, "The 'New Unionism'," pp. 509-29; Montgomery, "Workers' Control of Machine Production in the Nineteenth Century," *Labor History* 17 (Fall 1976): 485-86, 507-9; Hugh G. J. Aitken, *Taylorism at Watertown Arsenal: Scientific Management in Action, 1908-1915* (Cambridge, Mass.: Harvard University Press, 1960); Bryan Palmer, "Class, Conception, and Conflict: The Thrust for Efficiency, Managerial Views of Labor, and Working Class Rebellion," *Review of Radical Political Economics* 7 (Summer 1975): 31-49. The most recent discussion is Daniel Nelson, *Managers and Workers: Origins of the New Factory System in the United States, 1880-1920* (Madison, Wis.: University of Wisconsin Press, 1975), pp. 55-78. For developments in France, Germany, Belgium, and England see Peter Stearns, *Lives of Labour: Work in a Maturing Industrial Society* (London: Croom Helm, 1975), pp. 193-228. The English experience is treated in conjunction with German and American developments in Arthur Shadwell, *Industrial Efficiency: A Comparative Study of Industrial Life in England, Germany and America*, 2 vols. (New York: Longman's, 1906).

95. U.S. Congress, *Final Report and Testimony Submitted to Congress by the Commission on Industrial Relations*, 64th Congress, Senate Doc. no. 415, X (Washington: Government Printing, 1916), 9761; "Scheduling Locomotive Repair Work on the Canadian Pacific Railway," *Industrial Engineering and Engineering Digest* 8 (November 1910): 380-83.

96. Canada, Royal Commission on Industrial Training and Technical Education, *Report of the Commissioners*, IV (Ottawa: C. H. Parmalee, 1913), 2087.

97. *Industrial Canada*, 21 Jan. 1901; *Industrial Banner*, December 1901, September 1905, September 1906.

98. *Industrial Canada*, March 1911, March 1913, April 1913, May 1913.

99. Frederick Winslow Taylor, "The Principles of Scientific Management," in Canadian Club of Ottawa, *Yearbook, 1912-1913* (Ottawa: Canada Club, 1913), pp. 115-43. My thanks to Russell Hann for making this source available to me.

100. *Industrial Canada*, November 1907, and on the developing concern with standardization, ibid., 1 May 1902, December 1906, December 1908.

101. See Albert H. Leake, *Education and Industrial Efficiency* (Toronto: L. K. Cameron, 1906); Leake, *Industrial Education: Its Problems, Methods, and Dangers* (Boston and New York: Houghton, Mifflin, 1913); Peter H. Bryce, *National Social Efficiency: Annual Presidential Address of the Canadian Conference on Public Welfare, Ottawa, 25 September 1917* (Ottawa: J. de Labroquerie Tache, 1918).

102. *Industrial Canada*, May 1911. For a fuller discussion of the efficiency drive in Toronto see Wayne Roberts, "Boomers, Craftsmen, and Managers: Cultural and Technological Conflict in the Toronto Metal Trades, 1889-1914," chap. 3 of a forthcoming Ph.D. dissertation, University of Toronto.

103. On branch plants see Babcock, *Gompers in Canada*, pp. 28-37; *Labour Gazette* 3 (1903): 138; 4 (1904): 1207. On the merger movement see H. G. Stapells, "The Recent Consolidation Movement in Canadian Industry" (M.A. thesis, University of Toronto, 1922).

104. Herbert Lister, *Hamilton, Canada, Its History, Commerce, Industries and Resources* (Hamilton: Spectator, 1913), p. 43; "Hamilton — The Electric City of Canada," Souvenir Edition, *Magazine of Industry and Daily Times* (December 1910), p. 2; Max Jesoley, "Hamilton — Birmingham of Canada," *National Monthly* 2 (August 1903), pp. 77-80; *Hamilton Manufacturer* III (1912): 10-12.

105. *Hamilton Manufacturer* III (1912): 22, 24.

106. *HS*, 18 and 20 Jan. 1906.

107. "How Does it Strike You: Results of Experiments to Increase Producing Power of Skilled Workmen in Shops and Factories," ibid., 5 Dec. 1906.

108. William Kilbourn, *The Elements Combined: A History of the Steel Company of Canada* (Toronto: Clarke, Irwin, 1960), pp. 72, 75, 84-85. Robert T. Armstrong, "Memoir of Duncan Lithographing Company, Hamilton, 1882-1978," n.p. John Weaver kindly provided a xerox of this document. On American experts at Westinghouse see *HS*, 15 Apr. 1910. On the use of technical experts in the early iron and steel industry, many brought in from American universities, see Harold Bernard Ward, "Hamilton, Ontario, as a Manufacturing Center" (Ph.D. diss., University of Chicago, 1934), pp. 137, 147.

109. *Hamilton Manufacturer* III (1912): 24.

110. On the Greening Company see Ward, "Hamilton as a Manufacturing Center," p. 44; *Industrial Canada*, June 1906. The Frost Wire Company practices are discussed in *HS*, 6 Feb. 1908; *Industrial Canada*, December 1904, p. 327; Canada, Department of Labour, *Annual Report, 1907-1908* (Ottawa: C. H. Parmalee, 1908), p. 26. For a general discussion of paternalism see Heron and Palmer, "Through the Prism of the Strike," pp. 455-56. On other similar innovations in London and Toronto see *Industrial Canada*, May 1908, May 1909.

111. See *Life and Labor* 1 (May 1911): 131; *Typographical Journal*, August 1911, December 1911, January 1914; *Iron Molders' International Journal*, April 1911, August 1911; *Shoeworkers' Journal*, October 1911; *American Federationist* 18 (February 1911): 116-17; 18 (April 1911): 278-79; 18 (May 1911): 380-84; 18 (August 1911): 603-4; *Machinists' Monthly Journal*, September 1911; Jean Trepp McKelvey, *AFL Attitudes Towards Production, 1900-1932* (Ithaca, N.Y.: Cornell Studies in Industrial and Labor Relations, 1952), pp. 12-26; Milton J. Nadworny, *Scientific Management and the Unions, 1900-1932* (Cambridge, Mass.: Harvard University Press, 1955), pp. 23-29, 53-71; Robert Franklin Hoxie, *Scientific Management and Labor* (New York: D. Appelton, 1915); David J. Saposs, ed., *Readings in Trade Unionism* (New York: Arno Reprint, 1969), pp. 282-89; John R. Commons, "Organized Labor's Attitude towards Industrial Efficiency," *American Economic Review* 1 (September 1911): 463-72; Commons, "Is Class Conflict Growing in America and Is It Inevitable?' *American Journal of Sociology* 13 (May 1908): 756-83. The quote is from Commons, ed., *Trade Unionism and Labor Problems*, 2nd ser. (New York: Ginn and Co., 1921), p. 149.

112. *The Lance*, 29 Apr., 13 May 1911, 12 Feb. 1912; *Cotton's Weekly*, 8 June 1911. King, author of a sophisticated liberal tract aimed at uniting "Taylorist" aims and paternalistic modes of personnel management and welfare work (William Lyon Mackenzie King, *Industry and Humanity: Industrial Relations and Liberalism, 1918* [Toronto: University of Toronto Press, 1973; 1st ed., 1918]) came under attack in *Cotton's Weekly*, 18 Aug., 2 and 23 Sept. 1910.

113. Alan Sullivan, *The Inner Door* (New York: Century, 1917), pp. 133-34. Sullivan was a Canadian novelist trained as a civil engineer. Closely in touch with developments in the business community, he can be regarded as an astute commentator. In this novel he chronicles the attempts of an impersonal management to utilize efficiency experts and speed-up to elicit greater productivity. The result is a violent strike in which the workers seize the factory. On Sullivan see Michael Bliss' introduction to Sullivan's better-known novel, *The Rapids* (Toronto: University of Toronto Press, 1972), pp. vi-xx. The Dunlop Tire episode is discussed in *Toronto Star*, 26 Oct. 1906, cited in the conclusion to Wayne Roberts's forthcoming University of Toronto Ph.D. dissertation.

114. *Labor News* 1 Mar., 26 July, 2 Jan. 1912, 22 May 1914.

115. *HS*, 15 and 16 May, 1 Aug., 21 Sept. 1893.

116. *Labour Gazette* 1 (1901): 516-17.

117. Ibid., 3 (1903): 479, 566.

118. Ibid., 10 (1910): 1441; Strikes and Lockouts Records, vol. 297, Strike no. 3257; *Minute Book, Trades and Labor Council, 1910-1914*, pp. 11-12; *HS*, 14 May 1910.

119. *Labour Gazette* 11 (1911): pp. 1430-35; Strikes and Lockouts Records, vol. 298, Strike no. 3376.

120. *Labour Gazette* 13 (1913): 1000; Strikes and Lockouts Records, vol. 301, Strike no. 11. Cf. Strikes and Lockouts Records, vol. 304, Strike no. 19, on a 1914 garment workers' strike waged against a "task system." On similar strikes against managerial innovations in other cities see Heron and Palmer, "Through the Prism of the Strike," pp. 434-46. On the Watertown Arsenal conflict see Aitken, *Taylorism at Watertown Arsenal*, p. 151.

121. For a brief discussion of women workers see Patricia V. Schulz, "The Employees of Hamilton Cotton Company, 1900-1902" (typescript, York University, 1978).

122. On Hamilton founders see *HS*, 21 Nov., 1 Dec. 1884; Kilbourn, *Elements Combined*, pp. 33-35; *Report of the Royal Commission on the Relations of Labor and Capital in Canada*, "Ontario Evidence," II (Ottawa: Queen's Printer, 1889), 834-35. The quotation is from *Industrial Canada*, June 1914.

123. I have argued this position in my "Class, Conception, and Conflict," pp. 31-49.

124. Introductions to the open shop drive are provided in Michael Bliss, *A Living Profit: Studies in the Social History of Canadian Business, 1883-1911* (Toronto: McClelland and Stewart, 1974), pp. 74-94; Michael J. Piva, "The Decline of the Trade Union Movement in Toronto, 1900-1915," paper presented at the Canadian Historical Association meetings, 1975, pp. 8-17; Heron and Palmer, "Through the Prism of the Strike," pp. 446-56.

125. Dooley is quoted in *Industrial Canada*, 10 May 1907. The attack on union limitation of output is in *Industrial Canada*, October 1903, quoting CMA, *Report of a Special Committee on Labor*. Other attacks on restriction of output are found in ibid., October 1908, April 1909. For the trade union response to this kind

of attack see *Industrial Banner*, October 1911; *Minute Book, Trades and Labor Council, 1910-1914*, p. 40.

126. *Industrial Canada*, September 1903, November 1905, October 1904, April 1914.

127. These tactics are discussed in detail, with some reference to Hamilton, in Heron and Palmer, "Through the Prism of the Strike," pp. 446-56. On Kirby's role see *Industrial Canada*, November 1912; *The Toiler*, 6 Feb., 15 May 1903; *Industrial Banner*, February 1903, May 1903; *The Lance*, 22 May 1909.

128. See *Industrial Banner*, April 1909.

129. *American Federationist* 10 (September 1903): 821.

130. Ibid., 15 (June 1908): 447-48; 16 (September 1909):752-53. Cf. Bradley Rubin, "Mackenzie King and the Writing of Canada's (Anti) Labour Laws," *Canadian Dimension* 8 (January 1972): 42-48; Ramirez, *When Workers Fight*, pp. 160-73; A. B. Garretson, "The Attitude of Organized Labor Toward the Canadian Industrial Disputes Act," *Annals of the American Academy of Political and Social Science* 69 (January 1917): 170-72. The general context is outlined in Henry Ferns and Bernard Ostry, *The Age of Mackenzie King* (Toronto: Lorimer, 1976).

131. *Industrial Banner*, February 1907; Gompers to Landers, 22 June 1907, Gompers Letterbooks, vol. 125, pp. 539-40; R. Lee Guard to Flett, 28 Sept. 1909, vol. 150, p. 326.

132. On this phenomenon see Clarence E. Bonnett, *Employers' Associations in the United States: A Study of Typical Associations* (New York: Macmillan, 1922); Ray S. Baker, "Organized Capital Challenges Organized Labor: The New Employers' Association Movement in the United States," *McClure's* 21 (July 1904): 279-92; *Typographical Journal*, December 1905. Hamilton Associations are listed in *Labour Gazette* 6 (1906): 279-88.

133. Strikes and Lockouts Records, vol. 294, Strike no. 288; *Labour Gazette* 7 (1907): 1438.

134. *Hamilton Herald*, 29 May 1907, in Brian Henley, compiler, *Clippings from the Hamilton Herald*, "Labour File," Hamilton Collection, Hamilton Public Library.

135. *HS*, 11 Feb. 1905.

136. *Industrial Banner*, April 1905.

137. See *POL*, 12 Apr., 19 Sept. 1885, 27 Mar. 1886, and the discussion in chap. 6 above.

138. *Typographical Journal*, December 1905, January 1906.

139. Ibid., February 1906.

140. For a different perspective see Piva, "Decline of Toronto Union Movement."

141. See the brief introduction in Montgomery, "Workers' Control," pp. 504-7; and the earlier discussions in Fred S. Hall, *Sympathetic Strikes and Sympathetic Lockouts* (New York: Russell Sage, 1898); Helen Marot, *American Labor Unions* (New York: Henry Holt, 1914), pp. 112-20. On sympathetic strikes in New York see Philip Taft, *The A.F.L. in the Time of Gompers* (New York: Harpers, 1957), pp. 25, 29, 251.

142. See chaps. 3 and 6 above.

143. *Labour Gazette* 2 (1902): 674-75. On other important Canadian sympathetic strikes in this period see ibid., 1 (1901): 230; 3 (1903): 270; 5 (1905): 1147.

144. *Industrial Banner*, August 1905, October 1905.

145. Montgomery, "Workers' Control of Machine Production," p. 507; Mark Perlman, *The Machinists: A New Study in American Trade Unionism* (Cam-

bridge, Mass.: Harvard University Press, 1961), pp. 20-36, 48-50; Gompers to Flett, 11 June 1904, Gompers Letterbooks, vol. 89, p. 902; Gompers to Flett, 1 July 1904, vol. 90, p. 667.

146. *HS*, 7 and 11 Apr. 1900, 30 Mar. 1901.

147. See ibid., 12 June – 28 Aug. 1902.

148. Ibid., 22 and 23 Apr. 1903, 26 and 30 Apr. 1904.

149. *Hamilton Herald*, 7 and 29 May 1907, in *Clippings from Hamilton Herald*.

150. Strikes and Lockouts Records, vol. 299, Strike no. 3422A.

151. *Labor News*, 22 Mar., 5 Apr. 1912.

152. The above draws upon, "Labor Owes Much to the Fighting Quality of Allan Studholme," in Hamilton and District Trades and Labor Council, *60th Anniversary, Diamond Jubilee, 1888-1948* (Hamilton: Spectator, 1948), p. 13; Studholme's obituaries in *HS*, 28 July 1919; *Hamilton Herald*, 28 July 1919; William T. C. Bews to T. V. Powderly, 28 Dec. 1882, Powderly Papers, Letterbook 3, Catholic University, Washington, D.C.; J. A. Welch to Powderly, 18 Dec. 1884; *POL*, 31 May 1884, 21 March 1885. The following section on Studholme has benefited from discussions with Craig Heron.

153. The 1906 campaign is outlined in *HS*, 9-30 Nov. 1906; *Industrial Banner*, December 1906; January 1907; *Canadian Annual Review, 1906*, p. 319. On Landers's opportunism and Liberal sympathies see Gene Howard Homel, "James Simpson and the Origins of Canadian Social Democracy" (Ph.D. diss., University of Toronto, 1978), pp. 352-53; Martin Robin, *Radical Politics and Canadian Labour, 1880-1930* (Kingston, Ont.: Industrial and Labor Relations Centre, 1968), p. 223.

154. *HS*, 29 May – 9 June 1908; *Industrial Banner*, June 1908, July 1908.

155. *Industrial Banner*, November 1908; *HS*, 15 Sept. – 27 October 1908.

156. *HS*, 27 Nov. 1906.

157. Quoted in Homel, "Simpson," pp. 352-53.

158. On the 1911 and 1914 victories see *Hamilton Herald*, 30 June 1914; *HS*, 6-30 June 1914; *Industrial Banner*, 15 May, 12 and 26 June, 3 July 1914. On socialist – ILP antagonisms see Robin, *Radical Politics*, pp. 62-118; Homel, "Simpson," pp. 256-66, 354-55, 427-28, 611-12; Wayne Roberts, "Brothers, Citizens, Toilers, and Workers: The Rise of Socialism in Toronto, 1887-1914," in his forthcoming University of Toronto Ph.D. dissertation.

159. See *HS*, 4 Apr. 1908, 2 Apr. 1909, 7 Feb. 1910; *Industrial Banner*, March 1907, June 1908, March 1910; Homel, "Simpson," pp. 367-68, 380.

160. *HS*, 7 Mar. 1910, 9 Mar. 1909; *Hamilton Evening Times*, 27 Feb. 1911, in *Hamilton Evening Times Scrapbook*, "Labour," pt. II, p. iv. On the general movement to secure workmen's compensation see Michael J. Piva, "The Workmen's Compensation Movement in Ontario," *Ontario History* 67 (March 1975): 39-56.

161. *HS*, 12 Mar. 1909, 7 Mar. 1910; *Industrial Banner*, December 1911.

162. *Industrial Banner*, December 1911; *HS*, 7 Apr. 1909.

163. *Industrial Banner*, January 1907, February 1907, February 1910; *HS*, 21 Oct. 1909; Homel, "Simpson," p. 599.

164. See the comments on the British ILP in E. P. Thompson, "Homage to Tom Maguire," in Asa Briggs and John Saville, eds., *Essays in Labour History* (London: Macmillan, 1960), pp. 280-81.

165. See the comments and sources cited in Heron and Palmer, "Through the Prism of the Strike," pp. 452-55; *HS*, 8 May 1909, 18 and 22 Apr. 1913.

166. *HS*, 22 Oct. 1908, 8 May 1909; Trades and Labor Congress of Canada, *Proceedings of the Annual Convention, 1909*, pp. 33-34.

167. *HS*, 22 Oct. 1908.

168. As an introduction to the Hamilton context see Jane Synge, "Immigrant Communities — British and Continental European — in Early Twentieth Century Hamilton," *Oral History* 4 (1976): 38-51.

169. *HS*, 7 May 1912.

170. See, for instance, ibid., 2 June 1909, 4 Apr. 1910; and the sources cited in chap. 1, note 136.

171. *HS*, 28 Mar. 1908, 3 Sept.-28 December 1909.

172. Ibid., 1-4 Apr. 1910.

173. *Hamilton Evening Times*, 6 and 13 Jan., 15 and 17 Apr. 1914, in *Hamilton Evening Times Scrapbook*; *HS*, 21 and 27 Mar., 26 Nov. 1908.

174. William Morris in *Commonweal*, 21 Sept. 1889, quoted in E. P. Thompson, *William Morris: Romantic to Revolutionary* (New York: Pantheon, 1977), p. 530.

175. On some of these stoppages see Strikes and Lockouts Records, vol. 304, Strike nos. 19, 27A, 34; *Hamilton Evening Times Scrapbook*, "Labour," pt. I, pp. 41-49; pt. II, pp. 52-59, 81; Myer Siemiatycki, "Munitions and Labour Militancy: The Hamilton Machinists' Strike of 1916," *Labour/Le Travailleur* 3 (1978): 131-51.

176. *Hamilton Evening Times Scrapbook*, "Labour," pt. II, p. 55.

177. On one syndicalist upheaval of the reconstruction period see David Jay Bercusson, *Confrontation at Winnipeg: Labour, Industrial Relations, and the General Strike* (Montreal and London: McGill-Queen's University Press, 1974). A survey of strike activity in Canada in these years is found in Stuart Marshall Jamieson, *Times of Trouble: Labour Unrest and Industrial Conflict in Canada, 1900-1966* (Ottawa: Task Force on Labour Relations, 1968), pp. 158-91.

178. See for instance Irving Bernstein, *The Lean Years: A History of the American Worker, 1920-1933* (Baltimore: Pelican, 1960); Jamieson, *Times of Trouble*, pp. 192-211. On the blending of "Taylorist" practice and personnel/welfare management see Ordway Tead, *Instincts in Industry: A Study of Working Class Psychology* (Boston: Houghton Mifflin, 1918); Daniel Nelson, "The New Factory System and the Unions," *Labor History* 15 (Spring 1974): 163-78; David Brody, "The Rise and Decline of Welfare Capitalism," in John Braeman et al., *Change and Continuity in Twentieth Century America* (Columbus, Ohio: Ohio State University Press, 1968), pp. 147-78. In this context King's *Industry and Humanity*, first published in 1918, was a major statement. The subtle incorporation of scientific management, personnel management, and welfare capitalism establishes a major theme of Nelson's *Managers and Workers*, esp. pp. 79-162.

179. F. J. Roethlisberger and W. J. Dickson, *Management and the Worker: Technical vs. Social Organization in an Industrial Plant* (Cambridge, Mass.: Harvard University Press, 1934), pp. 16-17, quoted in Montgomery, "Workers' Control," p. 507. Cf. W. Lloyd Warner and J. M. Low, *The Social System of the Modern Factory* (New Haven, Conn.: Yale University Press, 1947), esp. pp. 66-89.

CHAPTER 8

1. Whale's painting hangs in the National Gallery of Canada and is reproduced in Dennis Reid, *A Concise History of Canadian Painting* (Toronto: Ryerson, 1973), p. 77. For later depictions of the city's industrial landscape see "Hamilton's Business Proclamation: The City of Hamilton — Past, Present, and Future," *HS*, 20 May 1908. Cf. William H. Care, *Art Work on Hamilton, Canada* (Montreal:

n.p., 1899); Hamilton Times, *The Birmingham of Canada* (Hamilton: Times, 1893), pp. 19, 38, 60, 65, 112, 124. The verse is from Alex. H. Wingfield, "Hamilton," in *Poems and Songs in Scotch and English* (Hamilton: Times, 1873), pp. 120-21.

2. See E. J. Hobsbawm, "From Social History to the History of Society," *Daedalus* 100 (Winter 1971): 21.

3. See the overviews, often marred by factual error, ideological bias, and overly blunt generalization, in D. G. Creighton, "George Brown, Sir John Macdonald and the 'Workingman'," *Canadian Historical Review* 24 (December 1943): 362-76; Bernard Ostry, "Conservatives, Liberals, and Labour in the 1870s," ibid., 41 (June 1960): 93-127; Ostry, "Conservatives, Liberals, and Labour in the 1880s," *Canadian Journal of Economics and Political Science* 27 (May 1961): 141-61; Martin Robin, *Radical Politics and Canadian Labour, 1880-1930* (Kingston, Ont.: Industrial and Labor Relations Centre, 1968).

4. The pacesetter has been Peter Laslett and his Cambridge Group for the History of Population and Social Structure. See his *The World We Have Lost* (London: Methuen, 1971); and Laslett, ed., *Household and Family in Past Time* (London: Cambridge University Press, 1972). Note the discussion in Michael B. Katz, *The People of Hamilton, Canada West: Family and Class in a Mid-Nineteenth Century City* (Cambridge, Mass.: Harvard University Press, 1975), pp. 209-308.

5. See for instance Philip Greven, *Four Generations: Population, Land, and Family in Colonial Andover, Massachusetts* (Ithaca and London: Cornell University Press, 1970); Herbert G. Gutman, *The Black Family in Slavery and Freedom, 1750-1925* (New York: Pantheon, 1976). A forthcoming study, focusing on many of the themes common to this treatment of Hamilton workingmen, uses family sketches to effectively probe the process of working-class cultural life and how it is used in conflict situations. See Daniel J. Walkowitz, "Worker City, Company Town: Adaptation and Protest within the Troy Iron Worker and Cohoes Cotton Worker Communities, 1855-1884" (typescript, Rutgers University, 1976).

6. See Edward Shorter, *The Making of the Modern Family* (New York: Basic Books, 1975); David Gagan, "The Prose of Life: Literary Reflections of the Family, Individual Experience, and Social Structure in Nineteenth Century Canada," *Journal of Social History* 9 (Spring 1976): 367-81. This kind of easy way out is attacked in Elizabeth H. Pleck, "Two Worlds in One: Work and Family," *Journal of Social History* 10 (Winter 1976): 178-95; Tamara K. Hareven, "Family Time and Industrial Time: Family and Work in a Planned Corporation Town, 1900-1924," in Hareven, ed., *Family and Kin in Urban Communities, 1700-1930* (New York: New Viewpoints, 1977), pp. 187-206.

7. Jane Synge, "Immigrant Communities — British and Continental European — in Early Twentieth Century Hamilton," *Oral History* 4 (1976): 38-51.

8. See the essays in Richard Cobb, *A Sense of Place* (London: Duckworth, 1976); Cobb, *Paris and Its Provinces, 1792-1802* (London: Oxford University Press, 1975).

9. E. J. Hobsbawm, "The Labour Aristocracy in Nineteenth Century Britain," *Labouring Men: Studies in the History of Labour* (New York: Basic Books, 1964), pp. 272-315, remains the essential discussion. John Foster, *Class Struggle and the Industrial Revolution: Early Industrial Capitalism in Three English Towns* (London: Weidenfeld and Nicholson, 1974), pp. 203-50 is perhaps the most recent provocative statement. The literature on the question is surveyed in Bryan D. Palmer, "Most Uncommon Common Men: Craft and Culture in Historical Per-

spective," *Labour/Le Travailleur* 1 (1976): 5-32; Michael J. Piva, "The Aristoc-racy of the English Working Class: Help for an Historical Debate in Difficulties," *Histoire Sociale/Social History* 7 (November 1974): 270-92. A recent effort to de-velop the concept in a Canadian context is Ian McKay, "Capital and Labour in the Halifax Baking and Confectionery Industry during the Last Half of the Nine-teenth Century," *Labour/Le Travailleur* 3 (1978): 63-108.

10. Quoted in E. P. Thompson, *William Morris: Romantic to Revolutionary* (New York: Pantheon, 1977), pp. 336-37. Cf. V. I. Lenin, *Imperialism, The High-est Stage of Capitalism: A Popular Outline* (Peking: Foreign Language Press, 1965), p. 9; Lenin, *On Britain: A Compilation* (New York: International, 1934); Karl Marx and Friedrich Engels, *Correspondence, 1846-1895: A Selection With Commen-tary and Notes* (New York: International, 1935), pp. 115-16.

11. *Labor News*, 26 July 1912.

12. Note the discussion in Neville Kirk, "Class and Fragmentation: Some Aspects of Working-Class Life in South-East Lancashire and North-East Cheshire, 1850-1870" (Ph.D. diss., University of Pittsburgh, 1974).

13. See Edward Young, *Labor in Europe and America: A Special Report on the rate of wages, the cost of subsistence, and the condition of the working classes, in Great Britain, France, Belgium, Germany, and other countries of Europe, also in the United States and British America* (Philadelphia: S. A. George & Co., 1875), pp. 828-32; Peter R. Shergold, "Wage Differentials Based on Skill in the United States, 1889-1914: A Case Study," *Labor History* 18 (Fall 1977): 485-508.

14. Foster, *Class Struggle and the Industrial Revolution*, pp. 233, 237.

15. Note the following critical assessments: John Saville, "Class Struggle and the Industrial Revolution," in Milliband and Saville, eds., *The Socialist Regis-ter, 1974* (London: Merlin Press, 1974), pp. 226-40; Gareth Stedman Jones, "Class Struggle and the Industrial Revolution," *New Left Review* 90 (March-April 1975): 35-70; E. P. Thompson, "Testing Class Struggle," *Times Higher Education Supplement*, 8 Mar. 1974; A. E. Musson and John Foster, "Class Struggle and the Labour Aristocracy, 1830-1860," *Social History* 3 (October 1976): 335-66.

16. Irwin Yellowitz, "Skilled Workers and Mechanization: The Lasters and the 1890s," *Labor History* 18 (Spring 1977): 197-213.

17. Note the argument in James Hinton, *The First Shop Stewards' Move-ment* (London: George Allen and Unwin, 1973); R. Q. Gray, *The Labour Aristoc-racy in Victorian Edinburgh* (Oxford: Clarendon Press, 1976), pp. 93, 120, 137.

18. My position thus corresponds closely to the argument in R. Q. Gray, "Styles of Life, the 'Labour Aristocracy', and Class Relations in Later Nineteenth Century Edinburgh," *International Review of Social History* 18 (1973): 428-52; Gray, *Labour Aristocracy*. For an assessment of the negative impact of upwardly mobile English artisans on the Canadian labour movement see *Supplement to the Labor News, Labor Day 1914, Annual Review* (Hamilton: Labor News, 1914), pp. 40-41.

19. Quoted in Thompson, *William Morris*, p. 682.

20. Jean Monds, "Workers' Control and the Historians: a new Econo-mism," *New Left Review* 97 (May-June 1976): 81-100.

21. V. I. Lenin, *What Is To Be Done?* (Moscow: Progress Publishers, 1969), pp. 78-79.

22. Note the remarkable discussion of shop-floor culture in Bruce E. Nick-erson, "Is There a Folk in the Factory?" *Journal of American Folklore* 87 (April-June 1974): 133-39.

23. See George Milton Janes, *The Control of Strikes in American Trade Unions* (Baltimore: Johns Hopkins, 1916).

24. *Labor News*, 5 Jan. 1912.

25. See, for instance, Ronald Radosh, "The Corporate Ideology of American Labor Leaders from Gompers to Hillman," *Studies on the Left* 6 (November-December 1966): 66-88.

26. Craig Heron and Bryan D. Palmer, "Through the Prism of the Strike: Industrial Conflict in Southern Ontario, 1901-1914," *Canadian Historical Review* 58 (December 1977): 423-58.

27. See Hinton's reply to the Monds critique in *New Left Review* 97 (May-June 1976): 100-4.

28. Peter Warrian, "The Challenge of the One Big Union Movement in Canada, 1919-1921" (M.A. thesis, University of Waterloo, 1971), pp. 120-21; Norman Penner, ed., *Winnipeg, 1919: The Strikers' Own History of the Winnipeg General Strike* (Toronto: James Lewis and Samuel, 1973), pp. 243-84; David J. Bercusson, *Confrontation at Winnipeg: Labour, Industrial Relations, and the General Strike* (Montreal: McGill-Queen's University Press, 1974).

29. Cited in David Millar, "The Winnipeg General Strike, 1919: A Reinterpretation in the Light of Oral History and Pictoral Evidence" (M.A. thesis, Carleton University, 1970), p. 57.

30. Stelco contract, 1976, cited in *Steel Shots*, January 1976. My thanks to Wayne Roberts for pointing me in the direction of this quotation.

31. Paul Kagan, *New World Utopias: A Photographic History of the Search for Community* (New York: Penguin, 1975), p. 85. Russell G. Hann and Gregory S. Kealey informed me of this source.

Index

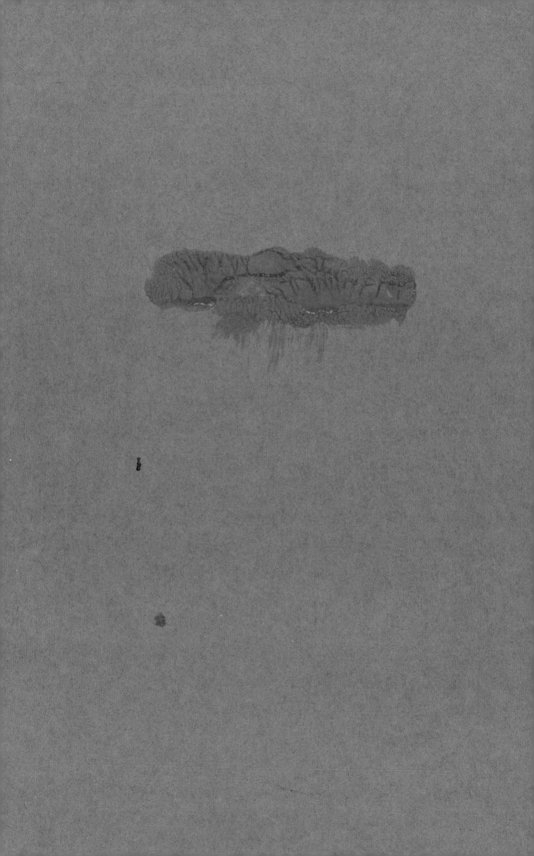